World Headquarters

Jones and Bartlett Publishers
40 Tall Pine Drive
Sudbury, MA 01776
978-443-5000
info@jbpub.com
www.jbpub.com

Jones and Bartlett Publishers Canada
6339 Ormindale Way
Mississauga, Ontario L5V 1J2
Canada

Jones and Bartlett Publishers International
Barb House, Barb Mews
London W6 7PA
United Kingdom

Jones and Bartlett's books and products are available through most bookstores and online booksellers. To contact Jones and Bartlett Publishers directly, call 800-832-0034, fax 978-443-8000, or visit our website www.jbpub.com.

Substantial discounts on bulk quantities of Jones and Bartlett's publications are available to corporations, professional associations, and other qualified organizations. For details and specific discount information, contact the special sales department at Jones and Bartlett via the above contact information or send an email to specialsales@jbpub.com.

The authors, editor, and publisher have made every effort to provide accurate information. However, they are not responsible for errors, omissions, or for any outcomes related to the use of the contents of this book and take no responsibility for the use of the products and procedures described. Treatments and side effects described in this book may not be applicable to all people; likewise, some people may require a dose or experience a side effect that is not described herein. Drugs and medical devices are discussed that may have limited availability controlled by the Food and Drug Administration (FDA) for use only in a research study or clinical trial. Research, clinical practice, and government regulations often change the accepted standard in this field. When consideration is being given to use of any drug in the clinical setting, the health care provider or reader is responsible for determining FDA status of the drug, reading the package insert, and reviewing prescribing information for the most up-to-date recommendations on dose, precautions, and contraindications, and determining the appropriate usage for the product. This is especially important in the case of drugs that are new or seldom used.

Production Credits

Publisher, Higher Education: Cathleen Sether
Acquisitions Editor: Shoshanna Goldberg
Senior Associate Editor: Amy L. Bloom
Production Manager: Julie Champagne Bolduc
Associate Production Editor: Jessica Steele Newfell
Associate Production Editor: Sarah Bayle

Associate Marketing Manager: Jody Sullivan
Composition: Publishers' Design and Production Services, Inc.
Cover Design: Scott Moden
Printing and Binding: Malloy, Inc.
Cover Printing: Malloy, Inc.

Library of Congress Cataloging-in-Publication Data
Cottrell, Randall R.
  Health promotion and education research methods : using the five-chapter thesis/dissertation model / Randall R. Cottrell, James F. McKenzie. — 2nd ed.
      p. ; cm.
  Includes bibliographical references and index.
  ISBN-13: 978-0-7637-7507-0 (casebound : alk. paper)
  ISBN-10: 0-7637-7507-X (casebound : alk. paper)
  1. Health promotion—Research—Methodology. 2. Health education—Research—Methodology. 3. Dissertations, Academic—Research—Methodology. I. McKenzie, James F., 1948– II. Title.
  [DNLM: 1. Health Education. 2. Authorship. 3. Health Promotion. 4. Health Services Research—methods. 5. Models, Theoretical. WA 590 C851h 2011]
  RA427.8.C686 2011
  610.72—dc22

2009042689

6048

Printed in the United States of America
14 13 12 11 10   10 9 8 7 6 5 4 3 2

Health Promotion & Education Research Methods

Using the Five-Chapter
Thesis/Dissertation Model

SECOND EDITION

Randall R. Cottrell, DEd, CHES
University of Cincinnati
Cincinnati, Ohio

James F. McKenzie, PhD, MPH, CHES
Ball State University
Muncie, Indiana

JONES AND BARTLETT PUBLISHERS
Sudbury, Massachusetts
BOSTON   TORONTO   LONDON   SINGAPORE

BRIEF CONTENTS

CONTENTS

Chapter 8 Instrumentation   145

**Chapter 9 Quantitative Research Methods: Experimental
            (Writing Chapter III)   171**

Chapter 12 Data Analysis and Reporting the Findings (Writing Chapters III and IV)   253

Chapter 13 Conclusions, Discussion, and Recommendations (Writing Chapter V)   271

PREFACE

There are many excellent research methods books available on the market. Two features separate this book, *Health Promotion and Education Research Methods: Using the Five Chapter Thesis/Dissertation Model, Second Edition*, from the others. First, this book was developed specifically for health education specialists. As research concepts are presented, all examples relate directly to health education. Learning research in the context of one's own professional frame of reference is advantageous. Other health professions will also benefit from this text with its health-related focus and emphasis on thesis and dissertation writing. Our colleagues in community nursing, health psychology, health communication, health policy, and the various public health disciplines may find that this book better meets their needs than other books on the market.

The second unique feature of this book is that it fully integrates the learning of research methods with the writing of a five-chapter thesis or dissertation. The purpose of writing a thesis or dissertation in graduate school is to teach students how to conduct a research project in a very systematic and prescribed manner, yet research methods courses are often divorced from the process of writing the thesis or dissertation. Students learn research methods in one or more courses and then often must learn how to write the thesis or dissertation through "osmosis," individual advisor meetings, or a separate seminar or course specifically designed to address thesis or dissertation writing. Each chapter of this book contains information relevant to the writing of one or more chapters of a thesis or dissertation. Because differences exist in thesis/dissertation requirements from university to university, students are reminded throughout this text to consult their committee chairs and departments to obtain the specific requirements for their academic program.

In *Health Promotion and Education Research Methods, Second Edition*, the reader will find many new health education examples to help illustrate various research concepts, as well as the components of a thesis or dissertation. New and updated references and citations have been used wherever possible. There are expanded discussions of mixed-methods research, evidence-based best practices, action research, telephone surveys, online surveys, multimode surveys, and effect size, as well as new information on research ethics and the health education code of ethics. As in the first edition, readers of the second edition will find comprehensive coverage of basic research methodologies.

Chapter 1 provides students with an overview of research and different approaches to research, while introducing them to the five-chapter thesis or dissertation format (by convention, any reference to chapters of this text will be in Arabic numerals, i.e., 1–14, and references to chapters in the thesis or dissertation will be in roman numerals, i.e., I–V). Chapter 2 is dedicated to helping students find a topic for their thesis or dissertation. We believe the information contained in Chapter 2 is unique and will greatly assist students in conceptualizing, narrowing, and selecting their topics. Chapter 3 focuses on the literature review and writing for Chapter II of the thesis or dissertation. Chapter 4 provides a brief overview of health education theories and models that should be considered when developing a thesis or dissertation. Theories or models used in developing a thesis or dissertation should be thoroughly discussed when writing Chapter II. Chapter 5 explains research questions, purpose statements, hypotheses, limitations, delimitations, assumptions, and operational definitions within the context of writing Chapter I of a thesis or dissertation. Chapter 6 provides a close examination of ethics in research, especially health education research. This chapter has relevance to the entire thesis/dissertation process, as well as any research endeavor. Chapter 7 focuses on the selection of research participants and is an integral part of the information presented in Chapter III of a thesis or dissertation. Data collection instruments are the focus of Chapter 8.

Chapters 9, 10, and 11 focus on different research methodologies and are necessary to fully understand the research process and to write the methodology section of a thesis or dissertation's Chapter III. These three chapters combined provide the meat of any research methods course. Chapter 12 focuses on data analysis and reporting of results. This chapter also includes information about writing Chapter IV of a thesis or dissertation. Chapter 13 explains how to develop and write Chapter V of a thesis or dissertation. It includes information about how to discuss findings, compare findings to the literature, and make appropriate recommendations related to professional practice, thereby improving the current research study and future studies needed on this topic. Finally, Chapter 14 presents information on how to share the findings from a thesis or dissertation with other health and health education professionals. It is our belief that quality thesis and dissertation research should be shared with others, and it is the responsibility of the graduate committee to mentor graduate students through this process. Publishing and professional presentations are both discussed in Chapter 14.

For those who do not require a thesis or dissertation in their graduate programs, chapters and chapter sections devoted to thesis and dissertation development can easily be identified and eliminated from assigned reading. Thus, the book can still serve those interested in teaching health education research methods courses that are not in the context of writing a thesis or dissertation.

We sincerely hope that you enjoy this book and find that it meets your needs. We welcome any feedback from users, positive or negative. It is through your input that we can improve future editions of this text.

ACKNOWLEDGMENTS

We would like to begin by thanking Dr. Kelli McCormack Brown for writing Chapter 11 on qualitative research. We were fortunate to have such a renowned researcher and expert in qualitative research assist us with this aspect of the book.

We would also like to thank the following people for their contributions to our book: R. Morgan Pigg, Jr., HSD, MPH, Professor, University of Florida, for his review and critique of Chapter 6; and James A. Jones, PhD, Assistant Director for Research Design, Ball State University, for his review and critique of Chapter 7.

We would like to acknowledge the following colleagues for their reviews of the manuscript: Sandra Minor Bulmer, PhD, CHES, ACSM HFD, Southern Connecticut State University; Michael Collins, EdD, Kennesaw State University; Bart Hammig, PhD, MPH, Southern Illinois University at Carbondale; Stephen Bezruchka, MD, MPH, University of Washington; Martha A. Bass, PhD, RD, Sam Houston State University; and the reviewers of the first edition: Brian Pritschet, PhD, Eastern Illinois University; Dr. Hyun-Duck Kim, Arkansas State University; Christopher A. Taylor, PhD, RD, LD, The Ohio State University; Sandra Minor Bulmer, PhD, Health Education, CHES, Southern Connecticut State University; Stacie M. Metz, PhD, MPH, MSW, MA, West Chester University; and Dr. Julia A. Watkins, University of North Florida.

A special thanks needs to go to all of our graduate students over the years who have helped us better conceptualize and understand research through their many projects, theses, and dissertations. In particular, we would like to thank those students who used the book while it was in the developmental stages, and in particular, Tiffany Brown, Julia Heitzer, Brittany Mathers, Todd Santabarbara, Phoebe Lubonovich, and Anna Torrens Salemi, who provided specific suggestions and critique. Our gratitude is also extended to Beth Miller and Sasi Chockalingam, who provided extensive assistance with the research and writing of the second edition.

We would also like to recognize Billie S. Kennedy, Debbie Morris, Linda Miller, Lennell Wade, and Pat Borusiewicz, our secretaries and administrative assistants, for their help and support.

We would also like to thank the administration and staff at Jones and Bartlett Publishers for their support in the development of this text. In particular, we would like to thank Kris Ellis and Jacqueline Geraci for their conceptual and editorial assistance, as well as Shoshanna Goldberg, Acquisitions Editor; Amy Bloom, Senior Associate Editor; Kyle Hoover, Senior Editorial Assistant; Julie Bolduc, Production Manager; Sarah Bayle, Associate Production Editor; and Jody Sullivan, Associate Marketing Manager, our "go-to" people for this project.

Finally, we would like to dedicate this book to those people most important in our lives who are always there to encourage and support us: our wives, Karen and Bonnie; our children, Kyle, Lisa, Kory, Anne, and Greg; our grandchildren, Kaylee, Mitchell, and Julia; and our parents, Russell and Edith Cottrell and Gordon and Betty McKenzie.

CHAPTER 1 | # Introduction to Research and the Research Requirement

Chapter Objectives

After reading this chapter and answering the review questions, you should be able to:

1. Define health education research.
2. Identify the two basic approaches to research.
3. Describe quantitative and qualitative research.
4. Explain similarities and differences between quantitative and qualitative research.
5. Define key terms listed below.
6. Describe the various research methods associated with quantitative research.
7. Describe the various research methods associated with qualitative research.
8. Explain what is meant by a mixed method study.
9. Identify at least five characteristics of good research.
10. Discuss the characteristics of good researchers.
11. Compare and contrast the various research requirements associated with graduate study.
12. Explain what is included in a five-chapter thesis or dissertation.

Key Terms

applied research
basic research
capstone experience
case studies
community-based participatory research
comprehensive exams
correlational research
deductive reasoning
descriptive research
doctoral dissertation
ethnographic studies
evaluation research
experimental research

explanatory mixed method design
exploratory mixed method design
ex post facto research
field research
grounded theory research
health education research
honors thesis
inductive reasoning
laboratory research
master's project
master's thesis
mixed method research
mixed method study
non-experimental research

participatory action research
phenomenological study
qualitative research
quantitative research
quasi-experimental research
random assignment
redundancy
reliable
saturation
scientific method
survey research
triangulation mixed method design
valid

Research is not owned by any one profession or discipline (DePoy & Gitlin, 2005). A car manufacturer may use research to determine if one particular engine design produces better gas mileage than another. A pharmaceutical company may use research to determine which drug works best to treat a specific ailment. Basketball coaches may use research to determine which training technique produces the greatest increase in vertical jump. Farmers may use research to determine which seed type produces the greatest yield at harvest time. The research process used to conduct any of the above studies would be similar; yet to actually do the research a background in automotive engineering, medicine, exercise physiology, or agriculture would be helpful. The purpose of this text is to assist in the teaching of research methods in the context of health education. Although there are many research methods books that could teach health education specialists the basic process of research, it seems likely that health education specialists will learn research methods best when doing so within the context of their own profession. An additional purpose of this text is to integrate the learning of research methods with the development of a thesis or dissertation. In essence, the writing of a thesis or dissertation is the process utilized by most graduate schools to teach students how to conduct research; yet most research methods textbooks do not discuss the thesis/dissertation process.

Research is a term that is used in a variety of ways (Leedy & Ormrod, 2010). When a fourth-grade student is asked to do a report on the food guide pyramid, it might be said she is doing research. When a high school or college student is asked to write a paper on HIV/AIDS, it is often called a research paper, indicating that the student did research to obtain the information needed to write the paper. When a middle-aged man searches the Internet to learn more about his high cholesterol levels, it is often said that he is researching the topic. In essence, none of these examples is true research (Schloss & Smith, 1999). What these individuals are doing might more accurately be termed information gathering, processing, and reporting. Someone else did the research that provided the information these individuals seek.

What, then, is research? As one might expect, there are numerous definitions for research. Kerlinger and Lee, in their classic research methods text *Foundations of Behavioral Research* (2000), defined research as a "systematic, controlled, empirical, a moral, public, and critical investigation of natural phenomena. It is guided by theory and hypotheses about the presumed relations among such phenomena" (p. 14). Kerlinger and Lee's definition implies that the only legitimate approach to research is systematic and controlled hypothesis testing. Although this is certainly a point of view held by some researchers, others have adopted somewhat different definitions. DePoy and Gitlin (2005) define research as "multiple, systematic strategies to generate knowledge about human behavior, human experience, and human environments in which the thinking and action processes of the researcher are clearly specified so that they are logical, understandable, confirmable, and useful" (p. 6). This definition tends to view research in terms of what the researcher does. Still others define research more broadly. Berg and Latin (2004) state that research "is a way to gather information and make a sound decision or judgment or develop new knowledge" (p. 4). Salkind (2009) notes that "research is a process through which new knowledge is discovered" (p. 3).

For the purpose of this text, which is designed to teach health education students about research, we have chosen to modify the definition of educational research found in a text by McMillan and Wergin (2002). Our definition for **health education research** is a systematic investigation involving the analysis of collected information or data that ultimately is used to enhance health education knowledge or practice and answers one or more questions about a health-related theory, behavior, or phenomenon.

Approaches to Research

There are two basic, fundamental types of research: quantitative and qualitative (Creswell, 2005; Gay, Mills, & Airasian, 2006; Patten, 2009). These two approaches to research may both be utilized in the same study, which is then called a **mixed method study** (Creswell, 2005, 2009; Gay *et al.*, 2006). Creswell (2009) actually goes so far as to describe mixed method approaches as a third type of research design. We believe, however, that mixed method designs are best considered a blend of the traditional quantitative and qualitative type designs and are not a unique third type of research. Creswell (2009) does make a good point however, in that "quantitative and qualitative research should not be thought of as polar opposites or dichotomies; instead, they represent different ends on a continuum" (p. 9), with mixed method research somewhere in the middle. Let's take a closer look at quantitative and qualitative research and then examine how the two can be used together.

Quantitative research is the more traditional form of research. It is also termed the positivist, experimental, or empiricist approach to research. Quantitative research is used to answer questions about relationships among measurable variables. It uses the time-honored procedure known as the **scientific method**. Steps in the scientific method include stating the problem, stating testable or measurable hypotheses, designing a study to test the hypotheses, conducting the study, analyzing the data using appropriate statistical tests, stating conclusions based on the findings, and identifying new research questions (Berg & Latin, 2004).

A health education–related example of a quantitative study might involve examining two diet programs to determine which is most effective at helping people to lose body fat. To test this problem, a group of similarly obese individuals would be randomly assigned to one of three different groups. Initial body fat measures would be taken on all participants. Two of the groups would be labeled experimental (or treatment), and each would be assigned to participate in one of the two diet programs being studied. The third group would be termed a control group and would get no treatment. After the diet programs were in effect for a specific period of time, all participants' body fat would again be measured. Statistical analysis would be completed on the body fat data obtained from the groups, and conclusions would be drawn about differences between the three groups and the effectiveness of the two diet programs.

Qualitative research is designed to answer questions about the complex nature of phenomena with the purpose of describing, explaining, and understanding the phenomena being researched. Other terms applied to qualitative research include interpretative, constructivist, postpositivist, and naturalistic. Whereas the quantitative researcher records numbers and conducts statistical tests, the qualitative researcher records words and phrases looking for meaning, concepts, or theory.

A health education example of a qualitative study might use participants in a similar diet program to the above example, but the purpose of the study would be different. Instead of trying to determine which diet program was most effective at reducing body fat, the qualitative researcher might want to know why people want to lose body fat, what attracted them to an organized weight loss program, how they felt while they were on the diet program, what their sources of support were, what roadblocks they encountered, how they felt when they were successful, how they felt when they were not so successful, and so on. To obtain answers to these questions, qualitative researchers might attend weight loss programs, perhaps even participating in the program themselves. Qualitative researchers might also do in-depth interviews with individuals in the program, following them over a period of months or even years. Throughout this process the qualitative researcher would be taking comprehensive notes, recording conversations, and writing detailed observations. The full and rich data obtained through qualitative studies cannot be obtained using quantitative methods. The questions answered through qualitative research are important questions that may provide valuable information and insight into the topic being studied.

Mixed method research is used when both quantitative and qualitative data provide a better, more thorough understanding of the research question being studied. Creswell (2005) identified three ways to combine the use of quantitative and qualitative approaches. Quantitative data can be collected first, and then based on these results qualitative data collection can be incorporated to provide more insight, depth, and understanding of the qualitative results. Creswell calls this the **explanatory mixed method design**. Essentially, qualitative data is used to help explain quantitative results. In an **exploratory mixed method design** qualitative data is collected first, and based on these findings quantitative data is collected to answer research questions that arose from the initial qualitative findings. In other words, by exploring the rich qualitative data new research questions emerge that can be answered through a quantitative research study. In a **triangulation mixed method design**, both quantitative and qualitative data are collected at the same time and the results are examined simultaneously to develop conclusions related to the initial research question.

The decision to use a quantitative, qualitative, or mixed method design is based primarily on the research question or questions being asked. See Box 1.1 for health education examples of research designs.

Community-based participatory research is a mixed method approach to research that has gained favor in public and community health and typically utilizes both quantitative and qualitative data collection strategies. According to Viswanathan and colleagues (2004), "Community-based participatory research (CBPR) is a collaborative approach to research that combines methods of inquiry with community capacity-building strategies to bridge the gap between knowledge produced through research and what is practiced in communities to improve health" (p. Abstract). It involves working in collaboration with community stakeholders to plan and conduct research resulting in action plans for community improvement. CBPR is closely akin to **participatory action research** (PAR), which has been used in educational settings and is focused on improving the quality of people's organizations, communities, and family lives (Creswell, 2005).

Quantitative/Qualitative Comparisons

At this point it is important to discuss more completely how quantitative and qualitative approaches are similar and how they are different. Quantitative and qualitative approaches are similar in that both are research, and as such we can use our definition of health education research to describe them. We can say that both approaches are systematic investigations involving the analysis of collected information or data that ultimately is used to enhance health education knowledge or practice and answers one or more questions about a health-related theory, behavior, or phenomenon.

The differences between qualitative and quantitative approaches are many (Creswell, 2005; Leedy & Ormrod, 2010). Figure 1.1 draws comparisons between the two methods in a number of areas. Quantitative researchers identify variables that can be observed and measured. These variables are recorded as numbers, and statistics can be used to determine relationships between and among the variables. Qualitative researchers use words instead of numbers to represent their data. The words describe their observations, interactions, and insights. Categories or variables emerge from the word data, and qualitative researchers use interpretive narratives to explain the phenomenon being studied (Leedy & Ormrod, 2010).

The thinking or reasoning process in quantitative and qualitative research is different

---

Box 1.1   Quantitative, Qualitative, and Mixed Method Approaches to Research

---

1. A health education specialist wants to know if growing a vegetable garden will have a positive impact on the diet of the gardeners and their immediate family. A study is designed that compares the diet of a group of vegetable gardeners and their families with the diet of a group of families that do not have a vegetable garden. What type of study is this? Given what you know about research, what do you think would be the strengths and weaknesses of this study? What questions would be answered in this study and what questions might still need to be answered?

2. A health education specialist wants to know more about people that garden. Why do they garden? What do they perceive as the benefits and drawbacks to gardening? How does gardening make them feel? What do they believe about gardening and health? The researcher collects data by volunteering to work in gardens with the gardeners over the course of a summer, conducting informal interviews while they work. What type of study is this? Given what you know about research, what do you think would be the strengths and weaknesses of this study? What questions would be answered in this study and what questions might still need to be answered?

3. The health education specialist in #1 above determines that indeed the gardeners and their families eat a better diet than those families that do not garden. The health education specialist now wants to know if there are other benefits to gardening. She wants to conduct in-depth interviews with the gardeners and their families to determine how gardening makes them feel, what they perceive as the benefits of gardening, what they believe to be negatives associated with gardening, and so on. She conducts these interviews while working with the gardeners in their gardens. What type of study is this (be specific)? Given what you know about research, what do you think would be the strengths and

weaknesses of this study? What questions would be answered in this study and what questions might still need to be answered?

4. The health education specialist in #2 above determines that gardeners are typically very positive toward gardening and feel their gardening allows them to eat a healthier diet and get more exercise, reduces their stress, and improves their mental health. He now designs a study comparing a group of gardeners with a group of non-gardeners to determine if the gardeners are healthier in terms of selected measures of health including percentage of body fat, cholesterol levels, blood pressure, and scores on an instrument to measure stress levels. What type of study is this (be specific)? Given what you know about research, what do you think would be the strengths and weaknesses of this study? What questions would be answered in this study and what questions might still need to be answered?

5. A health education specialist wants to explore gardening, and in particular the impact gardening has on the dietary behaviors of gardeners and their immediate families. The health education specialist designs a study that compares the diet of a group of vegetable gardeners and their families with the diet of a group of families that do not have a vegetable garden. At the same time, she selects several gardening families in the study and voluntarily works in gardens with the gardeners over the course of a summer, conducting informal interviews while they work. Data from gardener vs. non-gardener comparisons and from the interviews with gardeners is considered in developing conclusions about gardening and health. What type of study is this (be specific)? Given what you know about research, what do you think would be the strengths and weaknesses of this study? What questions would be answered in this study and what questions might still need to be answered?

Quantitative Characteristics	Steps in the Process of Research	Qualitative Characteristics
• Description and explanation oriented	Identifying a Research Problem	• Exploratory and understanding oriented
• Major role • Justification for the research problem and specification for the need for the study	Reviewing the Literature	• Minor role • Justificaton for the research problem
• Specific and narrow • Measurable, observable data	Specifying a Purpose	• General and broad • Participants' experiences
• Predetermined instruments • Numeric (numbered) data • Large number of individuals	Collecting Data	• General, emerging from • Text or image data • Small number of individuals or sites
• Statistical analysis • Description of trends comparison of groups, or relationships among variables • A comparison of results with predictions and past studies	Analyzing and Interpreting Data	• Text analysis • Description, analysis, and thematic development • The larger meaning of findings
• Standard and fixed • Objective and unbiased	Reporting and Evaluating Research	• Flexible and emerging • Reflexive and biased

FIGURE 1.1

Characteristics of quantitative and qualitative research in the process of research.

From: Creswell, J.W. (2005). *Educational Research: Planning, Conducting and Evaluating Quantitative and Qualitative Research*. Upper Saddle River, NJ: Pearson Education Inc. P. 44.

(Leedy & Ormrod, 2010). Quantitative researchers use more **deductive reasoning** than do qualitative researchers. Deductive reasoning involves the forming of conclusions based on gathered data by applying the rules of logic to a premise. In deductive reasoning the thinking processes and procedures are well defined. Qualitative researchers use more **inductive reasoning** than do quantitative researchers. This means they attempt to develop truths or to produce a universal claim or principle from their data. In other words, qualitative research involves the process of inducing a feeling, an insight, an idea, or an awareness from the information collected. In inductive reasoning the thinking and procedures are more free flowing and less well defined than in deductive reasoning.

The number of participants (subjects) in a study also varies between quantitative and qualitative studies. Quantitative studies tend to use a larger number of participants. The more participants used in a quantitative study, the more likely those studied will be representative of the larger population from which they are selected. Larger sample sizes are also important when participants are compared by subgroups such as age, gender, or race. Each subgroup must be large enough so that appropriate statistical comparisons can be made. Larger sample sizes also make it easier to obtain statistical significance between or among groups. In qualitative studies, larger numbers are not necessary because statistical analysis is seldom used and results are typically not generalized. Because of the nature of data collection and the large time investment with each participant, it is neither feasible nor necessary to use large numbers of subjects. Qualitative case studies have been completed with just one participant.

In general, quantitative studies take less time to complete than do qualitative studies. In quantitative studies, the period for data collection is fairly well defined. In most quantitative studies data are collected over a period of weeks or months. There are exceptions where subjects are followed over a period of years (longitudinal studies), but even in these cases the data collection from each individual usually takes only a short period of time each year. In qualitative studies, the period of data collection is typically much longer and may be unknown at the onset of the study. It is typical for data collection to take many months or even years in qualitative studies. With quantitative studies it is usually clear when data collection should end. It ends when enough completed questionnaires have been collected, enough people have been tested, or enough programs have been offered to make the needed

comparisons. In qualitative research it is sometimes difficult to determine when data collection should end. There is often a feeling that with just a few more weeks of observation or a few more in-depth interviews, additional insights could be achieved. Eventually the qualitative researcher should begin to notice **saturation** or **redundancy** in data collection. This means that he or she starts seeing or hearing the same things over again. When this happens, data collection should be terminated. The concepts of saturation and redundancy, although helpful to the qualitative researcher, are still more subjective than the criteria used in quantitative research.

In quantitative research, the procedures used to collect data are clearly identified and described prior to the actual data collection. Individuals charged with collecting the data should not alter the procedures. To do so could compromise the data and bring any findings from the research into question. In qualitative studies researchers can change the procedures as they go. If, for example, they find that a question they ask in an interview is not working well, they can reword the question, change the order in which the question is asked, or completely eliminate it without a negative impact on their research. In fact, by changing procedures when needed, the research will most likely be improved.

It is important for quantitative researchers to be able to generalize their findings. In other words, any findings they obtain from the participants in the study should also hold true or be generalized to the larger population from which the study participants were drawn. For example, if a particular antismoking campaign is found to be effective in a number of randomly selected pilot cities across the country that are representative of a larger group of cities, it should be effective in those other cities, as well. In qualitative research there is no attempt to generalize findings from study participants to other groups. Instead, the desire is to describe, explain, explore, and interpret the study group. Ultimately, the qualitative researcher may make generalizations only about the group being studied but may build new theories based on their findings. These new theories may then be tested using quantitative methods.

Finally, a major difference between quantitative and qualitative research is the role of the researcher in the research (Creswell, 2005). The quantitative approach requires the researcher to be independent of the research. The researcher should do nothing that might influence the participants in any way. The qualitative approach requires the researcher to interact with those in the study. This interaction may take the form of observing participants, living with participants, actually participating in some activity with the participants, or having long, in-depth conversations (interviews) with the participants. Perhaps these two approaches can best be summarized in a quote from Creswell (2005):

> Quantitative research is a type of educational research in which the researcher decides what to study; asks specific, narrow questions; collects numeric (numbered) data from participants; analyzes these numbers using statistics; and conducts the inquiry in an unbiased, objective manner. Qualitative research is a type of educational research in which the researcher relies on the views of participants; asks broad, general questions; collects data consisting largely of words (or text) from participants; describes and analyzes these words for themes; and conducts the inquiry in a subjective, biased manner (p. 56).

Quantitative/Qualitative Debate

Whether or not researchers want to admit it, there is and has been considerable discussion, debate, and controversy surrounding quantitative and qualitative approaches. Some quantitative researchers do not respect the work of qualitative researchers and vice versa.

Quantitative research is the more traditional form of research. It is based on the scientific model and is what most researchers learned in graduate school, until the 1990s when large numbers of qualitative research courses were introduced to graduate curricula. To some trained in quantitative

research the work of qualitative researchers is not scientific. They would maintain that qualitative research is not standardized, cannot be generalized, is based on personal opinion or interpretation of the researcher, uses small numbers of nonrepresentative subjects, and in general does not involve the rigor of quantitative research.

Some qualitative researchers, on the other hand, see quantitative research as merely the manipulation of numbers. They believe that the world is too complex to reduce everything to measurable variables that can then be recorded as numbers and statistically manipulated. They see the quantitative researcher as narrow in focus and likely to miss the beauty of the forest because of their interest in counting and categorizing the trees.

The problem is that those quantitative and qualitative researchers who are critical of and lack respect for the other research approach view it through the context of their own preferred method. Certainly, when qualitative research is critiqued based on the rules and guidelines for quantitative research, it does not hold up as sound research. Conversely, the same is true when quantitative research is judged by the criteria of qualitative research.

What all in the field of research need to realize is that the quantitative and qualitative approaches are two different types of research, each with its own accepted procedures and methodology. Each answers different types of questions; therefore, each serves to further the overall knowledge base in a given field. Quantitative and qualitative researchers are not in competition with each other but complement each other. Each approach to research is of value and should only be critiqued based on the accepted procedures and methodology of that approach.

Most current research methods texts are presenting both quantitative and qualitative approaches (Creswell, 2009; Leedy & Ormrod, 2010; Patten, 2009), and researchers often extol the advantages of integrating both approaches to answer difficult and complex research questions.

Quantitative Research Designs

Within both the quantitative and qualitative approaches to research, there are numerous designs that can be utilized. In the quantitative approach the methods can be divided into three groupings: experimental, quasi-experimental, and non-experimental. **Experimental research** is designed to establish a true cause-and-effect relationship (Salkind, 2009). In other words, the study design will allow the researcher to state at the end of the study whether or not one variable clearly caused something to happen in a second variable. For example, as a result of an experimental study that compared the hand-washing behavior of third-grade children receiving special hand-washing training to a group of third-grade children not receiving the special training, a researcher could state whether the special training increased the rate of hand washing among the third-grade students. For this to be an experimental design, the children would have had to be randomly assigned to either the special training group or the group not receiving the special training. **Random assignment** means that all participants had an equal chance of being assigned to either the treatment group or the nontreatment group. If intact classrooms were used instead of random assignment, the study design would be considered quasi-experimental. **Quasi-experimental research** designs attempt to control and manipulate variables just as in experimental designs, but they do not use random assignment.

In the broadest sense, **non-experimental research** is any quantitative research that does not look for cause-and-effect relationships. Non-experimental research studies can be **descriptive research**, meaning they are designed to describe, through the use of numbers, percentages, and averages, characteristics of a group of people or some other phenomena. If a health education specialist wanted to determine the exercise and nutritional behaviors of college females, descriptive research would be used.

Correlational research is non-experimental research that examines relationships between or among variables. A health education specialist, for example, wants to know if there is a relationship between exercise levels and stress levels. By doing a correlational study, the researcher might determine that as exercise levels increase, stress levels decrease. The researcher must be careful, however, and not conclude that increased exercise causes decreased stress levels. It is equally possible that people with low stress levels exercise more than people with high stress levels. What the researcher found was only a correlation or relationship between these two variables. To determine cause and effect, an experimental design would have to be employed.

Ex post facto (after the fact) **research** examines a phenomenon that has already occurred and attempts to infer cause-and-effect relationships. These studies are also called causal-comparative studies. An example of an ex post facto study completed for a master's thesis follows. The student wanted to determine if eating a high fat diet and race were associated with prostate cancer (Martinez, 1997). The student obtained permission from two local urological surgeons to use their patient lists. Patients were divided into two groups: those diagnosed with prostate cancer and those with normal prostate functioning. A random sample of each group was then sent a survey asking questions related to fat consumption. The student then compared the data obtained from the groups.

McMillan and Wergin (2002) state that ex post facto research is "a non-experiment dressed up to look like an experiment" (p. 5). The reason for their comment is that it is easy to misinterpret the results of ex post facto research. "Teasing out whether in fact any differences are due to the 'treatment' variable is very difficult in ex post facto studies" (McMillan & Wergin, 2002, p. 6). Although the student in the above example was not able to find any differences in fat consumption between the two groups, even if he had, he could not have said for sure that high-fat diets and race caused the prostate cancer. At best he could have said that there appeared to be a relationship between the variables and to call for additional research.

Other types of non-experimental quantitative studies include evaluation research and survey research. **Evaluation research** is a process through which the effectiveness of a program can be measured, usually by determining if the program's objectives have been achieved (Neutens & Rubinson, 2010). This is a common type of research in health education and will be thoroughly discussed in Chapter 10 of this book. **Survey research** involves using questionnaires or structured interviews for data collection with the intent of generalizing from a sample to a population (Aday & Cornelius, 2006; Creswell, 2005). Although we treat survey research as a separate type of non-experimental quantitative research, it is important to note that survey research methods can be used to collect data in many of the other research designs discussed above. Survey research is very common in health education.

Qualitative Research Designs

Qualitative researchers also have a variety of different designs to choose from in developing their research studies (Creswell, 2005; Leedy & Ormrod, 2010; McMillan & Wergin, 2002). A few are briefly presented here, but more detailed descriptions can be found in Chapter 11. **Case studies** involve the in-depth study of one individual, program, community, setting, or event for a defined period of time. For example, a health education specialist might want to study the health issues and problems of a homeless individual over a one-year period of time. Case studies are useful for learning more about a little-known or poorly understood situation and for investigating how programs or individuals change over time. Of course, the results of a case study are not generalizable beyond the case being studied. Case studies can be useful

in providing preliminary support for new theories, which can then be tested and refined.

A **phenomenological study** is one that tries to understand a small, selected group of people's perceptions, understandings, and beliefs concerning a particular situation or event. A health education specialist, for example, might study a group of homeless individuals at a group shelter. The question to be answered might be, "What are the health issues or problems of the homeless?" Upon completion of the study, the researcher could make some generalizations or summary statements about the health implications of being homeless for this particular group of people. Note that the researcher could not generalize these findings to other homeless people. It is important to keep in mind the difference between generalizing to other groups and making generalizations about the group being studied, as this is an important distinction between quantitative and qualitative research.

If the researcher in the above example were actually to live with the homeless or at least move in and out of their environment on a regular basis, the work might be considered an ethnographic study. **Ethnographic studies** involve direct engagement with the participants in their environment to obtain in-depth understandings of their behaviors and situations. The purpose of living with the homeless for a health education researcher might be to identify the cultural norms, beliefs, social structures, and behaviors related to the health of homeless people. The individual doing the study might actually live the life of the homeless in order to gain a better understanding of the group being studied.

In a **grounded theory** study, the intent is to discover or generate a theory related to a specific phenomenon based on the data collected. The term "grounded" arises from the notion that any theory conceived from the work is derived from and rooted in the data collected. For example, a health education specialist might seek to develop a theory related to homelessness and health. The health education specialist would begin by collecting field data on the homeless. Through careful synthesis and analysis of the data a theory may emerge.

Other Research Terminology

In addition to quantitative and qualitative, other distinctions can also be made of research. **Basic research**, also called pure research, is research with no immediate application. It is done primarily out of intellectual curiosity or "to advance human beings' theoretical conceptualizations about a particular topic" (Leedy & Ormrod, 2010, p. 44). For example, a chemist mixes a new combination of chemicals and creates a sticky substance. Only later is it determined that this new sticky substance has a commercial value as an adhesive. Health education specialists rarely do basic research.

Applied research is done with a specific question or application in mind (Leedy & Ormrod, 2010). This is the more likely approach for health education specialists. Consider the worksite health education specialist who does research to determine if one smoking cessation program is better than another. This research could be considered a quantitative experimental or quasi-experimental study. It is also applied research. The results of this research will be immediately applied by selecting the program that works best for broad-scale implementation.

Another distinction often made is that of field versus laboratory research (Berg & Latin, 2004). **Field research** is done in the real world of classrooms, worksites, and communities. In other words, it is research conducted where people actually live, work, and play. The level of control the researcher has in field research is usually limited in comparison to laboratory research. **Laboratory research**, as the name implies, is conducted in the tightly structured conditions of a lab. This allows the researcher to have greater control over the research. In a lab study on exercise, for example, the researcher can control the time of day, duration and intensity of exercise, temperature and humidity while exercising, amount of fluid consumed, and many other factors. In a field study, participants may be told to exercise a certain amount of time four days a week, but there is no control on whether the participants follow the instructions. It would be impossible to control for time of day, intensity of exercise, temperature and humidity while exercising, and amount of fluid consumed as in the lab. Although lab research may be more precise and pure, field research is more practical and applied. The vast majority of health education research would be considered field research.

Characteristics of Good Research

Not all research is good research. Studies are completed every day that, for a variety of reasons, are not well done and whose results are questionable. Regardless of the type of research or the specific research design utilized, there are some common, and generally agreed upon, characteristics of good research (see Table 1.1).

A review of existing related literature is always a part of good research. Quantitative research should begin with a thorough review of the literature. It is important for the researcher to learn what research has already been done and how it was done. Failure to review the literature can result in

Table 1.1   Characteristics of Good Research

It is based on previous work and a thorough review of literature.
It is based on theory.
It is apolitical, objective, and logical.
It is designed to answer a question or solve a problem.
It can be replicated and validated.
It can be generalized to other settings (quantitative).
It uses accurate observation and measurement.
It requires patient, unhurried activity.
It involves rigorous analysis of data.
Results are reported for others to utilize and critique.

repeating work that has already been accomplished or remaking mistakes that have already been made. The credibility of the researcher and the research will be questioned if the literature review is not well done. In qualitative studies a literature review is also important, but it may be used somewhat differently. A preliminary literature review is used to identify conceptual frameworks, broad areas of study, and scholarly concepts that provide the foundation for the qualitative research. Continual literature review takes place throughout the study to connect the work with previous studies and possibly to alter focus and methodology. By the end of the qualitative study, there is a complete review of related literature (McMillan & Wergin, 2002).

Understanding and utilizing theory is an important part of research (Leedy & Ormrod, 2010; Neutens & Rubinson, 2010; Salkind, 2009). Research is used to refine and substantiate theory, and theory is used to spawn additional research. Research projects are not just developed out of thin air. Good research is based on previous theory that has been developed over time through the testing of hypotheses (Neutens & Rubinson, 2010). Chapter 4 of this text will examine different theories that are commonly used when conducting health education research. Students are encouraged to consider how their research will test previous theory or contribute to the development of new theory.

Good research is apolitical, unbiased, and objective. Research must be above political, economic, and social influences. Anytime research results are biased or interpreted based on political, economic, or social agendas, the reputation and credibility of all research is called into question. Because of its very purpose, research must be independent and objective.

Research always starts with a question that needs to be answered or a problem that needs to be explored. How the question is worded and how well the question can be answered by the proposed research methodology are the foundation of good research. Chapter 5 of this text will provide information on how to develop good research questions, problem statements, and hypotheses.

For research to be considered good research, it must be designed in such a way that it can be replicated and validated. Several years ago there was a newspaper article reporting on research that found coffee caused pancreatic cancer. The study was not well designed and had been done on a very small number of subjects. When the actual research article from which the newspaper article had been written was reviewed, the researcher indicated that the findings were preliminary and that more research needed to be done to determine if the finding was valid. Additional studies have reported no such association. Had this original research not been replicated to determine if the results were valid, a false belief about coffee would have been accepted. Repeating studies that have already been completed is an important step in the research process. This example also shows that it is important to look at the original research and not rely on secondary reporting of research found in news stories.

Good quantitative research can be generalized to other settings. This means, for example, if a researcher finds that an ergonomics program was effective with secretaries for a given company, the program should also work for similar secretaries in other companies. If a program is effective in only one setting, it could mean that some aspect of that setting (participant motivation) or the program presenter (personable and dynamic) was responsible for the success and not the program being evaluated.

Research is only as good as the accuracy of its observations and measurements. If, for example, a researcher wanted to measure bone density and the calibrations of the equipment were off, the results of the research would also be off. This is a fairly obvious example. The same, however, is true for other types of measurements that health education researchers may use. If one wanted to measure the effects of a stress management program on perceived stress, the instrument used to measure perceived stress must also be accurate. If the instrument measured some other concept, such as anxiety, or if the instrument worked for females but not males, the results of the research would be just as poor as in the bone density example. All measurement instruments used in research must be valid and reliable. **Valid** means the instrument measures what it is supposed to measure (stress vs. anxiety), and **reliable** means the instrument is consistent in its measurement over time. In qualitative research it is just as important that any observations and recording of data be accurate. A detailed description of instrument validity and reliability will be presented in Chapter 8.

Research requires patient, unhurried activity. It takes time to do a thorough literature review, design a study, and collect and analyze data. Often barriers arise during a study that may affect an initial time line. When collecting survey data, for example, there are often problems with low response rates. In other words, the researcher fails to get back enough completed questionnaires to have valid results. Researchers may have to do additional mailings and follow-up phone calls to obtain the desired response rate. Although there may be a temptation to proceed without the needed number of respondents, to do so would jeopardize the results of the entire study.

Data must be thoroughly and rigorously analyzed before results can be presented. This involves cleaning the data so that input errors are corrected. It also means analyzing the data in different ways and looking for possible interactions between and among variables that could cause one to incorrectly interpret the results. Students are sometimes frustrated when advisors ask for the data to be reanalyzed or analyzed again in a slightly different way. This, however, is very important so that the data can be completely understood and the results accurately reported.

Once a research project is completed, it is important that the results be shared with the wider health education community. This means presenting the results at professional meetings and publishing the results in professional journals. Even if there are no statistically significant or new findings, these results are still important and should still be shared. What good is it to do research if others in the profession do not know what was learned?

Characteristics of Good Researchers

What makes good researchers? This is a reasonable question. As with all professional endeavors, certain personality types or characteristics help make some people more successful than others. The same is true about researchers. Table 1.2 summarizes traits found in good researchers.

First and foremost, good researchers are inquisitive. Researchers are constantly asking questions and seeking to answer those questions through the research process. Individuals who do not ask questions, do not wonder why something happened or failed to happen, and have no interest in exploring attitudes and behaviors probably will not make good researchers.

Good researchers must have patience and work in a deliberate and unhurried fashion. It takes time to carefully plan and conduct research. If researchers hurry through the planning phase, problems may arise in the implementation phase that can jeopardize the entire study. One student, for example, was in a hurry to get a mailing out

Table 1.2   Characteristics of Good Researchers

Inquisitive
Patient, unhurried, and deliberate
Perseverant and determined
Systematic and logical
Doubtful and skeptical
Independent, objective, impartial, and honest
Seek order and understanding
Courageous

prior to a self-imposed deadline. Unfortunately, he forgot to put an identification number on the return envelopes in the mailing. It was not until he started receiving the returns in the mail that he noticed the error. The research design required him to match responses and analyze the results in preestablished pairs. Because he did not have identification information on the envelopes, the responses could not be matched. The student's first response was to suggest changing the research design, but to do so would not have allowed him to answer the research questions he had posed and would have greatly weakened his study. Ultimately, he had to begin the entire process over. Had this student taken the time to check the mailing and perhaps have his advisor or fellow students look it over, he might have avoided the delay and cost of a second mailing. Patience and deliberateness are certainly important characteristics of good researchers.

Along with being patient and unhurried, good researchers are also perseverant and determined. When roadblocks present themselves, as in the previous example, researchers must persevere and find ways to complete the research. There are often stumbling blocks in research, but good researchers will find ways to overcome them.

Good researchers must be systematic and logical, because research is a systematic and logical process. Each step in the research process must be thoroughly completed before the next step can begin. For example, it does no good to send out questionnaires if the questionnaire has not been shown to be valid and reliable. Further, it is of no value to send out a valid and reliable questionnaire if the sample is not representative of the group being studied. One cannot have confidence in the results of research if the response rate from the sample is too low. Being systematic in completing every step and following a logical progression are the hallmarks of good research. Being systematic and logical means conforming to the accepted norms of research practice (DePoy & Gitlin, 2005).

This is true for both quantitative and qualitative researchers.

Researchers are doubters and skeptics. As researchers read the works of other researchers, they should be critical, raise doubts, and ask questions about the work. This is not done to put other researchers down and should not be thought of as a negative personality trait among researchers. The purpose is to seek alternative answers for questions, raise additional questions, and further the research endeavor. Conversely, as researchers share their research with other researchers, they should expect questions and doubts to be raised about the work. Ultimately, the discussion and debate that take place through such interchanges help to improve the quality of one's own research and the quality of all research within the health education field.

The very nature of the research endeavor requires researchers to be independent, objective, impartial, and honest. Researchers must deal with facts and not allow their own values to influence the results. They must be open to all possible outcomes. Good researchers must not permit themselves to be influenced by outside groups, funding agencies, or public opinion. To do so would be unethical. Anytime researchers allow their findings to be swayed, public confidence in all research is diminished.

Researchers try to seek order in their findings. It is important to determine how new research findings relate to the current body of knowledge in a given field. This is accomplished by relating research findings back to the literature to determine if the new findings support or refute previous findings. Researchers also seek order by trying to relate their research to theory. Research is used to originate, support, modify, and refute theory.

Finally, researchers are courageous. Every time new research findings are shared, the researchers conducting the work are opening themselves, their methodology, and their results to review and critique. It often takes "thick skin" to hear what reviewers have to say about one's work. Sometimes research results are not what researchers or funders expected; nevertheless, such results must be reported and published. Occasionally, research results are highly controversial and may contradict current thinking and belief systems. In such cases it takes real courage to report such results. Think of the courage it must have taken for John Snow to oppose the then-accepted miasmas theory of disease and forward his theory that an 1849 London cholera epidemic was being caused by the drinking water. To prove his point, Snow removed the handle of the water pump that served the infected area of London and the epidemic abated (Cottrell, Girvan, & McKenzie, 2009; see Figure 1.2).

FIGURE 1.2
London, England, 1849. John Snow interrupted a cholera epidemic by removing the handle from this pump, located on Broad Street.

Research Requirement

If you have been assigned to read this text, it is probably because you are in a required course that is designed to teach you how to conduct research. As a result of what you learn in this course, you will probably be required to develop and complete a capstone experience, honor's thesis, master's project, master's thesis, or doctoral dissertation, or at the very least pass comprehensive exams that will contain questions on research methods (Schloss & Smith, 1999). Although the specific requirements for the project, thesis, dissertation, or "comps" may vary from university to university, the requirement to learn about research will not. Research is one of the seven core responsibilities of health education specialists at the entry, advanced 1, and advanced 2 levels of practice (Cottrell et al., 2009). Learning about research methods is often the major distinction between undergraduate- and graduate-level health education programs. All health education specialists should be able to read, understand, and critique research. Those at the graduate level and some advanced undergraduates should also possess the skills to conduct research. See Box 1.2 for the research responsibility, competencies, and sub-competencies required of a health education specialist.

The type of research project undertaken may depend on the level of study. Undergraduate students may be required to complete a capstone experience. A **capstone experience** is a major project designed to conclude the undergraduate program. This project may involve conducting research. An **honors thesis** is usually completed by outstanding undergraduate students as either a capstone experience or an elective course.

Master's-level students are usually required to complete comprehensive exams and/or a project or thesis. **Comprehensive exams** are designed to assess a student's understanding of the responsibilities, competencies, and sub-competencies of a health educator as well as any content information

Box 1.2   Area IV: Conduct Evaluation and Research Related to Health Education

	Entry (Baccalaureate/master's, less than 5 years' experience)	Advanced 1 (Baccalaureate/master's, 5 years' experience or more)	Advanced 2 (Doctorate and 5 years' experience or more)
Competency A: Develop plans for evaluation and research	1. Synthesize information presented in the literature 2. Evaluate research designs, methods, and findings presented in the literature	1. Develop an inventory of existing valid and reliable tests and survey instruments	1. Assess the merits and limitations of qualitative and quantitative methods
Competency B: Review research and evaluation procedures	1. Evaluate data-gathering instruments and processes 2. Develop methods to evaluate factors that influence shifts in health status	1. Identify standards of performance to be applied as criteria of effectiveness 2. Identify methods to evaluate factors that influence shifts in health status 3. Select appropriate methods for evaluating program effectiveness	1. Establish a realistic scope of evaluation efforts 2. Select appropriate qualitative and/or quantitative evaluation design
Competency C: Design data collection instruments	1. Develop valid and reliable evaluation instruments 2. Develop appropriate data-gathering instruments	. . .	. . .
Competency D: Carry out evaluation and research plans	1. Use appropriate research methods and designs in health education practice 2. Use data collection methods appropriate for measuring stated objectives 3. Implement appropriate qualitative and quantitative evaluation techniques 4. Implement methods to evaluate factors that influence shifts in health status	1. Assess the relevance of existing program objectives to current needs	1. Apply appropriate evaluation technology 2. Analyze evaluation data
Competency E: Interpret results from evaluation and research	1. Analyze evaluation data 2. Analyze research data 3. Compare evaluation results to other findings 4. Report effectiveness of programs in achieving proposed objectives	1. Compare program activities with the stated program objectives 2. Develop recommendations based upon evaluation results	1. Determine the achievement of objectives by applying criteria to evaluation results 2. Communicate evaluation results using easily understood terms
Competency F: Infer implications from findings for future health-related activities	. . .	1. Suggest strategies for implementing recommendations that result from evaluation 2. Apply evaluation findings to refine and maintain programs	1. Propose possible explanations for evaluation findings

the program deems important. It would be unusual if such an exam did not have questions about research methods. A **master's project** involves program development, research, or evaluation that is usually specific to a work setting or agency. Projects typically involve just as much work as theses, but they may not be as tight in their methodology, and the results may not be generalizable or of interest to others outside of the agency in which the work takes place. A specific project to evaluate the effectiveness of a fitness program at a small midwestern company, for example, may not be publishable in most major research journals; however, the *Health Promotion Practice* journal and the Community Learning Ideas and Procedures (CLIPs) section of the *American Journal of Health Education* are intended to publish just such practitioner-oriented articles.

The master's project may also take different, less traditional forms than a master's thesis. Some programs, for example, may allow students to do projects that do not involve collecting primary data, such as a meta-analysis or a literature review with in-depth analysis. Others have allowed students to develop a new health education program or an educational video on a health-related topic. Typically, students electing non-traditional types of projects are still expected to write a modified project document containing the problem statement, literature review, methodology, and discussion. This document may or may not be in a five-chapter format as would most theses or dissertations. As always, it is important to check with one's academic program advisor to determine what is acceptable and what is not at any given institution.

The **master's thesis** is usually a well-designed study that will produce results of interest to others in the profession, and, therefore, the results should be published. The traditional thesis is written in five chapters and will be described later in this chapter. Since the master's thesis and master's project are often similar in nature, and to avoid confusion and the awkward wording associated with discussing projects and theses, from this point

forward the word "thesis" should be interpreted to incorporate the word "project."

A **doctoral dissertation** is a more complex research project conducted by doctoral students after they have been declared candidates for the degree. The scope of a doctoral dissertation is usually larger than that of a master's thesis. In particular, the sophistication of the design, amount of data collected, and level of data analysis are typically beyond what would be expected for the master's thesis. Intervention studies that may take longer to conduct are common at the doctoral level. Again, the results should be of interest to others in the profession and, therefore, publishable.

Regardless of which research requirement is undertaken, the ultimate goal within the academic program is to use the requirement to teach students the basic skills associated with conducting research. The process of developing and writing a project, thesis, or dissertation may seem long and arduous. Although it is true that the level of detail expected and the amount of writing involved in a thesis or dissertation may not be required when conducting research in the professional world, to go through the process as a graduate student is a valuable learning experience. Many students, in retrospect, say that completing the thesis or dissertation was one of the best learning experiences of their academic career. A Chinese proverb says, "I hear and I forget. I see and I remember. I do and I understand." The educational objective behind having students complete a thesis or dissertation is to have them "do and understand," while under the close supervision of a faculty advisor.

The Five-Chapter Thesis/Dissertation

Although there are variations among universities, most health education programs utilize some form of a five-chapter thesis/dissertation format. Conceptually the five chapters include the introduction to the problem (Chapter I), review of the literature (Chapter II), description of the methodology (Chapter III), presentation of the results (Chapter

IV), and finally a presentation of the conclusions and recommendations (Chapter V). Some programs utilize a four-chapter format by allowing Chapters IV and V to be combined into one chapter. Berg and Latin (2004) present a seven-chapter format in their research methods text. Essentially, they separate the introduction from the problem and the discussion from the summary and conclusions. Whether four, five, or seven chapters are required, the same information is presented. Students should always follow the guidelines of their respective academic programs when developing their thesis or dissertation.

By convention this book will always use roman numerals (I, II, III, IV, V) when referring to chapters in a thesis or dissertation. When referring to other chapters in this text, we will always use arabic numerals (1, 2, 3, 4, 5).

This textbook is designed to help students develop a five-chapter thesis or dissertation. When writing each chapter of the thesis or dissertation, one or more chapters in this text will help with this process (see Table 1.3).

Table 1.3   Thesis/Dissertation Chapters and Corresponding Chapters

Thesis/Dissertation Chapter No.	Chapters
Chapter I Introduction	Chapters 1–5
Chapter II Review of Literature	Chapters 3 and 4
Chapter III Methodology	Chapters 6–11
Chapter IV Results and Data Analysis	Chapter 12
Chapter V Conclusions and Recommendations	Chapter 13
Post Chapter V Sharing Thesis and Dissertation Findings	Chapter 14

Chapter I of a thesis or dissertation provides the reader with a brief synopsis of the most important background research on the topic and discusses any relevant theories to be utilized in the research. The problem statement or research question(s) is presented as well as any hypotheses, operational definitions, limitations, delimitations, and assumptions involved in the research. Chapters 1 through 5 of this book may all be helpful to students in developing Chapter I of the thesis or dissertation. In particular, Chapter 5 in this book discusses the specific sections included in Chapter I of the thesis or dissertation.

Chapter II of a thesis or dissertation provides a detailed description of the literature reviewed. Literature related to the topic as well as discussion of any relevant theories should be presented in this chapter. Often this chapter is actually written or at least presented in a detailed outline prior to writing Chapter I, as it is the literature review that helps develop the historical background, theory, research questions, and hypotheses included in Chapter I. Chapters 3 and 4 of this book should be most helpful to students in writing Chapter II of their thesis or dissertation.

Chapter III of a thesis or dissertation describes the methodology used in the study. This includes a description of the study population and sampling techniques, instruments used or developed, human subjects approval, pilot testing, study design, permissions from participants, cover letters, time lines, and procedures for data analysis. Not all studies will include all of the items just listed. In particular, qualitative studies may use very different headings. Regardless, it is important to write this chapter in great detail so that another researcher reading the document could follow exactly the procedures of the original researcher. To write Chapter III of the thesis or dissertation, students need to have a significant amount of information about research design and methodology. Chapters 6 through 11 in this book provide important information for students related to writing Chapter III of a thesis or dissertation.

Chapter IV of a thesis or dissertation presents the results of the research. This chapter is usually organized around the research questions and hypotheses (if appropriate). If the study is a quantitative study, reporting results typically involves presenting numbers and statistics in narrative and table/figure formats. Some universities may also have students discuss the results in this chapter. If such is the case, the discussion would not be included in Chapter V. If the study is qualitative, it may involve providing detailed lists or descriptions of responses/observations and synthesized analyses of study findings. Chapter 12 of this book will guide students in the development of Chapter IV of their thesis or dissertation.

Chapter V of a thesis or dissertation includes the conclusions, discussion, and recommendations. The conclusions should be based on the research questions or hypotheses and must be supported by the results presented in Chapter IV. In the discussion section, students interpret their findings in relation to other study findings and any theories that were utilized in the study. Recommendations are then made in three areas. First, recommendations are made concerning the practical implication of the research. In other words, how can the results of this research be used in real-world practice settings? Second, recommendations are made concerning the current research. What limitations were found in the study design? How could the study have been done better? Finally, recommendations are made concerning future research. Given the results of the current research, what are the next research steps to further this line of investigation? Chapter 13 of this book will help students develop Chapter V of their thesis or dissertation.

After the thesis or dissertation is completed and orally defended to the thesis or dissertation committee, the next step should be to share the results of the work with the broader health education profession. This involves presenting the findings at professional meetings and/or publishing the results in professional journals. Chapter 14 of this book provides information to students on presenting and publishing the results of their work.

Summary

In this chapter the concepts of research and health education research have been defined. Basic research approaches, methods, and terminology have been presented. Particular emphasis has been given to the similarities and differences between quantitative and qualitative research. While a major focus of this book will be on quantitative research, qualitative research will be presented as a viable option for health education research in answering questions that quantitative research cannot answer. In addition, this chapter exposed readers to the characteristics of good research and the characteristics of good researchers. The chapter ended by discussing the research requirement in undergraduate and graduate health education programs. The five-chapter thesis/dissertation was also presented as the framework for completing the graduate research requirement.

Review Questions

1. What is the definition of health education research?
2. Describe the essential characteristics of quantitative, qualitative, and mixed method research.
3. Explain the basic debate that exists between quantitative and qualitative researchers. Why does this debate continue to exist?
4. Identify and describe three research methods that are used by quantitative researchers.
5. Identify and describe three research methods that are used by qualitative researchers.
6. What research method appeals most to you? Why does it appeal to you?
7. Explain five characteristics of good research.

8. Analyze the characteristics of good researchers in light of your own perceived strengths and weaknesses.
9. Explain the differences between a master's project, master's thesis, and doctoral dissertation.
10. Describe what is covered in each of the five chapters of a thesis or dissertation.

References

Aday, L.A., & Cornelius, L.J. (2006). *Designing and conducting health surveys* (3rd ed.). San Francisco: Jossey-Bass.

Berg, K.E., & Latin, R.W. (2004). *Research methods in health, physical education, exercise science, and recreation* (2nd ed.). Philadelphia: Lippincott Williams & Wilkins.

Cottrell, R.R., Girvan, J.T., & McKenzie, J.F. (2009). *Principles and foundations of health promotion and education* (2nd ed.). San Francisco: Benjamin Cummings.

Creswell, J.W. (2005). *Educational research: Planning, conducting, and evaluating quantitative and qualitative research* (2nd ed.). Upper Saddle River, N.J.: Pearson Education, Inc.

Creswell, J.W. (2009). *Research design: Qualitative, quantitative and mixed methods approaches* (3rd ed.). Los Angeles: Sage Publications.

DePoy, E., & Gitlin, L.N. (2005). *Introduction to research* (3rd ed.). St. Louis: Elsevier Mosby.

Gay, L.R., Mills, G.E., & Airasian, P. (2006). *Educational research: Competencies for analysis and applications*. Upper Saddle River, N.J.: Pearson Education, Inc.

Kerlinger, F.N., & Lee, H.B. (2000). *Foundations of behavioral research* (4th ed.). Fort Worth, Tex.: Harcourt College Publishers.

Leedy, P.D., & Ormrod, J.E. (2010). *Practical research: Planning and design* (9th ed.). Upper Saddle River, N.J.: Pearson Education, Inc.

Martinez, T.F. (1997). Prostate cancer and dietary fat intake in African-American and Caucasian men. Unpublished master's thesis, University of Cincinnati.

McMillan, J.H., & Wergin, J.F. (2002). *Understanding and evaluating educational research* (2nd ed.). Upper Saddle River, N.J.: Merrill/Prentice Hall.

Neutens, J.J., & Rubinson, L. (2010). *Research techniques for the health sciences* (4th ed.). San Francisco: Benjamin Cummings.

Patten, M.L. (2009). *Understanding research methods: An overview of the essentials*. Glendale, Calif.: Pryczak Publishing.

Salkind, N.J. (2009). *Exploring research* (7th ed.). Upper Saddle River, N.J.: Prentice-Hall.

Schloss, P.J., & Smith, M.A. (1999). *Conducting research*. Upper Saddle River, N.J.: Merrill/Prentice Hall.

Viswanathan, M., Ammerman, A., Eng, E., Gartlehner, G., Lohr, K.N., Griffith, D., *et al.* (July 2004). *Community-based participatory research: Assessing the evidence*. Evidence Report/Technology Assessment No. 99 (Prepared by RTI—University of North Carolina Evidence-based Practice Center under Contract No. 290-02-0016). AHRQ Publication 04-E022-2. Rockville, Md.: Agency for Healthcare Research and Quality.

CHAPTER 2 | Finding a Topic and Getting Started

Chapter Objectives

After reading this chapter and answering the review questions, you should be able to:

1. Discuss why it is important to identify a good thesis or dissertation topic.
2. Describe at least five different ways to identify potential thesis or dissertation topics.
3. Relate any potential research topic to the 10 considerations to review prior to deciding on a research topic.
4. Discuss considerations to be made when selecting a committee chair.
5. Discuss considerations to be made when selecting committee members.

Key Terms

committee chair	institutional review board	modified replication
cross-sectional study	longitudinal study	PRECEDE/PROCEED model
health belief model	mentee	strict replication
human subjects committee	mentor	

Finding a research topic is one of the most important tasks for graduate students. The topic chosen will become an integral part of an individual's academic training. It may set the direction for future employment potential and establish an initial research agenda. At the very least, it is a topic the student will have to live with on a day-to-day basis for many weeks, months, or even years while completing the thesis or dissertation.

Some students enter graduate programs with a good idea of what they want to research. For example, one student's father had died of cancer and she knew she wanted to do research on some aspect of cancer when she first met with her academic advisor. Another student worked for a large company in its health and fitness program. He knew when entering the master's program that he wanted to do research on employee health using company employees as participants. Although these students had an idea of what they wanted to research, they still needed guidance to clarify and refine their research questions and develop acceptable research designs.

More common than students who know what they want to research, however, are students who have little or no idea of what they want to research. One of the most difficult tasks for graduate students is often finding a research topic. Some students agonize over this choice for months without making a decision. In one sense this is not bad, because it is an important decision and needs serious consideration. Such students, however, often become frustrated and feel they are not making progress toward their degree. They need to consider that the research process begins the minute one starts searching for and narrowing a topic. Finding, limiting, and refining a topic is not just spinning one's wheels; it is an important part of the research process (Blaxter, Hughes & Tight, 2002).

It is also possible, however, for students to spend too much time deciding on a topic. Some students resist making the final decision on a topic. Often an assignment in a research course pressures students to make a decision on their research topic. Although this may be what is needed to push an undecided student to make a decision, it is important to note that topics can typically be modified and revised throughout the development of the literature review and the writing of Chapters I, II, and III. Some students even totally change topics after completing their research course. It is not until the actual proposal hearing that students are fully committed to a topic and design.

The purpose of this chapter is to help students make this important decision and get started with their thesis or dissertation. Ideas will be presented on how to find a topic, considerations when choosing a topic, how to assemble a thesis or dissertation committee, and how to select a committee chair.

Finding a Topic

It is important to start to identify a research topic early in one's graduate program. One should not wait for the research methods class or research seminar to begin thinking about the thesis or dissertation topic. Since not all students are fortunate enough to enter a graduate program knowing what they want to research, the following suggestions for identifying a thesis or dissertation topic may be of help (see Table 2.1).

Table 2.1   Potential Sources of Research Topics

Literature reviews
Thesis and dissertation defense hearings
Local, state, regional, and/or national conventions
Existing theory
Coursework
Current work environment
Community contacts
Grant/foundation sources
Chance opportunities

Literature Review

A review of the literature is typically the first place to start looking for research topics. This is particularly helpful when students have a general topic area in mind but not a specific research question. In other words, if a student has an interest in physical fitness and exercise, for example, but is not sure what specifically to research, reading research articles about physical fitness and exercise is a good place to begin. At this point, reading anything about physical fitness and exercise will help. Later, when a specific research question has been identified, the literature review will become more focused.

Remember, all research starts with a question. Articles should be read not just to obtain the content but with the purpose of developing questions about the work or critiquing the work. What would I have done differently? What could be done to improve this work? How can variables be changed or new variables included to extend the research? Are there other population groups for which this study could be done? As a student is reviewing articles on a topic of interest, it is a good idea to have a notepad nearby with a page titled "Questions." When questions come to mind during the reading, they can then be written on the notepad.

See Box 2.1 for an example of how this process works. Box 2.1 contains a reprint of an article's abstract. Although it would be best for the student

---

Box 2.1 Reviewing Literature for Questions

Abstract

This study retrospectively examined physical activity patterns across three specific age periods (childhood, teenage, and young adulthood) in a cross sectional sample of young Caucasian undergraduate women ($N = 44$). All women (mean age = 22.27 ± 3.14 years) completed questionnaire packets assessing transtheoretical model of behavior change constructs. Additionally, each woman completed a detailed historical physical activity oral interview with the investigator. Physical activity decreased significantly across all age groups. Physical activity during ages 13 to 18 and 19 years and older, counter conditioning (i.e., substituting physical activity for other behaviors), self-liberation (i.e., making a commitment to adopt an active lifestyle), self-reevaluation (i.e., recognizing the personal importance of physical activity in one's life), reinforcement management (i.e., rewards associated with physical activity), physical activity during ages 6–12 years, and dramatic relief (i.e., experiencing negative emotions associated with physical inactivity) had the strongest relationship with current physical activity participation. Cons (i.e., costs associated with physical activity participation) were negatively correlated with current physical activity patterns. Results suggest a need to identify additional correlates and mediators of physical activity participation in this population.

Sample Questions

I wonder if there are other correlates (i.e., parental exercise patterns, sibling exercise patterns, self-concept, body image, self-efficacy) that might correlate with physical activity participation in this population?

I wonder if this study were repeated with a larger random sample of women instead of volunteers, if the results would be the same?

I wonder if the same correlates would be found in African American women?

I wonder if the same correlates would be found in a group of women in the same age group, but not attending college?

I wonder if the same correlates would be found in a group of older women?

I wonder if the same correlates would be found in college men?

Etc.

Source: Wallace, L.S. (2003). Correlates of lifetime physical activity in young women. *American Journal of Health Education*, 34, 41–46. Used with permission.

---

to read the entire article, because of space limitations only the abstract is provided here. Students are encouraged to read this abstract and develop potential questions while doing so. The students' questions can then be compared to sample questions developed by the authors while reading the same abstract. Note that at this point it is not necessary for questions to be worded in any type of formal research format. Rather, it is enough for questions to be written down in everyday language. Any of the questions identified in Box 2.1 could serve as the basis for developing formal research questions or problem statements used in a thesis or dissertation.

If in reviewing the literature one decides to do the same study as someone else but change the population being studied or the instrument used, this might be called a **modified replication** study. It is also possible to do a **strict replication** study, where the researcher tries to duplicate in every way the methodology of the original researcher to determine if the same results will occur. A strict replication would only be undertaken if the original research was thought to be important to the field and the results were questionable. For example, a study may have been completed with a small number of participants, and questions arose as to whether the same results would be obtained with a larger sample. Both modified replication studies and strict replication studies are valid research and can serve as excellent theses or dissertations (Patten, 2009).

Thesis/Dissertation Defense Hearings

Attending thesis and dissertation defense hearing presentations is another way to help identify potential research topics. The discussion that is part of a defense often raises questions about the research that could serve as the basis for additional research projects. In addition, it is always helpful to see how others have formulated research questions and

devised research methodologies to answer their questions.

It might also be helpful to review the titles of research projects recently completed in one's program. Some selected theses completed at the authors' institutions can be seen in Box 2.2, and some sample dissertation titles from selected U.S. universities can be seen in Box 2.3.

Professional Meetings

Another way to identify potential research topics is to attend local, state, regional, and/or national health education professional meetings. Health

---

Box 2.2   Completed Theses from Selected U.S. Universities

Atri, A. (2007). Role of social support, hardiness and acculturation as predictors of mental health among the international students of Asian Indian origin in Ohio. Unpublished master's thesis, University of Cincinnati.

Austin, A. (2006). Stress and quality of diet in adolescents and college students. Unpublished master's thesis, Cleveland State University.

Beyer, S.P. (2008). Examining the social and emotional impact of substance use on the users' family members. Unpublished master's thesis, Cleveland State University.

Bland, R. (2007). Medication compliance among hemodialysis patients and factors that contribute to non-compliance. Unpublished master's thesis, University of Cincinnati.

Browder, M.E.W. (2008). Sexuality education curriculum in secondary schools and its relationship to sexual knowledge, attitudes and behaviors of college students. Unpublished master's thesis, University of Cincinnati.

Byun, W.W. (2007). The physical activity levels of international college students. Unpublished master's thesis, Ball State University.

Cermak, M.A. (2009). Women's knowledge of HPV and their perceptions of physician educational efforts regarding HPV and cervical can-

cer. Unpublished master's thesis, University of Cincinnati.

Fondran, K.M. (2008). The effect of Surya Namaskara Yoga practice on resting heart rate and blood pressure, flexibility, upper body muscle endurance, and perceived well-being in healthy adults. Unpublished master's thesis, Cleveland State University.

Heitzer, J.G.-H. (2004). A descriptive analysis of patient education courses in undergraduate and graduate health education programs. Unpublished master's thesis, Ball State University.

Koski, J. (2003). Hepatitis A and B vaccination in matriculating college students: Knowledge, self-perceived risk, health risk behaviors, and theory of planned behavior constructs. Unpublished master's thesis, Oregon State University.

Smith, L.G. (2008). HPV knowledge of college females and their intention to receive the HPV vaccination. Unpublished master's thesis, Ball State University.

Walter, J.L. (2007). Determining attitude toward and level of involvement in health promotion and education programs in Greater Cincinnati faith communities. Unpublished master's thesis, University of Cincinnati.

Box 2.3   Completed Dissertations from Selected U.S. Universities

---

Bonetto, M. (2005). State legislators' knowledge and perceptions of medical savings accounts and the U.S. health care system: Identifying future compromises to health care reform. Unpublished doctoral dissertation, Oregon State University.

Carneiro, R.B. (2006). Barebacking among MSM Internet users. Unpublished doctoral dissertation, University of Georgia.

Della, L. (2006). Explaining variation in fruit and vegetable intake with a consumer marketing tool. Unpublished doctoral dissertation, University of Georgia.

Hendershot, C.H. (2008). Elementary school nurses' perceptions and practices regarding body mass index measurement in school children. Unpublished doctoral dissertation, University of Toledo.

Hirschler, C.A. (2008). An examination of vegans' beliefs and experiences using critical theory and autoethnography. Unpublished doctoral dissertation, Cleveland State University.

Leone, J.E. (2007). Predictors of body image dissatisfaction among selected adolescent males. Unpublished doctoral dissertation, Southern Illinois University at Carbondale.

Nevares, H.C. (2006). Cross cultural examination of factors influencing exercise during pregnancy. Unpublished doctoral dissertation, Oregon State University.

Thompson, M.M. (2007). Males and male hormonal contraception. Unpublished doctoral dissertation, Kent State University.

Tobler, A. (2009). Neighborhood context and alcohol use among urban, low-income, multiethnic, young adolescents. Published doctoral dissertation, University of Florida.

Torrens, A. (2006). The social construction of school refusal: An exploratory study of school personnel's perceptions. Unpublished doctoral dissertation, University of South Florida.

Wood, M.R. (2007). Parental/guardian predictors of well controlled and poorly controlled asthmatic African American youths. Unpublished doctoral dissertation, University of Toledo.

Yan, A.F. (2009). Environmental influences on physical activity and obesity in African American adolescents—a multilevel perspective. Unpublished doctoral dissertation, University of Maryland.

---

education students should look for state, regional, or national meetings of the American Association for Health Education (AAHE), the Society for Public Health Education (SOPHE), the American Public Health Association (APHA), the American School Health Association (ASHA), the American College Health Association (ACHA), and the American Academy of Health Behavior (AAHB), among others. Most of these meetings will have presentations and poster sessions on the latest research. This is a great place to brainstorm ideas with other students and researchers, which could lead to identifying a research topic. At such meetings, new information is presented that may stimulate questions needing to be answered. Issues and trends within the health education profession

are also a common topic for presentations and informal discussions. Students might very well be stimulated to do their thesis or dissertation on some aspect of the profession such as credentialing, accreditation, ethics, and so on.

Theories and Models

Existing health behavior theories or models are another source for research topics. For example, one might choose the **health belief model** (Rosenstock, 1966). The health belief model was originally devised to examine why people used or did not use health services. It has since been expanded to examine all types of health-related behaviors. A student might begin by reading as much as possible about this classic model. In particular, the student might want to examine how the model has been applied in past research projects. The student might then develop a research project around some application of this model to a health behavior not previously studied in this way. A student could also select a health planning model like **PRECEDE-PROCEED** (Green & Kreuter, 2005) and develop a study around an application of this model. Previous coursework a student may have taken could serve as the impetus for learning about these theories and models upon which a research study could be based. In particular, a behavioral theory course and/or a health planning course might be very helpful. Chapter 4 of this book will present information on theories in research that might also be of help in selecting a research topic.

In actuality, any course a student takes could serve as the springboard for the research project. As discussion occurs in classes and questions are raised, students should develop a system to keep track of any potential research topics. Some students have a page at the end of each class notebook dedicated to listing potential research questions. Other students write the ideas directly into their notes and then mark them with a special color of highlighter. Still others maintain a separate research notebook that they take to all of their classes in which they write potential research ideas.

Work Setting

Part-time students can often use their current work setting as a source of research problems, while full-time students may use a past work setting. Students are encouraged to think about their current or past employment settings and the types of health education–related questions that need to be answered. The advantage to doing such research is that students are often allowed to work on their thesis or dissertation while on the job. This provides for a very efficient use of time. Further, the work should be of real practical value to both the student researcher and the worksite.

Local Contacts

Another idea for identifying potential research projects is to contact health education specialists working in the area and ask if they have any programs that need to be evaluated or any ideas for research projects. This could include health education specialists working for a local health department, a corporate health/fitness center, a health care facility, any voluntary agency, or even a local school system. Often these health education specialists have ideas for research, but because of their job demands they do not have time to pursue the ideas themselves. They welcome students who can do the research that really needs to be done. One health education student, for example, contacted the local branch of the American Lung Association (ALA). He learned that the ALA had been offering smoking cessation programs using hypnosis for several years, but they had not done any evaluation on the program. After agreeing to conduct a retrospective evaluation study (looking back at past participants), he was given access to all ALA records in order to locate past participants, copying and mailing privileges, and a reading list from which to start his literature review. The ALA was thrilled to have someone to evaluate its program (which included the supervisory input of university faculty), and the student was thrilled to have identified a research topic in an area of personal interest.

Funding Sources

Foundations and other sources of grants and contracts are good places to look for potential research topics. Most universities subscribe to services that list potential funding agencies and their funding priorities. Looking over such lists may give students ideas for research that needs to be completed. An additional advantage in using this approach to identify potential research topics is that possible funding sources for the research are also identified. Oftentimes, however, students are not eligible for or do not have enough experience to compete for such funding. It may be possible for students to jointly seek funding with their faculty advisors, or they may just use a list of funding sources as an idea generator for their own research topic without actually applying for funding.

Serendipity

An additional source for identifying research topics is what might be termed serendipitous events or chance opportunities. An example might be a faculty member who has just been awarded a grant and is looking to turn part of the research over to a graduate student to use for his or her thesis or dissertation. By chance, a given student happens onto a great project that facilitates this faculty member's research. Although students cannot plan on this happening, they should always be on the lookout for any such opportunity that might arise.

Population Group/Topic Approach

Other ideas about research may come from reviewing Table 2.2. On the left side of the table is a partial list of population groups to study, and on the right side a partial list of potential topics. In addition to thinking of each topic area or population group as a potential research topic, it is also possible to take one population group and combine it with a topic area to develop research topics. For example, one might identify research questions related to the mental health issues of cancer survivors, the physical fitness levels of stay-at-home mothers, or advocacy issues related to diabetes.

Graduate students are strongly encouraged to look at groups other than college students to study for their theses and dissertations. Although college students are an easy group to access, studying other less studied groups might be of more value

to the field. For example, it is difficult to find research on persons in the 18–24 age range who do not attend college. This group may be quite different from traditional college students. Accessing this population can be more challenging than accessing college students, but the resulting information from studying this group may be most useful. Worksites, churches, shopping malls, or even local bars may be the best sites at which to access this group.

In essence, the number of research topics is limitless. As long as there are questions to be answered, there is research to be done. The key factor for students is to identify a topic that meets their needs as graduate students. The next section will present students with some helpful guidelines to follow when selecting a topic.

Considerations in Choosing a Topic

Numerous considerations should be made prior to deciding on a research project for the thesis or dissertation requirement. As students begin to narrow down topics to research, they are encouraged to compare each potential topic to the list of considerations in Table 2.3.

Contribution to the Profession

It is important that the research topic chosen contributes to the profession. It would make little sense to expend all the time and effort to complete a research study and have results that would be of little or no value to other health educators or the population being studied. Schloss and Smith (1999) note that "the most extensive literature review, elaborate sampling method, elegant analysis, and comprehensive conclusions are for naught if the topic is of little interest or utility to members or beneficiaries of your profession" (p. 31).

There are several ways studies contribute to the knowledge and practice of a profession (Creswell,

Table 2.2   Research Idea Starters

Population groups to research	Topical areas to research
Preschool children	Alcohol
Elementary school children	Tobacco
Secondary school children	Illicit drugs
Home-schooled children	Stress
College students	Nutrition
Non–college students	Sexuality
Dropouts	Cancer
Pregnant teens	Heart disease
Pregnant women	Sexually transmitted diseases
Cancer patients	HIV/AIDS
Cancer survivors	Health consumer behaviors
Heart disease patients	Mental health
Heart disease survivors	Environmental health
Working mothers	Physical fitness/exercise
Stay-at-home mothers	Communicable diseases
Homosexuals	Chronic diseases
Employee groups	Prevention behaviors
Unemployed persons	Behavior change strategies
Working poor	Safety
Rural, suburban, urban dwellers	Parental influences
Professional health educators	Peer influences
Professional association members	Media influences
Athletes	Internet usage
Recreational sports participants	Computer-assisted instruction
Elderly persons	Self-concept
Cultural/ethnic groups	Body image
Retirement home dwellers	Locus of control
Police and/or fire personnel	Eating disorders
Smokers	Advocacy issues
Diabetics	Health policy issues
Overweight individuals	Health education careers
Religious groups	Marketing health or health education
Nurses	Health education certification (CHES)

Table 2.3 Considerations in Choosing a Topic

Interest and enthusiasm
Time
Cost
Scope of the problem
Contribution to the profession
Support and expertise
Access issues/human subjects
Degree of control
Design
Values and comfort level of the researcher

2005). They can fill a void that exists in the literature or extend existing research. This is accomplished by studying new participants, new sites, new theories, or new variables that have not been researched. Studies can also contribute to the profession by replicating studies already completed with different participants at different sites. This helps to confirm and verify the results of the duplicated study. Studies also contribute to the literature if they examine "people not heard, silenced or rejected by society" (Creswell, 2005, p. 64). This is particularly important in community and public health settings where there are large groups of marginalized people at high risk for health-related problems who do not receive health care or important health information. Finally, a study contributes to the profession if it serves to improve practice. Anytime research can answer questions about how health education practitioners can best help people live happy, healthy, and productive lives, it is most certainly contributing to the profession.

Interest and Enthusiasm

Almost without exception, the authors of research methods texts implore students to select thesis or dissertation topics they are interested in and enthusiastic about (Leedy & Ormrod, 2010; Neutens & Rubinson, 2010; Salkind, 2000). This is really common sense. Students are going to be intimately involved with their research topic for an extended period of time. If they are not enthusiastic and passionate about their topic, it will be more difficult spending the time and energy needed to complete a thesis or dissertation.

Salkind (2000) warns, however, that "falling in love with your idea can be fatal" (p. 49). When this occurs, students may become so attached to their idea that they cannot bear to change anything about it. This could spell disaster in terms of completing the research, the student's relationship with the graduate committee, and the quality of the final product. Jung (2000) also warns about having too much "personal interest" in a topic. Her concern is that "Personal interest may cause bias in how you would research a topic. . . . You have to be willing to accept whatever your research finally shows, and if you can't present all your findings because they may conflict with how you want your research to come out, then you are not doing research the way it should be done" (p. 44).

While keeping these warnings in mind, it is still considered important to look for a thesis or dissertation topic that is of interest. In most situations, interest and enthusiasm will increase motivation, enhance the likelihood of completion, and improve the final product.

Time

The time required to complete a research project is an important consideration, especially for students who are looking to graduate and seek employment in a reasonable time period. Faculty also want to see students complete their thesis or dissertation and progress into the profession. It is therefore important to select a research project that is reasonable in terms of time. What might be considered reasonable? Although there is great variation in research projects, it is reasonable to expect that the data collection and analysis phase of a research project may take several months for master's students and several months to a year or more for doctoral students. This is in addition to the time it takes to develop the research question, write the literature review, locate or develop and test the instruments, obtain human subjects approval, and so on.

The data collection and analysis phases of research usually take the greatest amount of time. As a result, students should carefully examine what will be necessary in terms of data collection and analysis for any proposed research project. In general, quantitative studies typically take less time to complete than qualitative studies (Patten, 2009). Graduate students should consider conducting a **cross-sectional study** instead of a **longitudinal study** (Neutens & Rubinson, 2010). A cross-sectional study, for example, might compare the exercise behaviors of elementary school, middle school, and high school students at a given point in time, such as next week. A longitudinal study would follow the exercise behaviors of a specific group of elementary school children as they progress through middle school and high school. Unless students are willing to wait 12 years for their subjects to mature and data collection to be completed, this would not be a good research design choice for a thesis or dissertation. It might, however, be an excellent research project to begin after graduation.

To gauge the time needed to complete a study, students can review similar studies to determine the time they took to complete. Committee members and the committee chair should also be consulted, as they may have experience conducting or supervising other such studies. It is a good idea for students to develop a realistic time line for completion with at least a 25% "fudge factor" built in. In other words, if you plan that it will take 8 months to complete your study, give yourself 10 months in the time line you develop. The time line should list each step with an estimate of the amount of time it will take to complete that step (see Figure 2.1). Remember, a time line is not "written in stone." It is just an estimate of the time required to complete the thesis or dissertation, and it may have to be adjusted as one progresses through the process.

Cost

Do not forget that there is a cost to doing research. Unless you have your research fully funded (which few graduate students do), you will have to pay out of pocket to complete your research. Depending on the type of research, the costs can vary from several hundred to several thousand dollars. Consider a student who wants to conduct a mailed survey with 300 participants. The student will need to pay for 600 envelopes, 300 copies of the survey materials, postage to mail 300 packets, and postage for 300 return envelopes, plus copying and postage for any follow-up mailings needed to increase the return rate. This study is probably in the range of $400 to $1,000.

When considering any research topic, it is important to cost it out. Develop a budget and have your advisor review it. Some universities have special funds for which graduate students can apply that may pay part or all of the research costs. Ask your advisor if such funds exist at your institution. Typical costs associated with research can be seen in Table 2.4.

Scope of Problem

In selecting a topic for research in graduate school, the goal should be to pick a topic that is realistic and feasible yet contributes to the profession. This is not the time to solve all of the problems facing health promotion and education. Blaxter and colleagues (2002) describe what they term the Goldilocks strategy: "You want to select a topic which is not too big, and not too small, but just right (and one which will not break)" (p. 25). Thompson (2000) says, "As you select your topic and focus your research, be sure to maintain a good perspective on your most immediate goal: completing this particular research project to meet degree requirements" (p. 62). When students are in the planning stage for their thesis or dissertation, it is tempting to develop grandiose ideas for studies that address complex and sophisticated

Task	Jan	Feb	Mar	Apr	May	June	July	Aug	Sept	Oct	Nov	Dec
Literature review		X	X	X							X	
Develop proposal			X	X								
Present proposal					X							
Human subjects						X						
Mail survey instrument							X					
Mail follow-up								X				
Data entry									X			
Data analysis									X	X		
Write Chapters IV and V										X	X	
Defend thesis												X

FIGURE 2.1
Sample time line for completing a thesis.

Table 2.4   Costs Associated with Research

Book and journal purchases
Article reprints and interlibrary loan costs
Travel costs to and from research sites
Telephone and long distance or cellular fees
Postage
Purchase or rental of equipment (computer, printer,
    scanner, tape recorder, skin calipers, etc.)
Purchase of data collection instrument and
    scoring keys
Software (word processing, statistical package,
    spreadsheet, etc.)
Miscellaneous consumables (paper, envelopes,
    printer cartridges, tape, paper clips, staples,
    batteries, etc.)
Thesis/dissertation publication costs
Fees for degree registration and/or examination

questions facing the profession. Remember, however, that these studies then need to be carried through to completion, which may take more time, money, and expertise than you have. A good faculty advisor will assist students with refining topics so they are within the scope of a thesis or dissertation yet still worthy of study.

Support and Expertise

Various types of support are needed for students to successfully complete their graduate research requirement. First and foremost is faculty support. Students need to have the support of faculty with expertise in the type of research they are proposing. If, for example, students want to do a quantitative study, they need to have faculty supporting them who are familiar with quantitative research designs and statistical analyses. If a student is interested in doing a historical study, he or she needs to have faculty present who can guide and support historical research.

Students may also need the support and cooperation of the participants in the study. If participants are unwilling to provide needed information,

to complete a survey, or to be interviewed, the study will not proceed. Further, students will need the support of the supervisors or managers of participants in worksite or school settings.

In addition to academic and participant support, students also need personal and emotional support. Blaxter and colleagues (2002) note that "Undertaking research, or any kind of education, can threaten your personal, family, work or social life. Be aware of the demands which your research project may put on your loved ones, friends and colleagues" (p. 28).

It is a good idea for students to carefully consider the support needed and the support available before beginning the thesis or dissertation. If academic, administrative, participant, or personal support is questionable, students should establish the needed support or look for another research topic. Beginning a research study without adequate support can lead to disaster.

Access Issues

In deciding on a research topic, it is important to consider the accessibility of the group to be studied. Some groups of people, such as homosexuals, may try to remain anonymous and may be difficult to locate for study purposes. Other times, there are limitations on who can be studied and the types of questions that can be asked because of human subjects constraints. All colleges and universities have a **human subjects committee** or **institutional review board** (IRB) that approves research proposals utilizing human subjects before research can begin. These committees or boards are mandated by the Office for the Protection from Research Risk (OPRR) under the Department of Health and Human Services. Their task is to assure the safety and ethical treatment of those being studied by ensuring that federal guidelines for the treatment of human subjects are followed. Individual participants in a study who cannot legally or practically make informed consent decisions to participate in a research study, such as minors, the mentally impaired, and the incarcerated, are often difficult to access.

In some cases, approval must be obtained from multiple levels prior to collecting data. If one wanted to collect data on the health behaviors of public school students, for example, approval would most likely be needed from the human subjects committee, the school board, the superintendent, the parents of the children, and the children themselves. This is not to say it is impossible to collect data in schools. Rather, the point here is that graduate students should consider accessibility issues prior to deciding on a research topic. Obtaining the permissions necessary to do research can take considerable time, and this must be included in any estimates of time to degree completion. See Chapter 7 for more information on selecting study participants.

Degree of Control

Students should try to develop research studies that give them as much control as possible. Whenever one must rely on other people to return survey instruments, show up for appointments, agree to interviews, record their behaviors, send out a mailing, provide funding, and so on, one is opening the door to uncertainty. The fact that completion of a particular study relies on other people should not be seen as a red flag but as a yellow warning flag. Students should proceed with caution. At the very least, students should identify the areas where they lack control and do everything possible to maximize a positive result.

Design Considerations

Students need to consider carefully the research design they are planning to use in their study. The first and most important consideration is whether the design will answer the research question. If the research question cannot be adequately answered using a specified design, another design must be selected or there is no need to do the study.

A second consideration is how comfortable the student feels with the design. If, for example, the research design calls for students to do personal interviews and the student is shy talking to strangers, another equally effective methodology should be considered or another research study undertaken.

Values and Comfort Level of the Researcher

A final consideration to be made prior to deciding on a research topic is whether the research is in concert with the values and comfort level of the researcher. Although all research is supposed to be value free, Neutens and Rubinson (2002) point out that value-free research is a myth. All researchers have values that they bring to their research. Problems arise when values are so strong that the researcher's objectivity is lost. In other cases, one's personal values can make it difficult or uncomfortable to conduct some research projects.

Suppose, for example, a student is doing research on the impact of abstinence-only versus abstinence-based sex education. Suppose further that the student is an employee of Planned Parenthood and has a strong personal belief that abstinence-based sex education that includes specific information about condom use is superior to abstinence-only sex education that provides no contraceptive information. The student believes (and hypothesizes) that abstinence-based sex education is more likely to prevent unwanted pregnancy and sexually transmitted infections. After conducting the research, however, the results indicate no significant differences between the two approaches in reducing unwanted pregnancy or sexually transmitted infections. At this point the student's values could come into play. As a researcher, the student should accurately report the results of the study and publish or present the findings. Instead, the student chooses to ignore the findings and not promote them beyond the health education program in which the research was conducted. This student should have considered the strong values held on this topic prior to starting the research. It would probably have been better for this student to select another topic.

In an actual example, values were considered prior to conducting research. In this case, the student was given the opportunity to work on a grant to conduct research in the gay community on HIV/AIDS risk behaviors. The work was to be totally funded and would have served as his thesis topic. After initially accepting the opportunity, the student reconsidered his choice. It seems the student was brought up in a strong Christian home. His values and beliefs would have made it extremely uncomfortable for him to work in the gay community. He decided it best to let someone else work on the grant and selected another topic.

In summary, a multitude of factors need to be considered when deciding on a thesis or dissertation topic. Although no topic will be perfect in all regards, it is important to consider all factors prior to deciding on a topic. One factor overlooked in the decision-making process can end up being the barrier that prevents one from completing the research requirement.

Selecting a Committee Chair

In most health education programs, students will select a faculty member to serve as their primary advisor for the thesis or dissertation. This faculty member may be called the student's **committee chair,** major advisor, research advisor, research supervisor, or some similar title. This person is charged with "an academic responsibility for guiding and advising you on your research project" (Blaxter *et al.,* 2002, p. 138). It is this individual who will work most closely with students throughout the entire research process. From the beginning stages of conceptualization to the final defense hearing, this person is going to be highly involved. For that reason the selection of this person is very important (see Box 2.4).

As a first step in selecting a committee chair, the student should identify faculty who are qualified to serve in that capacity. At some institutions, any faculty member can chair a graduate committee. At other institutions, only those at the associate professor level or above can chair a committee. Some institutions make a distinction between graduate faculty and nongraduate faculty. Only graduate faculty are permitted to chair graduate committees, and some institutions may have different criteria for thesis versus dissertation chairs. Graduate faculty status can be granted based on a variety of considerations, including academic rank, previous research record, previous graduate committee work, and time spent at the institution.

Ideally, the committee chair should have knowledge in the topic area the student is studying. If a potential committee chair does not possess such knowledge, the student should either try to find another committee chair or identify a committee member with that content expertise. It is more difficult, but not impossible, for research to be completed when the committee chair has little or no knowledge of the topic being studied. In addition to topical knowledge, a committee chair should also have a good knowledge of the research methods proposed for a study. This helps to ensure that the research design, analysis, conclusions, discussion, and recommendations will be on target.

Another critical consideration in selecting a committee chair is that person's knowledge of the program, college, and university rules and regulations concerning theses and dissertations. This is critical. The specific requirements can vary considerably from one program to another and from one institution to another. Select a committee chair who is good with details and that person will probably be knowledgeable about the rules and regulations that apply to theses and dissertations. A faculty member who is not fully aware of such rules and regulations can cause additional rewrites and delays in completion of graduate research.

A graduate committee chair should be responsive to students. That means students should select

---

Box 2.4   Rabbit Story

One sunny day a rabbit came out of her hole in the ground to enjoy the fine weather. The day was so nice that she became careless and a fox snuck up behind her and caught her.

"I am going to eat you for lunch!" said the fox.

"Wait!" replied the rabbit. "You should at least wait a few days."

"Oh yeah? Why should I wait?"

"Well, I am just finishing my thesis on 'The Superiority of Rabbits Over Foxes and Wolves.'"

"Are you crazy? I should eat you right now! Everybody knows that a fox will always win over a rabbit."

"Not really, not according to my research. If you like, you can come into my hole and read it for yourself. If you are not convinced, you can go ahead and have me for lunch."

"You really are crazy!" But since the fox was curious and had nothing to lose, he went with the rabbit. The fox never came out.

A few days later the rabbit was again taking a break from writing and, sure enough, a wolf came out of the bushes and was ready to set upon her.

"Wait!" yelled the rabbit. "You can't eat me right now."

"And why might that be, my furry appetizer?"

"I am almost finished writing my thesis on 'The Superiority of Rabbits Over Foxes and Wolves.'"

The wolf laughed so hard that he almost lost his grip on the rabbit.

"Maybe I shouldn't eat you; you really are sick . . . in the head. You might have something contagious."

"Come and read it for yourself; you can eat me afterward if you disagree with my conclusions." So the wolf went down in the rabbit's hole . . . and never came out.

The rabbit finished her thesis and was out celebrating in the local lettuce patch. Another rabbit came along and asked, "What's up? You seem very happy."

"Yup, I just finished my thesis."

"Congratulations. What's it about?"

"'The Superiority of Rabbits Over Foxes and Wolves.'"

"Are you sure? That doesn't sound right."

"Oh yes, come and read it for yourself."

So together they went down into the rabbit's hole. As they entered, the friend saw the typical graduate abode, albeit a rather messy one after writing a thesis. The computer with the controversial work was in one corner. To the right there was a pile of fox bones, and on the left a pile of wolf bones. In the middle was a large, well-fed lion.

The moral of the story:

The title of your thesis doesn't matter.

The subject doesn't matter.

The research doesn't matter.

All that matters is who your advisor is.

—Author Unknown

---

a committee chair who has a reputation for providing students with prompt and thorough feedback on projects and papers. A thesis or dissertation is different from most academic work students have done. Typically, students submit projects or papers and receive a grade for the work submitted. With a thesis or dissertation, students submit a draft, receive feedback, revise, submit another draft, receive feedback, and so forth. It usually takes multiple submissions and rewrites of each chapter to get the thesis or dissertation into an acceptable form. If the committee chair does not provide prompt, thorough feedback, the time to complete the graduate degree will be extended. A good committee chair will keep students focused and on track with their research requirement.

Select a committee chair who is well respected in the program and gets along well with other faculty. Zhang (2000) notes, "If you happen to choose a professor who does not get along with many others in the department either academically or personally, you are likely to be a victim or scapegoat of their fights" (p. 16).

The mentor's reputation within the profession should also be a consideration for students selecting their committee chair. Who a health education student studies with may be as important as what the student studies. For a student to be able to say that Professor XXX chaired his or her thesis or dissertation can carry real weight when searching for a job. Further, a well-known professor with a good reputation will have a wider network of contacts and may be able to use those contacts to help secure good jobs for their students upon completion of their degrees.

Because of the nature of graduate research, students will probably develop a more personal relationship with their committee chair than with other committee members or other faculty. For that reason it is important that students select faculty members they like and with whom they feel comfortable to serve as committee chairs. Hopefully, a close, lifelong mentor-mentee relationship will be established through thesis or dissertation work. A **mentor** is usually an older, more experienced individual who provides advice and support to and fosters the progress of a younger, less experienced person or **mentee**. This should not be construed to mean that graduate students should only select older faculty to serve as their committee chairs. Often younger faculty members make excellent mentors, and because the graduate student experience is fresher in their minds, they may relate well to current graduate students.

To maintain a good mentor-mentee relationship, it is important that both parties have realistic expectations of the other. For a listing of realistic expectations of graduate committee chairs and graduate students, see Table 2.5.

Table 2.5   Student and Committee Chair Expectations

What students should expect of committee chairs:
1. Advice and assistance on selecting a topic
2. Advice and assistance in developing research design
3. Advice and assistance preparing for proposal hearing
4. Advice and assistance preparing human subjects proposal
5. Reasonable turn-around times when reading drafts
6. Accurate and thorough feedback on drafts
7. Advice and assistance with data analysis and conclusion development
8. Advice and assistance preparing for defense hearing
9. Advice and assistance in developing presentation proposals and manuscripts for publication

NOTE: Committee chairs offer advice and assistance—they *do not* do the work for the student.

What committee chairs should expect of students:
1. To keep chair informed throughout the entire research process
2. To work independently
3. To make continual progress toward completion
4. To request advice when needed
5. To accept constructive criticism
6. To make suggested changes
7. To do multiple rewrites as needed
8. To maintain a positive attitude

Selecting Committee Members

In addition to carefully selecting a committee chair, students should also carefully select the other committee members. Depending on the requirements of a given institution, the graduate committee may include one to three or more members in addition to the chair. As a general rule it is usually best to establish a committee of the minimum size allowed by the program. The fewer committee members, the fewer people who will need to be pleased and who will have to approve the final project. The exception is when a particular expertise is needed to complete the research requirement, in which case more members should be added to the committee.

The committee members do not work as closely with the student as does the chair; nevertheless, committee members should always be kept in the communication loop. Students should keep committee members informed of progress, time line, modifications, and the like. Committee members usually do not read every draft; rather, they are consulted when their expertise is needed, and they read documents just ahead of the proposal and defense hearing presentations. Typically, the committee chair will inform the student when he or she believes a thesis or dissertation is ready for reading by the other committee members. Committee members should always be given sufficient time to read and make suggestions on a given draft prior to scheduling a proposal or defense hearing.

Committee members should be chosen based primarily on their potential contributions to the project. For example, a committee member may be selected because of content, research design, or statistical expertise. Further, students should select committee members who will work well with other committee members and the committee chair. Schuetze (2000) notes that "It is not unusual to hear of students who had difficulty completing their requirements because committee members were unable to agree on various aspects of the project or because they refused or were unable to work together efficiently" (p. 35).

In selecting committee members and the committee chair, students should seek information from current and past students in the program. One's academic or program advisor can also serve as a resource when deciding on the committee. In addition, once a committee chair has been determined, that person can be consulted to help iden-

tify other committee members who would work well together and be an asset to the project.

Summary

This chapter has focused on helping students get started with their thesis or dissertation. First, the importance of selecting a good thesis or dissertation topic was discussed. Readers were presented with numerous ideas about how to identify potential research topics. This is often difficult for students to do, but the information presented in this chapter may stimulate some new ideas and ways of identifying research topics. Next, 10 different considerations were presented that students should review prior to making a decision on any research project. Failure to make these considerations could result in major problems for the student researcher. As most graduate theses and dissertations are supervised by a committee chair and several committee members, suggestions on how to select a committee chair and committee members were presented to end the chapter.

Review Questions

1. Why do the authors say, "Finding a research topic is one of the most important tasks for graduate students"?
2. When one is searching for a research topic and reading an article in a potential interest area, what should that person be thinking and doing while reading the article?
3. Other than reading through the literature, what are five ways to identify potential research topics of interest?
4. What problems could arise if a student "falls in love with a topic" or is too involved with a topic?
5. Suppose a student wanted to conduct a nationwide telephone survey of Americans regarding

their use of the Internet for health information. Compare this idea with each of the 10 considerations to be reviewed prior to deciding on a topic (see Table 2.3). How does this idea relate to each of the considerations? What additional information, if any, would you need to make a good decision?

6. Select an idea you have for a thesis or dissertation topic. Compare this idea with each of the 10 considerations to be reviewed prior to deciding on a topic. How does this idea relate to each of the considerations? What additional information, if any, would you need to make a good decision?

7. What considerations should be made prior to selecting a faculty member to serve as thesis or dissertation committee chair?

8. What considerations should be made prior to asking a faculty member to serve on a thesis or dissertation committee?

References

Blaxter, L., Hughes, C., & Tight, M. (2002). *How to research* (2nd ed.). Philadelphia: Open University Press.

Creswell, J.W. (2005). *Educational research: Planning, conducting and evaluating quantitative and qualitative research* (2nd ed.). Upper Saddle River, N.J.: Pearson Education, Inc.

Green, L.W., & Kreuter, M.W. (2005). *Health program planning: An educational and ecological approach* (4th ed.). Boston: McGraw-Hill.

Jung, B.C. (2000). Contribution 23. In F. Pryczak (Ed.), *Completing your thesis or dissertation* (pp. 43–44). Los Angeles: Pryczak Publishing.

Leedy, P.D., & Ormrod, J.E. (2010). *Practical research planning and design* (9th ed.). Upper Saddle River, N.J.: Pearson Education, Inc.

Neutens, J.J., & Rubinson, L. (2010). *Research techniques for the health sciences* (4th ed.). San Francisco: Benjamin Cummings.

Patten, M.L. (2009). *Understanding research methods* (7th ed.). Glendale, Calif.: Pryczak Publishing.

Rosenstock, I.M. (1966). Why people use health services. *Milbank Memorial Fund Quarterly,* 44, 94–124.

Salkind, N.J. (2000). *Exploring research* (4th ed.). Upper Saddle River, N.J.: Prentice-Hall.

Schloss, P.J., & Smith, M.A. (1999). *Conducting research.* Upper Saddle River, N.J.: Merrill/Prentice Hall.

Schuetze, P. (2000). Contribution 26. In F. Pryczak (Ed.), *Completing your thesis or dissertation* (pp. 34–35). Los Angeles: Pryczak Publishing.

Thompson, V. (2000). Contribution 48. In F. Pryczak (Ed.), *Completing your thesis or dissertation* (pp. 62–63). Los Angeles: Pryczak Publishing.

Wallace, L.S. (2003). Correlates of lifetime physical activity in young women. *American Journal of Health Education*, 34, 41–46. Used with permission.

Zhang, J. (2000). Contribution 13. In F. Pryczak (Ed.), *Completing your thesis or dissertation* (pp. 15–16). Los Angeles: Pryczak Publishing.

CHAPTER 3 | **The Literature Review**

Chapter Objectives

After reading this chapter and answering the review questions, you should be able to:

1. Define literature review.
2. Explain the need for a literature review.
3. Relate guidelines that can be used to determine the appropriate length of the literature review.
4. Determine if a particular source should be included in the literature review.
5. Utilize Boolean operators in conducting a literature search.
6. Quickly scan books, reports, and articles for relevance.
7. Adopt a system for reading and recording information.
8. Use relevant sources already obtained to locate additional relevant sources written either before or after the initial source.
9. Differentiate between primary and secondary sources of information.
10. Organize Chapter II of a thesis or dissertation.
11. Write Chapter II using appropriate detail when describing a given source.
12. Utilize an approved publication style manual to cite and reference sources.
13. Write an appropriate summary section in Chapter II.

Key Terms

abstract
bibliography
Boolean operators
citations
computerized searches
descriptors
electronic searches

index
library catalog
literature review
literature search
parameters
peer-reviewed journals

practical significance
primary source
refereed journals
reference list
running reference list
secondary source

In Chapter 2 of this text, we discussed the idea of using the literature to help identify and select a research topic for the thesis or dissertation. In this chapter we will assume that the reader has decided on a topic and is now ready to explore that topic more fully in preparation for conducting the research. This does not mean that the research questions and design are fully developed, only that a decision has been made on the general topic to research. The research questions and hypotheses may have been formulated in a general sense but very well could be modified as a result of reading relevant literature. Any reading one has done to this point to help decide on a topic has not been a waste of time as these sources can most likely be included as sources in the final literature review.

A **literature review** is "a synthesis of the literature on a topic" (Pan, 2008, p. 1). Creswell (2005) goes into more detail in noting that a literature review involves, "locating summaries, books, journals, and indexed publications on a topic, selectively choosing which literature to include in your review, and then summarizing the literature in a written report" (p. 9). The literature review helps to direct one's thinking and moves one toward developing a specific research question to be answered. It is a critical step in the research process. DePoy and Gitlin (2005) note that "reviewing the literature is a significant thinking and action process in the world of research. However, it is often misunderstood and undervalued" (p. 42).

Students often underestimate the importance of the literature review and feel that it delays the true beginning of their research. This may be because they do not have a clear idea of why they are doing a literature review, and they do not realize that they are doing research when they are working on it. In addition, some students find the literature review to be a daunting task: they do not know where to start the literature search, do not know when to stop, do not have a clear strategy for collecting and organizing data, and they experience frustration with the nebulous guidelines for completing the literature review. In the past, when doing research papers, students have often been given well-defined directions with a specific page guideline. For example, they were told to write a 10-page research paper using a minimum of 15 sources. No such guidelines exist when writing a literature review.

This chapter should help students understand why they are doing a literature review, give them guidelines for limiting the literature review by establishing appropriate parameters, provide strategies on how to collect and organize the information obtained, and give ideas on how to write Chapter II of the thesis or dissertation.

Why Do a Literature Review?

The answer to this question can vary depending on whether one is doing quantitative or qualitative research. In qualitative research, the literature serves a different purpose than in quantitative research. The literature may be mentioned at the beginning of a qualitative study to help justify the research problem's importance. This is not, however, as extensive a review as in a quantitative study. Qualitative researchers often desire to enter into a study without being constrained by what has been found in previous research. This allows them to observe and interpret findings without expectations or bias. They will, however, conduct a thorough literature review as their research progresses, and the skills needed to conduct the literature review are similar to those of quantitative researchers. The information from a qualitative researcher's literature review will be utilized at the end of the study to compare and contrast findings and to place the new study in the context of the body of knowledge in that area or field. (See Chapter 11 for further discussion of the literature review in qualitative research.)

In quantitative research the literature review is done at the very beginning of the study. It is used to justify the importance of the study, place the study in historical perspective, refine the research questions, and identify appropriate theory, methodology, and instrumentation. There is typically a full chapter on related literature (Chapter II) in a quantitative thesis or dissertation along with a discussion of the literature related to the results from the current research in Chapter V.

There are many reasons for doing a thorough literature review. It provides the historical structure for a given research area. In other words, it allows one to see how past research efforts have contributed to the current state of knowledge. This allows researchers to place their own research in context with the larger body of knowledge on a given topical area.

A solid literature review will help ensure that one does not unintentionally repeat work that has already been done. In addition, it will help avoid mistakes that have already been made by identifying research designs or instrumentation that did not work well in the past. At the same time, the literature review can help to identify research procedures and instruments that have been successfully utilized in the past. Imagine how frustrating it would be to go through the process of developing and validating a new instrument to measure some health-related variable only to find later that a similar instrument had already been developed.

The literature can also be utilized to justify the importance of a particular study. Most thesis and dissertation committees will require students to explain why their studies are important or needed. There are several ways to justify the importance of a study through the literature. A study might be seen as important if it will fill a gap in the literature. A study might also be seen as significant when it will help to clarify conflicting results in the literature. Committee members may also want to know why this study should be conducted, what the study will add to the body of knowledge, and the practical significance of doing the study. **Practical significance** refers to how those actually practicing in the profession will benefit from this work. A study may produce statistically significant results but lack practical significance.

Studies can also be justified if they test or develop theory. Developing an understanding of and grounding in theory is a critical aspect of the literature review. A student, for example, may have a general understanding of social cognitive theory from a behavioral theory class. This general understanding is probably not sufficient, however, to conduct a study based on social cognitive theory. By examining the literature on social cognitive theory, the student can gain a more thorough under-standing of this theory, where it came from, how it has developed, and how it has been used in previous research.

The literature review can also reveal studies closely related to the proposed study. In some cases these closely related studies may eventually serve as the source for a strict replication or modified replication study. If a replication study is not developed, the closely related studies can still be of help in clearly defining the research question or problem statement and identifying possible methods, procedures, and instruments for the proposed study. In Chapter V of a thesis or dissertation, students will need to compare their study results to those of related studies found through the literature review.

Validity of Health Information

In reviewing the health literature, it is especially important to determine the validity of the sources being used. As anyone who has spent much time reading the health literature knows, there is a lot of information printed that is of questionable quality. How can one decide what is valid information and what is not?

One guideline that can be used to determine the validity of health information is where it is published. One can be most confident in information contained in **refereed journals**. A refereed journal is one that only publishes articles that have been reviewed and accepted by an independent panel of reviewers or referees made up of individuals in the same or a closely related profession. Refereed journals are also known as **peer-reviewed journals**, because typically it is a panel of one's peers that reviews proposed manuscripts. Although review by such a panel is no guarantee of valid information in refereed journals, if the majority of independent reviewers believe it to be a good article, chances are better that the information is solid.

Selecting primary sources and minimizing the use of secondary sources is an excellent way to improve the likelihood of utilizing valid literature.

Primary sources are those written by the person or persons who actually conducted the research. Research articles published in professional health education journals such as the *Journal of the American Public Health Association,* the *American Journal of Health Education,* and the *Journal of School Health* are examples of primary sources. **Secondary sources** are those that report on or summarize primary sources. Books, summary articles, news reports, and encyclopedias are examples of secondary sources. When using secondary sources, any misinterpretations or biases of the secondary author are transferred to the literature review. It is always best to rely on primary sources if at all possible. Only when there are pivotal summary reviews of the literature or when a primary source is not available should a secondary source be used (Berg & Latin, 2004). If a secondary source is used, it must be referenced as a secondary source. The style manual approved by your program will explain how to write a secondary source reference. It is unethical to reference a secondary source as if it were a primary source.

When reading an article there are some other guidelines to consider. Most good articles contain citations of sources utilized in the body of the article and a reference list at the end of the article. An article with no references may indicate that the contents represent only the authors' opinions. The style of presentation is another clue that can be used to determine the validity of the information. If the style is more scientific and follows the format of other research-type articles, one can be more confident in the findings than if an article is written in a more conversational or sensational style, as might be found in a popular magazine. Articles that contain advertisements or personal testimonies should usually be avoided in a literature review.

Check to see if the authors' qualifications make sense related to the content of the article. Do they have academic degrees in the field about which they are writing? Having such a degree does not guarantee that an author is qualified, but it provides evidence to suggest good qualifications. If no information about an author is available, that is another indication that an article may be questionable. Beware of information written by individuals with degrees, qualifications, or positions outside of the area in which they are writing. Someone with a Ph.D. in electrical engineering, for example, is probably not qualified to write about nutrition. Sometimes persons completely outside a given profession or specialty with no academic training may write on health-related topics. This often happens when movie stars, sports figures, or other celebrities promote fitness programs, nutritional supplements, or weight loss plans that supposedly have worked for them. Such sources should not be included in a literature review.

The newness of information is also a consideration when determining the validity of an article. When students read about some new finding they have neither seen in other sources nor discussed in their classes, a caution flag should be raised. This is especially true if the information contradicts current thinking or accepted practice. For new information to become accepted, it must pass the test of time. Other researchers must validate the findings in independent research studies to establish the true value of new information. Although new information reported in recognized sources should be included in the literature review, it should only be reported with appropriate cautions indicating it as emerging or new findings. The validity of new information must be of concern, but the further testing of new information or concepts might make a good research topic for a thesis or dissertation.

Health Information on the Internet

The validity of health information found on the Internet is of special concern. Anyone with basic computer skills can develop a Web page and post information to the Internet. Much health information on the Internet has never been peer-reviewed by health experts, is designed to sell health products, only represents the thoughts of a given individual or group, and is not suitable for use in a literature review. Given the plethora of questionable health information available on the Internet, author information is extremely important to help determine the validity of a source. We believe it imperative that either corporate or individual author information be provided for all Internet references listed in a health education literature review.

Many other factors also need to be considered when determining whether to include an Internet source in the literature review. MedlinePlus, a Web site developed by the U.S. National Library of Medicine and the National Institutes of Health, has a guide for "healthy Web surfing" that can be seen in Figure 3.1. Readers are encouraged to familiarize themselves with the criteria included in this evaluation and utilize them when considering Internet health sources.

Although some information on the Internet is questionable, there is also much good information to be found on the Web. There are full-text peer-reviewed articles and some books available in electronic formats that may be of importance to a literature review. Information from governmental sources such as the Centers for Disease Control and Prevention (CDC) and the National Institutes of Health (NIH) is often available via the Internet and would be appropriate for a literature review. As a general rule of thumb, those sites that have a URL ending in .gov, .org, or .edu may be of more value than those ending in .com.

Since this book was first published five years ago, the availability of online electronic journals has greatly increased. With the flexibility and convenience of electronic journals have also come some interesting referencing issues. Some journals, for example, now make accessible manuscripts of accepted works in advance of their actual publication. One should always cite the latest edition of a work that is available. If an advanced copy of the manuscript is all that is available, then cite it. When the final version is available change your citation to reflect the newer advanced version if possible. There is also the possibility that electronic journal articles may have lengthy attachments, embedded videos, or other resources to augment the actual article. In referencing these supplemental materials, cite the most recent edition of the article to which they are attached (American Psychological Association, 2010).

While there are many intricacies and unusual cases in referencing electronic sources, the *Publication Manual of the American Psychological Association* (2010) does a nice job of providing direction for referencing dilemmas. As a general rule of thumb, they state, "We recommend that you include the same elements, in the same order, as you would for a reference to a fixed-media source and add as much electronic retrieval information as needed for others to locate the sources you cited" (American Psychological Association, 2010, p. 187). Electronic information that should be included would include either a uniform resource locator (URL) or a digital object identifier (DOI). For further information on URLs and DOIs, see the *Publication Manual of the American Psychological Association* (2010).

Evidence-Based Research

Due to the large body of published health research that lacks methodological rigor, a group of medical researchers in the 1990s developed the concept of evidence-based medicine. Evidence-based medicine involves a systematic process to locate, evaluate, and apply quality research to clinical practice. Essentially it is a system to evaluate the quality of research (Neutens & Rubinson, 2010).

The concept of evidence-based medicine has since been expanded to include evidence-based research in a more general sense, and is utilized in health education. Like medical doctors, health education specialists want to make their program decisions based on the best evidence available. Suppose

What should you look for when evaluating the quality of health information on Web sites? Here are some suggestions based on our experience.

Consider the source—Use recognized authorities.

Know who is responsible for the content.

- Look for an "about us" page. Check to see who runs the site: is it a branch of the federal government, a non-profit institution, a professional organization, a health system, a commercial organization, or an individual.
- There is a big difference between a site that says, "I developed this site after my heart attack" and one that says, "This page on heart attack was developed by health professionals at the American Heart Association."
- Web sites should have a way to contact the organization or webmaster. If the site provides no contact information, or if you can't easily find out who runs the site, use caution.

Focus on quality—All Web sites are not created equal.

Does the site have an editorial board? Is the information reviewed before it is posted?

- This information is often on the "about us" page, or it may be under the organization's mission statement, or part of the annual report.
- See if the board members are experts in the subject of the site. For example, a site on osteoporosis whose medical advisory board is composed of attorneys and accountants is not medically authoritative.
- Look for a description of the process of selecting or approving information on the site. It is usually in the "about us" section and may be called "editorial policy" or "selection policy" or "review policy."
- Sometimes the site will have information "about our writers" or "about our authors" instead of an editorial policy. Review this section to find out who has written the information.

Be a cyberskeptic—Quackery abounds on the Web.

Does the site make health claims that seem too good to be true? Does the information use deliberately obscure, "scientific" sounding language? Does it promise quick, dramatic, miraculous results? Is this the only site making these claims?

- Beware of claims that one remedy will cure a variety of illnesses, that it is a "breakthrough," or that it relies on a "secret ingredient."
- Use caution if the site uses a sensational writing style (lots of exclamation points, for example).
- A health Web site for consumers should use simple language, not technical jargon.
- Get a second opinion! Check more than one site.

FIGURE 3.1
MedlinePlus guide to healthy Web surfing.

Taken From: MedlinePlus Guide to Healthy Web Surfing. Produced by the U.S. National Library of Medicine and the National Institutes of Health.

continued

Look for the evidence—Rely on medical research, not opinion.

Does the site identify the author? Does it rely on testimonials?

- Look for the author of the information, either an individual or an organization. Good examples are "Written by Jane Smith, R.N.," or "Copyright 2003, American Cancer Society."
- If there are case histories or testimonials on the Web site, look for contact information such as an email address or telephone number. If the testimonials are anonymous or hard to track down ("Jane from California"), use caution.

Check for currency—Look for the latest information.

Is the information current?

- Look for dates on documents. A document on coping with the loss of a loved one doesn't need to be current, but a document on the latest treatment of AIDS needs to be current.
- Click on a few links on the site. If there are a lot of broken links, the site may not be kept up-to-date.

Beware of bias—What is the purpose? Who is providing the funding?

Who pays for the site?

- Check to see if the site is supported by public funds, donations, or commercial advertising.
- Advertisements should be labeled. They should say "Advertisement" or "From our Sponsor."
- Look at a page on the site, and see if it is clear when content is coming from a non-commercial source and when an advertiser provides it. For example, if a page about treatment of depression recommends one drug by name, see if you can tell if the company that manufactures the drug provides that information. If it does, you should consult other sources to see what they say about the same drug.

FIGURE 3.1 *Continued*

for a moment you are the health education specialist for a large inner city school district and you have been charged with finding the best program to reduce teen sexual involvement, pregnancies, and STDs. You begin reading the literature, but find there is a great variation in the quality of the research, which ranges from mere testimonials to well-controlled research studies. A system to stratify the research and weight it would be helpful in your decision-making process. The U.S. Preventive Services Task Force (U.S. Department of Health and Human Services, 2009) developed such a system for ranking categories of evidence for an article under review, and the system has been modified by Neutens and Rubinson (2010, p. 38) to apply better to health education:

Level I	Controlled and randomized
Level II-1	Controlled but not randomized
Level II-2	Cohort or case control
Level II-3	Multiple time series
Level III	Expert opinion or case study

Determining the quality and level of research available related to sexuality education programs would allow the health education specialist to make the best evidence-based decision related to program selection for this school district.

Literature: Where to Look

A **literature search** involves identifying and obtaining relevant resources to include in a literature review. Many tools are available to assist with literature searches. An **index** is a listing of all articles published in the journals cataloged within that index. Articles are listed in an index by title and organized by topical areas. Basic bibliographical information is provided on each index entry so that one may access articles of interest. In an index only the article title is available to help users determine if an article is appropriate for their search. An **abstract** is a listing of articles published in a topical area that includes basic bibliographic information as well as a brief summary of article content. Abstracts make it easier to determine if the content of an article will be helpful for a given literature search. A **library catalog** lists books, reports, and other nonjournal resources by author, title, call number, or subject. Most indexes, abstracts, and library catalogs are now available either online or via CD-ROM databases found in libraries. This allows for **computerized** or **electronic literature searches** that are less time consuming and often more accurate than manual searches. Online databases provide quick access to current, high-quality research by notable authors and respected publications (Wilhelm & Kaunelis, 2005). A listing of some of the more common indexes, abstracts, and databases used in health education literature searches can be seen in Table 3.1. Keep in mind that no database is all encompassing; therefore, researchers should become familiar with the strengths and limitations of each database and perform literature searches using a variety of databases (Wilhelm & Kaunelis, 2005).

One final resource that should never be overlooked when conducting a literature search is the reference librarian. DePoy and Gitlin (2005) emphatically state that, "Working with an experienced librarian is the best way to learn how to navigate physical and virtual libraries, find the best search words for your area of interest, and access the numerous databases that open the world of literature to you" (p. 47).

Table 3.1   Useful Resources for Health Education Literature Searches

Health and medical
Index Medicus
MEDLINE
GENMED
Biological Abstracts
Cinahl
Web of Science
SCOPUS

Psychology/sociology
Psych Abstract
Psych Articles
PsychINFO
Sociological Abstracts
Socindex

Education
Resources in Education (RIE—part of ERIC)
Current Index to Journals in Education (CIJE—part of ERIC)
Dissertation Abstracts International

Miscellaneous
Social Sciences Citation Index
Science Citation Index
Statistical Abstract of the United States
Health and Psychosocial Instruments

The Literature Search

There are several steps involved in conducting a literature search (see Figure 3.2). A systematic, structured approach to the literature search is recommended and provides a guide to your topic. According to Timmins and McCabe (2005), the search strategy should be noted in great detail. This ensures that the search is focused, purposeful, comprehensive, and rigorous. It also helps the

- Determine the topic of interest and establish the parameters of the literature search.
- Determine the style manual recommended or required by your program, obtain a copy, and become familiar with its content.
- Identify databases to be searched and keep an accurate record of each database and descriptor used. Spend time identifying the best key words or descriptors for each database.
- Conduct electronic and/or manual searches.
- Review all resources obtained from the searches and evaluate each as to their appropriateness for your study.
- Obtain full-text copies of all resources that are appropriate.
- Determine the headings and sub-headings that will be used in your study.
- Take notes on all appropriate sources using a system that is accurate and efficient. Utilize a bibliographic citation software program if available.
- Organize notes into groupings based on headings and sub-headings.
- Begin writing the methods/strategies section of the literature review describing all databases you searched and key words or descriptors used.
- Write each section of the literature review as per the headings and sub-headings identified above. Be sure to use good transitions between paragraphs and sections.
- Write your summary of the literature review.
- Develop your reference list and double check to be sure all citations and references are correct.

FIGURE 3.2
Steps in conducting a literature review.

researcher to reconnect to the search after having been away from it for some time (Wilhelm & Kaunelis, 2005).

Once the search strategy approach is outlined, the next step is to identify the descriptor words related to the topic. **Descriptors** or key terms are the words under which articles are cataloged in a given database (Creswell, 2005). Selecting and using appropriate key words is critical to an effective search (Timmins & McCabe, 2005). Descriptors need to be selected carefully so that literature closely related to the study will be revealed. For example, a researcher may want to find articles on stretching exercises, but if "stretching" is not a recognized descriptor, no articles will be identified. The terms "fitness" or "exercise" may be the descriptors that will include articles related to stretching. Different databases may use different descriptors, so it is important to look at the descriptors available for each database searched. A list of the descriptors for each database may be included with the index or presented in a separate volume.

Once descriptors have been identified, the next step is to determine how best to use the descriptors so as to obtain a listing of articles that most precisely represent the topic being searched. To accomplish this, students need to become familiar with **Boolean operators** (Gay, Mills, & Airasian, 2006). Boolean operators are syntax terms used in the search line that help the computer to identify more precisely the articles of value to a specific search.

Suppose, for example, a health education researcher wants to research the advertising of vitamin supplements. The person might begin by entering the word "vitamin" and find that thousands of sources are identified. That is far more than can be reviewed, and most of the identified sources will not deal with the desired topic of advertising. To narrow the search, the researcher might use the word AND in the search line to connect "vitamin AND advertisement." Now only those sources that contain both terms will be selected. If the researcher has reason to believe that some articles are being missed because the word "supplements" is sometimes used instead of "vitamins," another Boolean operator can help. A search could be run using "vitamin OR supplement AND advertisement." Now articles will be selected that contain either the word "vitamin" or "supplement" and "advertisement." If the researcher were concerned that plurals or derivatives of the word "supplement," such as "supplements" or "supplementation," may be used in articles, an asterisk (*) can be placed after the word "supplement"—"vitamin OR supplement* AND advertisement." This will instruct the computer to look for all derivatives and plural forms of the word. Suppose further that the researcher is finding numerous articles that deal with the advertising of "natural vitamins," and these articles are not desired in this particular search. By using the Boolean operator NOT, the search can be further refined. The search line might read "vitamin OR supplement* NOT natural AND advertisement." Now any article with "natural" in it will be eliminated and those with either "vitamin" or "supplement" and "advertisement" will be listed. Other possibilities exist for using Boolean operators. For example, it is possible to limit searches to specific years, to look for certain combinations of words, and to require words to be in certain proximity of each other. Most databases contain information on how to use Boolean operators, and librarians will also provide assistance if needed.

Scanning Potential Sources

Once potential sources have been identified through either computer or manual searches, the researcher is ready to begin locating, reading, and evaluating the sources to determine whether or not they are helpful for the literature review. This will require obtaining an abstract or full-text version of the articles and documents. Many journal articles are now available via Web sites. Some of these are free to researchers and some require a fee to download articles. Many articles can also be found in the library's collection of journals. If not available at a given library or online, interlibrary loans are often required to obtain needed materials. It can take several days, weeks, or months to locate and retrieve all of the needed materials, so plan accordingly.

Once abstracts and articles are located, the next step is to carefully review them for relevance to the literature review. Even the most effective searches will reveal sources that are unhelpful or only marginally helpful for a given review. To determine if an article or book will be helpful, it is not necessary to read the entire document. To do so would be impractical and a waste of time. The effective researcher will become proficient at determining the value of an article or book in a short time. Blaxter and colleagues (2002) state that "You should, with some practice, be able to get the gist of a book, report or article in five minutes" (p. 112). Wilhelm and Kaunelis (2005) suggest that the abstract from the online database can be easily skimmed for relevance to make a decsion about selecting the article. If the full-text version of the article is available it can be downloaded or exported using reference management software. Read the introduction and the conclusion of the article to determine the relevance to your topic. Any books, articles, or reports that appear to contain valuable information related to the topic of investigation should be either read immediately or set aside for more careful reading and note taking later.

Reading and Recording Relevant Literature

An initial consideration is to determine when and where valuable resources identified through the search process will be read. Some students prefer to do their reading and note taking in the library. For these students, the library has the advantages of being relatively quiet and a better place to concentrate than one's home. Also, resources can be used in the library without requiring any copying costs. Other students prefer to copy or print out sources in the library and take them home to read at another time. This allows students to work in the comfort of their home environment, to take advantage of smaller blocks of time when it would be impossible to get to the library, and to be able to spread materials out and not have to remove them after each session. Downloading full text versions of the articles directly to a laptop allows students to view articles on the computer or to print them out. Having personal copies of articles also means that articles can be written on and highlighted, which cannot be done with original library sources. However, distractions associated with roommates or family can be an issue when working at home.

Regardless of where students decide to do their work, it is important to get organized. How will important information be recorded and cataloged for future use? There are many answers to this question, but students must adopt a system and stick with it. Being meticulous in following a system or process from beginning to end of the literature review will save much time and many hassles throughout the thesis or dissertation process. Pan (2008) suggests that before writing, the articles should be grouped together in broad categories; within each category, the articles then should be arranged chronologically. Start taking notes on the oldest article first.

One system many students use involves writing note cards to record important information about each resource. All information written on note cards must be neat and legible so that students can easily read and understand it when writing the literature review. The first thing that should be written on the note card is a full bibliographic reference for that resource. In most cases this should include the names of all authors; the date of publication; the title of the article, book, or report; a volume and issue number for articles; page numbers; and for books, the publisher and the place of publication. If the source will be directly quoted in the litera-

ture review, a page number for the quote will also be needed on the card. Web site sources require a URL address and the date you accessed the site.

For more information on how each source should be referenced, students should refer to the publication manual approved by their institutions. In most health education programs and professional health education journals, the *Publication Manual of the American Psychological Association* (APA, 2009) has been used. Some journals and programs, however, are now utilizing the *AMA Manual of Style* of the American Medical Association (2007). In 2005, the *American Journal of Health Education* and the *International Electronic Journal of Health Education* changed their style from APA to AMA (Price & Murnan, 2004). Whichever publication manual your program approves, be sure to follow it closely. Paying careful attention to detail when referencing sources at this point in the process can save much time looking up material again to retrieve missing or incorrect information.

After writing the full bibliographic reference on the card, a topical title should be placed at the top of the card to help when organizing for the actual writing of the literature review. For example, if a literature search is being conducted on dental health and the researcher intends to write a section in the literature review on nutrition and dental health, the topical title might be "nutrition." As the researcher begins to organize note cards for the actual writing of Chapter II, all note cards with the topical title "nutrition" can be placed together.

Next, important information about the report, article, or book should be written on the card. This might include details of the study's design, the population being studied, instrumentation, and important findings and conclusions. The more closely related a resource is to the literature review, and in particular the proposed research study, the more detail should be included on the card. In addition to a description of the article, the researchers should also note any comments or critique they might have of the work. For example, they might want to note that the sample size was small, the response rate was low, or participants were not randomly selected. If one card will not hold all the information from a given resource, additional cards can be utilized for that resource and stapled to the first. If one source contains information that can be used in several sections of the literature review, multiple cards can be written and placed in the appropriate sections. For example, if when conducting a literature review on dental health, one article reviewed contains useful information on both nutrition and flossing, two separate cards should be developed; one with the heading "nutrition" and the other with the heading "flossing." That way when the health education researcher is organizing the cards, one card can be physically placed with other cards on nutrition and the other card can be physically placed with other flossing cards.

One convenience with using note cards is that they can be manually moved about to help with organization within each section when actually writing the literature review. When researchers are finally ready to begin writing, they can review all the note cards in each section and type directly from them into the computer.

A variation on using note cards is to develop a data collection sheet. A data collection sheet is nothing more than a template of headings for information that needs to be collected for each resource (see Figure 3.3). Researchers can utilize the sample data collection sheet or customize a data collection sheet with headings to best meet their needs. Once a template is developed, multiple copies can be made. A new sheet is used for each resource instead of a note card. The advantage to data collection sheets is that the headings are always there as reminders of important information that needs to be recorded for each resource.

Another system to record data from relevant resources is to enter notes directly into the computer. Different files can be started for each different section of the literature review. Notes on individual resources within each section can be

stored on different pages within the files. The information recorded for each resource should be the same as that described above for the note cards. Data collection sheets can also be used with a computer system by pasting in a template data collection sheet before taking notes on each source. When ready to begin writing the first draft of the literature review, the notes or data sheets within each file can be used to develop that section. Often, large sections of notes or data sheets can be cut and pasted directly into the literature review. This system has the advantages of eliminating the initial handwriting of the notes or data sheets and minimizing possible errors when transferring the information from cards/data sheets to the computer. The disadvantage is that one must be at the computer whenever recording any information for the literature review.

There are many variations on the two general systems for reading and taking notes described above. The important thing is to identify a system that is comfortable and stick with it. Imagine the frustration of having to return to the library and relocate an article to find missing information, the page number of a quote, or the volume number of a given issue. Organization is key to conducting a thorough, efficient literature review.

Finding More Literature

Conducting an initial computer and/or manual search for resources does not end the process of locating relevant literature. As one reads and takes notes on the relevant articles one has found through the initial literature search, those articles can be used to find additional relevant articles. By using the reference list at the end of an article or book, one can identify relevant resources read by the initial authors. These relevant resources should then be obtained and read by the researcher. Even if a thorough electronic and/or manual search has been completed, reviewing reference lists will often identify articles that were not identified in the

Author(s)

Date

Title

Publication Information

Purpose/Research Questions/Hypotheses

Population of Study

Instrumentation

Methodology

Results/Conclusions

Critique

FIGURE 3.3
Sample data collection sheet.

original search. Remember that if a journal is not listed in a specific index or abstract, or if an appropriate descriptor is not used in the search, valuable resources can be missed.

Although using reference lists to identify potential resources allows one to go back further in the literature to find additional sources, there is also a way to identify newer articles written after a specific article has been published. This involves using the *Social Sciences Citation Index* and/or the *Science Citation Index*. These two sources work in the same way but, as their names imply, index different journals. Suppose the researcher locates a valuable article for the literature review that was written in 2004. The article may describe a study that is very close to what the researcher plans to do, may use the same theoretical base, or may contain instrumentation that can be utilized in the current research. Because the article is so helpful, it is possible that other researchers since 2004 may also have found this article helpful and might have referenced the 2004 article in their work. The *Social Sciences Citation Index* and the *Science Citation Index* allow one to look up the 2004 article by author and view a list of all articles since 2004 that have referenced the 2004 article. This might allow the researcher to identify other important articles on the topic written since 2004 but missed in the initial search.

When to Stop the Literature Search

How do I know when to stop collecting literature? How do I know if I have covered the literature? How do I know when to start writing the literature review? These are questions thesis and dissertation advisors hear every year. Unfortunately, there are no easy responses to these questions. The length of the literature review will depend on the size of the literature and the limitations placed on the review process. The authors of this text have personally supervised student literature reviews that ranged from 10 pages to 70

pages in length. The 10-page review was an athletic training student conducting research on the treatment of a specific type of injury, and the 70-page review was a health education student studying the issue of adolescent obesity.

In the absence of specific page requirements, there are some guidelines students can use to help determine the scope of the literature review. First, enough literature needs to be reviewed to be able to write all the necessary components of a literature review. For example, most literature reviews will produce information that will identify the problem and justify the proposed study. This might involve some epidemiological data related to the problem being studied. Literature is also needed to identify and explain any theories used in the proposed study with examples of how each theory has been applied to similar studies in the past. Finally, literature is needed to describe to the reader what research has led to the proposed study. This could include information on the selected population, instrumentation, and methodology as well as studies on the same or a similar topic.

It is necessary to establish **parameters** in a literature review. These might be called limits or boundaries of the literature review. Aaron (2008) reported that it is important to give the reader a description of how articles were selected and what criteria were used to eliminate articles. For example, if one was studying the stress levels of teachers, it would be important to find articles dealing with the responsibilities, challenges, and ultimately stress levels of teaching. If articles were found dealing with the stress levels of other occupations, they should be eliminated unless direct comparisons were made between those professions and teaching. The literature review should also be limited to examining studies where stress levels were measured. Studies dealing with other indicators of health such as nutrition or smoking behaviors would be of little use. In other words, one parameter that should be used in every situation is to limit the literature review to the key components being studied.

Even after limiting the search to studies dealing with stress levels and information on teaching, there still may be a need to further limit the review. One option is to restrict the review to specific years. Experts disagree on how many years should be covered in a literature review. Creswell (2005) notes, "In many searches, reviewing material for the last 10 years will suffice for school- or university-based research reports" (p. 97), but DePoy and Gitlin (2005) believe that "most researchers search the literature for articles written within the previous 5 years" (p. 49). Wilhelm and Kaunelis (2005) write "although there is no hard and fast rule for selecting publications by date, publications that are more than 10 years old can be suspect as to their currency in a research area such as computer technology, but may be perfectly acceptable in an area such as ethics" (p. 102). The decision to restrict the literature search to a certain period of time should depend on the scope of the literature rather than an artificially contrived fixed period of time. An extensive literature might be reduced to include fewer years, but a sparse literature might be extended to include more years. The need to establish historical significance will also impact the number of years searched. Student researchers are encouraged to discuss the issue of establishing topical and time-related parameters with their thesis or dissertation committees.

A final guideline for determining when to stop searching and begin writing is redundancy or repetitive patterns in the literature (Leedy & Ormrod, 2010). When one is working through the literature and keeps seeing the same key sources that have already been reviewed appearing over and over again in reference lists, it is probably time to stop searching and begin writing. This does not mean, however, that the search process ends at this point. Researchers need to keep abreast of the literature while they are doing their studies. New articles, books, or reports may appear at any time that could be important to the literature review. It is always a good idea to do a quick scan of the most current literature prior to submitting the final draft of the thesis, dissertation, or article for publication.

Writing Chapter II

Organization

After literature has been collected, reviewed, and written in note format, it is time to begin writing the first draft of a thesis or dissertation's Chapter II. This chapter is typically titled "Literature Review" or "Review of Literature." Usually this chapter is written prior to Chapter I, the introductory chapter, because information from the literature review is needed to fully develop Chapter I.

After writing an introductory paragraph that describes the study and the topic being studied, a brief but detailed section on the methods or strategies used to conduct the literature review should be included (Pan, 2008). This should include information on the steps undertaken in the search process, databases searched, and key words or descriptor words that were used (Aaron, 2008).

Once the methods or strategies used in the literature review have been presented, it is time to begin reporting on the findings of the literature review.

A problem often faced by students is that so much data have been collected that it is difficult to know how or where to begin. Organization is the key to developing a good Chapter II. Students can begin by developing an outline of the section headings and sub-headings and then sorting articles into these headings. Headings and sub-headings also will help the reader follow the flow of the research presented (Pan, 2008). Ideally, the process of identifying headings should have been happening as students were reading through the literature. During the review process students should constantly be asking themselves how a particular resource will fit into the literature review and what similar resources have been found. For example, a student is looking at literature concerning the effectiveness of health fairs in promoting knowledge, attitude, and behavioral changes. Through reading the student determines that there is information on health fairs at worksite settings and different information on health fairs in community settings. The student decides that there is sufficient information to make each setting a different section of the literature review. Subsequent articles describing health fairs are placed in the appropriate sections.

Pan (2008) encourages "generous" use of headings and sub-headings. He suggests "As a general rule, whenever there is a large block of material (say, five more paragraphs) that is distinct in content from the preceding material, consider adding a main heading or sub-heading" (p. 59).

After the complete list of section headings and sub-headings has been developed, they next need to be organized into some logical order for presentation. Although there may be no one right way to organize a Chapter II, students should have a rationale for how they order the information they present in the chapter. As a general rule, students are encouraged to begin with broad general concepts and progress toward specific, detailed information (Galvan, 1999). Broad, general information might include information about a specific health problem, behavior, or disease. Readers of the thesis or dissertation should be convinced that this is an important issue to study. Next, information on the theoretical basis of the study could be presented. Explain the historical basis of the theory and describe the theory and how it has been applied. Report any applications of the theory to the topic of the proposed research. As writing progresses, research articles that are most closely related to the topic and/or methodology of the proposed study should be presented at the end of the chapter. A way to visualize the organization of Chapter II is to think of it as a funnel. Epidemiological data, broad concepts, and theoretical information are at the top of the funnel or

the beginning of the chapter, narrowing toward specific studies related to the current proposed study at the bottom of the funnel or the end of the chapter.

See Figure 3.4 for two examples of working heading outlines utilized in thesis-level literature reviews. These are termed working headings because they may not be the exact headings used in the final literature review. At this point they are primarily for organizational purposes. See Box 3.1 for a listing of working headings that were developed for a study on smoking and hypnosis. These headings are in random order. Try to organ-

---

Box 3.1 Organizing the Chapter II Literature Review

Organize the following nine working headings into order from broad to specific. Hint: four of these headings are actually sub-headings under a higher-level heading.

Self-Help Programs
Smoking Prevalence in Ohio and Hamilton County
Nicotine Replacement
Previous Smoking/Hypnosis Studies
Harmful Effects of Smoking
Hypnosis
Behavior Modification
Smoking Prevalence in the U.S.
Smoking Cessation Programs

Below are the headings as they were actually organized. How close was your organization to the actual organization?

Smoking Prevalence in the U.S.
Smoking Prevalence in Ohio and Hamilton County
Harmful Effects of Smoking
Smoking Cessation Programs
　Behavior Modification
　Self-Help Programs
　Nicotine Replacement
　Hypnosis
Previous Smoking/Hypnosis Studies

Women's knowledge of HPV and their perceptions of physician educational efforts regarding HPV and cervical cancer [Cermak, M. (2009). Unpublished thesis, University of Cincinnati].

Human Papillomavirus
  Prevalence of HPV
  Prevention of HPV
  New HPV Vaccine
Cervical Cancer
  Prevalence of Cervical Cancer
  Primary Prevention
  Secondary Prevention
  Tertiary Prevention
  Treatment Options

Awareness and Knowledge of HPV and Cervical Cancer
  Women with Abnormal Results
  Socioeconomic Status
  Race and/or Ethnicity
  Education
  Age
  Clinicians

Determining attitude toward and level of involvement in health promotion and education programs in faith communities in the Greater Cincinnati Consolidated Metropolitan Statistical Area [Walter, J.L. (2007). Unpublished master's thesis, University of Cincinnati].

Health Care in the United States
  Health Care Crisis
  Causes of Death and Illness
  Healthy Behaviors to Improve Quality of Life
  National Objectives for Understanding and
    Improving Health
  Improvements in Health Care Due to
    Prevention Programs
Health Promotion in the Community
Religion and Health
Health by Denomination
Biblical Basis for Health Promotion
Health Promotion in Faith Communities
  Adolescent Ministries
  Aging Ministries

Caregiving Ministries
Community Ministries
Family Ministries
Health Clinics
HIV/AIDS Ministries
Homeless Ministries
Mother and Children's Ministries
Mental Health Ministries
Addiction Ministries
Violence Prevention
Women's Ministries
Parish Nursing
Partnerships
Summary

FIGURE 3.4
Sample Chapter II main heading outlines.

ize them using the broad-to-specific guidelines presented above. The actual outline used in the study is then presented. See how close your organization is to the actual organization used.

Writing

Prior to beginning the writing of Chapter II, be sure to review several other theses or dissertations written for your program. Note how articles are summarized, how they are referenced, the style of writing, and so on. A sample page from a Chapter II can be seen in Figure 3.5. Any questions about what is expected in your program should be directed to the chair of your thesis or dissertation committee.

Actually putting the first words to paper can sometimes be difficult. If it is easier to begin

The AWMA (1999) believed that while men faced more immediate life-threatening occupational hazards, women appeared to be more vulnerable to stress-induced illnesses for a variety of reasons. First, they were socialized to be caretakers, and as such they almost automatically took on responsibilities that men might not even consider. This alone added to the stress load they carried. Second, women as a whole were less likely to be in positions of power and were not as able to control what was going on in their environment as men. Sociologists speculated that many women were disadvantaged because they incorporated a male standard for achievement in the work world with an old-fashioned female standard for perfection at home (AMWA, 1999). In studies of stress, women tended to report more distress than men (Baum & Grunberg, 1991; Culberson, 1997). Furthermore, Hammen (1991) observed that not only were women affected by stressful events, but that they also played a role in the generation of their stressors.

Women with medium or high stressors and low assertiveness, low hardiness, or the inability to express their feelings were more likely to report physical symptoms of stress than women who were stronger in these personality traits. Also, women with medium or high stressors and low to medium trust or love relationships were very likely to report high emotional symptoms of stress, as were women with high trust or love who did not express their feelings. The amount of women's stressors and their personality traits may increase or diminish their stress response and affect their health (Kenny & Bhattacharjee, 2000).

Many young women and middle-aged women in the United States were at greater risk for developing stress-related illnesses than their predecessors because they were exposed to more and different types of stressors (Ader, 1995; Dreher, 1995; Elliot, 1995). Many women tried to balance the demands of family, housework, and career. Collins (1997) found that half of working women thought stress had some effect on their health. Verbrugge (1989) reported that womens' roles and stressors contributed to poor health, overall stress, low job mastery, and a sense of vulnerability to illness.

FIGURE 3.5
Sample page from Chapter II literature review.

Reproduced by permission from Vertin, B.E. Stress and social support among college students by gender. Unpublished master's thesis, University of Cincinnati, 2002.

writing another section of Chapter II rather than the introduction, do so. Some students find it easier to write all the individual sections and then go back and write the introduction. The important thing is to begin writing.

Of course, as with any writing, it is important to follow grammar and punctuation rules. See Box 3.2 to glimpse some of the typical writing errors seen by thesis and dissertation committee members. Taking the time to make certain that grammar and punctuation are correct will go a long way in reducing the number of rewrites and will expedite the approval of Chapter II.

Tense is especially important when writing Chapter II. Essentially, Chapter II should be written in the past tense. Remember that everything you report in Chapter II has already been com-

pleted. It is in the past; therefore, it must be written about in past tense. Note how the sample literature review page in Figure 3.5 was written in the past tense.

Write Chapter II as if you were telling the reader a story. Do not just report one study after another without connecting them. This style of writing is boring and monotonous. If you have found three articles, for example, that relate to the same topic and make similar points, do not write a paragraph on each article. Instead, think of the major concepts that these three articles convey, write one or more paragraphs to explain these concepts, and cite all three articles together. Readability is also improved when students make good use of introductory sentences, transition sentences, and summary sentences. Transitional terms provide

Box 3.2   Rules of Good Writin

12 Rules of good writin
- Verbs HAS to agree with subjects.
- Prepositions are *not* words to end sentences with.
- And don't start a sentence with a conjunction.
- It is wrong to ever split an infinitive.
- Avoid clichés like the plague (they're old hat).
- Be more or less specific.
- Parenthetical remarks (however relevant) are (usually) unnecessary.
- Also, too, never use repetitive redundancies.
- No sentence fragments.
- Don't use no double negatives.
- Proofread carefully to see if you any words out, and to check spellin.
- Do not write one-sentence paragraphs.

—Author unknown

coherence in writing. Some examples of transitional words are additionally, again, besides, equally important, moreover, alternatively, conversely, and however (Pan, 2008).

How much detail should be included about each source is a common question. As a general rule, articles that are only tangentially associated with the proposed research can be briefly summarized. "Briefly summarized" means providing only a sentence or two stating a finding associated with the current literature review. For example:

> Smith and Jones (2008), in their work with teen smokers, found that smoking was related to a desire to appear more adult. Other researchers have found that smoking is more closely associated with youths' desires to express their independence and rebel (Adams & Smith, 2004; Bramble, 2005; McKnight & Kirby, 2007).

Note in this hypothetical example that four articles have been referenced in just two sentences.

At the opposite end of the spectrum are those sources that are closely aligned to the proposed research study in terms of topic, instrumentation, or methodology. These sources should be described

in more detail. It would not be unusual to spend a page or more of space to describe a study fully if important to the current study.

Building on the previous smoking example, suppose the researcher was actually interested in the effectiveness of the nicotine patch in helping college students to stop smoking. The information above about why students started smoking as teens might be considered tangential and only briefly covered. In the literature search, however, an article is discovered that examines the effectiveness of the nicotine patch with a group of military men. The methodology, instrumentation, and research design are similar to what is being proposed. This article would be explained in detail in the literature review. If one follows the broad-to-specific organization in writing Chapter II, the early part of the chapter will contain more brief summarizations of articles while the later parts will contain more detailed article descriptions.

How much analysis and critique of the literature should be included in Chapter II? Some authors contend that the researcher must critique articles as part of the literature review. Neutens and Rubinson (2010) note that, "contradictory results among studies arise from differing definitions of important terms, varying instruments and methodologies of science, and utilizing different data analyses. As you review and write the literature section of your proposal with a critical eye, you will certainly be challenged but will also make a very important contribution to your field of study" (p. 31). Blaxter and colleagues (2002) state, "A key point to note is that good literature reviews go beyond the stage of simply listing sources to offer an analytical study of the area, through which you can develop you own position, analysis and argument" (p. 122). Although these authors were describing the research process in general, Manning, Algozzine, and Antonak (2003) speak directly about critiquing literature in Chapter II of a thesis or dissertation. They state, "The second chapter provides an analysis of the relevant literature used to support the need, rationale, and purpose of the research. . . .

The objective is to analyze the literature, not simply report a series of index card summaries of articles or other publications" (p. 36).

Analyzing the literature is an important skill to obtain in graduate-level study. Entire books have been written on how to analyze or interpret research (Hittleman & Simon, 2005; Pryczak, 2008). Analysis can involve several different tasks such as noting relationships between different sources, identifying common problems or disagreements, summarizing the state of knowledge, and critiquing specific articles (Manning *et al.*, 2003). Although it is easy to say that the literature should be critiqued, to actually critique the literature can be difficult. This is particularly true not only of students at the master's degree level but also of many at the doctoral level. Students typically have limited knowledge about sample size, sample selection, instrument quality, and research design. Often students are writing their literature review while they are still enrolled in their research methods class or classes. Students might, for example, see lack of randomization as a fatal flaw in a study when in reality the study could only be done using intact groups, and this technique has been used and accepted by the profession in previous research. The point here is that students should provide analysis and critique of the literature, but to use caution and reason when doing so.

At this point it is important to note that writing the literature review is a fairly complex task that must be completed with considerable thought and deliberation. Galvan (1999) noted that the literature review chapter of a thesis or dissertation is the most complex type of literature review, far more involved than literature reviews for term papers or journal articles. It is expected that you (the student) will not only provide a "comprehensive and up-to-date review of the topic" but also "demonstrate that you have a thorough command of the field you are studying" (p. 13). In addition, the writing of a thesis or dissertation requires absolute adherence to style manual rules for citations, references, headings, quotations, numbers, tables, figures, and statistical reporting. Students should expect to do several rewrites of Chapter II before it is finally accepted. Writing the literature review is a complex skill and it is unusual that anyone gets it right with the first try. Mitchell (2000) noted that "There is no problem that cannot be resolved by a willingness to cheerfully rewrite" (p. 61).

Referencing

In a thesis or dissertation, a reference list is provided at the end of the document. A **reference list** is an alphabetical listing by first author's last name of all sources cited in an article, thesis, or dissertation. This differs from a **bibliography,** which lists all sources read, whether or not they are cited. **Citations** are essentially brief in-text references that provide the author(s) and date of a publication (if using APA style). Readers use citations to obtain complete references from the reference list. Students must be meticulous in citing sources and recording an accurate bibliographical reference for each source.

Referencing is a critical aspect of writing Chapter II, because most of the references appearing in the thesis or dissertation will be found in this chapter. Almost everything written in Chapter II will have a citation and be referenced, because the student is reporting on what other people have done. The purpose of referencing is to attribute any ideas, findings, or results to the proper source and to provide future readers of the thesis or dissertation with needed information to obtain the original source should they desire to do so.

One way to keep track of references is by keeping a running reference list. The **running reference list** is simply a way of developing the reference list as one writes. As students begin writing and place the first citation in the chapter, they begin a new computer file titled "References" or "Running Reference List." They now place a reference for the first citation in that new file. Each time a citation for a new source is listed, a new reference is placed in the running reference list. New references should be inserted in the appropriate alphabetical order in the list so that the reference list will be completed when the writing is completed. Note that if a numerical referencing system such as that of the American Medical Association (2007) is used, references are listed in the order in which they appear in the thesis or dissertation and not in alphabetical order. Regardless of what style of referencing is used, students should always do a final check when they finish writing to be sure all cited sources have been referenced and none were accidentally left out. Also, if any references are missing information, that information will have to be obtained prior to completing the thesis or dissertation.

An option for maintaining a running reference list is to purchase a computer-based bibliography software program such as EndNote or RefWorks. These software programs assist in correctly formatting footnotes, endnotes, and bibliographies. They save large amounts of time in preparing thesis and dissertation manuscripts. They work in conjunction with a word processing program such as Microsoft Word (Kiernan, 2006). The programs can be used on both Macintosh and Windows computers. RefWorks may be easier to use for beginners and may be provided for free or at reduced cost by colleges and universities. It is Web-based so the student can access it from any computer, but because of its Web-based nature, the program is slower than End-Note. EndNote is software that is loaded onto a personal computer. It costs approximately $250, but again universities may have deals that allow students to purchase it at a discount price. EndNote allows one to link a PDF article directly to the reference within the computer. Exporting citations from databases directly into the thesis or dissertation is fast and easy. There is also a newer Web-based version of EndNote now available.

These programs allow students to establish a separate record for each source. Records contain preestablished or customized fields for entering data. Fields can be used to collect such data as author, date, publisher, title, and any notes one may

wish to include. When writing the final document, the software program works to insert the appropriate citations automatically in whatever style is used. The reference for every citation is automatically placed in a reference list, and manual cross-checking to be sure every source is included is not necessary. Computer-based bibliography programs also make it easy to modify the references when writing future articles for publications that use different style requirements.

One caution needs to be made in terms of citations. Depending on the style manual used, sources are often cited differently the first time they appear in a document than when they are subsequently cited. For example, when using the *Publication Manual of the American Psychological Association* (2010), if an article has five authors, all are listed in the first citation, but only the first author and *et al.* are used in subsequent citations. Since Chapter I is often written after all or part of Chapter II, and since some sources cited in Chapter II are also cited in Chapter I, it may be necessary to change a citation in Chapter II to the *"et al."* format if a first citation listing all authors is placed in Chapter I.

Summarizing Chapter II

At the end of the literature review chapter, a separate section with the heading "Summary" should be included. The summary should not be more than one page in length. Students may want to structure the summary based on the headings contained in Chapter II. Students should ask themselves, "What are the major results and findings from all the studies I reviewed?" (Creswell, 2005, p. 110). The purpose of the summary is not to reiterate what each study said but to synthesize and condense the findings. Since the summary is the student's perception of what the literature reports, there would typically be no citations in the summary. In addition to summarizing what was found, the student may make summary statements pointing out gaps or weaknesses in the literature and specify what is needed to bolster the literature. This should logically lead to support for the proposed research.

Summary

In this chapter we have discussed why it is important to do a thorough literature review as part of any research project. We then discussed the need to be sure that the literature reviewed contains valid sources of health information. In the health area there is much written that is of questionable quality, particularly among Internet sources. Readers were then provided with information about how to conduct a literature review with emphasis placed on searching for appropriate literature using electronic databases and Boolean operators.

Once a list of potential resources has been generated and the appropriate documents located, the next procedure discussed was how to scan through this list for those resources most relevant to the proposed research. When these relevant sources have been identified, suggestions were presented on how to best organize oneself to read and record important information. Using the reviewed literature to extend one's search and identify additional sources was presented as well as knowing when to stop the literature search.

At the end of the chapter, specific information was presented to readers concerning the development of Chapter II for a thesis or dissertation. Ideas about organizing, writing, referencing, and summarizing Chapter II were presented.

Review Questions

1. How would you describe the literature review to a friend who has no background in research methods?
2. Explain to the same friend why one needs to do a literature review.
3. Explain why it is difficult for thesis or dissertation advisors to give students specific length requirements for Chapter II.
4. You have just found a new resource for the literature review that presents some very novel and different ideas. What guidelines can be followed to determine if this is a valid source that should be included in your literature review?
5. Explain how the Boolean operators "AND," "OR," "NOT," and "*" can be used.
6. You have just picked up an article with a promising title for your literature review, but you are not sure if it is really relevant. What sections of the article should you review to make a quick determination on whether the article will be of help?
7. Select a system for reading and recording information that makes the most sense to you. Explain how the system is used and why you like it.
8. Explain how you can use relevant sources already obtained to locate additional relevant sources written either before or after the initial source.
9. Discuss the difference between primary and secondary sources. Which is most appropriate to use in a literature review and why?
10. Discuss how Chapter II should be organized.
11. What is a reference list? What is a citation? Why are these important when writing Chapter II?
12. Explain how programs like EndNote and RefWorks can help when developing the literature review.
13. What is the difference between a reference list and a bibliography?
14. What is the purpose of the summary section of Chapter II? What should be included in the summary section?

References

Aaron, L. (2008). Writing a literature review article. *Radiologic Technology*, 80(2), 185–186.

American Medical Association. (2007). *AMA Manual of style* (10th ed.). New York: Oxford University Press.

American Psychological Association. (2010). *Publication manual of the American Psychological Association* (6th ed.). Washington, D.C.: American Psychological Association.

Berg, K.E., & Latin, R.W. (2004). *Essentials of research methods in health, physical education, exercise science, and recreation* (2nd ed.). Philadelphia: Lippincott Williams & Wilkins.

Blaxter, L., Hughes, C., & Tight, M. (2002). *How to research* (2nd ed.). Philadelphia: Open University Press.

Creswell, J.W. (2005). *Educational research: Planning, conducting, and evaluating quantitative and qualitative research.* Upper Saddle River, N.J.: Pearson Education, Inc.

DePoy, E., & Gitlin, L.N. (2005). *Introduction to research: Understanding and applying multiple strategies* (3rd ed.). St. Louis: Elsevier Mosby.

Galvan, J.L. (1999). *Writing literature reviews.* Los Angeles: Pryczak Publishing.

Gay, L.R., Mills, G.E., & Airasian, P. (2006). *Educational research: Competencies for analysis and applications.* Upper Saddle River, N.J.: Pearson Education, Inc.

Hittleman, D.R., & Simon, A.J. (2005). *Interpreting educational research* (4th ed.). Upper Saddle River, N.J.: Merrill/Prentice Hall.

Kiernan, V. (2006). Toss out the index cards. *Chronicle of Higher Education*, 52(40), A29–A30. Retrieved April 16, 2009, from Library, Information Science & Technology Abstracts with Full Text database.

Leedy, P.D., & Ormrod, J.E. (2010). *Practical research: Planning and design* (9th ed.). Upper Saddle River, N.J.: Pearson Education, Inc.

Manning, T., Algozzine, B., & Antonak, R. (2003). *Guide for preparing a thesis or dissertation.* Morgantown, W.Va.: PNG Publications.

Mitchell, C.L. (2000). Contribution 46. In F. Pryczak (Ed.), *Completing your thesis or dissertation* (p. 61). Los Angeles: Pryczak Publishing.

Neutens, J.J., & Rubinson, L. (2010). *Research techniques for the health sciences* (4th ed.). San Francisco: Benjamin Cummings.

Pan, M.L. (2008). *Literature reviews: Qualitative and quantitative approaches* (3rd ed.). Glendale, Calif. Pryczak Publishing.

Price, J.H., & Murnan, J. (2004). Referencing style of health education journals. *American Journal of Health Education*, 35(5), 258–259.

Pryczak, F. (2008). *Evaluating research in academic journals: A practical guide to realistic evaluation* (4th ed.). Glendale, Calif.: Pryczak Publishing.

Timmins, F., & McCabe, C. (2005). How to conduct an effective literature search. *Nursing Standard*, 20(11), 41–47.

U.S. Department of Health and Human Services. (2009). Methods and background: U.S. Preventive Services Task Force (USPSTF). Retrieved June 12, 2009, from http://www.ahrq.gov/clinic/uspstmeth.htm.

Vertin, B.E. (2002). *Stress and social support among college students by gender.* Unpublished master's thesis, University of Cincinnati.

Wilhelm, W.J., & Kaunelis, D. (2005). Literature reviews: Analysis, planning and query techniques. *The Delta Pi Epsilon Journal*, 47(2), 91–106.

CHAPTER 4 | **Theory and Research**

Chapter Objectives

After reading this chapter and answering the review questions, you should be able to:

1. Define and explain the differences among theory, concept, construct, variable, and model.
2. Differentiate between planning models and the theories/models of change.
3. Name the five components that seem to be common to most planning models.
4. Define theory-based research.
5. Describe what is meant by theory-based endeavors.
6. Explain the relationship among theory, research, and practice.
7. List and explain the four categories of theory-based research.
8. Describe four methods of developing theory.
9. Describe what is meant by the terms best practices, evidence, evidence-based interventions, and evidence-based health education practice.

Key Terms

best practices
concepts
construct
evidence
evidence-based health education
    practice

evidence-based interventions
models
planning models
theories/models of change

theory
theory-based endeavors
theory-based research
variable

As you have probably discovered by now, the range of research topics is almost limitless, and one of the most difficult tasks embedded in the larger research process is narrowing your research topic to a manageable project. As you continue to narrow and define the topic of your research project, one question you need to ask yourself is "Does my topic lend itself to **theory-based research**?" That is, should my research project be planned using a theory or model as its foundation? As you have reviewed the literature, we are sure you have come across some research that is theory-based and some that is not. For example, if a health education specialist has an interest in studying the impact of an intervention on a specific group of people, it would make sense to use an intervention based on a theory that has been shown to be useful in creating change in other similar situations. However, if a health education specialist is interested in conducting a study that tracks the prevalence of a specific disease or health behavior in a given group of people over a period of time, there is probably no need to base one's study on a theory.

In this chapter, we present information to help researchers in deciding whether their research should be theory-based research. Specifically, this chapter includes definitions of terms associated with the use of theory and models, a very brief overview of the theories and models that are commonly used in health education research and practice, and a discussion of the possibilities for theory-based research, including a brief discussion of evidence-based research and practice. Also, it should be noted that this chapter is presented with the assumption that the reader has an understanding of the theories and models commonly used in the practice of health education. If you are not familiar with these theories and models, it is suggested that you seek out the sources that provide a comprehensive presentation of them. [Note: Original sources are presented in Table 4.1, and summaries of many of the theories and models can be found in DiClemente, Crosby, and Kegler (2009); Glanz and Rimer (1995); Glanz, Rimer, and Viswanath (2008a); McKenzie, Neiger, and Thackeray (2009); and Nutbeam and Harris (1999).]

Definitions of Key Terms

In order to better understand the use of theory and models in the research process, it is important to be familiar with some of the key terms. We begin with one of the most frequently quoted definitions of **theory** in which Glanz, Rimer, and Viswanath (2008b) modified an earlier definition presented by Kerlinger (1986). It states, "A theory is a set of interrelated concepts, definitions, and propositions that present a *systematic* view of events or situations by specifying relations among variables in order to *explain* and *predict* the events or situations" (p. 26). Green and colleagues (1994) have stated, "The role of theory is to untangle and simplify for human comprehension the complexities of nature" (p. 398). In other words, a theory is a systematic arrangement of fundamental principles that provide a basis for explaining the behavior of individuals. As applied to health education, theories are "tools to help health educators better under-

stand what influences health—relevant individual, group, and institutional behaviors—and to thereupon plan effective interventions directed at health-beneficial results" (Hochbaum, Sorenson & Lorig, 1992, p. 298).

Nutbeam and Harris (1999) have stated that a fully developed theory would be characterized by the explanation of three major elements:

- the major factors that influence the phenomena of interest, for example those factors that explain why some people are regularly active and others are not;
- the relationship between these factors, for example the relationship between knowledge, beliefs, social norms and behaviours such as physical activity; and
- the conditions under which these relationships do or do not occur: the how, when, and why of hypothesised relationships, for example, the time, place, and circumstances which, predictably, lead to a person being active or inactive. (p. 10)

Another word that is used when people talk about theory is "model." It is not uncommon for laypeople, as well as some professionals, to use the words "theory" and "model" interchangeably, yet they are different. **Models** are a subclass of theories. They "are generalized, hypothetical descriptions, often based on an analogy, used to analyze or explain something" (Glanz & Rimer, 1995, p. 11). "Models draw on a number of theories to help understand a specific problem in a particular setting or context" (Glanz *et al.,* 2008b, p. 27). "They are not always as specific as theory" (Rimer & Glanz, 2005, p. 4) and often are created using more than one theory (Glanz *et al.*, 2008b).

There are a number of different ways of categorizing the theories and models associated with health education research and practice. For the purpose of this chapter, we present the theories and models in two groups: planning models and theories/models of change. **Planning models** are those that are used for planning, implementing, and evaluating health education/promotion programs. Planning models provide practitioners with a framework on which to develop a health education/promotion program plan. A number of planning models have been developed over the years. Although some of the models have common elements, the vocabulary used to describe the elements in the various models is often unique. In fact, "the underlying principles that guide the development of various models are similar; however, there are important differences in sequence, emphasis, and the conceptualization of the major components that make certain models more appealing than others to individual practitioners" (Simons-Morton, Greene & Gottlieb, 1995, pp. 126–127). However, most planning models revolve around five basic components: (1) assessing needs, (2) setting goals and objectives, (3) developing an intervention, (4) implementing the intervention, and (5) evaluating the results (McKenzie *et al.*, 2009).

Theories/models of change "specify the relationships among causal processes operating both within and across levels of analysis" (McLeroy, Steckler, Goodman, & Burdine, 1992, p. 3). In other words, they help explain how change takes place. Like planning models, a number of theories/models of change have been created over the years. Most theories/models of change have their roots in the field of psychology. Table 4.1 presents a listing of many of the planning models and theories/models of change that have been used in health education/promotion.

The major components of the theories and models are known as **concepts** (Glanz *et al.*, 2008b). When a concept has been developed, created, or adopted for use with a specific theory, it is called a **construct** (Kerlinger, 1986) (see Table 4.2 for selected constructs and examples of their application). The empirical counterparts or operational (practical use) forms of constructs are known as **variables** (Glanz *et al.*, 2008b; McKenzie *et al.*, 2009). Variables "specify how a construct is to be measured in a specific situation" (Glanz *et al.*, 2008b, p. 28) (see Box 4.1 for examples of how constructs are measured).

Here is an example of the application of the key terms defined above using the social cognitive theory (SCT). Let's suppose that researchers want to determine the impact of a new intervention in getting sedentary adults to become more active. From previous research, it has been shown that people's confidence in their ability to exercise is an important predictor of future exercise behavior. That is, the greater their confidence in being able to exercise, the greater the probability that they will exercise. Confidence is the *concept*, and as part of the SCT it is identified as the *construct* of self-efficacy. Therefore, the intervention being planned by the researchers is aimed at enhancing the self-efficacy of the participants in the study. However, if self-efficacy is going to be enhanced, the researchers have to be able to measure it both before and after the intervention. When the researchers are able to measure the construct of self-efficacy, it is then known as a *variable*. Results of the research may show that the construct of self-efficacy cannot fully explain why people do or do not exercise. Thus, a *model* that includes concepts from several theories may be needed to help further understand sedentary lifestyles.

Theory-Based Research

As we begin our discussion of theory-based research, we would like to clarify the use of the word "theory" in the term "theory-based." Earlier in this chapter we made a distinction between the words "theory" and "model," yet when discussing the term "theory-based" it is commonly understood in our profession that the word "theory" is used in a general way to mean either a theory *or* a model. Thus, as we use the term "theory-based" throughout the remainder of this book, we use it to be inclusive of endeavors based on either a theory *or* a model.

Table 4.1 Selected Planning Models and Theories/Models of Change Used in Health Education/Promotion Practice

Planning model	Author(s)
Assessment Protocol for Excellence in Public Health (APEX/PH)	NACHO (1991)
CDCynergy	CDC (2003)
Comprehensive Health Education Model	Sullivan (1973)
Generalized Model for Program Planning	McKenzie, Neiger, & Thackeray (2009)
Generic Health/Fitness Delivery System	Patton, Corry, Gettman, & Graff (1986)
Health Communication Model	NCI (2002)
Healthy Plan-It	CDC (2000)
Intervention Mapping	Bartholomew, Parcel, Kok, & Gottlieb (2006)
Mobilizing for Action through Planning and Partnerships (MAPP)	NACCHO (2001)
Model for Health Education Planning	Ross & Mico (1980)
Model for Health Education Planning and Resource Development	Bates & Winder (1984)
Multilevel Approach to Community Health (MATCH)	Simons-Morton, Greene, & Gottlieb (1995)
Planned Approach to Community Health (PATCH)	CDC (no date)
Planning, Program Development, and Evaluation Model	Timmreck (2003)
PRECEDE-PROCEED	Green & Kreuter (2005)
Social Marketing Assessment and Response Tool (SMART)	Neiger & Thackeray (1998)

Theories/models of change	Author(s)
Cognitive-behavioral model of the relapse process	Marlatt & Gordon (1980)
Elaboration likelihood model of persuasion	Petty, Wheeler, & Bizer (1999)
Diffusion theory	Rogers (2003)
Health belief model (HBM)	Rosenstock (1966)
Precaution adoption process model (PAPM)	Weinstein (1988)
Social cognitive theory (SCT)	Rotter (1954) and Bandura (1977)
Stimulus response theory	Thorndike (1898); Watson (1925); Hall (1943)
Theory of freeing	Freire (1973)
Theory of planned behavior (TPB)	Ajzen (1988)
Theory of reasoned action (TRA)	Fishbein (1967)
Transtheoretical model (TTM)	Prochaska (1979)

The term **theory-based endeavors** refers to processes (e.g., theory-based research, theory-based practice, and theory-driven programs) in which theoretical constructs serve as the foundation or framework for the endeavor. For example, a researcher might plan a study testing different methods of smoking cessation based on the *stages of change* construct of the transtheoretical model. Or a practitioner may create a tailored health education intervention for young mothers to remind them of the need to have their children properly immunized based on the theory

Table 4.2   Selected Theories: Their Constructs, Descriptions, and Examples

Theory of planned behavior[a, b]		
Construct	**Description**	**Quitting smoking example**
Attitude toward performing the behavior	Beliefs about outcomes or attributes of performing the behavior	Has positive attitude about quitting and feels that it would be good for him
Subjective norm	Belief about whether most people approve or disapprove of the behavior	Thinks others whom he values believe it would be good for him to quit
Perceived behavioral control	Perceived personal control over the behavior	Perceives that he has control over whether he quits
Behavioral intention	Perceived likelihood of performing a behavior	Likely to quit if he has a good attitude about quitting, others believe it is good for him, and he feels as if he has control over quitting

Health belief model		
Construct	**Description**[c]	**Exercise example**[b]
Cues to action	Strategies to activate "readiness"	She sees a public service announcement on television about the importance of exercise in preventing heart disease.
Perceived susceptibility	Belief about the chances of experiencing a risk of getting a condition or disease	She discovers from a health risk appraisal she is at higher risk of heart disease.
Perceived severity	Belief about how serious a condition and its sequelae are	She knows if she gets heart disease it can be very serious.
Perceived benefits	Belief in the efficacy of the advised action to reduce risk or seriousness of impact	She knows that exercise can help to prevent heart disease and increases her chances of surviving a heart attack.
Perceived barriers	Belief about the tangible and psychological costs of the advised action	She knows that an exercise program takes time and that it is not always easy to exercise in bad weather.
Self-efficacy	Confidence in one's ability to take action	She feels confident that she can exercise regularly, and if she does so it will be good for her.

[a] = Adapted from Montano and Kasprzyk (2008).
[b] = Adapted from McKenzie, Neiger, and Thackeray (2009).
[c] = Source: Champion and Skinner (2008).

continued

Table 4.2   *Continued*

Transtheoretical model		
Construct	**Description**[d]	**Stress management example**
Stages of change	Temporal dimension of change represented by six stages: pre-contemplation, contemplation, preparation, action, main-tenance, and termination	He is planning to start a stress management program next month (preparation).
Decisional balance	Relative weighing of the pros and cons of behavioral change	He has made a list of the pros and cons of practicing stress management and finds more pros than cons on his list.
Self-efficacy	Internal belief in one's own abil-ity to perform a behavior successfully; includes the concepts of confidence and temptation	He feels confident that he can manage his stress, and if he does so it will be good for him.
Processes of change	Covert and overt activities that people use to progress through the stages	He has made a firm commit-ment in front of his friends to manage his stress.
Social cognitive theory		
Construct	**Definition**[e]	**Weight loss example**[e]
Behavioral capability	Knowledge and skills necessary to perform a behavior	If people are going to exercise aerobically, they need to know what it is and how to do it.
Expectations	Beliefs about the likely out-comes of certain behaviors	If people enroll in a weight-loss program, they expect to lose weight.
Expectancies	Values people place on expec-ted outcomes	How important is it to people that they become physi-cally fit?
Locus of control	Perception of the center of con-trol over reinforcement	Those who feel they have con-trol over reinforcement are said to have internal locus of control; those who perceive reinforcement under the con-trol of some external force are said to have external locus of control.

[d] = Adapted from Prochaska, Redding, and Evers (2008).
[e] = Source: Cottrell, Girvan, and McKenzie (2009), p. 130.

Table 4.2   *Continued*

Social cognitive theory		
Construct	**Definition**[e]	**Weight loss example**[e]
Reciprocal determinism	Behavior changes result from an interaction between the person and the environment; change is bidirectional (Glanz & Rimer, 1995).	Lack of use of vending machines could be a result of the choices within the machines; notes about the selections from the nonusing consumers to the machines' owners could change the selections and the behavior of the consumers to that of users.
Reinforcement (direct, vicarious, self-management)	Responses to behaviors that increase the chances of recurrence.	Giving verbal encouragement to those who have acted in a healthy manner.
Self-control or self-regulation	Gaining control over one's own behavior through monitoring and adjusting it.	If clients want to change their eating habits, have them monitor their current eating habits for seven days.
Self-efficacy	People's confidence in their ability to perform a certain desired task or function.	If people are going to engage in a regular exercise program, they must feel confident or believe they can do it.
Emotional coping response	For people to learn, they must be able to deal with the sources of anxiety that surround a behavior.	Fear is an emotion that can be involved in learning, and people would have to deal with it before they could learn a behavior.

[e] = Source: Cottrell, Girvan, & McKenzie (2009), p. 130.

of planned behavior construct *attitude toward performing the behavior*. In each example, the construct guides the researcher or practitioner as he or she plans the intervention for his or her programs.

Though the above examples illustrate the use of theory-based endeavors, you may remember that earlier in the chapter we indicated that not all research is theory-based, nor should it be. For example, descriptive research, research that describes the status of a situation or condition such as the number of cases of a specific disease in a given population, is often not theory-driven. However, one of the criticisms of the health education profession over the years has been that not enough of the practice of health education, research included, is theory-based. Burdine and McLeroy (1992) have pointed out that health education practice is too loosely linked to theory and lacks the necessary field tests for efficacy. There are a number of reasons why theory has not been included more in the practice of health education, but this is not the place nor is there space to discuss them here. [If you are interested in the reasons, see discussions in Burdine and McLeroy (1992); Glanz *et al.* (2008a); Green *et al.* (1994); Hochbaum *et al.* (1992); McLeroy *et al.* (1992); Rimer, Glanz, and Rasband (2001); and van Ryn & Heaney (1992).]

Box 4.1   Examples of How Constructs Have Been Measured

Construct	Measure
Stages of change[a]	Do you exercise three times a week for at least 20 minutes each time?
Maintenance	a. YES, I have been for *MORE than 6 months.*
Action	b. YES, I have been, but for *LESS than 6 months.*
Preparation	c. NO, but I intend to in the *next 30 days.*
Contemplation	d. NO, but I intend to in the *next 6 months.*
Precontemplation	e. NO, and I do *NOT* intend to in the *next 6 months.*

Construct	Measure
Internal locus of control[b]	(Note: These six questions are scored using the following scale: Strongly disagree = 1, moderately disagree = 2, slightly disagree = 3, slightly agree = 4, moderately agree = 5, strongly agree = 6. The scores are summed and the higher the score, the more internal the locus of control.)

1. If I get sick, it is my own behavior that determines how soon I get well again.
2. I am in control of my health.
3. When I get sick, I am to blame.
4. The main thing which affects my health is what I myself do.
5. If I take care of myself, I can avoid illness.
6. If I take the right actions, I can stay healthy.

Construct	Measure
Stage[c]	What are your intentions for receiving the HPV vaccination?
Acting	I have already had the vaccination.
Decided to act	I have decided that I will receive the vaccination.
Decided not to act	I have decided that I will not receive the vaccination.
Deciding about acting	I am still trying to decide if I will receive the vaccination.
Unengaged by the issue	I really haven't thought about receiving the vaccination.
Unaware of the issue	I was unaware that there was a vaccination for HPV.

Sources: [a] = Laforge *et al.* (1999); R.G. Laforge, personal communication, April 23, 1999; [b] = Wallston, Wallston, and DeVellis (1978); [c] = Smith (2008).

Suffice it to say, theory should be integral to the practice of health education because it assists health education specialists in understanding the nature of targeted health behaviors as well as guiding them through the various tasks of planning, implementing, and evaluating an intervention (Glanz & Rimer, 1995). In other words, "Theories can provide answers to program developers' questions regarding *why* people aren't already engaging in a desirable behavior of interest, *how* to go about changing their behaviors, and *what* factors to look for when evaluating a program's focus" (van Ryn & Heaney, 1992, p. 326). Effective practice depends on using the most appropriate theory or theories and practice strategies for a given situation (Glanz *et al.*, 2008b).

When discussing theory-based research, it is important to recognize that "Theory, research, and practice are interrelated" (Crosby, Kegler, & DiClemente, 2009, p. 10). The relationship is by no means simple or linear in nature (Glanz *et al.,* 2008b) but rather dynamic, complex, and circular. Crosby and colleagues (2009) summarize this dynamic relationship well when they say:

> as theories become less useful (that is, they explain an insufficient amount of variance in particular risk behaviors) or are found wanting as a foundation for guiding the design and implementation of behavior change interventions, they are modified or even discarded in favor of potentially more useful theories. This process of development, elimination, and replacement is gradual. As new theories are synthesized and embraced, they too are subject to empirical validation, and if they are found lacking, they are similarly discarded. (p. 12)

The examination of the circular nature of theory, research, and practice can assist health education specialists in identifying potential opportunities to conduct theory-based research. As such, several major categories for thinking about theory-based research have been identified (Glanz *et al.,* 2008b; Hiatt & Rimer, 1999; Rimer *et al.,* 2001). They include: (1) basic or fundamental research to develop and test theories, (2) intervention research to develop and test evidence-based interventions, (3) surveillance research to track trends, and (4) research dealing with application and program delivery. Each of these categories will be discussed in the sections that follow.

Basic or Fundamental Research to Develop and Test Theories

Basic or fundamental research to develop and test theories is research that either creates new theories or further tests the usefulness of existing theories. Such research can occur in several different ways. Kegler, Crosby, and DiClemente (2002) have identified four different methods for developing theory. The first is adding new constructs to existing theory. That is, researchers may find that another construct, such as a new original one or one from another theory, when combined with a theory's existing constructs helps to further explain the

processes of change being studied. Using statistical language, we say that we are able to explain more of the variance for a specific behavior. For example, the construct of *perceived behavioral control* was added to the theory of reasoned action (TRA) to help create the theory of planned behavior (TPB). In earlier research, the TRA had proved to be most successful when dealing with purely volitional behaviors, but the theory was not as useful when it was applied to behaviors that were not fully under volitional control, such as when a smoker is unsuccessful in quitting. Even though the smoker's intentions to quit are high, nonmotivational factors, such as lack of requisite opportunities, skills, and resources, could prevent success in quitting (Ajzen, 1988). By adding the construct of *perceived behavioral control* to the TRA, a greater amount of the variance in a number of health behaviors could be explained.

A second means of theory development is refining existing theory to create a new, more parsimonious approach. When the health belief model (HBM) was created back in the early 1950s, it was created to help explain why people were not participating in a free chest x-ray program offered by the Public Health Service to diagnose tuberculosis. The model was useful in helping explain behavior change that required a single step, such as getting an x-ray or immunization. In the years that followed, a number of health researchers began to use the HBM to study other health behaviors, including some that took more time to accomplish, such as weight loss and a change in diet. Because the HBM was not created with such behaviors in mind, it was in need of some refinement. Thus, in the late 1980s, it was suggested that the construct of *self-efficacy* be added to the HBM to help explain the lifestyle behaviors requiring more long-term changes (Rosenstock, Strecher, & Becker, 1988).

The third method of developing theory identified by Kegler and colleagues (2002) is the application of existing theory from other disciplines. As an eclectic applied science, much of health education's body of knowledge has come from other disciplines (Galli, 1976). Examples include the application of the elaboration likelihood model of persuasion (ELM) and the cognitive-behavioral model of the relapse process. The ELM originated in the discipline of social psychology. It has been used to study attitudes associated with health behavior [see Petty, Barden, and Wheeler (2009) for examples of its application]. Whereas the cognitive-behavioral model of the relapse process was first used by psychologists to study relapse as it applied to substance abuse (i.e., alcohol and other drugs), it is also now applied to health behaviors more often studied by health education specialists, such as exercise, dieting, and weight loss.

The fourth method of developing theory is based on approaches that have evolved from the work of practitioners. That is, hypotheses for theory can arise as practitioners apply common-sense principles to reach the objectives of the programs they have planned, implemented, and evaluated. For example, practitioners working for a local health department may find that they have been very successful in getting the new mothers in their health district to participate in breastfeeding. When they look closely at the methods they have used in doing so, it may reveal ideas and concepts that cannot be explained by existing theory and thus provide the basis for hypotheses that may create new theory.

Regardless of the method researchers use to develop theory, their goal is to develop the most robust theory possible. Such theories are flexible (Crosby et al., 2009) and retain parsimonious explanatory and predictive power when applied to a variety of health issues, settings, and populations (Kegler et al., 2002).

Intervention Research to Develop and Test Evidence-Based Interventions

Few health education graduate students take on basic or fundamental research to develop and test theories for their thesis or dissertation project, primarily because of the time and experience necessary to do such research. It is much more likely that graduate students in health education will get involved in intervention research to develop and test evidence-based interventions. **Evidence-based interventions** are those that are most likely to be based on theory and have been shown through empirical study to be effective. "The use of theory-based interventions, evaluated through appropriate designs, contributes to understanding why interventions do or do not work under particular conditions" (Rimer et al., 2001, p. 244). Such research is needed not only to "prove" the effectiveness of health education practice, but also to continue the maturation of the profession. Evidence-based interventions are a part of the larger concept of evidence-based health education practice. Using the definitions of evidence-based medicine (Rosenberg & Donald, 1995) and evidence-based public health (Jenicek, 1997) and the work of Rimer and colleagues (2001), **evidence-based health education practice** can be defined as the process of systematically finding, appraising, and using contemporaneous quantitative and qualitative research findings as the basis for decisions in the practice of health education. The gold standard for testing theory-based interventions' effectiveness is the randomized controlled trial (RCT) (Kegler et al., 2002). (See Chapter 9 for a discussion of experimental research methods and Box 4.2 for a framework for rating the strength of scientific evidence and suitability of study designs for assessing effectiveness.)

Here is an example of intervention research to develop and test evidence-based interventions. Suppose through some earlier pilot testing, a researcher found that a 10-minute health education intervention grounded in the TPB and delivered by a health education specialist showed promise in getting women at risk for breast cancer in a specific setting to get a mammogram. Using this information, the researcher designed an RCT in which women who received their health care at a given clinic and met the rest of the

Box 4.2   Framework for Rating the Strength of Scientific Evidence and Suitability of Design for Assessing Effectiveness

Strength of evidence[a, b]

I: Evidence from at least one properly designed randomized controlled trial.

II-1: Evidence from well-designed controlled trials without randomization.

II-2: Evidence from well-designed cohort or case control analytic studies.

II-3: Evidence from multiple time series with or without the intervention. Dramatic results in uncontrolled studies (e.g., introduction of penicillin) could be regarded as evidence.

III: Opinions of respected authorities, descriptive studies, or reports of expert committees.

Suitability of study designs for assessing effectiveness[c]

Greatest: Concurrent comparison groups and prospective measurement of exposure and outcome.

Moderate: All retrospective designs *or* multiple pre- or postmeasurements but no concurrent comparison group.

Least: Single pre- and postmeasurements and no concurrent comparison group *or* exposure and outcome measured in a single group at the same point.

Taken from: Rimer, B.K., Glanz, K., & Rasband, G. Searching for evidence about health education and health behavior interventions. *Health Education and Behavior,* 28 (2), p. 236, copyright 2001 by Sage Publications. Reprinted by Permission of Sage Publications, Inc.

Original sources: [a] = Canadian Task Force on Periodic Health Examination (1994); [b] = U.S. Preventive Services Task Force (1996); [c] = Briss *et al.* (2000)

mation as the first group, again based on the constructs of the TPB, but this group received the intervention via a series of e-mail messages. Thus, these first two groups received an educational intervention that included content that revolved around three key constructs of the TPB: *attitude toward performing the behavior, subjective norm,* and *perceived behavioral control.* The third group, or the control group, received the "normal" health education intervention provided by the clinic prior to the beginning of the RCT. The variables measured in the study were intention to get a mammogram and whether a mammogram was received. Data on these variables were gathered by telephone interviews at 2, 4, and 10 weeks after the interventions. The findings of the RCT were then reported. In reporting the results, the researchers were providing information about the effectiveness of an evidence-based intervention.

The results, or data generated, from the above noted RCT are part of the **evidence** that can lead to decisions by planners for future programming efforts (McKenzie *et al.*, 2009). The concept of using the evidence that results from the critical review of multiple research and evaluation studies that substantiate efficacy of an intervention in a certain population is referred to as **best practices** (Green & Kreuter, 2005). The concept of best practices got its start in U.S. manufacturing, and since its beginning has been applied to a number of different fields. It got its start in the health fields in medicine. The incorporation of best practices in health education has come more recently, and because of the nature of health education practice the concept cannot be applied the same as in these other professions, especially medicine. "The relative predictability of the human organism's response to medical or surgical interventions compared with the relative unpredictability of social and psychological factors that modify the response to health promotion or public health interventions make the 'evidence-based best practices' exercise qualitatively different" (Green, 2001, p. 172). In other words, generating evidence that leads to best

inclusion criteria (see Chapter 7 for a discussion of inclusion criteria) were invited to participate in the study. The women were randomly assigned to one of three groups. One group received the promising intervention based on the TPB and delivered in face-to-face interaction with the health education specialist. A second group received the same infor-

practices for health education/promotion programming is not as easy as it is in some other professions because of the variations of populations (e.g., cultures and socioeconomic circumstances) and the multiple settings where health education/ promotion takes place (e.g., communities and clinics). Because of these variations in population and settings, theory-driven research may produce evidence that is indeed internally valid but may lack external validity (see Chapter 9 for a discussion of these terms). In the end, "if we want more evidence-based practice, we need more practice-based evidence" (Green, 2006, paragraph 1). Table 4.3 provides several sources for evidence-based recommendations.

Surveillance Research to Track Trends

Probably the category of research with the least potential for theory-based research is that of surveillance research to track trends. Such research is often descriptive research and follows people over time to track, for example, attitudes and behaviors or epidemiological data such as incidence and prevalence of various health conditions. Yet even surveillance data can be theory-based. For example, the stage construct of the transtheoretical model (TTM) could be used in designing a surveillance project examining the adoption of health

behavior change over time. Such a study could follow those in a priority population who have been exposed to a mass media campaign to increase exercise behavior. Thus, at two-month intervals, simple random samples could be drawn from the priority population and surveyed by telephone to determine what stage they were in with regard to exercise behavior.

Research Dealing with Application and Program Delivery

The potential for theory-based research also exists with research dealing with application and program delivery. That is, once evidence-based interventions are identified, they must be made available to those who may deliver them (i.e., health practitioners, lay consumers, the media, other researchers, and other potential users), and they "must be delivered to the right people at the right time if impact is to be achieved" (Rimer et al., 2001, p. 239). Only then can evidence-based research be turned into evidence-based practice. Depending on the type of evidence-based intervention identified, the right people would be a priority population that is the same as or similar to those from which the evidence-based research was generated. The right time would be when the priority population is most in need of the inter-

Table 4.3   Sources for Evidence-Based Recommendations

Title	URL
Agency for Healthcare Research and Quality: Evidence-Based Practice	http://www.ahrq.gov/Clinic/epcix.htm
Best Practices for Comprehensive Tobacco Control Programs—2007	http://www.cdc.gov/tobacco/tobacco_control_programs/ stateandcommunity/best_practices/
The Community Guide (recommendations and findings to improve public health)	http://www.thecommunityguide.org/about/index.html
HIV/AIDS Prevention Research Synthesis (PRS) project	http://www.cdc.gov/hiv/topics/research/prs/index.htm
SAMHSA's National Registry of Evidence-Based Programs and Practices (NREPP)	http://nrepp.samhsa.gov

vention. Examples of a research project falling into this category would be either the dissemination or evaluation of the program used in the mammogram RCT described above. For the purpose of this explanation, let's suppose the results of that research suggested that the 10-minute health education session by a health education specialist was far superior to both the e-mail messages and "normal" care in prompting women to get a mammogram. One study could be designed to examine the dissemination of results of the evidence-based results of the RCT—in other words, examining the process by which the evidence-based program can be placed in the "hands" of practitioners who can deliver the program. Such a dissemination study could be designed using constructs from the theory of diffusion, in which some practitioners get the information via a packet of materials sent to them that includes all the information and materials to implement the intervention. A second group could be invited to attend a half-day workshop to receive the information and materials. The outcome measures for such a study might include the self-efficacy of practitioners to deliver the intervention and the adoption rate for using the intervention.

Another study could be created in this category of research dealing with application and program delivery in which the right people (or the priority population) are the focus of the study. The right people could include the women in need of a mammogram but be further segmented (e.g., by race and ethnicity, or by different age groups over 50 years, or by place of residence). Thus, a study may use the evidence-based intervention to determine with which group of women (e.g., 50–59 years, 60–69 years, or 70+ years) the intervention is most useful.

As can be seen in the above discussion, the possibilities for designing theory-based research projects exist in all aspects of health education. Whether the research is aimed at basic/fundamental research to develop and test theories or at research dealing with application and program delivery or some-

where in between, "more research is needed at all points along the research continuum" (Glanz *et al.*, 2008b, p. 36).

Summary

This chapter began with the definitions of the terms theory, concept, construct, variable, and model. Included in these definitions was a brief presentation of the various planning models and the theories/models of change. These definitions were followed by a discussion of theory-based endeavors and the relationship among theory, research, and practice. The chapter concluded with a discussion of the four different categories of theory-based research and evidence-based health education practice.

Review Questions

1. Define each of the following and explain how they relate to each other: (a) theory, (b) concept, (c) construct, (d) variable, and (e) model.
2. What is the difference between a construct and a variable?
3. What is the difference between planning models and the theories/models of change?
4. What five components seem to be common to all planning models?
5. What is meant by theory-based endeavors?
6. What is it that makes health education research theory-based?
7. Explain the relationship among theory, research, and practice.
8. Briefly describe the four categories of theory-based research.
9. Name and briefly describe the four methods for creating theory.
10. Define each of the following: (a) best practices, (b) evidence, (c) evidence-based interventions, and (d) evidence-based health education practice.

11. What is meant by the terms evidence-based interventions and evidence-based health education practice?

References

Ajzen, I. (1988). *Attitudes, personality, and behavior.* Chicago: Dorsey Press.

Bandura, A. (1977). *Social learning theory.* Englewood Cliffs, N.J.: Prentice-Hall.

Bartholomew, L.K., Parcel, G.S., Kok, G., & Gottlieb, N.H. (2006). *Planning health promotion programs: An intervention mapping approach* (2nd ed.). San Francisco, Calif.: Jossey-Bass.

Bates, I.J., & Winder, A.E. (1984). *Introduction to health education.* Palo Alto, Calif.: Mayfield.

Briss, P.A., Zaza, S., Pappaioanou, M., Fielding, J., Wright-De Agero, L., Truman, B.I., Hopkins, D.P., Mullen, P.D., Thompson, R.S., Woolf, S.H., Carande-Kulis, V.G., Anderson, L., Hinman, A.R., McQueen, D.V., Teutsch, S.M., & Harris, J.R. (2000). Task Force on Community Preventive Services: Developing an evidence-based guide to community preventive services—methods. *American Journal of Preventive Medicine,* 18(1S), 35–43.

Burdine, J.N., & McLeroy, K.R. (1992). Practitioners' use of theory: Examples from a workgroup. *Health Education Quarterly,* 19(3), 331–340.

Canadian Task Force on Periodic Health Examination. (1994). *Clinical preventive health care.* Ottawa: Minister of Supplies and Services.

Centers for Disease Control and Prevention (CDC), U.S. Department of Health and Human Services (USDHHS). (2003). *CDCynergy 3.0: Your guide to effective health communication (CD-ROM version 3.0).* Atlanta, Ga.: Author.

———. (2000). *Healthy Plan-It: A tool for planning and managing public health programs. Sustainable Management Development Program.* Atlanta, Ga.: Author.

———. (no date). *Planned approach to community health: Guide for local coordinator.* Atlanta, Ga.: Author.

Champion, V.L., & Skinner, C.S. (2008). The health belief model. In K. Glanz, B.K. Rimer, & K. Viswanath (Eds.), *Health behavior and health education: Theory, research, and practice* (4th ed., pp. 45–65). San Francisco, Calif.: Jossey-Bass.

Cottrell, R.R., Girvan, J.T., & McKenzie, J.F. (2009). *Principles and foundations of health promotion and education* (4th ed.). San Francisco: Benjamin Cummings.

Crosby, R.A., Kegler, M.C., & DiClemente, R.J. (2009). Theory in health promotion practice and research. In R.J. DiClemente, R.A. Crosby, & M.C. Kegler (Eds.), *Emerging theories in health promotion practice and research* (2nd ed.). (pp. 4–17). San Francisco: Jossey-Bass.

DiClemente, R.J., Crosby, R.A., & Kegler, M.C. (Eds.) (2009). *Emerging theories in health promotion practice and research* (2nd ed.). San Francisco: Jossey-Bass.

Fishbein, M. (1967). *Readings in attitudes theory measurement.* New York: Wiley.

Freire, P. (1973). *Education: The practice of freedom.* London: Writer's and Reader's Publishing.

Galli, N. (1976). Foundations of health. *Journal of School Health,* 46(3), 158–165.

Glanz, K., & Rimer, B.K. (1995). *Theory at a glance: A guide for health education practice* [NIH Pub. No. 95–3896]. Washington, D.C.: National Cancer Institute.

Glanz, K., Rimer, B.K., & Viswanath, K. (Eds.). (2008a). *Health behavior and health education: Theory, research, and practice* (4th ed.). San Francisco: Jossey-Bass.

Glanz, K., Rimer, B.K., & Viswanath, K. (2008b). Theory, research, and practice in health behavior and health education. In K. Glanz, B.K. Rimer, & K. Viswanath (Eds.), *Health behavior and health education: Theory, research, and practice* (4th ed., pp. 23–40). San Francisco: Jossey-Bass.

Green, L.W. (2006). *Lawrence W. Green.* Retrieved June 7, 2009, from http://www.lgreen.net/authors/lwgreen.htm.

———. (2001). From research to "best practices" in other settings and populations. *American Journal of Health Behavior,* 25(3), 165–178.

Green, L.W., Glanz, K., Hochbaum, G.M., Kok, G., Kreuter, M.W., Lewis, F.M., Lorig, K., Morisky, D., Rimer, B.K., & Rosenstock, I.M. (1994). Can we build on, or must we replace, the theories and models of health education? *Health Education Research,* 9(3), 397–404.

Green, L.W., & Kreuter, M.W. (2005). *Health program planning: An educational and ecological approach* (4th ed.). Mountain View, Calif.: Mayfield.

Hall, C.L. (1943). *Principles of behavior.* New York: Appleton-Century-Crofts.

Hiatt, R.A., & Rimer, B.K. (1999). A new strategy for cancer control research. *Cancer, Epidemiology, Biomarkers, and Prevention, 8,* 957–964.

Hochbaum, G.M., Sorenson, J.R., & Lorig, K. (1992). Theory in health education practice. *Health Education Quarterly, 19*(3), 295–313.

Jenicek, M. (1997). Epidemiology, evidence-based medicine, and evidence-based public health. *Journal of Epidemiology, 7,* 187–197.

Kegler, M.C., Crosby, R.A., & DiClemente, R.J. (2002). Reflections on emerging theories in health promotion practice. In R.J. DiClemente, R.A. Crosby, & M.C. Kegler (Eds.), *Emerging theories in health promotion practice and research: Strategies for improving public health* (3rd ed., pp. 386–395). San Francisco: Jossey-Bass.

Kerlinger, F.N. (1986). *Foundations of behavioral research* (3rd ed.). Austin, Tex.: Holt, Rinehart & Winston.

Laforge, R.G., Rossi, J.S., Prochaska, J.O., Velicer, W.F., Levesque, D.A., & McHorney, C.A. (1999). Stage of regular exercise and health-related quality of life. *Preventive Medicine, 28,* 349–360.

Marlatt, G.A., & Gordon, J.R. (1980). Determinants of relapse: Implications for maintenance of behavior change. In P.O. Davidson & S.M. Davidson (Eds.), *Behavioral medicine: Changing health lifestyles* (pp. 410–452). New York: Brunner/Mazel.

McKenzie, J.F., Neiger, B.L., & Thackeray, R. (2009). *Planning, implementing, and evaluating health promotion programs: A primer* (5th ed.). San Francisco: Benjamin Cummings.

McLeroy, K.R., Steckler, A., Goodman, R., & Burdine, J.N. (1992). Health education research, theory, and practice: Future directions. *Health Education Research, Theory, and Practice, 7*(1), 1–8.

Montano, D.E., & Kasprzyk, D. (2008). The theory of reasoned action and the theory of planned behavior. In K. Glanz, B.K. Rimer, & K. Viswanath (Eds.), *Health behavior and health education: Theory, research, and practice* (4th ed., pp. 67–97). San Francisco: Jossey-Bass.

National Association of County and City Health Officials (NACCHO). (2001). *Mobilizing for action through planning and partnerships (MAPP).* Washington, D.C.: Author.

National Association of County Health Officials (NACHO). (1991). *APEX/PH: Assessment protocol for excellence in public health.* Washington, D.C.: Author.

National Cancer Institute (NCI). (2002). *Making health communication programs work* [NIH Publication No. 02–5145]. Washington, D.C.: U.S. Department of Health and Human Services.

Neiger, B.L. & Thackeray, R. (1998). *Social marketing: Making public health sense.* Paper presented at the annual meeting of the Utah Public Health Association, Provo, UT.

Nutbeam, D., & Harris, E. (1999). *Theory in a nutshell: A guide to health promotion theory.* Sydney, Australia: McGraw-Hill.

Patton, R.P., Corry, J.M., Gettman, L.R., & Graff, J.S. (1986). *Implementing health/fitness programs.* Champaign, Ill.: Human Kinetics.

Petty, R.E., Barden, J., & Wheeler, S.C. (2009). The elaboration likelihood model of persuasion. In R.J. DiClemente, R.A. Crosby, & M.C. Kegler (Eds.), *Emerging theories in health promotion practice and research* (2nd ed., pp. 185–214). San Francisco: Jossey-Bass.

Petty, R.E., Wheeler, S.C., & Bizer, G.Y. (1999). Is there one persuasion process or more? Lumping versus splitting in attitude change theories. *Psychology Inquiry, 10,* 156–163.

Prochaska, J.O. (1979). *Systems of psychotherapy: A transtheoretical analysis.* Homewood, Ill.: Dorsey Press.

Prochaska, J.O., Redding, C.A., & Evers, K.E. (2008). The transtheoretical model and the stages of change. In K. Glanz, B.K. Rimer, & K. Viswanath (Eds.), *Health behavior and health education: Theory, research, and practice* (4th ed., pp. 97–121). San Francisco: Jossey-Bass.

Rimer, B.K., & Glanz, K. (2005). *Theory at a glance: A guide for health promotion practice* (2nd ed.) [NIH Pub. No. 05-3896]. Washington, D.C.: National Cancer Institute.

Rimer, B.K., Glanz, K., & Rasband, G. (2001). Searching for evidence about health education and health behavior interventions. *Health Education and Behavior, 28*(2), 231–248.

Rogers, E.M. (2003). *Diffusion of innovations* (5th ed.). New York: Free Press.

Rosenberg, W., & Donald, A. (1995). Evidence-based medicine: An approach to clinical problem-solving. *British Medical Journal, 310,* 1122–1126.

Rosenstock, I.M. (1966). Why people use health services. *Milbank Memorial Fund Quarterly, 44,* 94–124.

Rosenstock, I.M., Strecher, V.J., & Becker, M.H. (1988). Social learning theory and the health belief model. *Health Education Quarterly,* 15(2), 175–183.

Ross, H.S., & Mico, P.R. (1980). *Theory and practice in health education.* Palo Alto, Calif.: Mayfield.

Rotter, J.B. (1954). *Social learning and clinical psychology.* New York: Prentice-Hall.

Simons-Morton, B.G., Greene, W.H., & Gottlieb, N.H. (1995). *Introduction to health education and health promotion* (2nd ed.). Prospect Heights, Ill.: Waveland Press.

Smith, L.G. (2008). HPV knowledge of college females and their intention to receive the HPV vaccination. Unpublished master's thesis, Ball State University.

Sullivan, D. (1973). Model for comprehensive, systematic program development in health education. *Health Education Report,* 1(1), 4–5.

Thorndike, E.L. (1898). Animal intelligence: An experimental study of associative processes in animals. *Psychology Monographs,* 2(8).

Timmreck, T.C. (2003). *Planning, program development, and evaluation* (2nd ed.). Boston, Mass.: Jones & Bartlett.

U.S. Preventive Services Task Force. (1996). *The report of the U.S. Preventive Services Task Force* (2nd ed.). Baltimore, Md.: Williams & Wilkins.

van Ryn, M., & Heaney, C.A. (1992). What's the use of theory? *Health Education Quarterly,* 19(3), 315–330.

Wallston, K.A., Wallston, B.S., & DeVellis, R. (1978). Development of the multidimensional health locus of control (MHLC) scales. *Health Education Monographs,* 6, 160–170.

Watson, J.B. (1925). *Behaviorism.* New York: W.W. Norton.

Weinstein, N.D. (1988). The precaution adoption process. *Health Psychology,* 7, 355–386.

CHAPTER 5 | Research Questions and Hypotheses (Writing Chapter I)

Chapter Objectives

After reading this chapter and answering the review questions, you should be able to:

1. Use relevant literature to write an introduction to Chapter I.
2. Write appropriate problem statements and/or research questions.
3. Write hypotheses and null hypotheses.
4. Define the delimitations of a study.
5. Identify potential limitations of a study.
6. Explain assumptions made in a given research study.
7. Operationally define relevant terms.

Key Terms

assumption
control variable
correlative hypothesis
delimitations
dependent variable
directional hypothesis

extraneous variable
hypothesis
independent variable
limitation
nondirectional hypothesis
null hypothesis

operational definition
purpose statement
research problem
research question
variable

In Chapter 2 of this text, we provided suggestions for identifying a topic of interest to study. In Chapter 3 the literature was discussed as a means of providing historical perspective, establishing a rationale, identifying theory, learning about what has already been done, and identifying potential research designs and instrumentation for the proposed study. Chapter 4 provided additional information supporting theory-based research and identified common theories used in health education research. It is now time to further refine ideas about the proposed study and to state clearly the research problem and purpose of the research. This is accomplished in writing Chapter I of a thesis or dissertation. Chapter I is typically called "The Problem." The multiple purposes of Chapter I can be seen in Table 5.1.

Students often ask why the literature review is not the first chapter of a thesis or dissertation since it is typically written first and used to develop Chapter I. To understand the answer to this question, one needs to think as a reader of the thesis or dissertation instead of the writer. Readers typically need to know what a thesis or dissertation is about, and they want to obtain that information quickly. That is, they want to know a little background on the topic and specifically the purpose of the research. They do not want to read an in-depth review of the literature and then find out that the purpose of the research is of little value to what

Table 5.1   Purposes of Chapter I

Introduce problem
- Stimulate reader interest in the problem
- Demonstrate importance of the problem
- Provide current status of the problem
- Provide background to the problem
- Introduce any relevant theory examined in the study
- Place the study within context of literature
- Identify the population to study

Clearly express the problem as a purpose statement and/or research questions (or questions) to be answered

Clearly state hypotheses (if appropriate)

Present delimitations

Identify limitations

Identify assumptions

Operationally define terms unique to the study

they are studying. On the other hand, if they read the purpose and find it is applicable, then they may want more in-depth information about the literature and how it supports the study.

Introduction to Chapter I

An introductory section that summarizes information concerning the thesis or dissertation's problem is used to begin Chapter I. The introduction uses relevant literature to support the need for and importance of the research. This could include epidemiological data such as incidence and prevalence statistics, relative rates, years of potential life lost, and so forth. In addition, it may be helpful to provide information on the cost of the problem to inflicted individuals, their families, the community, the public health infrastructure, the insurance industry, and/or society as a whole. Essentially, the writer needs to establish who is susceptible to this problem and the seriousness of the problem.

At this point it would be important to introduce any theory that might be necessary to understand this problem and ultimately to the study being pro-

posed. A brief history of the theory and a short explanation of its major tenets should suffice in Chapter I. Once the importance of the topic has been clearly established and relevant theory introduced, the writer should next discuss previous attempts to solve the problem. This should include those that have worked as well as those that have not worked. Ultimately, this section should lead the reader to see that a next logical step would be to undertake the research being proposed in the current study. Those studies that are most similar to the proposed study should be discussed just ahead of moving to the next section of Chapter I, which is presenting the research question or problem.

The information needed to write the introductory section of Chapter I should be taken primarily from the literature review. Much, if not all, of the information will also be presented in Chapter II. In the introductory section of Chapter I, however, the presentation will be much briefer than when presented in Chapter II with many fewer sources cited. Remember, in this first section of Chapter I the purpose is to introduce the reader to the problem, not to review the literature. Only the most salient sources are presented and in only enough detail to convey the essence of the work. Organizationally, one can think of the introduction to Chapter I as an inverted triangle beginning with the broad global problem leading to the specific problem of the study (see Figure 5.1). Although it is risky to give page length guidelines, because there are always exceptions to the rules, most introductory sections to Chapter I can be written in 4 to 10 pages. It might help to think of the introductory section of Chapter I as the *Reader's Digest* version of Chapter II.

The introductory section should be written in past tense. Again, as in Chapter II, you are writing about research that has been completed. All sources discussed in the introductory section should be carefully cited and referenced. Prior to starting their own writing, students are encouraged to read the introductory sections of several theses or dissertations written by previous students from

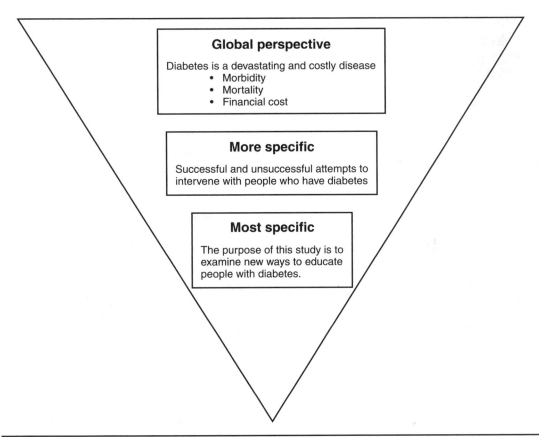

FIGURE 5.1
Chapter I introductory section organization.

their program. This may help current students to better understand the style, tone, and information included in the introductory section of Chapter I.

The Problem

Following the introductory section of Chapter I is the problem section. This is usually titled "Statement of the Problem" or just "The Problem." A **research problem** is exactly what it sounds like: a problem that someone wants to research (Fraenkel & Wallen, 2006). The way the problem is articulated, however, is very important. DePoy and Gitlin (2005) stated that "How one frames and states the problem is critical to the entire research endeavor and influences all subsequent thinking and action processes" (p. 38). Essentially the research problem is the foundation upon which the remainder of the thesis or dissertation work will be based. It is the first substantial step in developing the thesis or dissertation, and much thought should be given to writing it in a clear, concise, and meaningful way.

The research problem is typically written as a purpose statement. A **purpose statement** is a declarative statement that clearly and succinctly describes the overall direction or focus of the research. Purpose statements are present in both quantitative and qualitative research (Creswell, 2009). A purpose statement is typically one or two sentences in length and worded in the past tense, since the study will be completed when the reader actually reads the study. One exception to the past tense rule occurs when developing a grant or funding proposal; future tense can then be used because the researcher is presenting a plan of study that has yet to happen (Creswell, 2009). The purpose statement is not only a critical part of a thesis or dissertation, but also an essential component of research articles for professional journals.

An alternative to writing a purpose statement is to write one or several research questions (Neutens & Rubinson, 2010). **Research questions** are interrogative sentences that clearly and succinctly state the major question or questions to be answered in the study. Research questions are often used in place of hypotheses and may indicate that a study is non-experimental (Neutens & Rubinson, 2010). The decision to write the problem as a purpose statement or research question(s) is a matter of personal preference; both are acceptable in the scientific community. Students should be sure to check with their committee chairs to determine if their programs state a preference or requirement related to the writing of purpose statements or research questions.

In some situations, both purpose statements and research questions are used. In these cases, the purpose statement provides the broad, overall purpose of the study and the research questions are really sub-problems that when answered will fulfill the purpose of the study. Using multiple research questions stemming from a purpose statement often occurs when a study does not involve the use of hypotheses (Neutens & Rubinson, 2010). Hypotheses will be discussed later in this chapter.

At this point, we would like to describe a hypothetical research problem and provide examples of purpose statements and research questions. XXX University has become troubled about high levels of alcohol consumption by some spectators at basketball and football games. There is concern that these individuals may be involved in vandalism, violence, and drunken driving incidents after the games. The XXX University Alcohol Awareness Committee would like to know the characteristics of individuals who consume large amounts of alcohol at these events so as to better direct intervention efforts. Thus, we have a problem or potential problem and a question about who the individuals are that consume large amounts of alcohol.

A health education specialist at XXX University, who is a member of the Alcohol Awareness Committee, has agreed to take the lead on a research study. After reviewing the literature, she writes the purpose statement as follows:

> The purpose of this study was to determine the characteristics of persons who consume large quantities of alcohol at XXX University basketball and football games.

She could just as easily have written the purpose statement as a research question:

> What are the characteristics of persons who consume large quantities of alcohol at XXX University basketball and football games?

Either of the above would be acceptable for a study. It is also possible to use the purpose statement or research question as stated above and then develop several sub-research questions as follows:

1. What is the gender profile of those persons who consume large quantities of alcohol at XXX University basketball and football games?
2. What is the racial profile of those persons who consume large quantities of alcohol at XXX University basketball and football games?
3. What is the age profile of those persons who consume large quantities of alcohol at XXX University basketball and football games?
4. What are the ticket characteristics (box seat, reserved, grandstand, student) of those persons

who consume large quantities of alcohol at XXX University basketball and football games?

Remember that the wording of the research question or problem statement is very important. Simply changing one word can affect the direction of the research and the way data are analyzed. Students should expect to spend a great deal of time considering, writing, and rewriting their research question(s) or problem statement to obtain the desired wording. The thesis or dissertation committee chair will typically work with the student to make certain the wording is appropriate. See Figure 5.2 for additional samples of problem statements and research questions from previously completed theses.

Variables

Before we discuss the next section of Chapter I, hypotheses, it is important to have an understanding of the terminology surrounding variables used in quantitative research. In the previous chapter we

---

Sample Purpose Statements

The purpose of this study was to determine the role of social support, hardiness, and acculturation as predictors of mental health among international students of Asian Indian origin enrolled at two large public universities in Ohio (Atri, 2007).

The purpose of this study was to examine the relationship between sexual knowledge, attitudes, and behaviors of college students based upon the approach to sexuality education they received in junior and senior high school (Browder, 2008).

The purpose of this study was to determine the faith community's attitude toward and level of involvement in community health promotion and education programs in the Greater Cincinnati Consolidated Metropolitan Statistical area (GCCMSA). Differences between the number and variety of programs, collaboration with other faith communities and agencies, coordination of programs, perceived health status, attitude, denomination, location, size, educational background, ethnic composition, member age, and annual and health budgets of faith communities were explored (Walter, 2007).

The purpose of this study was to determine what factors contributed to medication noncompliance in hemodialysis patients. Further, it examined the variables of age, race, gender, and educational level as they related to noncompliance (Bland, 2007).

Sample Research Questions

Will there be a higher rate of detection of dual substance use and severe mental illness disorders following the introduction of the new Dartmouth Integrated Dual Disorder Treatment (IDDT) Model than prior to initiation of the IDDT Model (Viorst, 2008)?

How do women rate their physician's educational efforts regarding HPV and the new HPV vaccine (Cermak, 2009)?

FIGURE 5.2
Sample purpose statements/research questions.

discussed variables as means of measuring or operationalizing constructs. To provide further explanation, a **variable** "is a characteristic or attribute of an individual or an organization that can be measured or observed by the researcher and varies among individuals or organizations studied" (Creswell, 2005, p. 600). In the alcohol consumption example above, variables would include alcohol consumption levels, gender, race, age, and ticket characteristics.

Many different types of variables exist and are useful in developing purpose statements, research questions, and hypotheses. An **independent variable** is the variable being examined or tested. It is the variable of interest in a study. A **dependent variable** is the measured or observed variable. The dependent variable can also be considered the outcome variable. By observing the dependent variable, the impact of the independent variable can be seen. In other words, the independent variable is designed or manipulated so as to have an effect on the dependent variable, and the dependent variable is observed to determine if the independent variable had the desired effect. If we wanted to know the effect of practicing relaxation techniques on stress levels, what would be the independent and dependent variables? If you said relaxation was the independent variable and stress level was the dependent variable, you were correct.

It is important to keep in mind that it is acceptable and often desirable to examine the effects of multiple independent variables on one or more dependent variables. In fact, to do so is often more representative of reality than to study one single independent variable. In the stress example, relaxation techniques, exercise levels, nutrition, gender, and age could all be independent variables used to determine their impact on the dependent variable of stress levels. Using multiple independent variables increases the complexity of the statistical analysis, so studies of this type are more often seen at the doctoral level than at the master's level.

A **control variable** is a variable that has the potential to impact the dependent variable as well

as the independent variable, but its effects are removed or controlled by research design or statistical manipulation. If in the initial stress example above we were concerned that time of day might impact stress levels in addition to relaxation techniques, we could control time of day by testing stress levels at the same time of day for all participants.

An **extraneous variable** is one that has an unpredictable or unexpected impact on the dependent variable. Fraenkel and Wallen (2006) state that an extraneous variable is, "A variable that makes possible an alternative explanation of results; an uncontrolled variable" (p. G-3). For example, suppose a health education specialist was examining factors that allow one to successfully manage the stress of losing a job. Several independent variables are being examined including hardiness, exercise behaviors, social support, and self-efficacy. During the course of this study it is determined that education level, which is not an independent variable being studied, also explains one's ability to manage the stress of losing a job. Education level would be an extraneous variable. Extraneous variables might also be considered contaminating, intervening, or confounding variables because of their effect on the results of the research. In some cases extraneous variables may mask the true results of a study or render the results of a study useless. For that reason, it is important to plan research meticulously, being careful to select the best design, sampling, and instrumentation possible.

Hypotheses

A **hypothesis** is "a logical supposition, a reasonable guess, an educated conjecture" (Leedy & Ormrod, 2010, p. 4). In essence, a hypothesis is the researcher's best guess at predicting the results of the research findings. Hypotheses are always directly related to the purpose statement and are developed to answer the research questions posed. Hypotheses transform the purpose statement or research questions into statements that are testable. Remember, all hypotheses written for a study must be tested and the results reported in Chapter 4.

As a general rule, qualitative researchers do not state formal hypotheses at the onset of their studies, as do quantitative researchers (Gay, Mills, & Airasian, 2006). The results of qualitative research, however, may suggest new problems and hypotheses for future studies.

Not all quantitative research will involve the use of hypotheses. Only studies that involve comparisons between conditions need hypotheses. For example, if one wanted to determine which child car safety seat program, A or B, was most effective in getting first-time parents to use child car safety seats, a hypothesis would be needed. If one wanted to compare the child car safety seat usage behaviors of first-time parents based on demographic characteristics such as gender, age, race, education level, or the like, hypotheses would be needed to make comparisons between different genders, races, age groups, and education levels. If one wanted to compare the safety seat knowledge of new parents prior to and after the safety seat program, a hypothesis would be needed. If, however, one simply wanted to determine the child car safety seat usage behaviors of first-time parents, hypotheses would not be needed because only one group, first-time parents, is being examined and no comparisons are being made. This is a descriptive study, in which research questions replace hypotheses.

Hypotheses can be either nondirectional or directional (Patten, 2009). **Nondirectional hypotheses** predict a difference between groups but do not specify what that difference might be. Using the above safety seat example, a nondirectional hypothesis might read: "The child car safety seat usage behaviors of first-time parents exposed to program A will be different from the child car safety seat usage behaviors of first-time parents exposed to program B." **Directional hypotheses** also predict a difference between groups, but they go further to predict the nature of that difference. Using the same safety seat example, a directional

hypothesis might read, "The rate of child car safety seat usage of first-time parents exposed to program A will be higher than the rate of child car safety seat usage of first-time parents exposed to program B." As one might expect, nondirectional hypotheses are used when the researcher has no reason to suggest that one program or treatment will be better than another. Directional hypotheses are used when the researcher has reason to believe that one program or treatment might be better than another.

In addition to directional and nondirectional hypotheses, correlative hypotheses can also be developed (Berg & Latin, 2004). **Correlative hypotheses** predict that there will be a relationship between variables but do not specify the exact nature of that relationship. Correlative hypotheses differ from nondirectional hypotheses in that they are exploring relationships instead of differences between variables. A sample correlative hypothesis might read, "There will be a relationship between family income and child car safety seat usage behaviors." The statistical tests used to determine significance will differ depending on whether a nondirectional or correlative hypothesis is utilized.

A final form of hypothesis to discuss is the null hypothesis. The **null hypothesis** essentially states the opposite of the three types of hypotheses noted above, or that there will be no difference or no relationship between groups. It is the null form of the hypothesis that is statistically tested to determine the significance of observed differences. A sample null hypothesis related to child car safety seats might be, "There will be no difference in child car safety seat utilization rates of first-time parents exposed to program A and child car safety seat utilization rates of first-time parents exposed to program B."

To further understand how and why null hypotheses are used, suppose we find that 80% of first-time parents exposed to program A use child car safety seats and 70% of first-time parents exposed to program B use child car safety seats. Why does this 10-percentage-point difference exist? There are three possible explanations for this difference (Patten, 2009).

1. The 10-percentage-point difference represents a real difference between program A and program B. In other words, program A is better than program B at stimulating first-time parents to use child car safety seats.
2. The difference could be the result of bias in the methods, procedures used to study the problem, or sampling techniques used to select the participants. Maybe different health educators presented the two programs and the one presenting program A was more dynamic and convincing. Perhaps sampling errors were made so that the samples were not truly random. Those first-time parents exposed to program A were different in some way that made them more open to child car safety seats (e.g., their parents always made them sit in a safety seat) from those first-time parents exposed to program B (e.g., their parents did not make them sit in safety seats). These factors could be eliminated or reduced by utilizing proper research design and sampling procedures.
3. The difference between the groups is the result of chance variation and is not related to the effectiveness of the program. Given any two groups, it is likely there would be differences in child car safety seat usage rates because of chance or normal variations in the groups.

Is the difference in usage rates large enough to convince us that it is the result of differences between program A and program B and not simply chance or normal variation? Testing the null hypothesis answers this question. Statistical tests are used to determine the probability that the null hypothesis is true or that there really is no difference between the groups. By convention, if the probability (p) is less than 5 in 100 ($p < 0.05$), we reject the null hypothesis, indicating that there is really a difference between the two groups. Sometimes more stringent criteria such as $p < 0.01$ or

$p < 0.001$ are used to determine if the null hypothesis can be rejected. Occasionally, studies are less stringent, using $p < 0.10$, but this is rare and not encouraged. If the null hypothesis is rejected, it means that explanation 1 or 2 above must be the real reason for the observed differences. In studies that are well designed using appropriate sampling strategies, explanation 1 is the most likely reason for the observed differences. If the statistical probability is anything greater than 0.05, we would fail to reject the null hypothesis. (Note: a null hypothesis is never accepted.) This does not mean for certain that there are no differences between the groups. It does mean the probability that the differences could be the result of chance or normal variation is too high to believe that program A is better than program B in stimulating child car safety seat use.

Hypotheses are typically written in the future tense, indicating that there will be differences (or no differences) and/or relationships (or no relationships) between variables. In addition, hypotheses should be written using parallel construction so that groups and differences or relationships can be clearly identified. The following hypothesis does not use good parallel construction: "The rates of child car safety seat usage of first-time parents exposed to program A will be higher than those in program B." It would be better worded as, "The rates of child car safety seat usage of first-time parents exposed to program A will be higher than the rates of child car safety seat usage of first-time parents exposed to program B."

See Figure 5.3 for additional examples of well-written hypotheses.

Delimitations

Delimitations are parameters or boundaries placed on a study by the researcher. These are very important because they are used to limit and clarify the scope of the study. Delimitations are reported in a separate section of Chapter I titled "Delimitations,"

Hypothesis #1: Asian Indian students with higher acculturation, social support, and hardiness scores will exhibit higher levels of mental health than Asian Indian students with lower acculturation, social support, and hardiness scores when controlled for age and time spent in the United States (Atri, 2007).

Null Hypothesis #1: There will be no significant difference in mental health levels between Asian Indian students with higher acculturation, social support, and hardiness scores and Asian Indian students with lower acculturation, social support, and hardiness scores when controlled for age and time spent in the United States (Atri, 2007).

Hypothesis #2: The contraception knowledge level of students that participated in an abstinence-focused sexuality education program will be lower than the contraception knowledge level of students that participated in a comprehensive sexuality education program (Browder, 2008).

Null Hypothesis #2: There will be no difference in the contraception knowledge level of students that participated in an abstinence-focused sexuality education program and the contraception knowledge level of students that participated in a comprehensive sexuality education program (Browder, 2008).

Hypothesis #3: There will be a positive relationship between family history of breast cancer and the Health Belief Model variables of susceptibility, seriousness, and benefits (Collins, 2005).

Null Hypothesis #3: There will be no relationship between family history of breast cancer and the Health Belief Model variables of susceptibility, seriousness, and benefits (Collins, 2005).

FIGURE 5.3
Sample hypotheses and null hypotheses.

which is typically only one to two paragraphs in length. Sometimes delimitation sections begin with a short introductory sentence that is followed by a listing of the delimitations.

Student researchers often want to undertake large research efforts that are beyond the scope of a thesis or dissertation. Sometimes these large research efforts can be narrowed and focused to a more manageable size by using delimitations. Delimitations may involve delimiting a study by geographic location, time, population traits, population size, or similar considerations. For example, if we wanted to conduct a study on the health behaviors of patients following coronary bypass surgery, we could limit it to male patients in a three-county area who have had surgery in the past year, have completed cardiac rehabilitation, are between the ages of 60 and 70 years, have had no recurrent symptoms of heart disease, and like Mickey Mouse cartoons.

We were obviously just kidding about the Mickey Mouse cartoons, but we use Mickey to point out that there needs to be good rationale for any delimitations placed on a study. Needless to say, delimitations should be used because they make a study better or more feasible and not just for the convenience or interest of the researcher. It is possible that a study can be delimited so much that the results are not valuable or it is difficult to find subjects to meet all the inclusion or exclusion criteria stated in the delimitations. See Figure 5.4 for a sample Chapter I delimitation section, and

Chapter I
The Problem

Introduction (outline of topics covered)
- Psychological distress and mental pathologies among migrant populations
- Why study the Asian Indian population
- Growth of immigrant populations in the United States
- Acculturation issues and concerns of international students in the United States
- Summary of studies relating mental health with acculturation, social support, and hardiness

Statement of the Problem

Given that migration of the Asian Indian population to the United States had come to the forefront as a complex and important phenomenon with significant effects on U.S. demographics (Barringer, 1991; Holmes, 1995; Mehta, 1998) and that the unique mental health concerns and issues of international students from this population had received scant attention from the scientific community (Al-Sharideh & Goe, 1998; Mehta, 1998) the purpose of this study was to determine the role of social support, hardiness, and acculturation as predictors of mental health among international students of Asian Indian origin enrolled at two large public universities in Ohio.

Research Question (One research question selected from seven in this study)
1. To what extent did Asian Indian international students' social support predict their mental health status?

Hypotheses (One hypothesis set selected from seven hypothesis sets in this study)

Hypothesis #1: Asian Indian students with higher levels of social support will have higher levels of mental health when compared to Asian Indian students with lower levels of social support.

Null Hypothesis #1: There will be no significant differences in mental health status between Asian Indian students with higher levels of social support and Asian Indian students with lower levels of social support.

Delimitations

The study was delimited to international Asian Indian university students attending classes at two large public universities in the State of Ohio. To be included in the study, participants had to be natural Indian citizens currently studying and residing at one of the two universities. Verification of their citizenship status was not done; their reported citizenship was considered sufficient. Participants had to be enrolled either as part-time or full-time students between the dates of 10/12/06 and 01/30/07 because the responses were collected during that period. The ownership of at least one university e-mail account by each participant was a necessary condition imposed by the structure of the study. The data was collected primarily during the winter quarter of 2006 with the assumption that many such students do not travel back to their country but still take classes. The data collection was extended to early spring quarter to capture students who may have missed the winter term. The survey was available only for a period of four months during the year.

FIGURE 5.4
Sample Chapter I.

Source: Reproduced by permission from Atri, A. (2007). Role of social support, hardiness and acculturation as predictors of mental health among the international students of Asian Indian origin in Ohio. Unpublished master's thesis, University of Cincinnati.

Limitations (3 selected from 10 listed in the study)
1. The results were based on self-reported responses and could have included both participant bias and dishonesty.
2. The psychometric properties of all instruments except the American International Relations Scale had not been studied on the Asian Indian population.
3. Participants were not randomly selected and represented only two large universities in Ohio.

Assumptions

      It was assumed that all participants could read and understand the survey instrument and that they responded in an open and honest manner. It was also assumed that the number of students answering the questionnaire two or more times would be miniscule and not impact study results. It was believed that the recall of the participants would not be flawed since the survey design was essentially based on current life events surrounding the respondents and not events long past. . . .

Operational Definitions (Three selected from six listed in the study)
- Asian Indian origin—Respondents had to be natural Indian citizens, with both parents of Indian origin.
- Mental health—For the purpose of this study, mental health was defined as the well-being and psychological distress of the study population as measured through the Kessler Psychological Distress Scale, K-6 (Kessler, 2003).
- Social support—For the purpose of this study, social support was defined as a social network's provision of psychological and material resources to a person and would be assessed through the 12-item version of the Interpersonal Support Evaluation list (ISEL-12).

FIGURE 5.4 *Continued*

see Chapter 7 of this text for more information on inclusion and exclusion criteria.

Limitations

Limitations are parameters or boundaries of the research established by factors or people other than the researcher (Neutens & Rubinson, 2010). These are factors that are beyond the control of the researcher but might impact the results of the research. As such, they should be identified for the readers.

For example, suppose we wanted to conduct a study using a random sample of school districts in a given state. Each selected school district would obviously have to give its permission to participate in the study. Most likely, some school districts will not grant permission, forcing the researcher to select replacement school districts. This refusal to participate would be considered a limitation of the study.

If we were asking study participants to remember everything they had eaten for the past three days and were to use this information to analyze the nutritional behaviors of these participants, what limitations might we need to report? If you answered that this study would be limited by the memory and honesty of participants, you would be correct. These would be limitations of the study and should be reported in Chapter I in a section titled "Limitations." This section is usually only one to two paragraphs in length or may be formatted as an introductory sentence followed by a listing of limitations. See Figure 5.4 for a sample of limitations.

By identifying the limitations of a study, the researcher is essentially informing the reader that these problems have already been considered but were not thought to be of such importance as to prohibit conducting the study. Any study results, however, should be viewed with consideration of the limitations.

Assumptions

"An **assumption** is a condition that is taken for granted and without which the research effort would be impossible" (Neutens & Rubinson, 2010, p. 19). Assumptions are thought to be true but cannot be verified. Often assumptions are made in response to identified limitations. In the three-day dietary recall study mentioned in the previous section on limitations, it would be necessary to make an assumption that the participants answered honestly and to the best of their ability. This cannot be verified, but unless the assumption is made, there is no need to conduct the study. Stated another way, if knowledge or information exists that participants are not answering honestly and to the best of their ability, then the assumption could not be made. The results of the study would be questionable and of little value.

Readers of the thesis or dissertation need to be made aware of any assumptions used in the study through the development of a section in Chapter I titled "Assumptions." Leedy and Ormrod (2010) note that "All assumptions that have a material bearing on the problem should be openly and unreservedly set forth. If others know the assumptions a researcher makes, they are better prepared to evaluate the conclusions that result from the assumptions" (p. 59). See Figure 5.4 for sample assumptions.

Operational Definitions

In the final section of Chapter I, terms that have special meanings or are unique to the study are defined. These definitions are called **operational definitions** and are included in a section titled "Operational Definitions," "Definition of Terms,"

or simply "Definitions." The important thing to remember with operational definitions is that they are unique to your study. In most cases dictionary definitions are not included in this section unless there are terms that might be completely unfamiliar to a reader. Typically, terms that need to be operationally defined are found as variables in the purpose statement, research questions, or hypotheses.

Consider the example that was provided at the beginning of this chapter concerning large quantities of alcohol consumed at football and basketball games. The term "alcohol" would not need to be defined as it is not unique to the study. The concept of "large quantities of alcohol" would have to be operationally defined. What does large quantities of alcohol mean? The researcher would need to adopt a specific definition that would be applied consistently throughout the study. The researcher could simply define large quantities of alcohol by the number of drinks consumed. From this perspective, large quantities of alcohol could be operationally defined as being more than three drinks during the course of the game. If this were the case, there should be some rationale supported by the literature to defend the selection of three drinks instead of two or four or some other number. Another possibility would be for the author to define large quantities of alcohol based on estimated blood alcohol levels using the number of drinks and body weight to calculate the estimated blood alcohol levels. Real blood alcohol levels could also be obtained by using portable blood alcohol analysis equipment. In the latter two cases, the operational definition would define large quantities of alcohol as having a blood alcohol level above some established limit such as 0.08 or 0.10.

The point here is that there are often different ways to operationally define terms, and it is important that researchers be very specific in how terms are defined for a given study. Researchers also need to have a rationale or justification for why a particular operational definition was selected. Additional samples of operational definitions can be seen in Figure 5.4.

Summary

In this chapter the authors have presented detailed information to help students write a solid first draft of a thesis or dissertation's Chapter I, along with examples of its components. The first section of Chapter I is the introductory section, which contains background information on the problem, a justification for the proposed research, an introduction to relevant theory, and an explanation of closely related studies. It is organized from the broad global perspective to the specific problem statement. A clear and concise writing of the purpose statement and/or research questions follows this section. The exact wording of these is critical to the direction of the study. Everything that follows is directly related to the purpose statement and/or research questions. In quantitative studies, hypotheses may be developed that relate directly to the purpose statement or research questions. Writing hypotheses can be tricky, and wording is very important. One needs to decide whether to write directional, nondirectional, or correlative hypotheses. Null hypotheses should also be developed and used to test for statistical significance. At this point it is important that the researcher identify any delimitations that will be placed on the study. These are boundaries or parameters placed on the study by the researcher. In addition, limitations that may exist in conducting the study should be reported. Limitations are boundaries or parameters of the study that are beyond the control of the researcher. Assumptions necessary to complete the study and operational definitions complete the writing of Chapter I. A review of Figure 5.4 will demonstrate all components included in Chapter I of a thesis or dissertation and how these components work together to give the reader a complete picture of the problem to be studied.

Review Questions

1. What is the purpose of the introductory section of a thesis or dissertation's Chapter I?
2. Write a potential purpose statement or research question for a study you are planning. Share it with fellow students and your professor for feedback.
3. What is wrong with the following research question: Are people living in the inner city afraid of violence? Improve this research question by rewording it.
4. Differentiate between independent variables and dependent variables.
5. If someone wanted to examine dental flossing rates of third graders after they are exposed to two different programs promoting flossing, what would be the independent variable? What would be the dependent variable?
6. Write a directional and a nondirectional hypothesis related to whether males or females have higher internal health locus of control scores.
7. Write a null hypothesis for the locus of control example in question 6.
8. Explain how a nondirectional hypothesis differs from a correlative hypothesis.
9. What are extraneous variables? Explain how they impact research.
10. Explain the difference between delimitations and limitations. Give an example of each for a study of college students and the medications they use.
11. Using the study noted in question 10, provide an operational definition for medications.
12. What are assumptions, and why are they important to a research study?

References

Atri, A. (2007). Role of social support, hardiness and acculturation as predictors of mental health among the international students of Asian Indian origin in Ohio. Unpublished master's thesis, University of Cincinnati.

Berg, K.E., & Latin, R.W. (2004). *Research methods in health, physical education, exercise science, and recreation* (2nd ed.). Philadelphia: Lippincott Williams & Wilkins.

Bland, R. (2007). Medication compliance among hemodialysis patients and factors that contribute to non-compliance. Unpublished master's thesis, University of Cincinnati.

Browder, M.E.W. (2008). Sexuality education curriculum in secondary schools and its relationship to sexual knowledge, attitudes and behaviors of college students. Unpublished master's thesis, University of Cincinnati.

Cermak, M.A. (2009). Women's knowledge of HPV and their perceptions of physician educational efforts regarding HPV and cervical cancer. Unpublished master's thesis, University of Cincinnati.

Collins, C. (2005). Correlates of breast self-examination: Application of the Transtheoretical Model of Change and the Health Belief Model. Unpublished master's thesis, University of Cincinnati.

Creswell, J.W. (2005). *Educational research: Planning, conducting, and evaluating quantitative and qualitative research* (2nd ed.). Upper Saddle River, N.J.: Pearson Education, Inc.

Creswell, J.W. (2009). *Research design: Qualitative, quantitative, and mixed methods approaches* (3rd ed.). Los Angeles: Sage Publishers.

DePoy, E., & Gitlin, L.N. (2005). *Introduction to research: Understanding and applying multiple strategies* (3rd ed.). St Louis: Elsevier Mosby.

Fraenkel, J.R., & Wallen, N.E. (2006). *How to design and evaluate research in education* (6th ed.). Boston: McGraw-Hill.

Gay, L.R., Mills, G.E., & Airasian, P. (2006). *Educational research: Competencies for analysis and applications* (8th ed.). Upper Saddle River, N.J.: Pearson Education, Inc.

Leedy, P.D., & Ormrod, J.E. (2010). *Practical research: Planning and design* (9th ed.). Upper Saddle River, N.J.: Pearson Education, Inc.

Neutens, J.J., & Rubinson, L. (2010). *Research techniques for the health sciences* (4th ed.). San Francisco: Benjamin Cummings.

Patten, M.L. (2009). *Understanding research methods* (7th ed.). Glendale, Calif.: Pryczak Publishing.

Vorst, D.A. (2008). The impact of an integrated dual disorder treatment model in detecting substance use disorders and referral to community services in a population with severe mental illness. Unpublished master's thesis, University of Cincinnati.

Walter, J.L. (2007). Determining attitude toward and level of involvement in health promotion and education programs in Greater Cincinnati faith communities. Unpublished master's thesis, University of Cincinnati.

CHAPTER 6 | **Research Ethics**

Chapter Objectives

After reading this chapter and answering the review questions, you should be able to:

1. Define ethics, professional ethics, and research ethics.
2. Provide a brief history of research ethics by noting the importance of each of the following: Nuremberg Code; Helsinki Declaration; Universal Declaration of Human Rights; Tuskegee Syphilis Study; National Research Act of 1974 (Public Law 93-348); *The Belmont Report;* Title 45, Code of Federal Regulations, Part 46, Protection of Human Subjects (45 CFR Part 46).
3. Explain the benefits of a code of ethics.
4. Discuss the ethical issues associated with the selection of a research topic and research participants.
5. Explain the meaning of informed consent and the difference between consent and assent.
6. State the purpose of an institutional review board (IRB).
7. Explain why deception is an ethical concern in research.
8. Describe the difference between active and passive deception.
9. Differentiate between the ways of dealing with privacy in a research setting: anonymity and confidentiality.
10. Identify some ethical issues associated with an untreated control group and data analyses.
11. Explain the terms duplication, fragmentation, plagiarism, authorship, and external sponsorship as they relate to publishing research findings.

Key Terms

active deception
anonymity
assent
Belmont Report
code of ethics
Code of Ethics for the Health Education Profession
coercion
confidentiality
corresponding author
debriefing
deception
duplication
ethical issues
ethics
exempt from review

expedited review
fragmentation
full review
Health Insurance Portability and Accountability Act of 1996 (Public Law 104-191)
Helsinki Declaration
honorary authorship
human subject
implied consent
informed consent
institutional review board (IRB)
National Research Act of 1974 (Public Law 93-348)
Nuremberg Code
passive deception

plagiarism
privacy
professional ethics
research ethics
research participant
Title 45, Code of Federal Regulations, Part 46, Protection of Human Subjects (45 CFR Part 46)
Tuskegee Syphilis Study
undue influence
Universal Declaration of Human Rights
untreated control group
voluntary participation
vulnerable groups

At this point, you should have a fairly firm idea for the research project you are planning and awareness of what should be included in Chapters I and II of your thesis or dissertation. In addition, if you are planning to conduct theory-based research, you should have identified the constructs of the specific theory or model on which you plan to base your project. Prior to proceeding to Chapter III of your thesis or dissertation, where your research methods are delineated, you need to be aware of some of the ethical issues you may face as you continue to plan, carry out, and report on your research project.

As you began your study of research methods, probably one of the furthest thoughts from your mind was your concern for ethical issues related to the research process. Yet almost every step of the research process can be associated with some type of ethical issue (or some would say ethical dilemma). By **ethical issues** we mean situations where competing values are at play and the researcher needs to make a judgment about what is the most appropriate course of action. For example, a health education specialist may want to conduct an observational study of cancer support groups to better understand how such groups work and make recommendations for improvement. In selecting the appropriate methods for this study, the researcher must weigh the benefits and ethics of conducting the study using obtrusive observation (telling group participants that he or she will be attending the support group for the purpose of "watching and studying" their behavior) versus unobtrusive observation (not telling participants the "real" purpose of attending the support group but instead taking on the role of a cancer patient in order to "observe"). "Dealing with ethical issues rarely involves applying a set of hard and fast rules" (Crowl, 1993, p. 271). That is, "the distinction between ethical and unethical behavior is not dichotomous" (Kimmel, 1988, p. 34). Thus, conducting research often becomes "a balancing act. Researchers must balance their general obligation to promote knowledge with the general obligation

to treat others fairly" (Dane, 1990, p. 58). The study of ethics helps with this balancing act. It "helps to prevent research abuses and it assists us in understanding our responsibilities as ethical scientists. Ethically educated investigators can become better able to anticipate ethical problems in their studies before they occur, in order to avoid them entirely or else to become skillful in coping with them" (Kimmel, 2007, p. 24).

The purpose of this chapter is not to present information on the various ethical theories; that information can be found elsewhere (Cottrell, Girvan, & McKenzie, 2009). Rather, in this chapter we will explore the ethical issues that surround the research processes. More specifically, we will begin with definitions of ethics and research ethics, followed by a brief history of ethics as it relates to research. Then we will present some standards that can be used to help guide researchers as they face ethical issues during the research processes. Finally, we will examine the ethical issues and dilemmas that confront the researcher while planning the research project, while carrying out the research project, and after the research project.

Ethics, Professional Ethics, and Research Ethics Defined

Ethics, the study of moral behavior (Morrison, 2006), is one of the three major areas of philosophy. The other two are *epistemology,* the study of knowledge, and *metaphysics,* the study of nature and reality (Thiroux, 1995). Ethics is often referred to as moral philosophy. Yet Thiroux (1995) has made a distinction between ethics and morals, saying that ethics "seems to pertain to the individual character of a person or persons, whereas morality seems to point to the relationship between human beings" (p. 3). Since both the character of researchers and their relationships with other human beings are integral to the research process, in this chapter we will use "ethical" and "moral" to mean the same thing. "The important thing to remember here is moral, ethical, immoral, unethical, essentially mean, good, right, bad, and wrong, often depending on whether one is referring to people themselves or to their actions" (Thiroux, 1995, p. 3).

When the study of ethics is applied to the practice of health education, or for that matter the practice of any profession, it is referred to as professional ethics. **Professional ethics** "seeks to determine what the role of the professions is and what the conduct of professionals should be" (Bayles, 1989, p. 13). Within the larger realm of professional ethics is **research ethics**, which "comprises principles and standards that, along with underlying values, guide appropriate conduct relevant to research decisions" (Kimmel, 2007, p. 6).

Brief History of Research Ethics

"From the earliest days of philosophy in ancient Greece, people have sought to apply reason in determining the right course of action for a particular situation and explaining why it is right" (Morrison, 2009, p. 3). It was Socrates (470–399 B.C.), "the ancient Greek philosopher, who spent his days in the marketplace challenging people to think about how they lived" (White, 1988, p. 7). It was also during this time, in 460 B.C., that the Greek physician Hippocrates was born. Hippocrates, referred to as the "Father of Medicine," was known for developing the art of ethical bedside care. It is he who is credited with the Hippocratic oath. This oath, which has served as an ethical guide to the medical profession, is still often used at graduation ceremonies of medical colleges. Over the years and prior to more formal regulations and professional codes of ethics, the treatment of individuals by others was guided by the unwritten rule of acting fairly and compassionately (Kimmel, 2007). However, "history has taught us that without moral principles, protective measures, and a system of ethical standards that oblige researchers to follow certain rules, scientific misconduct and dishonesty will occur" (Baumgartner & Hensley, 2006, p. 93).

It was not until after the Nuremberg war crime trials following World War II that the treatment of research participants, as we know it today, first received attention. During those trials, it came out that many of the atrocities that occurred in Germany were justified by the defendants as "medical research." As a result of these trials, the **Nuremberg Code** was created in 1947. The Code, which set forth 10 conditions, attempted to outline permissible guidelines for medical experimentation (Kimmel, 2007). The 10 conditions are presented in Box 6.1. Since its development, the Code has provided the foundation for a number of other research ethics guidelines, documents, and codes of ethics that have been adopted by various regulatory groups and professional organizations (National Commission, 1979).

Though the Nuremberg Code became the prototype for many later documents, it was not all-encompassing. It made "no provisions for any special treatment of children, the elderly, or the mentally incompetent" (Haber, 2002, p. 266). Recognizing the need for guidelines broader in scope, in 1964 the World Medical Association adopted *The Declaration of Helsinki: Recommendations Guiding Medical Doctors in Biomedical Research Involving Human Subjects* (National Institutes of Health [NIH], 2004). The **Helsinki Declaration**, most recently revised in 2000 and currently in use throughout the world (NIH, 2004), compels "government officials who administer research funds to monitor the manner in which research is conducted" (Norwood, 2000, p. 58).

In 1948, a year after the Nuremberg Code was created, the General Assembly of the United Nations adopted and proclaimed the Universal Declaration of Human Rights (United Nations, 1948). The **Universal Declaration of Human Rights** represented the world's first effort to create a collective view of the rights that go along with human existence. Although the Universal Declaration of Human Rights did not specifically include the word "ethics," many of the documents specifically created for human subjects and research

Box 6.1   Nuremberg Code: Directives for Human Experimentation

1. The voluntary consent of the human subject is absolutely essential. This means that the person involved should have legal capacity to give consent; should be so situated as to be able to exercise free power of choice, without the intervention of any element of force, fraud, deceit, duress, over-reaching, or other ulterior form of constraint or coercion; and should have sufficient knowledge and comprehension of the elements of the subject matter involved as to enable him to make an understanding and enlightened decision. This latter element requires that before the acceptance of an affirmative decision by the experimental subject there should be made known to him the nature, duration, and purpose of the experiment; the method and means by which it is to be conducted; all inconveniences and hazards reasonable to be expected; and the effects upon his health or person which may possibly come from his participation in the experiment.

    The duty and responsibility for ascertaining the quality of the consent rests upon each individual who initiates, directs, or engages in the experiment. It is a personal duty and responsibility which may not be delegated to another with impunity.

2. The experiment should be such as to yield fruitful results for the good of society, unprocurable by other methods or means of study, and not random and unnecessary in nature.

3. The experiment should be so designed and based on the results of animal experimentation and a knowledge of the natural history of the disease or other problem under study that the anticipated results will justify the performance of the experiment.

4. The experiment should be so conducted as to avoid all unnecessary physical and mental suffering and injury.

5. No experiment should be conducted where there is an *a priori* reason to believe that death or disabling injury will occur; except, perhaps, in those experiments where the experimental physicians also serve as subjects.

6. The degree of risk to be taken should never exceed that determined by the humanitarian importance of the problem to be solved by the experiment.

7. Proper preparations should be made and adequate facilities provided to protect the experimental subject against even remote possibilities of injury, disability, or death.

8. The experiment should be conducted only by scientifically qualified persons. The highest degree of skill and care should be required through all stages of the experiment of those who conduct or engage in the experiment.

9. During the course of the experiment the human subject should be at liberty to bring the experiment to an end if he has reached the physical or mental state where continuation of the experiment seems to him to be impossible.

10. During the course of the experiment the scientist in charge must be prepared to terminate the experiment at any stage, if he has probable cause to believe, in the exercise of the good faith, superior skill, and careful judgment required of him, that a continuation of the experiment is likely to result in injury, disability, or death to the experimental subject.

Source: The National Commission for the Protection of Human Subjects of Biomedical and Behavioral Research. (1979). *The Belmont Report of ethical principles and guidelines for the protection of human subject research.* Retrieved May 9, 2009, from http://ohsr.od.nih.gov/guidelines/nuremberg.html.

Originally published in *Trials of war criminals before the Nuremberg military tribunals under Control Council Law No. 10,* Vol. 2, pp. 181–182. Washington, D.C.: U.S. Government Printing Office, 1949.

emerged from the broader context of rights created by the Universal Declaration.

Although most people are aware of the atrocities carried out in Germany during World War II, most are not aware of medical experiments in the United States that breached research ethics. The incidents in the United States should not be compared to the atrocities carried out in Germany, because they were carried out within the legal and cultural parameters and precedents of the time, but in retrospect they were not ethical by today's standards. Some of those experiments that have gained the most attention are ones that have been sponsored by the U.S. government. The **Tuskegee Syphilis Study**, which began in 1932, was sponsored by the U.S. Public Health Service. The study investigated the long-term effects of untreated syphilis in poor, semiliterate African American men of Macon County, Alabama. The participants of the study, which included approximately 400 men with syphilis and another 200 without, were not correctly informed of the nature of the experiment or the disease. The participants with syphilis were told "that they were being treated for 'bad blood,' a term allegedly understood by the researchers to be a local euphemism for syphilis, but which the local blacks associated with unrelated ailments" (Kimmel, 2007, p. 4). In order to recruit and maintain participation in the study, the participants were induced with such things "as free physical examinations, free treatment for minor health problems, food, transportation to and from the clinic, and a burial stipend of $50. . . . The burial stipend was needed in order to obtain permission to perform autopsies upon the death of the research participants" (Baumgartner & Hensley, 2006, p. 94). It was not long before it became clear that those in the "experimental group" were suffering many more health complications and experiencing much higher death rates than those without syphilis (Kimmel, 2007). In addition, these men were systematically denied penicillin even after its introduction in the 1940s as the standard treatment for the disease (NIH, 2004) in order to preserve the "integrity" of the study. It was not until 1972, when exposed by a newspaper reporter, that the study was ended and the surviving participants were finally treated. A congressional investigation followed in 1974 and led to an out-of-court settlement with the participants and their families. Finally, in 1997, President Clinton, on behalf of the U.S. government, formally apologized for the study (Baumgartner & Hensley, 2006).

Another breach of research ethics, as we know them today, sponsored by the U.S. government took place in the 1940s and 1950s, under the direction of the U.S. Energy Department. During this period of time, some 1800 individuals involved in several different studies were given radioactive isotopes (Kong, 1994). "Among the participants, who received no apparent medical benefits and in some cases suffered harmful consequences as a result of the experimental treatments, were pregnant women, infants, terminally ill patients, poor people, and other vulnerable groups" (Kimmel, 2007, p. 2). As with the Tuskegee Syphilis Study, information about the radiation studies was brought to the public's attention by a newspaper reporter. And also like the Tuskegee study, in 1995, after reacting to a government report documenting the radiation studies, President Clinton offered an apology to those who had been subjected to the experiments (Neutens & Rubinson, 2010).

As a result of these and other visible breaches of research ethics in the United States, the **National Research Act (Public Law 93-348)** was passed by Congress in 1974. As a part of this act, two important events took place. First, the Department of Health, Education, and Welfare (HEW) (renamed the Department of Health and Human Services [HHS] in 1981) was required to codify its policy for the protection of human subjects into federal regulations, which it did in 1974 (NIH, 2004). One of the major provisions of these regulations was the "regulation mandating that an institutional review board (IRB) functioning in accordance with specifications of the department must review and approve all studies" (Haber, 2002, p. 267).

Second, the National Commission for the Protection of Human Subjects of Biomedical and Behavioral Research was formed. One of the tasks given to the Commission was to identify the basic ethical principles that should underlie research involving human subjects and to develop guidelines to be followed to ensure that research is conducted in accordance with those principles (National Commission, 1979). During its existence, the Commission issued several reports, with the publication in 1979 of *The Belmont Report: Ethical Principles and Guidelines for the Protection of Human Subject Research* being the most notable. Unlike the Nuremberg Code and the Helsinki Declaration, which consist of guidelines or rules, the *Belmont Report* identified three fundamental ethical principles that are relevant to all research involving human subjects: respect for persons, beneficence, and justice (NIH, 2004) (see Box 6.2).

As the knowledge and use of the principles of research ethics matured, there became a need to revise the 1974 HEW regulations for the protection of human subjects. In 1981, the HHS gave approval to **Title 45, Code of Federal Regulations, Part 46, Protection of Human Subjects** (45 CFR Part 46). Initially, these regulations were applicable only to research supported by the HHS, but in June 1991, 45 CFR Part 46 was revised and became the basic policy that now governs all federally supported research (NIH, 2004). The policy reaffirmed that all research studies involving human subjects and funded by federal funds must be reviewed by an

---

Box 6.2   The Ethical Principles of the *Belmont Report*

The *Belmont Report* establishes three fundamental ethical principles that are relevant to all research involving human subjects: Respect for Persons, Beneficence, and Justice. Although other important principles sometimes apply to research, these three provide a comprehensive framework for ethical decision-making in research involving human subjects.

1. The principle of Respect for Persons acknowledges the dignity and autonomy of individuals, and requires that people with diminished autonomy be provided special protection. This principle requires that subjects give informed consent to participation in research. Because of their potential vulnerability, certain subject populations are provided with additional protections. These include live human fetuses, children, prisoners, the mentally disabled, and people with severe illnesses.

2. The principle of Beneficence requires us to protect individuals by maximizing anticipated benefits and minimizing possible harms. Therefore, it is necessary to examine carefully the design of the study and its risks and benefits including, in some cases, identifying alternative ways of obtaining the benefits sought from the research. Research risks must always be justified by the expected benefits of research.

3. The principle of Justice requires that we treat subjects fairly. For example, subjects should be carefully and equitably chosen to insure that certain individuals or classes of individuals—such as prisoners, elderly people, or financially impoverished people—are not systematically selected or excluded, unless there are scientifically or ethically valid reasons for doing so. Also, unless there is careful justification for an exception, research should not involve persons from groups that are unlikely to benefit from subsequent applications of the research.

Source: National Institutes of Health (NIH). (2004). *Guidelines for the conduct of research involving human subjects at the National Institutes of Health.* Page 19. Retrieved May 9, 2009, from http://www.nihtraining.com/ohsrsite/guidelines/index.html.

institutional review board (IRB) to ensure compliance with the requirements set forth in the policy (Baumgartner & Hensley, 2006).

Code of Ethics

In addition to the ethical regulations for research put forth by both international and national governmental agencies, many professional organizations have also set forth their guidelines as a portion of their code of ethics for the profession (see Box 6.3). A **code of ethics** (or professional moral consensus, as some refer to it) outlines the norms of expected ethical behavior for the members of that profession. In other words, an ethical code sets standards "for honor, virtue, and dignity" (Iammarino, O'Rourke, Pigg, & Weinberg, 1989, p. 101) and "helps professionals become aware of what is generally considered right or wrong professionally" (Richardson & Jose, 1983). It also provides consumers of health

education services with an understanding of what they should expect from the provider.

The profession of health education has had a code of ethics since 1976. Since that time, two professional health education organizations, the Society for Public Health Education (SOPHE) and the American Association for Health Education (AAHE), have had codes. However, in 1995, the National Commission for Health Education Credentialing, Inc. (NCHEC) and Coalition of National Health Education Organizations (CNHEO) cosponsored a conference, *The Health Education Profession in the Twenty-First Century: Setting the Stage,* at which it was recommended that efforts be expanded to develop a profession-wide code of ethics. Soon after that conference the CNHEO began work on such a code. After several years of work, in 1999, the **Code of Ethics for the Health Education Profession** was created and approved by all members of CNHEO, thus replacing the earlier codes developed by SOPHE

Box 6.3 **Sources of Professional Codes of Ethics**	
Association/Organization	**Source**
American Anthropological Association	http://www.aaanet.org/committees/ethics/ethcode.htm
American College of Healthcare Executives	http://www.ache.org/ABT_ACHE/code.cfm
American College of Sports Medicine	http://www.acsm.org/AM/Template.cfm?Section=Search&template=/CM/HTMLDisplay.cfm&ContentID=2385
American Counseling Association	http://www.counseling.org/Resources/CodeofEthics/TP/HOME/CT2.aspx
American Nurses Association	http://www.nursingworld.org/MainMenuCategories/EthicsStandards/CodeofEthics.aspx
American Pharmaceutical Association	http://ethics.iit.edu/codes/coe/amer.pharmaceutical.assoc.coe.html
American Psychological Association	http://www.apa.org/ethics/
American Sociological Association	http://www.asanet.org/cs/root/leftnav/ethics/code_of_ethics_table_of_contents
Coalition of National Health Education Organizations	http://www.cnheo.org
Public Health Leadership Society	http://phls.org/home/section/3-26/

and AAHE. (See Appendix A for a copy of the code and more information on its development.)

As you can see from Appendix A, just a small portion of the Code of Ethics for the Health Education Profession, Article V, is dedicated to research ethics. The seven sections of this article should be thought of as the minimal standards of practice for those conducting health promotion and education research.

Ethical Issues Encountered During the Research Planning Process

In the remaining portions of this chapter, we will present ethical issues that often confront health education researchers as they engage in the research process. We begin with those issues encountered during the planning process.

Researcher's Qualifications

It should be obvious that no research project should begin unless the researcher is qualified to conduct the proposed research. In other words, "Does the researcher have the competence to conduct the research? Is the researcher aware of alternative approaches for meeting the research objectives? Is the researcher knowledgeable about the ethical guidelines, legal requirements, and local customs and norms?" (Kimmel, 2007, p. 11). Because this book is written for students learning the research process, some may question whether students are qualified to conduct many different types of research based upon the questions posed above. It is our belief that the students, as they proceed through the learning process, will obtain the knowledge and skills to be competent researchers under the guidance of their mentors and advisors. For example, students may feel that they can create and administer a written questionnaire using survey research methodology without much guidance, yet not be aware of a number of ethical issues associated with the process such as selecting partici-

pants, using incentives to increase response rates, obtaining consent to participate, analyzing the data, and sharing the results. It is the responsibility of the mentors/advisors to ensure their students' work meets all ethical guidelines, legal requirements, and local customs and norms.

Selecting a Research Topic

Chapter 2 of this book went into great detail regarding how and where a researcher could find an appropriate research topic to study. After identifying possible topics and prior to making a final decision on the topic to be studied, an ethical issue the researcher must consider is weighing the benefits and risks of conducting the study; that is, how much risk of potential harm is justifiable given the importance of the knowledge to be gained from carrying out the study (Crowl, 1993)? The requirement that research be justified on the basis of a favorable risk/benefit ratio is based on the *Belmont Report* principle of beneficence.

"The term 'risk' refers to a possibility that harm may occur. However, when expressions such as 'small risk' or 'high risk' are used, they usually refer (often ambiguously) both to the chance (probability) of experiencing a harm and the severity (magnitude) of the envisioned harm. . . . the term 'benefit' is used in the research context to refer to something of positive value related to health or welfare" (National Commission, 1979, p. 9). The types of harms that are often associated with the research conducted in our field of study include psychological (e.g., increased stress because of participation), social (e.g., being embarrassed in front of peers), economic (e.g., loss of income because of participation), legal (e.g., protection of confidential information), or physical (e.g., injury resulting from participation).

As an example, one such risk/benefit ethical issue may arise in a study where the researcher is testing a new intervention to improve youths' refusal skills to the use of tobacco. After a review of the literature, a researcher might come to the conclusion that a specific type of role-playing intervention used with other substance abuse has the potential to help youth say "no" when faced with the decision to use or not use tobacco in a social situation with peers. However, the role-playing technique has come under some criticism because of the stress (potential psychological harm) that is sometimes caused in youth. Thus, the researcher is faced with determining if the potential benefit (refusing tobacco) outweighs the risk (increased stress). In making such a decision the researcher should consider all the relevant data, including alternative ways of obtaining the benefits sought in the research (National Commission, 1979).

Recruiting Research Participants

There are several ethical issues related to the recruitment of participants for a research study, but before we present them we first need to define a research participant. A **human subject** or **research participant** "is a living individual about whom an investigator obtains either (1) data through interaction or intervention with the individual, or (2) identifiable private information. In many cases, the determination of whether a particular research activity involves human subjects is not difficult, but in some cases, the line is blurred" (NIH, 2004, p. 4). For example, say that a researcher is interested in studying the patient education practices of primary care physicians. Further, suppose the method chosen to do so is to study the written notes that the physicians place in patients' charts after the office visit. Clearly, the physicians are "human subjects" because the researcher is studying their behavior, but are the physicians' patients also human subjects since the researcher has to look at their charts? There are some who would say yes and others who would say no.

In the previous paragraph we used both the terms "human subjects" and "research participants" for the individuals who may take part in a research study. The reason for doing so is that the

National Institutes for Health's guidelines for conducting research that involves people uses the term "human subjects." However, more recently some professional groups (e.g., American Psychological Association) have chosen to use the term "research participants" because of the pejorative connotations associated with the word "subject," including the subordinate role (Kimmel, 2007). The term "participant" connotes people who are willing and more actively involved in the research process. For these reasons we recommend that the term "research participants" be used in health promotion and education research. Let's look more closely at some of the ethical issues associated with the selection of research participants.

VOLUNTARY PARTICIPATION

An accepted norm of all research that includes people is that participation in the research must be voluntary. "The term **voluntary participation** refers to the participants' rights to freely choose to subject themselves to the scrutiny inherent in research" (Dane, 1990, p. 39). The requirement that participation in research be voluntary is based on the *Belmont Report* principle of respect for persons.

Two ethical issues associated with voluntary participation are coercion and awareness (Dane, 1990). **Coercion** is seen as those acts that include the use of threats, force, or undue influence to get people to participate (Dane, 1990; National Commission, 1979). **Undue influence** is thought of as an excessive, unwarranted, inappropriate, or improper reward or other overture in order to get someone to participate (National Commission, 1979). Here are a couple examples of coercion. Biomedical researchers could threaten to withhold a proven treatment from people who are not willing to also "volunteer" to participate in a study that is testing the treatment. Or college professors can coerce their students to participate in a research study by offering an undue influence (100 extra credit points) for doing so. Obviously, these two scenarios are pretty clear examples of coercion, but that is not always the case, especially when there are choices. For example, is it coercion if the college professor says to the students that they can complete this requirement for the course by either participating in the research study or writing a three-page paper?

Being aware that one is involved in a research study is another component of voluntary participation (Dane, 1990). As with coercion, there is a continuum of possibilities, and it is not always clear what is and is not ethical behavior. For example, some would agree that it is unethical for a researcher to collect data for a research study from participants in a diabetes support group through observation when the researcher, who does not have diabetes, is participating in the group by acting as if he or she was a person with diabetes and has not disclosed such to the other participants. Others would say that it is unethical for a college professor to add "questions" to a written examination that are really not examination questions but rather questions to collect data for a research study he or she is conducting. Still others would say it is unethical for researchers to sit at a busy street corner to observe safety belt use as a part of their safety belt research study. Depending on how one looks at the situation, a case could be made for and against each of these scenarios.

USING VULNERABLE GROUPS AS RESEARCH PARTICIPANTS

Ethical issues can also arise in research studies when there is an exploitation of persons from vulnerable groups (Kimmel, 2007). Of prime concern is the ability (or lack of ability) of these vulnerable individuals to "volunteer" to participate. Often identified **vulnerable groups** include the elderly, minors, pregnant women, the unborn, institutionalized persons, the emotionally or physically disabled, prisoners (Haber, 2002; Kimmel, 2007; Melton & Stanley, 1996), the poor, the illiterate, or those with terminal diseases. Individuals in some of the groups noted above would be considered vulnerable because of being mentally (e.g., elderly or

emotionally disabled) or developmentally (e.g., minors) incompetent to make a decision even when presented with complete information about the research project. Others who are competent to make a decision about participation (e.g., prisoners or students) may be vulnerable because they see researchers in positions of authority or commanding influence and feel they can enhance their position by participating or are afraid of the consequences if they do not participate. "Also, inducements that would ordinarily be acceptable may become undue influences if the subject is especially vulnerable" (National Commission, 1979, p. 8). This latter situation could occur when a nominal amount of money, say $5, is used to induce people who see $5 as a lot of money (e.g., the poor) to participate (Dane, 1990). Thus, researchers must give extra attention to the process of selecting participants when potential participants are vulnerable to ensure that they indeed participate voluntarily. It has been suggested that one way of judging the ethical issues of using vulnerable groups in research studies is to determine if there is a therapeutic or nontherapeutic benefit to the participants (Ramsey, 1976).

Gaining Approval to Carry Out the Research Project

In addition to gaining the approval of one's thesis/dissertation committee to carry out a research project, students, like all others conducting research projects, must have their research protocol approved by an institutional review board.

INSTITUTIONAL REVIEW BOARD

As noted earlier in this chapter, Title 45, Code of Federal Regulations, Part 46, Protection of Human Subjects (45 CFR Part 46) outlined procedures that must be followed by institutions receiving funding from the federal government to conduct research with human subjects. As a part of that federal policy, institutions must establish an **institutional review board** (IRB) (sometimes referred to as a human subjects' committee, an ethical review board, or a research advisory committee). The purpose of an IRB is "to protect the rights and well-being of subjects asked to participate" (Torabi, 1994, p. 8). An IRB accomplishes this purpose by reviewing and approving, requiring modifications before approving, or rejecting all research protocols relevant to the policy (Kolbe, 1994). As such, most colleges and universities and health care systems have their own IRBs. In fact, at some very large, diverse institutions (e.g., very large universities) it would not be uncommon to find multiple IRBs for various units within the institution. In situations where it would be impractical to have an IRB because of limited research activity, institutions may create an interinstitutional IRB (Norwood, 2000) or ask an IRB from another institution to review a research proposal in order to be in compliance with the federal policy. An example of this latter situation could occur when a small community hospital asks a university IRB to review a proposal. Though the federal policy requiring a research protocol to be reviewed by an IRB pertains to federally funded research, most institutions that have IRBs have voluntarily decided to review all research protocols in their institution regardless of the funding source.

According to federal guidelines, an IRB must be composed of at least five members with varying backgrounds in order to be able to provide a complete and adequate review of the research activities commonly conducted at the institution. Among its members, an IRB must include: (1) persons who are sufficiently qualified through experience and expertise to serve; (2) persons who represent diverse groups (i.e., race, sex, cultural backgrounds); (3) persons knowledgeable enough to ensure that the proposed research projects are consistent with institutional commitments and regulations, applicable law, and standards of professional conduct and practice; and (4) an individual who is not otherwise affiliated with the institution and who is not part of the immediate family of a person who is affiliated with the institution. If nec-

essary, the IRB, at its discretion, may invite persons with competence in special areas to assist in the review of issues that require expertise beyond or in addition to those already available on the IRB (Office of Human Subjects Research [OHSR], 2005). Obviously, it would be difficult for most institutions to constitute a 5-member IRB that has representation from all the groups noted above, so it is not uncommon to have IRBs with 10 to 20 or more members.

Though 45 CFR Part 46 outlines the general procedures for IRBs to follow, each IRB has its own application of the procedures for operation. As you move forward in the planning of your research project, it would be prudent for you to find out how the IRB at your institution functions. Most have their own forms that must be completed along with instructions you must follow as you prepare your proposal for review. Many IRBs have a checklist for researchers to follow when preparing a proposal for review, and many IRBs now have their procedures and forms posted online, and many require IRB applications to be submitted online. One important detail to find out about your IRB is how often it meets. In institutions where much research takes place, some IRBs may meet weekly, but others that review only a few proposals a year may meet on an as-needed basis. There is nothing more frustrating for a researcher than to prepare a proposal for review only to find out that the IRB just met and thus the researcher has to wait another month or more before having the proposal reviewed.

Once the research proposal is in the hands of the IRB, the members will review it based on both 45 CFR Part 46 guidelines (see Box 6.4) and any guidelines specific to the institution. According to the 45 CFR Part 46 guidelines, proposals can be placed into three categories for review based on the amount of risk to which the research participants will be exposed. These categories are exempt from review, expedited review, and full review. "Exempt from review does not mean that the researcher can simply ignore IRB guidelines and

---

Box 6.4   Criteria for IRB Approval of Research

In order to approve research covered by this policy the IRB shall determine that all of the following requirements are satisfied:
(1) Risks to subjects are minimized.
(2) Risks to subjects are reasonable in relation to anticipated benefits, if any, to subjects, and the importance of the knowledge that may reasonably be expected to result.
(3) Selection of subjects is equitable. In making this assessment the IRB should take into account the purposes of the research and the setting in which the research will be conducted and should be particularly cognizant of the special problems of research involving vulnerable populations, such as children, prisoners, pregnant women, mentally disabled persons, or economically or educationally disadvantaged persons.

(4) Informed consent will be sought from each prospective subject or the subject's legally authorized representative.
(5) Informed consent will be appropriately documented.
(6) When appropriate, the research plan makes adequate provision for monitoring the data collected to ensure the safety of subjects.
(7) When appropriate, there are adequate provisions to protect the privacy of subjects and to maintain the confidentiality of data.

When some or all of the subjects are likely to be vulnerable to coercion or undue influence, such as children, prisoners, pregnant women, mentally disabled persons, or economically or educationally disadvantaged persons, additional safeguards have been included in the study to protect the rights and welfare of these subjects.

Source: Office of Human Subject Research (OHSR). (2005). *Title 45 CFR Part 46: Protection of human subjects.* Retrieved May 10, 2009, from http://ohsr.od.nih.gov/guidelines/45cfr46.html 46.111.

---

not submit required forms; it means that the proposed research is exempt from the full review process established by the IRB" (Baumgartner & Hensley, 2006, p. 108). Research proposals are **exempt from review** when there is no risk to the research participants and when the proposed project meets certain "exempt criteria" identified in 45 CFR Part 46 (see Box 6.5). However, if the research involves prisoners, fetuses, pregnant women, minors, or human in vitro fertilization, or uses deception (see information about deception later in the chapter), the exempt category does not apply. Typically most exempt reviews are conducted by just one individual, such as the chair of the IRB or another designated person (i.e., the staff person assigned to administer the IRB).

An **expedited review** is completed when the risk to a participant is minimal. Some examples of minimal risks include but are not limited to

(1) collection of personal data using survey methods that can be linked to the research subjects, (2) collection of specimens (i.e., hair and nail clippings) through noninvasive techniques, or (3) collection of data from video recordings made for research purposes. Often a small subcommittee (e.g., two to four people) conducts such reviews. (Note: Readers should refer to 45 CFR 46.110 for a more detailed description of what studies qualify for an expedited review.) A **full review** is required when research participants will be exposed to more than minimal risk and the research does not fall into the expedited review category. The result of most reviews is that the IRB approves the proposal with required changes, referred to as stipulations. However, IRBs are obliged to reject any protocol that does not meet the criteria noted in Box 6.4 (NIH, 2004).

Box 6.5   Criteria for an Exempt Review

The following types of studies meet the criteria for "exempt review":

(1) Research conducted in established or commonly accepted educational settings, involving normal educational practices, such as (i) research on regular and special education instructional strategies, or (ii) research on the effectiveness of or the comparison among instructional techniques, curricula, or classroom management methods.

(2) Research involving the use of educational tests (cognitive, diagnostic, aptitude, achievement), survey procedures, interview procedures or observation of public behavior, unless: (i) information obtained is recorded in such a manner that human subjects can be identified, directly or through identifiers linked to the subjects; and (ii) any disclosure of the human subjects' responses outside the research could reasonably place the subjects at risk of criminal or civil liability or be damaging to the subjects' financial standing, employability, or reputation.

(3) Research involving the use of educational tests (cognitive, diagnostic, aptitude, achievement), survey procedures, interview procedures, or observation of public behavior that is not exempt under paragraph (2) of this section, if: (i) the human subjects are elected or appointed public officials or candidates for public office; or (ii) federal statute(s) require(s) without exception that the confidentiality of the personally identifiable information will be maintained throughout the research and thereafter.

(4) Research involving the collection or study of existing data, documents, records, pathological specimens, or diagnostic specimens, if these sources are publicly available or if the information is recorded by the investigator in such a manner that subjects cannot be identified, directly or through identifiers linked to the subjects.

(5) Research and demonstration projects which are conducted by or subject to the approval of department or agency heads, and which are designed to study, evaluate, or otherwise examine: (i) Public benefit or service programs; (ii) procedures for obtaining benefits or services under those programs; (iii) possible changes in or alternatives to those programs or procedures; or (iv) possible changes in methods or levels of payment for benefits or services under those programs.

(6) Taste and food quality evaluation and consumer acceptance studies, (i) if wholesome foods without additives are consumed or (ii) if a food is consumed that contains a food ingredient at or below the level and for a use found to be safe, or agricultural chemical or environmental contaminant at or below the level found to be safe, by the Food and Drug Administration or approved by the Environmental Protection Agency or the Food Safety and Inspection Service of the U.S. Department of Agriculture.

Source: Office of Human Subject Research (OHSR). (2005). *Title 45 CFR Part 46: Protection of human subjects.* Retrieved May 10, 2009, from http://ohsr.od.nih.gov/guidelines/45cfr46.html 46.101.

Ethical Issues Encountered During the Research Process

After the research topic has been selected, research participants have been selected for a study, and the research protocol has been approved by the IRB, there are a number of ethical issues that could confront researchers as they begin the actual research procedures of the study. They begin with properly informing the participants about what participation in the study would include so they can make an informed decision of whether to participate.

Informed Consent and Assent

Unless otherwise waived by an IRB, no research study that uses human participants can begin unless the potential participants (or their legally authorized representatives for those not competent and/or of legal age) have been properly informed about the study and agree to participate. Such action is covered by informed consent and assent. Both are based on the ethical principle of respect for persons.

INFORMED CONSENT

Earlier in the chapter, the ethical issues surrounding the selection of participants for a study, mainly voluntary participation and use of vulnerable groups, were presented. These issues are central to informed consent, but informed consent is more comprehensive in nature and takes place after participants have been selected but before participation begins. **Informed consent** has been defined as

> the voluntary agreement of an individual, or his or her authorized representative, who has the legal capacity to give consent, and who exercises free power of choice, without undue inducement or any other form of constraint or coercion to participate in research. The individual must have sufficient knowledge and understanding of the nature of the proposed research, the anticipated risks and potential benefits, and the requirements of the research to be able to make an informed

decision. (Levine, 1988, as stated in NIH, 2000, ¶ 1)

"Valid informed consent requires: (1) Disclosure of relevant information to prospective subjects about the research; (2) their comprehension of the information, and (3) their voluntary agreement, free from coercion and undue influence, to research participation" (OHSR, 2006, p. 1).

Disclosure of relevant information about the research includes providing in writing all information that the potential participants, or their legally authorized representatives, need to make an informed decision about participation. The information that researchers must provide to the potential participants is presented in Table 6.1. Further, it is recommended that when the informed consent document is created, it should be formatted using headings to promote comprehension and readability (OHSR, 2006).

The second part of valid informed consent is ensuring that potential participants comprehend the information provided. "For example, presenting information in a disorganized and rapid fashion, allowing too little time for consideration or curtailing opportunities for questioning, all may adversely affect a subject's ability to make an informed choice" (National Commission, 1979, p. 7), which is not acceptable. Because potential participants' ability to comprehend may vary depending on their level of intelligence, rationality, maturity, and language skills, it is necessary to ensure that the presentation of the information about the study is adapted according to the capacities of the potential participants (National Commission, 1979). This means presenting the information in a clear and easy-to-understand way, in the appropriate language (e.g., Spanish for Hispanic participants), and at a reading level understandable to people with less than a high school education (OHSR, 2006). It is the researchers' responsibility to ensure that the research participants comprehend the information (National Commission, 1979).

Table 6.1   Information That Must Be Provided to Potential Participants for Informed Consent

Basic elements of informed consent.
The following information shall be provided to each subject:

1. A statement that the study involves research, an explanation of the purposes of the research and the expected duration of the subject's participation, a description of the procedures to be followed, and identification of any procedures which are experimental;
2. A description of any reasonably foreseeable risks or discomforts to the subject;
3. A description of any benefits to the subject or to others which may reasonably be expected from the research;
4. A disclosure of appropriate alternative procedures or courses of treatment, if any, that might be advantageous to the subject;
5. A statement describing the extent, if any, to which confidentiality of records identifying the subject will be maintained;
6. For research involving more than minimal risk, an explanation as to whether any compensation and an explanation as to whether any medical treatments are available if injury occurs and, if so, what they consist of, or where further information may be obtained;
7. An explanation of whom to contact for answers to pertinent questions about the research and research subjects' rights, and whom to contact in the event of a research-related injury to the subject; and
8. A statement that participation is voluntary, refusal to participate will involve no penalty or loss of benefits to which the subject is otherwise entitled, and the subject may discontinue participation at any time without penalty or loss of benefits to which the subject is otherwise entitled.

Additional elements of informed consent. When appropriate, one or more of the following elements of information shall also be provided to each subject:

1. A statement that the particular treatment or procedure may involve risks to the subject (or to the embryo or fetus, if the subject is or may become pregnant) which are currently unforeseeable;
2. Anticipated circumstances under which the subject's participation may be terminated by the investigator without regard to the subject's consent;
3. Any additional costs to the subject that may result from participation in the research;
4. The consequences of a subject's decision to withdraw from the research and procedures for orderly termination of participation by the subject;
5. A statement that significant new findings developed during the course of the research which may relate to the subject's willingness to continue participation will be provided to the subject; and
6. The approximate number of subjects involved in the study.

Source: Office of Human Subject Research. (2005). *Title 45 CFR Part 46: Protection of human subjects.* Retrieved May 10, 2009, from http://ohsr.od.nih.gov/guidelines/45cfr46.html, #46.116.

The third part of valid informed consent is ensuring that participation is indeed voluntary. The principles about volunteerism presented earlier in the chapter in the section on identifying and selecting participants apply here as well.

Generally, informed consent is a process that includes: (1) the researcher discussing the research study with the research participants, (2) research participants having an opportunity to ask questions about the study, and (3) the participants signing a written informed consent document (see Figure 6.1 for an example) that has been reviewed and approved by an IRB. However, it is not uncommon in health education research to obtain consent without completing all three items in the informed consent process. For example, there are times when the researcher and the potential participants will not be face to face for a discussion of the study. This

Consent Form for the Diabetes Reminder Study

Please read (listen to) the following information.

Introduction: Dear potential participant: You are being invited to participate in a research study on ways to improve glucose control in people with diabetes. As you are aware, the key to controlling diabetes is self-management. This study has been approved by the Institutional Review Board at XYZ University in Anytown, Nice State.

The purpose of this study is to determine which of several different methods of reminders (i.e., e-mail messages, letters, telephone calls, or a combination of two or more) after diabetes education programs best help people with diabetes control their blood glucose levels.

Research tests or procedures for this study: If you consent to participate in this study, you will receive one or more of the types of reminders once a month for six months. In addition, you will be asked to return to the ABC Clinic in six months to have a blood test performed in the clinic lab, at our expense, to measure your blood glucose level.

Risks and discomforts to you if you take part in this study: Your participation in the study will put you at no greater risk than the normal daily risks you encounter as a person with diabetes.

The benefits to you of taking part in this study: Other than the free blood test you will receive in six months, there are no direct benefits to you from participating in this study. The results of this study may give us knowledge to change the way we handle reminders in the future for you and other individuals with diabetes.

Specific things you should understand about confidentiality: All information gathered for the study, including the results of the blood test, will be kept confidential with regard to individual identity, and only group data will be reported. A random identification number will be assigned to you at the beginning of the study and only that number will be used on the data forms. All collected data will be kept in a secure location and destroyed once the study is complete.

What to do if you decide you want to withdraw from the study: Your participation in the study is entirely voluntary. You may choose not to take part, or you may withdraw from the study at any time. In either case, you will not lose any benefits to which you are otherwise entitled from the ABC Clinic. If you have any questions regarding your rights as a research participant, the following person may be contacted: Ms. Jane Doe, Coordinator of Research Compliance, Office of Academic Research and Sponsored Programs, XYZ University, Anytown, Nice State, 12345, (987) XXX-XXXX.

Thank you for your consideration of this request and for your interest in this study.

Investigators:

Randall R. Cottrell, DEd, CHES
Professor
Department of Health Promotion
XYZ University
Anytown, Nice State 12345
(987) XXX-XXXX

James F. McKenzie, PhD, MPH, CHES
Professor
Department of Health Promotion
XYZ University
Anytown, Nice State 12345
(987) XXX-XXXX

I give my consent to participate in the research project entitled "Diabetes Reminder Study." The researchers have discussed the research project with me and I have read the description of the project. I have also had a chance to ask questions about the study and they have been answered to my satisfaction. I understand that I will receive a copy of this consent form to keep for future reference.

_____   _____   _____
Participant's Name Printed   Participant's Signature   Date

This example was created using information available from: Office of Human Subject Research (2006). *Guidelines for writing informed consent documents.* Retrieved May 12, 2009, from http://ohsr.od.nih.gov/info/sheet6.html.

FIGURE 6.1
Example informed consent document.

occurs frequently when conducting a study using survey methodology where the data are collected using an instrument that is sent through the U.S. mail or the Internet. In such cases, the written informed consent document acts in place of the researcher. In other research studies, depending on the nature of the research, participants may not have to sign a consent form. For example, in survey research, when participants are asked to complete a questionnaire after being informed about the study, they are often presented with a statement that says, "Your consent to participate is implied by your decision to complete the questionnaire," or for an Internet survey, "Your consent to participate in this study is implied by your decision to link to the Web site and complete the questionnaire." As is indicated in these statements, this type of consent is referred to as **implied consent** and is acceptable in place of an actual consent form. That is, if after being informed about the study, the participants complete the research instrument, it is assumed that they consent.

Finally, before completing our discussion of informed consent, we want to briefly discuss a special ethical issue involving informed consent that comes up often in health education research. It occurs when trying to conduct field (i.e., nonlaboratory) research projects. Often field research involves observing unsuspecting participants in natural settings (e.g., foods ordered and eaten in restaurants or smoking behavior in public). "The problem with informed consent in field settings, of course, is that much field research involves situations in which informed consent is either not feasible or is detrimental to the interests of the research" (Kimmel, 2007, p. 123). An example of "not feasible" would be getting consent from passing motorists to observe their safety belt use, and an example of "detrimental to the interests of the research" would be getting the consent of individuals involved in some form of illegal behavior, such as an illicit drug purchase. The ethical issue that arises here is the right of researchers to "watch" public behavior versus the right of the

potential participants to their privacy. Therefore, when researchers are planning research protocols and IRBs are approving them, they will need to weigh the need for informed consent in light "of the specific research methodologies and the circumstances under which they are employed" (Kimmel, 2007, p. 123).

ASSENT

Assent is the "willingness to participate in research by persons who are by definition too young to give informed consent but who are old enough to understand the proposed research in general, its expected risks and possible benefits, and the activities expected of them as subjects" (NIH, 2000, ¶ 2). Assent does not replace informed consent. If assent is given, informed consent must still be obtained from the participant's parent(s)/guardian (NIH, 2000). Typically, assent would be used with study participants who range in age from the upper elementary school grades up to a state's legal age for an adult. An example of assent occurred in a study that examined the sleep behaviors of fifth-grade students (Amschler & McKenzie, 2005). In that study, the IRB approved a protocol that first required the researchers to obtain informed consent from the students' parents/guardians, and then have the students sign an assent statement after being appropriately informed. The assent statement in that study read:

I, _____, have had the research study explained to me by my teacher. I have been given the opportunity to ask questions regarding my participation in the research. I understand what I am to do as a participant and agree to participate.

_____ _____
Signature   Date

Deception

Researchers have long debated the ethical issues associated with the use of deception in research studies. By **deception**, we mean "the deliberate withholding of, or misinforming about, important information" (Kimmel, 1988, p. 34) associated with the research. Deception can be further broken down into two categories: active and passive deception. **Active deception** is deception by commission, when researchers deliberately mislead the research participants about some aspect of the study, such as the purpose of the study or the procedures of the study (Kimmel, 2007). Some have referred to active deception as not telling the truth or just not *truthtelling*. An example of active deception would be a study where participants are asked to complete a questionnaire on their tobacco use and to provide a saliva sample after doing so. The subjects are told that the saliva sample will be analyzed in a lab to determine the amount of cotinine (a measure of nicotine) in their blood. Even though the researchers tell the participants this, they have no intention of carrying out this expensive laboratory test. Their reason for telling the participants this is to make them think their saliva will be analyzed and thus get the participants to answer more truthfully on the questionnaire.

Passive deception, is deception by omission, when the researchers purposely withhold relevant information from the participants (Kimmel, 2007). "With passive deception, a lie is not told; rather, a truth is left unspoken" (Kimmel, 2007, p. 63). Such situations can arise when informing the participants about a pertinent part of the research is likely to jeopardize the validity of the study. For example, as you will read in Chapter 9, we know that it is not unusual for research participants to "act differently" than they normally would if they know they are being watched (i.e., Hawthorne effect). Therefore, there are times when it may be sufficient to tell the participants that they are being invited to participate in a research study of which some features will not be revealed to them until the study is completed.

In all cases of research involving incomplete disclosure, such research is justified only if it is clear that (1) incomplete disclosure is truly necessary to accomplish the goals of the research, (2) there are no undisclosed risks to subjects that are more than minimal, and (3) there is an adequate plan for debriefing subjects, when appropriate, and for dissemination of research results to them. Information about risks should never be withheld for the purpose of eliciting the cooperation of subjects, and truthful answers should always be given to direct questions about the research. Care should be taken to distinguish cases in which disclosure would destroy or invalidate the research from cases in which disclosure would simply inconvenience the investigator. (National Commission, 1979, p. 7)

Privacy

One of the most basic concepts of conducting research with people is privacy. The requirement that the privacy of research participants be protected is based on the *Belmont Report* principle of respect for persons. **Privacy** has been defined as "the claim of individuals, groups, or institutions to determine for themselves when, how, and to what extent information about them is communicated to others" (Westin, 1968, p. 7). Thus, when an individual, group, or institution has agreed to participate in a study, it becomes the duty of the researcher to protect the information provided by the research participants.

The importance of privacy for those researchers working with health care studies was further emphasized in April 2003 with the enactment of the *Standards for Privacy of Individually Identifiable Health Information* section (the Privacy Rule) of the **Health Insurance Portability and Accountability Act of 1996** (officially known as Public Law 104-191 and referred to as HIPAA). The Privacy Rule sets national standards that health plans, health care clearinghouses, and health care providers who conduct certain health care transactions electronically must implement to protect and guard against the misuse of individually identifiable health information. Failure to implement the standards can lead to civil and criminal penalties

(U.S. Department of Health and Human Services [USDHHS], 2003).

The two techniques that are used to protect the privacy of research participants are anonymity and confidentiality.

ANONYMITY

Anonymity exists when there is no link between personal information and the research participant's identity (McKenzie, Neiger, & Thackeray, 2009). Thus, information (also called data) associated with a research participant may be considered anonymous when such information cannot be linked to the participant who provided it. In applying this concept to a research project, the researcher would need to ensure that the data collected had no identifying information attached to it such as the participant's name, social security number, or any other less common information.

Even though a researcher has indicated in the study protocol that the data will be collected in an anonymous manner, depending on the information collected, certain responses could still be linked to an individual. For example, suppose a researcher was collecting information on a written questionnaire from a small group of people (< 50) and one of the questions asked the respondents their age. If the group is rather homogeneous with regard to age with the exception of one person, it would not be difficult to link that person to his or her data. In such a case, if the researcher does indeed want an anonymous study, then the question may have to be reworded so that the respondents could not be identified (e.g., "Are you older than or less than or equal to 35 years old?") or dropped from the instrument. If the researcher absolutely needs to know the respondents' ages, then he or she may need to change from an anonymous to a confidential protocol.

CONFIDENTIALITY

There are studies in which the researcher needs to know who the participants are and therefore cannot conduct an anonymous study. Such studies may include protocols when the researcher needs to collect data from the same group of people more than once (e.g., to establish test–retest reliability), or when the protocol calls for some type of follow-up with the participants after an intervention. For example, suppose a researcher wanted to determine the long-term effects of two different smoking cessation programs. For this study, the researcher would need to know what participants are in what group and have a means to contact them after the cessation programs are over. Because the research participants are known and the data collected from them can be linked to them, the study would not have an anonymous protocol but rather a confidential protocol. **Confidentiality** exists when there is a link between personal information and the research participant's identity but that information is protected from others (McKenzie *et al.*, 2009). When conducting confidential studies, researchers need to take every precaution to protect the participants' information. Often this means keeping the information "under lock and key" while the study is being conducted, then destroying (i.e., shredding) the information when the study is complete.

It is not unusual for a beginning researcher to ask if it is better to use an anonymous or a confidential protocol. We just pointed out two of the real advantages of using a confidential protocol: the ability to be able to collect data from the same group of people more than once and the ability to follow up. Probably the greatest advantage to conducting an anonymous study is that often many people are more likely to tell the truth or share personal information if such information cannot be linked back to them. For example, suppose a researcher wanted to study the teaching ability of high school health education teachers. As part of the study, the researcher wants to collect information from the teachers' students. Many of the students may fear that confidential responses may somehow get linked back to them and possibly impact their grade in the course. An anonymous protocol could prevent this from happening.

Untreated Control Group

Often in research, when using experimental or quasi-experimental designs (see Chapter 9 for a discussion of these designs), it is not uncommon for some of the participants in the study to receive the treatment (intervention) being examined while others do not. For example, suppose a researcher wanted to conduct a study to test the impact of a new health education program that had showed promise in earlier pilot testing. Suppose further that the design that the researcher selected to test the new program randomly divided the study participants into two groups. One group, called the treatment group, would receive the new program and the other group, called the control group, would not. This latter group is referred to as an **untreated control group** since it was not being exposed to the new, or any other, program. If the results of this study show that this new program was indeed beneficial to those in the treatment group, how can the *Belmont Report* principle of justice (the fair treatment of participants) be upheld by researchers? McDermott and Sarvela (1999) have indicated that an untreated control group can be ethically justified in at least two ways: "(1) the assumption that resource limitations prohibit the dissemination of an intervention to all groups simultaneously; and/or (2) the promise that the untreated control or comparison group can be offered the intervention at the end of the experiment if it proves to be beneficial" (p. 47).

Data Analyses

Once a study has been carried out and the data collected, researchers must next analyze the data. Like the other steps in the research process, data analyses can also create ethical issues. These ethical concerns can arise from lack of knowledge about appropriate analyses, carelessness in conducting the analyses, or deliberate misuse of analyses. Although the ethical issues associated with each of these situations vary, the resulting impact on the researchers, the research participants, and the users of study results can have lasting effects. Inappropriate data analyses can lead to, among other problems, harm to person or property, implementation of inappropriate policies or procedures, and the waste of time, effort, and resources. "Regardless of the purposes to which our research results may be put, we have the ethical obligation to ensure that we do not mislead anyone who may rely on them" (Dane, 1990, p. 52).

Torabi (1994) has identified several specific ethical issues related to analyses of data. They include using data in an ignorant or careless way, direct manipulation of data, selective use or elimination of data, and overanalysis of data. An example of ignorant use of data would be reporting the mean of a data set when the median or mode would be the most appropriate, and an example of using data in a careless way would be not double-checking data that is entered into a computer from a written questionnaire. Manipulation of data involves subjecting data to multiple statistical techniques until one achieves the desired outcome.

Selective use or elimination of data could occur in a survey research study when researchers have asked the participants to answer a number of questions and some of the analyzed data support the research questions or hypothesis and others do not. In such cases, some researchers have reported only those results that support their work. The final ethical issue noted by Torabi (1994) dealing with data analyses is overanalysis of data. There are times in the analyses of data that advanced statistical techniques need to be used to deal with complicated studies that include many variables. These advanced techniques should not be used just to impress others. "A general principle of data analysis recommends using the most appropriate, yet simplest, statistical techniques in research so findings can be better understood, interpreted, and communicated" (p. 11). A simple way to avoid overanalysis is to remember the old saying "Don't use Cadillac statistics with Volkswagen data."

In addition to this old saying, there are several ways to avoid ethical situations associated with data analyses. The first is to seek assistance from statistical experts if you lack the knowledge and skills needed to complete the data analyses (Torabi, 1994). Second, understand the nature of the data prior to beginning the analysis (Torabi, 1994). What type of data have you collected (nominal, ordinal, interval, ratio, or qualitative) and what are the limitations of each? (See discussions in Chapters 8 and 11.) Third, always double-check your data entry and the results of your data analyses. And fourth, always report *all* your findings, not just the ones that turned out the way you wanted them to turn out.

Ethical Issues Encountered After the Research Process

After a research study has been completed, it is indeed possible that the researchers could still face ethical issues when disseminating the findings. In fact, Winslow (1996) has indicated that not attempting to disseminate research findings can, in itself, be unethical since researchers have an implicit contract with research participants, coinvestigators, colleagues in the scientific community, and others who could use the research findings to promote the knowledge base of their respective disciplines. Then, when researchers report their research findings, they have the obligation to report them as accurately as possible (Dane, 1990). "Science progresses through honesty and openness, and is retarded by ego defenses and deception" (Babbie, 1995, p. 454). With this in mind, some of the issues associated with reporting and publishing research results are presented in the following sections.

Reporting Research Results

Reporting the findings of research can take many different forms, such as preparing a manuscript for publication in a professional journal, presenting a paper at a professional meeting or conference, preparing a technical report for the funding or sponsoring agency, releasing the findings to the press via a press conference or news release, and, for graduate students, preparing the final copy of a research report, thesis, or dissertation (Baumgartner & Hensley, 2006). A number of authors (e.g., Baumgartner & Hensley, 2006; Kimmel, 2007; Neutens & Rubinson, 2010; Pigg, 1994; Torabi, 1994) have identified several ethical issues researchers must deal with when preparing to disseminate their research. Some of the more common ones include deciding what the report should and should not contain; sharing the results with the research participants; and protecting confidentiality of participants.

WHAT TO INCLUDE AS PART OF THE REPORTING

Probably the biggest ethical issue facing researchers when reporting their findings is what to include in their report. Traditionally, a manuscript includes an introduction with background and related literature, a description of the methods used in the research, the results, a discussion of the results in relation to the existing literature, the implications of the research, and conclusions. Though all of this information should be presented in an accurate and honest way, researchers must also report any factor that could be interpreted as a conflict of interest in the study (Norwood, 2000). Examples of conflict of interest might include: (1) researchers conducting a ranking of the best health education programs in the United States and the programs where they are employed come out high in the rankings; (2) a researcher presenting the findings of a study that examined the status of the various professional health associations and the researcher happens also to be the president-elect of one of the associations; and (3) researchers conducting a study that is funded by a commercial company for which they are also paid consultants or hold financial interests. In each of these cases, "the scientific methodology must be held to the highest standards" (Torabi, 1994, p. 13), and as a part of the reporting on the studies, the ethical behavior would be for the researchers to disclose their affiliation with the involved organizations/institutions.

To assist institutions, IRBs, and researchers with the ethical issues surrounding conflicts of interest, in the spring of 2004 the U.S. Department of Health and Human Services released new guidance for protecting research participants from possible harm caused by financial conflicts of interest that may arise in research studies, called "Financial Relationships and Interests in Research Involving Human Subjects: Guidance for Human Subject Protection" (USDHHS, 2004).

Another ethical issue dealing with what to include in the reporting of the results is whether to report negative findings; that is, should results of a study that turn out differently than the hypotheses established by the researchers be reported? Some researchers might be inclined not to report the negative findings because of their bias (Torabi, 1994), and others may not report them because they feel negative findings are unimportant. However, researchers have the ethical obligation to report negative findings if they are related to the study analysis (Babbie, 1995). "It is often as important to know that two variables are not related as to know that they are" (Babbie, 1995, p. 453).

Researchers also have the ethical obligation to report the limitations of their research. Researchers "should be more familiar than anyone else with the technical shortcomings and failures of the study" (Babbie, 1995, p. 453), and as such they should include them in their reporting. However, some researchers do not report limitations of their work because they are embarrassed to do so, thinking it is showing the flaws of their work. But as with the other items noted above, the researchers have an ethical obligation to note the limitations in their reporting so that those who use the results of their work do not misinterpret the findings, and so that other researchers will not limit their studies in the same way.

SHARING THE RESULTS WITH THE PARTICIPANTS

Since research participants play an integral part in the research process, researchers have the ethical obligation of sharing the results of their work with the participants. Researchers can share the results by holding a meeting for the participants, sending them a shortened final report, or publishing information in a newsletter or newspaper that the participants receive. A special process referred to as debriefing is an important obligation of the researcher when any type of deception is used in the study. **Debriefing**, also sometimes referred to as *dehoaxing, desensitization,* or *disabusing* (Kimmel, 2007), has been defined as "a procedure by which any relevant information about the project that has been withheld or misrepresented is made known to the participants" (Dane, 1990, p. 49).

There are exceptions to sharing the results with the participants. If the number of participants is very large (e.g., 5,000), the participants are legal minors, or the participants are spread over a large geographic area (e.g., throughout the United States), sharing results can be close to impossible. Having said this, whenever possible, an attempt to share the results should be made.

In addition, by sharing the results with the participants they can learn about themselves and others and, possibly, how to do things better. Oftentimes, especially in the case of survey research, research participants could also be the consumers of the research findings. Since many research participants are not compensated for their participation, one way of thanking them for their participation is to share the results with them first. For example, a researcher may survey local health department (LHD) administrators to find out the status of health education efforts at the local level. In doing so, the researchers are likely to find some education initiatives in one or more LHDs that would be useful for the others. As such, it is appropriate for the researchers to offer to share their findings with all LHDs prior to disseminating the findings in a more general way (i.e., through publication).

PROTECTING CONFIDENTIALITY

The procedures to protect the confidentiality of participants should be spelled out in the materials submitted to the IRB and, in an abbreviated form, in the informed consent documents. Suffice it to say, researchers have the ethical obligation of protecting the privacy of their participants when reporting the results. Therefore, all the steps noted earlier in this chapter about protecting privacy should be followed when reporting the results. As such, it is not uncommon to see in the write-up of a research project the research participants described using language like "the participants included students enrolled at a midsize, midwestern university during the spring of 2010" instead of "the participants included students enrolled at Ball State University during the spring of 2010."

Publishing Research Results

Because of the heavy emphasis placed on the publication of research findings in the academic community, we felt it was important to provide a more in-depth presentation of the ethical issues associated with publication of one's research. A thorough overview of a number of ethical issues associated with publishing research has been presented by Pigg (1994), and much of what we are presenting here comes from his work. However, before presenting that information we wanted to clarify what we mean by the term "manuscript," since we use the term often in this section of the chapter. The term is given to a piece of scholarly work that has been submitted to a publisher or journal for review for possible publication.

DUPLICATION

Duplication can occur in two different ways. It can result from either "submitting the same manuscript or its essence to two or more journals for simultaneous consideration, or submitting a previously published paper or its essence for consideration by another journal without disclosing the prior publication" (Pigg, 1994, pp. 31–32). As

noted by Pigg (1994), duplication creates an ethical issue for at least three different reasons. First, as part of the submission process, most publishers ask the author(s) to sign a copyright release form, indicating that the manuscript is an original work and has not been published elsewhere, nor is it currently being considered for publication elsewhere. Thus, signing such a document when it does not represent the truth is an ethical breach on the part of the author(s).

Second, publications "exist to serve a unique mission and readership" (Pigg, 1994, p. 32). Editors have an obligation to their readership to accept manuscripts that are consistent with their mission and will be useful to the readers. Therefore, editors assume that when they receive a manuscript for review, the author(s) have decided to submit their manuscript for publication based on their knowledge of the uniqueness of the journal reviewing it. Authors who do not carefully consider the nature of each journal but instead just "shop their manuscript around" until they find someone to publish it are acting irresponsibly to the profession. (See Article II of the Code of Ethics in Appendix A.)

Third, duplication contributes to the waste of resources connected to the review process (Pigg, 1994). Often authors are not aware of all that goes into the process of getting a manuscript into print. Typically, when a manuscript is submitted for review, the editor receives it and considers its appropriateness. If inappropriate, it is returned to the author(s) with an explanation. If appropriate, it is then prepared for peer review and sent to (usually) a minimum of three reviewers. The reviewers read and prepare their critiques of the manuscript and send it back to the editor. If the reviewers agree on the disposition of the manuscript (i.e., all or a majority of the reviewers say accept with no revisions, accept with revisions, do not accept, or revise and resubmit for a second review), the editor then notifies the author(s) of the decision, at which time the author(s) take the necessary next step. If reviewers do not agree on the disposition of the manuscript, then there may be a need to involve other reviewers in the process, followed by appropriate notification. Once a manuscript is finally accepted for publication, the publishing staff commits its resources to formatting the manuscript for the printed journal page, proofreading the typeset pages, and printing, binding, and distributing the final product. Duplication doubles these efforts.

Finally, if the manuscript is accepted for publication by two different journals, it can be embarrassing for all associated with the journals and, of course, the author(s) (Pigg, 1994). But even worse than embarrassment, the reputation of the author(s) will be affected, and there is the possibility that the author(s) would be banned from submitting works to these journals in the future.

FRAGMENTATION

The one area associated with publishing that may generate the most discussion about ethical and unethical practices is fragmentation. "**Fragmentation** involves the preparation of multiple manuscripts regarding a topic that could be reported in one paper" (Pigg, 1994, p. 32). Fragmentation has also been referred to as least publishable unit (Broad, 1981), partitioning data (Torabi, 1994), or milking the data (Pigg, 1994). Fragmentation causes so much ethical debate because there are times when fragmentation is appropriate and other times when it is not. For example, most would say that fragmentation is indeed ethical in studies that are large-scale, multifaceted, and long-term in nature, such as the reporting on the data collected as part of the Youth Risk Behavior Surveillance System (YRBSS) (Centers for Disease Control and Prevention, 2009). However, if a researcher conducted a study of fifth graders' health behaviors in a single school district and reported the results of the girl participants in one manuscript and the results of the boys in another, most would see that as unethical fragmentation. Determining what is "ethical fragmentation" is not all that clear; much gray area surrounds the topic, and Pigg (1994) feels that "individual scientists ultimately

must determine to their own satisfaction whether or not they fragmented their work" (p. 33).

PLAGIARISM

We are sure that most, if not all, readers are familiar with plagiarism. Though not always presented as an ethical issue, it is a concern introduced to writers at a very young age. "**Plagiarism**, whether intentional or unintentional, involves the inappropriate and unauthorized use of the 'intellectual property' of others" (Pigg, 1994, p. 33). In other words, one who plagiarizes does not give credit to the original author and therefore presents the material as if it were his or her own (Pigg, 1994). Several steps can be taken to help avoid plagiarizing [the first four come from Pigg (1994)]: (1) keep "complete and accurate bibliographic information on all sources used as references" (p. 34); (2) keep records of all communiqués (i.e., voice, written, electronic, etc.) that include any intellectual property; (3) carefully document sources within the manuscript, giving special attention to direct quotations and paraphrasing; (4) whenever possible, use primary rather than secondary sources (see Chapter 3 for a discussion of these sources); and (5) always err on the side of caution when using the intellectual property of others. If you think it might be unethical, it more than likely is.

AUTHORSHIP

Several ethical issues can arise when determining who is an author and how much recognition each contributor should get (i.e., in what order the authors' names should be listed on the manuscript or final report). It is not uncommon these days, with the complex nature of much of the research being conducted in health education, to have collaborative research efforts. For example, a research project may bring together a person with expert knowledge in health behavior theory, a specialist in research design, and a statistician. Two of the three may contribute equally to the project while the third contributes considerably less but is still a vital component of the project. In addition, a fourth person may help in the writing of the final manuscript. Should all four be listed as authors? Of the two who contribute equally, who should be listed as first author? Unless these and other questions are answered at the outset of a project, a number of ethical conflicts could arise between and among authors.

Most in our profession would agree that in order for a person to be considered a coauthor on a project, he or she must make a meaningful (Pigg, 1994) or substantial contribution to the project (i.e., conception of the study, design of the study, implementation of an intervention, data collection, or data analysis/interpretation) or the publication of the project (i.e., writing, revising, reviewing, and preparing final copy). Authorship is clear-cut in many situations, but a number of gray areas arise, such as in situations where one gives an idea for a project but does nothing else, one proofreads a manuscript and suggests editorial and grammatical changes, or one provides either financial or in-kind support for a project. Making a person a coauthor for contributing (or supporting) in less than a meaningful or substantial way has been referred to as **honorary authorship**, in other words, a way of saying "thank you" for the contribution. A general rule for determining whether one should be an author is that "any author (first or last) should be prepared to explain and defend the project before colleagues" (Pigg, 1994, p. 37) and be able to explain and defend his or her role in the project. Based on these premises, "the practice of courtesy, nominal, and honorary authorship becomes increasingly difficult to defend" (Pigg, 1994, p. 37). In lieu of honorary authorship, individuals should be thanked with a note of acknowledgment, if the journal permits acknowledgments. An example of such a note may read, "The authors would like to thank Ms. Jane Doe for her assistance in the final preparation of the manuscript."

Once it has been determined who is an author, the issue of who should be given the most recog-nition for the work must be addressed. This recognition is given via the ordering of the authors' names on the publication. The first author's name should indicate that that person made the greatest contribution, and the last person's name should indicate that he or she contributed the least. Ahmed, Maurana, Engle, Uddin, and Glaus (1997) have put forth an authorship scale to determine the ordering of authors' names on a publication. Their scale takes into consideration the following components: conception of the idea, design of the research, implementation of the activities to carry out the project, data analysis/interpretation, drafting the article, revising/reviewing the article, and public responsibility (i.e., is accountable for the research and content being reported). With their scale, each of these seven items is given a score of 1 for minimal, 3 for some, and 5 for significant. The summed score of these items determines the order of names on the published article. In the case of a tie score for first author, the conception score would be used to break the tie. If the tie remains after considering conception, they recommend using a committee of others to make the decision. A less formal way of breaking the tie for first author would be to have the person who is willing to coordinate submitting the work for publication (also referred to as the **corresponding author**) become the first author. Ahmed and colleagues (1997) would recommend having the first author break the ties for second and subsequent authorship.

In some long-term studies, with multiple reports produced by the same project or laboratory over an extended period, the project or laboratory director's name goes last on every publication coming out of the project or lab as an acknowledgment of that person's overall contribution to the papers and projects, especially in the life and basic sciences (R. M. Pigg, Jr., personal communication, September 11, 2003).

One final issue associated with authorship arises when faculty and students collaborate on research projects. No matter who is the principal investigator, the faculty member or the student, the general guideline of differentiating between honorary authorship and coauthorship noted above would apply here, too. The ethical issues that arise when determining authorship for the possible publication of a graduate student's thesis or dissertation with the involvement of one student and several faculty members become more complex. We would like to refer the readers to Rienzo (1994), who has presented a good discussion of this ethical issue. Also, please note that Appendix B of this text presents the policy that the Department of Health Education and Behavior at the University of Florida uses to guide their behavior in this area.

EXTERNAL SPONSORSHIP

Externally sponsored research projects include all those in which "a sponsor or benefactor provides funding or other support" (Pigg, 1994, p. 37). Possible ethical issues associated with the sponsorship arise when the "sponsor holds a vested commercial, political, or philosophical interest in the outcome of the research" (Pigg, 1994, p. 37), and the said interest influences the outcomes or reporting of the research. For example, suppose that a chemical company is working to develop a new insect repellent to keep the mosquitoes that carry West Nile virus from biting humans and other animals. The laboratory tests have proved beneficial, and now the chemical company would like to fund a public health department to conduct some field research using the repellent. Obviously, the company is vested in the outcomes of such research in that the outcomes could have a big impact on the marketability of the new repellent. In such a case, the researchers have the ethical obligation to ensure that the sponsorship would not affect the outcomes. In other cases, sponsors have been known to pressure researchers to withhold negative research results or bypass the normal peer review process for dissemination by releasing results through news conferences, press releases, or informational publications (Pigg, 1994).

PROTECTING AGAINST UNETHICAL BEHAVIOR WHEN DISTRIBUTING RESEARCH FINDINGS

Because publishing is such an important component of the research process, researchers need to take the necessary steps to avoid possible ethical issues. Table 6.2 presents a short list of items [developed by Pigg (1994)] that researchers need to consider when distributing their research findings.

Ethical Issues Encountered When Using Animals

Before closing this chapter, we need to speak briefly about the ethical issues associated with the use of animals in research studies. Though few health education studies involve the use of animals, it is indeed possible that someday you may encounter such a situation. As when using human participants, researchers must also abide by

Table 6.2   Avoiding Unethical Behavior Associated with Publishing

1. Familiarize yourself with the topic of ethical conduct in research and professional practice, particularly in publishing, either through formal coursework or self-study;
2. Carefully study and comply fully with the author guidelines for publications to which you submit manuscripts;
3. Agree clearly and specifically with colleagues—in advance—concerning your role, responsibilities, and recognition as a member of a research or writing team;
4. Ask knowledgeable colleagues for advice when you have unanswered questions about appropriate ethical conduct, particularly regarding publishing; and
5. Accept the fact that maintaining personal integrity generally, and professional ethics specifically, resides with each of us as individuals.

Source: Pigg (1994), p. 41.

certain ethical standards when animals are the "study participants." The National Institutes of Health and the U.S. Department of Agriculture have guidelines for the use and care of animals in research studies. In addition, several professional associations have adopted policy statements or guidelines for the care and use of animals in research. Those most closely aligned with health education are the American Psychological Association and the American College of Sports Medicine. These guidelines, along with any special guidelines set forth by local IRBs, should be reviewed prior to planning research involving animals.

Summary

This chapter began with the definitions of the terms ethics, professional ethics, and research ethics. These definitions were followed with a brief history of research ethics by identifying the major events that helped shape research ethics as we know it today. Included were discussions of the Nuremberg Code, the Helsinki Declaration, the Universal Declaration of Human Rights, the Tuskegee Syphilis Study, the National Research Act of 1974 (Public Law 93-348), the *Belmont Report,* and HHS's Title 45, Code of Federal Regulations, Part 46, Protection of Human Subjects (45 CFR Part 46). The need for and use of the Code of Ethics for the Health Education Profession in the research process was also discussed. In addition, this chapter presented a number of different ethical issues that researchers may face while planning their research, during the implementation of their research, and after the research is completed.

Review Questions

1. Define ethics, professional ethics, and research ethics.
2. What significance do each of the following have to the history of research ethics?
   a. Nuremberg Code
   b. Helsinki Declaration
   c. Universal Declaration of Human Rights
   d. Tuskegee Syphilis Study
   e. National Research Act of 1974 (Public Law 93-348)
   f. *Belmont Report*
   g. Title 45, Code of Federal Regulations, Part 46, Protection of Human Subjects
3. Why does a profession need a code of ethics?
4. When was the Code of Ethics for the Health Education Profession developed? What professional group is responsible for its development?
5. What are some of the ethical issues associated with the selection of a research topic?
6. Why is there such a concern about ethical issues surrounding the selection of research participants?
7. What items should be included in valid informed consent?
8. What is the difference between consent and assent?
9. Briefly explain the purpose of an institutional review board (IRB). What institutions typically have IRBs?
10. Explain the difference between exempt from review, expedited review, and full IRB review.
11. Why is deception an ethical concern in research?
12. Describe the difference between active and passive deception and give an example of each.
13. How do anonymity and confidentiality differ?
14. Why is an untreated control group an ethical issue? How can a researcher deal with it?
15. Why is overanalysis of data an ethical concern?
16. What is meant by the term "debriefing"? When would a researcher need to use it?
17. Define each of the following terms and give an example of how each can be avoided:
    a. duplication

b. fragmentation

c. plagiarism

18. Provide examples of how authorship and external sponsorship can lead to ethical dilemmas.

References

Ahmed, S.M., Maurana, C.A., Engle, J.A., Uddin, D.E., & Glaus, K.D. (1997). A method for assigning authorship in multiauthored publications. *Family Medicine,* 29(1), 42–44.

Amschler, D.H., & McKenzie, J.F. (2005). Elementary students' sleep habits and a comparison of their habits to teachers' observation of sleep-related problems: A preliminary study. *Journal of School Health,* 75(2), 50–56.

Babbie, E. (1995). *The practice of social research* (7th ed.). Belmont, Calif.: Wadsworth.

Baumgartner, T.A., & Hensley, L.D. (2006). *Conducting and reading research in health and human performance* (4th ed.). Boston, Mass.: McGraw-Hill.

Bayles, M.D. (1989). *Professional ethics* (2nd ed.). Belmont, Calif.: Wadsworth.

Broad, W.J. (1981). The publishing game: Getting more for less. *Science,* 211, 1137–1139.

Centers for Disease Control and Prevention (CDC). (2009). *YRBSS: Youth risk behavior surveillance system.* Retrieved May 12, 2009, from http://www.cdc .gov/HealthyYouth/yrbs/index.htm.

Cottrell, R.R., Girvan, J.T., & McKenzie, J.F. (2009). *Principles and foundations of health promotion and education* (4th ed.). San Francisco: Benjamin Cummings.

Crowl, T.K. (1993). *Fundamentals of educational research.* Madison, Wis.: WCB/Brown & Benchmark.

Dane, F.C. (1990). *Research methods.* Pacific Grove, Calif.: Brooks/Cole Publishing Company.

Haber, J. (2002). Legal and ethical issues. In G. LoBiondo-Wood & J. Haber (Eds.), *Nursing research: Methods, critical appraisal, and utilization* (5th ed.) (pp. 265–292). St. Louis: Mosby.

Iammarino, N.K., O'Rourke, T.W., Pigg, R.M., & Weinberg, A.D. (1989). Ethical issues in research and publication. *Journal of School Health,* 59(3), 101–104.

Kimmel, A.J. (1988). *Ethics and values in applied social research.* Newbury Park, Calif.: Sage.

Kimmel, A.J. (2007). *Ethical issues in behavioral research: Basic and applied perspectives* (2nd ed.). Malden, Mass.: Blackwell Publishing.

Kolbe, L.J. (1994). The public health perspective. In R.M. Pigg, Jr. (Ed.), *The Eta Sigma Gamma Monograph Series: Ethical issues of scientific inquiry in health science education* (pp. 44–53). Muncie, Ind.: Eta Sigma Gamma.

Kong, D. (1994, February 20). 1800 tested in radiation experiments. *The Boston Globe,* pp. 1, 22.

Levine, R.J. (1988). *Ethics and regulations of clinical research.* New Haven, Conn.: Yale University Press.

McDermott, R.J., & Sarvela, P.D. (1999). *Health education evaluation and measurement: A practitioner's perspective* (2nd ed.). St. Louis: WCB/McGraw-Hill.

McKenzie, J.F., Neiger, B.L., & Thackeray, R. (2009). *Planning, implementing, and evaluating health promotion programs: A primer* (5th ed.). San Francisco, Calif.: Pearson Benjamin Cummings.

Melton, G.B., & Stanley, B.H. (1996). Research involving special populations. In B.H. Stanley, J.E. Sieber, & G.B. Melton (Eds.), *Research ethics: A psychological approach* (pp. 177–202). Lincoln: University of Nebraska Press.

Morrison, E.E. (2009). *Health care ethics: Critical issues for the 21st century* (2nd ed.). Sudbury, Mass.: Jones and Bartlett.

———. (2006). *Ethics in health administration: A practical approach for decision makers.* Sudbury, Mass.: Jones and Bartlett.

National Commission for the Protection of Human Subjects of Biomedical and Behavioral Research. (1979). *The Belmont Report of ethical principles and guidelines for the protection of human subject research.* Retrieved May 9, 2009, from http://ohsr .od.nih.gov/guidelines/belmont.html.

National Institutes of Health (NIH). (2004). *Guidelines for the conduct of research involving human subjects at the National Institutes of Health.* Retrieved May 9, 2009, from http://www.nihtraining.com/ohsrsite/ guidelines/index.html.

———. (2000). *Protomechanics: What is informed consent and assent?* Retrieved May 12, 2009, from http://www.medtran.ru/eng/trials/protomechanics/ch3 .htm, #whatareinformca.

Neutens, J.J., & Rubinson, L. (2010). *Research techniques for the health sciences* (4th ed.). San Francisco, Calif.: Benjamin Cummings.

Norwood, S.L. (2000). *Research strategies for advanced*

practice nurses. Upper Saddle River, N.J.: Prentice-Hall.

Office of Human Subject Research (OHSR). (2006). *Guidelines for writing informed consent documents.* Retrieved May 12, 2009, from http://ohsr.od.nih.gov/info/sheet6.html.

————. (2005). *Title 45 CFR Part 46: Protection of human subjects.* Retrieved May 10, 2009, from http://ohsr.od.nih.gov/guidelines/45cfr46.html.

Pigg, Jr., R.M. (1994). Ethical issues in writing for scientific publications. In R.M. Pigg, Jr. (Ed.), *The Eta Sigma Gamma Monograph Series: Ethical issues of scientific inquiry in health science education* (pp. 31–44). Muncie, Ind.: Eta Sigma Gamma.

Ramsey, P. (1976). The enforcement of morals: Non-therapeutic research on children. *Hastings Center Report, 6,* 21–29.

Richardson, G., & Jose, N. (1983). Ethical issues of school health: A survey. *Health Education,* 14(2), 5–9.

Rienzo, B.A. (1994). Guidelines for ethical faculty/student collaboration in health science education. In R.M. Pigg, Jr. (Ed.), *The Eta Sigma Gamma Monograph Series: Ethical issues of scientific inquiry in health science education* (pp. 18–30). Muncie, Ind.: Eta Sigma Gamma.

Thiroux, J.P. (1995). *Ethics: Theory and practice* (5th ed.). Englewood Cliffs, N.J.: Prentice-Hall.

Torabi, M.R. (1994). Fundamental principles of ethical research in health science education. In R.M. Pigg, Jr. (Ed.), *The Eta Sigma Gamma Monograph Series: Ethical issues of scientific inquiry in health science education* (pp. 6–17). Muncie, Ind.: Eta Sigma Gamma.

United Nations, General Assembly of (UN). (1948). *Universal Declaration of Human Rights.* Retrieved May 10, 2009, from http://www.un.org/en/documents/udhr.

U.S. Department of Health and Human Services (USDHHS). (2004, May 12). *HHS provides guidance on financial relationships and interests in research involving human subjects.* News release. Retrieved May 12, 2009 from http://www.hhs.gov/news/press/2004pres/20040512.html.

————. (2003). *Health information privacy.* Retrieved May 12, 2009, from http://www.hhs.gov/ocr/privacy/index.html.

Westin, A.F. (1968). *Privacy and freedom.* New York: Atheneum.

White, T.I. (1988). *Right and wrong: A brief guide to understanding ethics.* Englewood Cliffs, N.J.: Prentice-Hall.

Winslow, E.H. (1996). Failure to publish research: A form of scientific misconduct? *Heart & Lung,* 25(3), 169–171.

CHAPTER 7 | Selecting Study Participants

Chapter Objectives

After reading this chapter and answering the review questions, you should be able to:

1. Define inclusion and exclusion criteria.
2. Define census and sample.
3. Explain the difference among universe, population, study population, and sample.
4. Describe how a sample can be obtained from a population.
5. Explain the relationship among sample, sampling frame, and sampling unit.
6. Differentiate between probability and nonprobability samples.
7. Define sampling error.
8. Explain the significance of randomization and random selection to probability sampling.
9. Explain how to select a simple random sample (SRS) using a table of random numbers.
10. List seven different methods of probability sampling and seven methods of nonprobability sampling.
11. Determine the appropriate sample size for quantitative and qualitative studies.
12. Briefly explain central limit theorem, precision, and power analysis as they relate to sample size.
13. Explain the relationship of statistical significance and practical significance to the outcomes of a study.

Key Terms

census
central limit theorem (CLT)
cluster (area) sampling
confidence interval (CI)
convenience sampling
effect size (ES)
exclusion criteria
fishbowl sampling
frame
grab sampling
homogeneous sampling
inclusion criteria
judgmental (purposive) sampling
matrix sampling
multistage cluster (area) sampling
nonprobability sampling

nonproportional stratified random
    sample
population
power
power analysis
practical significance
probability sampling
proportional stratified random
    sample
quota sampling
random assignment
random selection
randomization
sample
sampling
sampling bias

sampling error
sampling frame
sampling unit
simple random sample (SRS)
snowball (chain) sampling
standardized effect size
statistical inferences
strata
stratified random sample
study population
systematic sampling
type I error
type II error
universe
volunteer sampling

At this point, you should have a fairly well-developed draft of Chapters I and II of your thesis or dissertation. If you are not writing your chapters as you proceed through this text, you should at least have a good idea of how to develop your Chapters I and II. In addition, you have been exposed to relevant theory and ethical concerns related to research. It is now time to develop your Chapter III, which is typically titled "Methods."

In Chapter III you should very briefly reintroduce your problem and repeat your purpose statement or research question exactly as it was written in Chapter I. This introduction should be no longer than one page. Next, you will need to describe the participants that will be involved in the study. Since you have yet to collect data on the participants, you cannot give exact numbers included in your study or describe any of the participants' demographic characteristics. You do, however, need to describe them in general terms and describe any inclusion or exclusion criteria for participation in the study. For example, "Participants for this study will consist of a random sample of practicing family physicians and internists in a three-county area of East Central Indiana," or "This study will examine the physical fitness levels of telephone service representatives from XXX Company who have worked in their positions for more than one year and have no history of heart disease."

Next, any measures and instrumentation are introduced to the readers. The measures may include physiological measures such as percent body fat or blood pressure, and the instruments used to collect such data would be skinfold calipers and sphygmomanometers. In health education research, the data collected often include one or more of the following measures: demographic variables, awareness variables, cognitive (knowledge) variables, psychosocial variables, skill variables, behavioral variables, environmental variables, health status variables, and/or quality of life (QoL) variables. Such measures are often collected on self-reporting, written questionnaires.

After describing the measures and instrumentation, the next section of Chapter III provides a detailed description of the procedures used in the study. This section, as well as all previous sections, must be written in great detail. Essentially, someone not familiar with your work should be able to read your procedures section and replicate your study. The final section of Chapter III describes how the collected data will be analyzed.

The knowledge and skills needed to write Chapter III are extensive and cannot be contained in one chapter of this book. For that reason, the next five chapters of this text will all focus on aspects of research that may be needed to write Chapter III of a thesis or dissertation. It is these five chapters that provide the nuts and bolts of how to actually conduct appropriate research that will answer your research questions and solve research problems.

In this chapter we will explore the processes used to select participants for a research project. More specifically, we examine how to identify the participants, whether to collect data from all or some of the participants and the advantages and disadvantages associated with each, the various means of selecting just some of the participants, and finally how many participants need to be selected.

Identifying the Participants

At this point of the research process, the problem of your study has been identified and you have had an opportunity to read much of the literature related to the problem. As such, you probably have a pretty good idea of who you would like the participants of your study to be. For example, you may have a problem that deals with clinical health education and know that the participants of your study will be patients at the XXX Clinic. However, since most clinics have patients with a variety of different demographic (i.e., age, ethnicity, race, sex, socioeconomic levels, etc.) and other defining variables (i.e., diagnoses, types of health insurance, time since last visit, etc.), you will need to further identify those individuals to be included in your study. This process is carried out by determining the **inclusion** (those to include participants) and **exclusion** (those to exclude participants) **criteria** for the participants (see Chapter 5 for the discussion on study delimitations). Thus, returning to the clinic population, you may want the participants in your study to *include* anyone who has been admitted to the ABC Hospital in the last 24 months with an ICD-9-CM (*International Classification of Diseases*, 9th edition) code of 410.x (acute myocardial infarction), but you want to *exclude* any individuals who may have a history of hypertension or diabetes, or who had an earlier cardiac event. As you decide on the inclusion/exclusion criteria you want to use, remember that the greater the number of inclusion/exclusion criteria, the more restrictive the selection process becomes and, depending on the number of potential participants, the more difficult it may become to identify the study participants.

Census versus Sample

Once the decision has been made on the inclusion/exclusion criteria, then a decision must be made as to how the specific participants for the study will be selected. Depending on the number of potential participants, your accessibility to these people, and the resources you have to collect data, you may want to try to collect data from all the participants with the given inclusion/exclusion criteria (referred to as a **census**) or from just some of the participants (referred to as a **sample**). Each of the participants is referred to as a sampling unit. A **sampling unit** is the element or set of elements considered for selection as part of a sample (Babbie, 1995). A sampling unit "may be an individual,

an organization, or a geographical area" (Bowling, 2002, p. 166).

Figure 7.1 illustrates the relationship among groups of individuals who have the potential to be in your study. The participants represented in the outer ring of the figure make up the universe. The **universe** is composed of all the participants with the given inclusion/exclusion criteria in an unspecified place and time. For example, our universe may be all Americans over the age of 50 years. The second ring of the figure, called the **population**, represents those individuals in the universe in a specified time and place, such as those Americans over the age of 50 years who are physically located within one of the 50 states on January 1, 2010.

The third ring of Figure 7.1 represents the **study population** (Babbie, 1995). This group of individuals includes those in the population who are accessible to the researcher. For example, suppose that the researcher is interested in collecting data from those in the population by way of the telephone. Any American over 50 years old and located within one of the 50 states on January 1, 2010, is a potential participant, but if a person cannot be contacted by telephone (e.g., does not have a phone or will not share an unlisted telephone number), then he or she is not accessible and is not part of the study population.

Even with a well-defined study population, the number of potential participants may make it impractical to include everyone in the study because of lack of resources to collect the data (i.e., not enough money to make a large number of long-distance calls). In such a case, researchers can take a sample from the study population, which is represented by the innermost ring of Figure 7.1. The process by which the sample is taken is referred to as **sampling**. The major advantage of taking a sample is the reduction in costs for the researcher. For example, using a sample can reduce the amount of researcher time needed to collect data, the cost of postage or telephone calls, travel costs, and paper

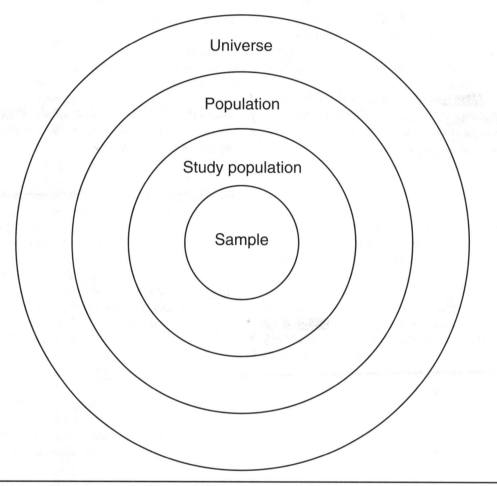

FIGURE 7.1
Relationship of groups of individuals.

Source: McKenzie, J.F., Neiger, B.L., & Thackeray, R. (2009). *Planning, Implementing and Evaluating Health Promotion Programs: A Primer* (5th ed.). San Francisco: Benjamin Cummings. p. 128.

and reproduction costs for a written questionnaire. Also, if the sampling and data collection are done properly, the precision of the data collected from a sample can very closely approximate that of a census.

"If done properly" is a key to sampling and the accuracy of the resulting collected data. Whenever a sample is taken, the researcher must ask how accurately the collected sample data approximates the true value in the study population. In other words, is the sample representative of the study population? For example, suppose we want to find the average age of the junior class at XXX High School. The class has approximately 500 students, but we do not have the resources to do a census and instead select a sample of 50. After asking these 50 people their age and calculating the mean, we find that their average age is 16.7 years. How closely does this mean represent the average age of all 500? The mean age of the sample will deviate from the actual average age of the study population by a certain amount because of chance variations in selecting the sample (Isaac & Michael, 1995). The difference between the sampling estimate (the statistic) and the actual study population value (the parameter) is referred to as the **sampling error** (Backstrom & Hursh-Cesar, 1981), also known as standard error (McDermott & Sarvela, 1999). Sampling error can be caused by a number of determining factors, but it often results from samples that are too small, poorly drawn (known as **sampling bias** or selection bias—see Chapter 9 for a discussion of selection bias as a threat to internal validity), or misrepresentative of important variables in the study population—overrepresenting some and underrepresenting others (Backstrom & Hursh-Cesar, 1981). The ability to generalize the results of data collected from the sample to the study population is greater when the sampling error is reduced, and much of the sampling error can be minimized by how the sample is selected.

Sampling

There are a number of different ways in which a sample can be selected from a study population. These sampling methods are categorized into two major groups—probability and nonprobability sampling. **Probability sampling** uses random selection of participants and assures that each person in the study population has an equal chance and known probability of being selected. There are, however, times when participants cannot be selected at random or there is not a need to select participants at random. In such cases, **nonprobability sampling** methods are used. In this form of sampling, all individuals in the study population do not have an equal chance and a known probability of being selected to participate in the study.

Probability Sampling

As noted in Table 7.1, there are a number of different methods of selecting a probability sample. The common element of all probability sampling

Table 7.1   Summary of Probability Sampling Procedures

Sample	Primary descriptive elements
Simple random	Each subject has an equal chance of being selected if a table of random numbers and a random start rate are used.
"Fishbowl" (or "out of a hat")	Approximates simple random sampling but not as precise. Can be done with or without replacement.
Systematic	Using a list (e.g., membership list or telephone book), subjects are selected at a constant interval (N/n) after a random start.
Nonproportional stratified	The population is divided into subgroups based on key characteristics (strata), and subjects are selected from the subgroups at random to ensure representation of the characteristic.
Proportional stratified	Like the nonproportional stratified random sample, but subjects are selected in proportion to the numerical strength of strata in the study population.
Cluster or area	Random sampling of groups (e.g., teachers' classes) or areas (e.g., city blocks) instead of individuals.
Matrix	The responses of several randomly selected subjects to different items are combined to form the response of one.

Source: McKenzie, J.F., Neiger, B.L., & Thackeray, R. (2009). *Planning, Implementing, and Evaluating Health Promotion Programs: A Primer* (5th ed.). San Francisco: Benjamin Cummings. p. 131. Originally adapted from Babbie (1995); Cozby (1985); Leedy (1993); McDermott and Sarvela (1999).

methods is the **random selection** of participants. Random selection helps ensure the representativeness of the sample to the study population about which generalizations will be made, and it shows that the researcher was unbiased as to which members of the study population were selected for the study (Baumgartner & Hensley, 2006).

Although the use of random selection increases the chances of representativeness of a sample and decreases the chances of sampling bias, in research studies that require more than one group of participants (see Chapter 9), another process called random assignment can be used. **Random assignment** occurs after the selection of participants, and is the assignment of the participants to groups such that each participant has an equal chance of being assigned to any of the groups (Neutens & Rubinson, 2010). The process of randomly assigning research participants to groups is known as **randomization.** The reason for using random assignment is to equalize characteristics among the groups (Baumgartner & Hensley, 2006). That is, if we had 100 participants for a study, 60 male and 40 female, and we randomly assigned them to two groups, we would expect 30 males and 20 females to end up in each of the groups. "It is especially desirable that groups are equivalent prior to the introduction of a treatment condition, thus providing greater confidence in attributing post treatment differences to the treatment. Random assignment is important to internal validity of a study, particularly in experimental research" (Baumgartner & Hensley, 2006, p. 118). (See Chapter 9 for more information about internal validity.)

The process of selecting a probability sample includes the following steps: (1) defining the population, (2) careful definition of the survey population (sampling frame), (3) determining the needed sample size (note: sample size will be discussed later in the chapter), and (4) selection of sample using appropriate procedures (see Table 7.1) (McDermott & Sarvela, 1999; McMillan, 2008).

The procedures for various probability sampling procedures are presented in the paragraphs that follow.

SIMPLE RANDOM SAMPLING

The most basic of the probability sampling methods is selecting a **simple random sample (SRS)**. In order to select an SRS, or for that matter any probability sample, the researcher must have a list of all sampling units in the study population. This list is referred to as the **sampling frame** or just the **frame**. Oftentimes, sampling frames have the names and contact information for all members of the study population (e.g., membership lists, class rosters, patients of a clinic, parents of children enrolled in a certain school or program). But other times the frame may be just the title of an individual or organization, such as the directors of nursing in the 94 local health departments in Indiana or a list of all the service clubs in the county.

Once the sampling frame has been identified for the study, the researcher can proceed with the process of selecting an SRS. It begins with assigning an identification (ID) number with an equal number of digits to each sampling unit in the frame. Suppose, for example, we have a frame of 100 individuals. The first person in the frame would be given the ID number 000. The rest of the individuals in the frame would be assigned consecutive numbers, ending with the last person in the frame receiving the number 099. Next we need to decide how many people we want to select in our sample. The guidelines for determining the sample size will be discussed later in the chapter, but for the purpose of our example here, let's suppose we want a sample size of 10. To select these 10 individuals, we could program a computer to randomly select 10 numbers between 000 and 099, or we could do it manually using a table of random numbers (see Table 7.2).

To use a table of random numbers, we first need to specify in what order we will proceed through the table. Since the table was generated

Table 7.2 Abbreviated Table of Random Numbers

Row/column	A	B	C	D	E
1	74 51	02 19	71 02	33 96	26 61
2	42 75	76 22	23 87	56 54	84 68
3	00 46	37 58	08 55	23 80	22 41
4	74 01	23 19	55 59	49 09	69 82
5	66 22	62 40	15 96	74 90	75 89
6	08 23	34 41	00 67	72 19	71 36
7	89 21	10 22	62 64	78 76	47 32
8	50 27	23 02	13 92	44 13	96 51
9	17 18	01 34	10 98	37 48	93 86
10	02 27	54 69	01 10	28 34	54 31

randomly (by computer), it really does not matter which way we move through it as long as we do so in a consistent manner. So for our example here, suppose we plan to: (1) use the first three digits in the columns of numbers (because we have a frame in which all individuals have a three-digit ID number), (2) proceed down the columns (as opposed to up or across the rows), (3) proceed to the top of the next column to the right when we get to the bottom of a column, and (4) proceed in this same manner until the 10 individuals are selected. To ensure that this process is indeed random, the process must begin with a random start. That is, the researcher cannot just pick the first number at the top of column 1 and proceed down through the column, because every individual in the study population would not have an equal chance of being selected. The researcher can accomplish the random start by closing his or her eyes and pointing to a place on the table of random numbers, and then proceeding through the table in the way that was set forth above.

Finally, we want to speak to the practicality of using an SRS with a large study population. Wang, Fitzhugh, and Westerfield (1995) have stated that the use of an SRS with a large study population "can be tedious and expensive. Under normal circumstances, we will consider a simple random-sampling design practical when the population size is 50,000 or fewer" (p. 53).

FISHBOWL OR "OUT OF A HAT" SAMPLING

Fishbowl or "out of a hat" **sampling**, as it is sometimes called, is similar to simple random sampling but is not as precise. This is a type of sampling that most people probably have used at one time or another. For this method of sampling, everyone in the sampling frame is represented on a piece of paper by a number, name, or other identifying characteristic. The pieces of paper are then placed in a container (i.e., fishbowl, hat) and someone draws them out one at a time until the desired sample size is obtained. To ensure that all have an equal chance of being selected using this method, the pieces of paper should be placed back in the container (called "with replacement") after being drawn so there is always the same number from which to draw. This process is not as precise as selecting an SRS because, typically, the pieces of paper may not have been mixed well or the paper is of different sizes or textures.

SYSTEMATIC SAMPLING

As with simple random sampling, **systematic sampling** also begins with a sampling frame. This process is "systematic" because participants are selected from the frame at a constant interval determined by dividing the study population size *(N)* by the desired sample size *(n)*, beginning with a randomly selected individual from the frame. For example, suppose that we want to choose a sample of 10 health education specialists from our professional association's membership list of 50 (the study population). We start by randomly choosing a number between 00 and 49, such as 24, using a table of random numbers. We then choose every fifth *(N/n = 50/10 = 5)* person (24, 29, 34, 39, 44, 49, 04, 09, 14, and 19) until we have the 10 members for the sample.

STRATIFIED SAMPLING

If it is important that certain groups should be represented in a sample, a stratified random sample can be selected. Such a method would be used if the researchers felt that a certain variable (i.e., size, income, age) might have an influence on the data collected from the participants. A stratified random sample might also be used if it is believed that because of the small numbers of a certain group in the study population, representatives from that group may not be selected using a simple random sample. That is, you may have a study population of 100 participants among which there are only 5 of one group. If you were to select a sample of 10 from the 100, there is a good chance that none of the 5 from the small group might be selected.

Let's look at an example. To select a stratified random sample, the researchers first must divide the study population into groups (or **strata**), and then select a simple random sample from each group. Suppose we were interested in collecting data from school districts in a particular state concerning the number of health elective classes offered in high schools. Based on the review of the literature, we thought the size of the school district (i.e., number of students enrolled) would affect the data we wanted to collect; that is, small districts might have fewer elective classes in general than

large districts. Also, we know that there are only a couple of school districts in the state that have large enrollments. We could then divide the school districts into groups by size, such as small (1–1,000 students), medium (1,001–8,000 students), and large (8,001+).

Once the researchers have decided how many to select from each group, they have to decide whether to conduct a proportional stratified random sample or a nonproportional stratified random sample. A **proportional stratified random sample** would be used if the researchers wanted the sample to mirror, in proportion, the study population—in other words, draw out the school districts in the same proportions at which they are represented in the study population. Suppose in our example that there are 600 small school districts, 350 medium districts, and 50 large districts, and the desired sample size is 100. The researchers would then select simple random samples of 60 small districts, 35 medium districts, and 5 large districts.

A **nonproportional stratified random sample** may be used if the researchers want equal representation from the different groups within the study population. For example, suppose we wanted to collect information about the opinions of college students on a small liberal arts campus (the study population) about a new health policy that was put in place by the administration, and we wanted to hear equally from the different level of students (freshmen: $N = 400$; sophomores: $N = 300$; juniors: $N = 200$; and seniors: $N = 100$) because we thought that the policy would affect each class differently. If a sample size of 100 was desired, we would randomly select (using a simple random sample method) 25 students from each of the classes.

CLUSTER (OR AREA) SAMPLING

Cluster or **area sampling** is a variation of simple random sampling in which the study population is composed of groups (or clusters or areas). Cluster or area sampling is especially useful when the study population is infinite in size, there is no sampling frame of individual participants, or the geographic distribution of the study population is widely scattered (Neutens & Rubinson, 2010). Clusters often used in health education research include sections of students in college/university courses; classes of children in K–12 schools; congregations of churches, temples, mosques, and synagogues; defined patient populations; types of businesses; counties; neighborhoods; service and fraternal groups; or census tracts.

To select a cluster sample, researchers need to create a sampling frame of all the clusters in a study population and then randomly select the desired number of clusters from the frame. For example, suppose you wanted to survey a sample of students enrolled in general education courses on your campus about their health behaviors. Because of confidentiality laws, a sampling frame that included the names of all students enrolled in these courses would not be easy to obtain. Yet using the course offerings booklet, you could create a list (sampling frame) of all the sections of all general education courses offered this semester. Then from this frame, you could select a simple random sample of course sections (clusters).

A more advanced use of the cluster sampling method is the multistage cluster sampling method. **Multistage cluster** (or **area**) **sampling** is a combination of cluster sampling and simple random sampling techniques "in which a series of random selections is made from units of progressively smaller size" (Crowl, 1993, p. 285). This method is often used in situations where the study population is very large and/or spread over a large geographic area. For example, suppose that the state

department of education was interested in measuring the impact of the state's new nutrition education program on fourth graders. There is no sampling frame that includes the names of all the fourth graders in the state, but we do have frames for all the counties in the state, all the school districts in each county, all the elementary schools in each district, and all the fourth-grade classrooms in each elementary school. From the list of counties we would first select a simple random sample of counties. From this list of selected counties, we would select a simple random sample of school districts. From the list of selected school districts, we would select a simple random sample of elementary schools. Finally, from the list of selected elementary schools, we would select a simple random sample of the desired number of fourth-grade classes. We would then administer our data collection process to the children in these classes. (See Figure 7.2 for a schematic diagram of multistage cluster sampling.)

MATRIX SAMPLING

Matrix sampling is a special type of probability sampling that is not often used in health education research. It is used when data collection involves having a large number of participants respond to a large number of questions and when researchers are only interested in making inferences about the study population (as opposed to individuals) (McDermott & Sarvela, 1999). For example, suppose you are interested in collecting data about the health behaviors of college students, and the instrument you want to use is very lengthy, say, 200 questions. Completing such an

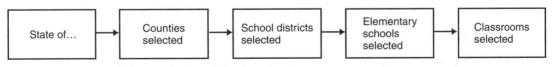

FIGURE 7.2
Schematic diagram of multistage cluster sampling.
Adapted from McDermott & Sarvela (1999).

instrument may take the participants an hour or more. To use matrix sampling you could divide the 200-item instrument into 10 smaller instruments, each containing 20 questions from the original instrument. Now, instead of one participant answering all 200 questions, 10 randomly selected participants will answer 20 questions each. The answers from these 10 participants will comprise one completed response.

Nonprobability Sampling

As noted earlier, there are times when a probability sample cannot be obtained or is not needed. For example, suppose there is no sampling frame available or it is difficult to identify participants with certain inclusion criteria, such as those who have participated in a 10K race at some time in their life. In such cases, researchers can use nonprobability sampling methods to identify the participants. "Participants can be included on the basis of convenience (because they have volunteered or because they are available or can be easily contacted) or because they have a certain characteristic" (McKenzie et al., 2009, p. 131). In other words, "Nonprobability samples are samples that use human judgment in selecting respondents" (Backstrom &

Hursh-Cesar, 1981, p. 64). When using such methods it must be remembered that there is an increased chance of sampling bias and there is no theoretical basis for estimating study population characteristics (Backstrom & Hursh-Cesar, 1981). Having said this, nonprobability sampling methods are often used in qualitative studies (see Chapter 11 for more information on qualitative research), and their power lies in selecting information-rich cases for in-depth study from which researchers can learn the most about issues central to the purpose of the research (Patton, 1990). Table 7.3 contains a summary of nonprobability sampling methods that are discussed in the following sections.

CONVENIENCE SAMPLING
Convenience sampling selects participants based on certain inclusion/exclusion criteria (usually few in number) and their accessibility and proximity to the researcher. It is the weakest of all sampling methods (Isaac & Michael, 1995) yet perhaps the one that is most frequently used (McDermott & Sarvela, 1999). It is used so often because of time and money savings (Neutens & Rubinson, 2010) and the ability to collect large amounts of data in a short period of time (McDermott & Sarvela, 1999). A convenience sample is drawn by selecting

Table 7.3   Summary of Nonprobability Sampling Procedures

Sample	Primary descriptive elements
Convenience	Includes any available subject meeting some minimum criterion, usually being part of an accessible intact group.
Volunteer	Includes any subject motivated enough to self-select for a study.
Grab	Includes whomever investigators can access through direct contact, usually for interviews.
Homogeneous	Includes individuals chosen because of a unique trait or factor they possess.
Judgmental	Includes subjects whom the investigator judges to be "typical" of individuals possessing a given trait.
Snowball	Includes subjects identified by investigators, and any other persons referred by initial subjects.
Quota	Includes subjects chosen in approximate proportion to the population traits they are to "represent."

Source: McDermott, R.J., & Sarvela, P.D. (1999). *Health education evaluation and measurement: A practitioner's perspective* (2nd ed.) New York: McGraw-Hill. p. 271. Reproduced with permission of the McGraw-Hill Companies.

any available participant from an intact group. Examples of intact groups often used by health education specialists are people who have to be at a certain place (e.g., students in a college classroom or employees of a certain company), or people who voluntarily show up at a certain place for a specific reason (e.g., members of a support group or those receiving free flu shots from the health department).

VOLUNTEER SAMPLING

There are times when researchers want to study a specific problem and know who the participants should be based on the inclusion/exclusion criteria, but they are unable to identify the study population. In such cases it is necessary to get volunteers to participate. Thus, the process that results in a sample that includes participants motivated enough to self-select for the study is referred to as **volunteer sampling** (McDermott & Sarvela, 1999). For example, a researcher who was interested in studying the exercise behaviors of people when they have colds would have a hard time identifying a suitable study population. That researcher may place an ad in a local newspaper asking for volunteers to participate, or he or she may ask health care providers to tell their patients with colds about the study in hopes of getting volunteers. Because of the difficulty of getting some people to volunteer in a study, it is not unusual to see researchers offer an incentive (i.e., money, free health care, or a T-shirt) to potential participants to get them to volunteer. For example, clinical research studies of the effects of a new drug on insomnia or indigestion often use volunteer sampling because participants are eager for treatment. The resulting participants of such a sampling method would include those who are really interested in the study, the incentive, or both and are probably not representative of those who do not volunteer.

GRAB SAMPLING

Have you ever been walking through a shopping mall when you spot a person (an interviewer) ahead with a clipboard in hand, asking people questions? Typically, these individuals are asking people questions about their shopping habits as a part of some marketing research. The sampling method the interviewer is using is referred to as grab sampling. **Grab sampling**, also known as chunk sampling (Backstrom & Hursh-Cesar, 1981), includes whomever researchers can access through direct contact (McDermott & Sarvela, 1999) and is representative of no study population.

HOMOGENEOUS SAMPLING

There are certain research problems that pertain only to a very specific group of individuals who possess a unique trait or factor. When such individuals are selected because of this trait, it is referred to as **homogeneous sampling**. Health education researchers might use this sampling method in qualitative studies in which they want to study a specific group of people in detail. An example of such a study would be in-depth interviews with those individuals who have been named the outstanding school health educator in their state during the past 10 years.

JUDGMENTAL SAMPLING

Judgmental or **purposive sampling** is a method in which researchers select participants that they judge to be "typical" of individuals possessing a given trait (McDermott & Sarvela, 1999). For example, an investigator who is conducting evaluation research to determine why employees have enrolled in the worksite health promotion program would want to interview "typical" enrollees to find the answers. Obviously, the greatest concern with this method of sampling is deciding what is typical. A way to deal with this is to try to achieve broad consensus about what is typical so that the selection of participants reflects the criteria (Isaac & Michael, 1995).

SNOWBALL SAMPLING

Snowball or **chain** (Backstrom & Hursh-Cesar, 1981) **sampling** is a multistage sampling method that literally "snowballs" (Neutens & Rubinson, 2010, p. 141). It is a method that is used when it may be difficult to identify the study population because of the sensitive nature of the research problem (e.g., issues dealing with sexuality or diseases that carry a social stigma). It begins when participants with certain characteristics are identified and interviewed. These individuals are then asked if they know others with the same characteristics who could be included in the sample. This second group of people is sought out, interviewed, and asked if they know of others. This process continues until the desired number of participants are contacted.

QUOTA SAMPLING

When researchers want a sample to be representative of certain characteristics of a study population and are unable to select a probability sample, they can use quota sampling. A **quota sample** includes those participants who are "chosen in approximate proportion to the population traits they are to represent" (McDermott & Sarvela, 1999, p. 271). Neutens and Rubinson (2010) have referred to quota sampling as "the nonprobability sampling equivalent of stratified sampling" (p. 141). This sampling method could be used when the population parameters are known and a probability sample cannot be selected. Suppose we know the enrollment in grades 9–12 at a high school is 55% female and 45% male and we want to select a quota sample of 200 students. We would select 110 females (55%) and 90 males (45%). When using this sampling method, as with all other forms of nonprobability sampling, the researchers "know nothing of sampling error and precision findings" (Backstrom & Hursh-Cesar, 1981, p. 65).

Determining Sample Size for Quantitative Studies

When preparing to select a sample from a study population (sampling frame), researchers must turn their attention to the size of the sample. There are two reasons why researchers need to be concerned about the size of a sample. "The first has to do with how large the sample must be to be an accurate representation of the population from which it was drawn" (Crowl, 1993, p. 280); that is, does the sample represent the study population so that reliable **statistical inferences** (estimating parameters from statistics) (Backstrom & Hursh-Cesar, 1981) can be made about the study population? In other words, will the characteristics identified in the sample be the same (or very similar) to those of the study population? The second has to do with how many research participants are needed to obtain a statistically meaningful result (Kuzma & Bohnenblust, 2005). In general, the larger the sample, the smaller the sampling error (other things being equal) and the greater the chance of getting statistically significant results (Borg & Gall, 1989; Bowling, 2002).

In most research projects, sample size is determined by balancing both statistical (i.e., probability level, power analysis, type of data) and practical (i.e., financial and time restrictions, manageability of participants) considerations (Borg & Gall, 1989; Bowling, 2002; Isaac & Michael, 1995; Neutens & Rubinson, 2010). "An ideal study would have a sample large enough to represent the population so generalization may occur, yet small enough to save time and money as well as to reduce the complexity of data analysis" (Neutens & Rubinson, 2010, p. 141). There are certain times and factors that require a large sample size (see Table 7.4). However, there are also times when one can or must use a small (or smaller) sample, such as when resources are limited, when studies are exploratory or pilot in nature, when in-depth case studies are being used (Isaac & Michael, 1995), or when other time-consuming data collection techniques are used (Borg & Gall, 1989).

It should be noted that in many studies finding statistical significance is important; however, statistical significance may not mean that the results have **practical significance**. For example, a researcher may be comparing two large groups of individuals on their knowledge of HIV/AIDS. On

Table 7.4   Times When Larger Samples Are Needed

- When the sampling units are highly heterogeneous on variables being studied
- When researchers want the sample estimates to be more precise
- When small differences in results (effect sizes) are anticipated
- When survey research methods (versus experimental methods) are used
- When high attrition (i.e., mortality, dropouts, nonrespondents) among the sampling units is expected
- When a large number of uncontrolled variables (also known as extraneous or confounding variables) are present
- When the samples being studied must be broken into subsamples
- When the level of statistical significance, statistical power, or both must be high
- When the reliable measures of the dependent variable are not available or when there is great variation in the dependent variable
- When a larger number of variables are being analyzed

Created from information in Backstrom & Hursh-Cesar (1981); Baumgartner & Hensley (2006); Borg & Gall (1989); Isaac & Michael (1995); Norwood (2000).

a 100-point test, the mean score of one group may be just 1–2 points higher than the mean of the second group. These scores may turn out to be statistically different, but what is the practical significance of having knowledge scores that are 2 points apart? How much more HIV/AIDS knowledge does the group with the higher score have than the one with the lower score? We believe most would say for all practical purposes, none. From a practical perspective, the 2-point difference would not indicate a need to develop HIV/AIDS educational programs for the lower-scoring group.

With this general understanding of the factors that affect sample size, let's now look at the specifics of determining sample size. There are three major theoretical considerations that form the basis for determining sample size for quantitative studies: central limit theorem, precision and reliability, and power analysis (Norwood, 2000). Researchers could make a case for selecting their sample sizes on any of the three.

Central Limit Theorem

The **central limit theorem (CLT)** "states that the distribution of means of samples taken from any population will tend toward the normal distribution as the size of the sample increases" (Bowling, 2002, p. 179). Further, it has been proven mathematically (Norwood, 2000) that the means of the samples approximate the mean of the study population with sample sizes of 30 or more (Bowling, 2002). Stated another way, the CLT affirms that the mean of a randomly selected sample of 30 or more sampling units approximates the study population's mean for a specified characteristic (Hinkle, Wiersma, & Jurs, 1988). For example, suppose we calculated the average age of a random sample of 30 students selected from a group of 200 students to be 12.5 years old (the statistic). According to the CLT, we could expect the mean age of the study population to be approximately 12.5 years old (the parameter). Although the CLT provides the researcher with a rationale for using a sample size of 30 per variable or group (Norwood, 2000), remember that sampling error is reduced (i.e., the difference between the parameter and statistic) and representativeness is increased as the sample size increases. "In other words, '30 per variable' should always be considered only the minimum acceptable size for accurately describing a characteristic of a population" (Norwood, 2000, p. 224).

Precision and Reliability

Precision is a statistical statement of how close the statistic (value in the sample) is to the parameter (value of the characteristic in the study population). Determining the precision of a statistic is based on two factors: (1) "how much error we can tolerate before the estimate might lead us astray; and (2) how confident we must be that the sampling error is not greater than we specify" (Backstrom & Hursh-Cesar, 1981, p. 72). The first factor, "how much error," refers to how much sampling error we can tolerate. (Note: Remember that sampling error is measured by calculating the standard error.) How close to the population parameter do we want the statistic to be? Within 1%? 2%? 5%? 10%? The size of the standard error (SE) is a function of the study population parameter and the sample size. Suppose we were interested in calculating the sampling error for a survey we are conducting using a probability sample of 400 college students to determine if they were in favor of having smoke-free residence halls. An estimate of the sampling error can be calculated by taking the square root of $(P \times Q/n)$, where P is equal to some proportion (e.g., those who are in favor), Q is equal to $1 - P$, and n represents the sample size (McDermott & Sarvela, 1999). Since we have no prior indication of whether the students are in favor of or against smoke-free residence halls, we assume they will be evenly split at 50% for and 50% against. Using the 50–50 split is common practice because researchers often are unable to estimate in advance the study population proportions. "Furthermore, surveys are most often interested in a number of variables to be estimated, rather than a single variable. We can seldom predict the population proportions on these variables before the survey" (Wang *et al.,* 1995, p. 54). Using the value 0.50 for P is a conservative approach that will "obtain the maximum sample size that will accommodate all ranges of population-proportion estimates" (Wang *et al.,* 1995, p. 54). Thus, returning to our example and using $P = 0.50$, $Q = 0.50$, and $n = 400$, the following calculations can be made:

a. $(P \times Q)$ is: $0.50 \times 0.50 = 0.25$
b. $(P \times Q/n)$ is: $0.25/400 = 0.000625$
c. The square root of 0.000625 is: 0.025
d. $0.025 \times 100\%$ is: SE of 2.5%

So what does an SE of 2.5% mean? It means, in this example, using a sample size of 400, any findings we get studying the sample (the statistic) would be within 2.5% of the actual value (the parameter) in the population. If we repeat the SE calculations with a sample of 800, the SE would be 1.77%. The larger sample size decreases the SE. Likewise, if the SE were calculated with a sample size of 200, the SE would be 3.54%. The smaller sample size would increase the SE.

The second factor in precision is how confident we are that the standard error is not greater than what we calculated. The indication of our confidence is expressed using a **confidence interval (CI)**. "In practical terms, a CI calculated from a sample is interpreted as the range of values which contains the true population value with the probability specified" (Bowling, 2002, p. 180). For example, if the 95% CI for the scores on a cancer knowledge test for a sample of college students was 68–83%, there is a 95% chance that the true study population is somewhere between 68% and 83%. Or stated another way, the mean score for 95% of all samples of the same size randomly selected from the study population of college students would be between 68% and 83% (Norwood, 2000). The two most commonly used CIs in health education research are 95% and 99%. They are calculated as follows (Bowling, 2002):

$$CI_{95} = \text{sample estimate} \pm (1.96 \times SE)$$
$$CI_{99} = \text{sample estimate} \pm (2.58 \times SE)$$

"The 1.96 value reflects that, in a normal distribution, 95% of all the cases lie within ± 1.96 standard deviations of the mean. The 2.58 value reflects that 99% of all the cases lie within ± 2.58 standard deviations of the mean. In both equations, $SE = sd/\sqrt{n}$" (Norwood, 2000, pp. 345–346). Using the SE calculated in the example above about the survey of 400 college students and their opinions about smoking in the residence halls (remember that we are estimating that 50% would be in favor of no smoking in residence halls), the following CI_{95} would be calculated:

$$CI_{95} = 50 \pm (1.96 \times 2.5)$$
$$CI_{95} = 50 \pm 4.9$$
$$CI_{95} = 45.1–54.9$$

Before leaving our discussion of confidence intervals, we wanted to note that CIs "are generally used in estimations of sample size for descriptive research (e.g., social, health and epidemiological surveys)" (Bowling, 2002, p. 168).

Power Analysis (or Calculation)

As has been noted earlier, the ability to find a statistical difference between groups in a research study is at least in part a function of both the size of the difference of the measure and the number of participants being studied. No researcher wants to conduct a study that may have a difference between the groups, but the difference goes undetected because there are not enough participants in the study for the statistical test being used to detect the difference. To help ensure that the sample sizes are large enough to detect relationships of a specific magnitude (also referred to as effect size), researchers can use a statistical technique called **power analysis**. "Power analysis enables a researcher to determine, based on the assumption that the research hypothesis is true, the number of subjects needed to give the hypothesis a chance of being accepted" (Norwood, 2000, p. 224). Such a power analysis would be considered an a priori analysis; that is, the power analysis was conducted before the study took place. A power analysis can also be calculated post hoc (after the study) for studies that have not found a difference to "validate the accuracy of their findings—and to excuse the inability to detect an intervention's effectiveness" (Norwood, 2000, pp. 224–225).

To conduct a power analysis to determine the appropriate sample size, researchers must consider the following factors: type I (alpha or α) error, type II (beta or β) error, power $(1 - \beta)$, effect size, and the directionality/nondirectionality ("one-tailed"/"two-tailed") of the statistical test. Each of these factors is discussed below.

The rejection of a null hypothesis by researchers when the hypothesis is actually true is known as a **type I error**. (See Chapter 5 for a discussion of hypotheses.) In other words, the data generated in a study suggests that there is a statistical difference in reality there is no difference. If, on the other hand, researchers fail to reject a null hypothesis that is false, it is referred to as a **type II error**. That is, if the data generated in a study suggests there is no statistical difference when in reality there is a difference, a type II error has been committed (see Figure 7.3)

To minimize the probability of making type I and II errors, researchers can subjectively set the alpha and beta levels, respectively, for use with the various statistical tests of significance at levels with which they feel comfortable. But because type I and type II errors are inversely related (i.e., as the risk of one goes down, the risk of the other goes up), it makes setting the levels a balancing act. As we noted in Chapter 5, the alpha level (sometimes referred to as the level of significance or the p level) in health education research is typically set at 0.05 (and sometimes 0.01 but rarely at 0.001), indicating that researchers want to be certain 95% of the time that they will not commit a type I error. The literature suggests (Windsor, Baranowski, Clark, & Cutter, 1994) setting the type II error rate at four times the alpha rate. Thus, with an alpha level of 0.05, the beta error rate would be 0.20. "This means the probability of failing to detect a relationship that actually exists is 20%" (Norwood, 2000, p. 225).

The next factor that needs to be considered when conducting a power analysis is power. The **power** of a statistical test is the probability of rejecting the null hypothesis when it is actually false (Isaac & Michael, 1995)—in other words, having a statistical test that is able to detect a difference when one exists (Valente, 2002) or the

The Truth

		Null hypothesis (H_0) is true	Null hypothesis (H_0) is not true
Researcher's conclusion based on the results of test of significance	Not statistically significant (fail to reject null)	Correct conclusion	Type II error
	Statistically significant (reject null)	Type I error	Correct conclusion

FIGURE 7.3
Illustration of type I and type II errors.

probability of making a correct decision (Stevens, 2002). Power is calculated by subtracting the probability of making a type II or beta error from one (i.e., $1 - \beta$). Therefore, with an alpha level of 0.05, beta would be 0.20, and the power would be 0.80. Having a "power of .80 means there is an 80% probability of detecting a relationship when one exists" (Norwood, 2000, p. 225).

The fourth factor to consider when conducting a power analysis is the effect size. **Effect size (ES or Δ) is the magnitude of a difference between groups or between the sample and the population.** Effect size is calculated differently for each type of statistical test (see Table 7.5 for examples) and is often determined based upon previous research studies. However, when such studies are not available, Cohen (1988) has offered the **standardized effect size** (expressed in standard deviation units) of small, medium, and large. Cohen (1992) provided the following rationale for the operational definitions of small, medium, and large values:

> My intent was that medium ES represent an effect likely to be visible to the naked eye of a careful observer. (It has since been noted in effect-size surveys that it approximates the average size of observed effects in various fields.) I set small ES to be noticeably smaller than medium but not so small as to be trivial. I set large ES to be the same distance above medium as small was below it. (p. 156)

If researchers are unsure of the expected effect size, Hinkle and colleagues (1988) recommend using medium.

Before leaving the discussion of effect sizes, it should be noted that there has been a call for the standard use of effect sizes in the health education literature. Buhi (2005) has recommended that calculating and reporting of effect sizes should be one of three practices (the other two being using judgment to assign importance to research results and providing evidence of result replicability) used by health education specialists in addition to reporting the results of statistical significance testing. In addition, Watkins, Rivers, Rowell, Green, and Rivers (2006) have recommended that effect sizes be both reported and interpreted in health education research findings. These authors state that such procedures would allow the consumers

Table 7.5   Approximate Effect Size for Selected Statistical Tests

Test	Small	Medium	Large
	Effect size		
1. m_A vs. m_B for independent means	0.20	0.50	0.80
2. Significance of product-moment r	0.10	0.30	0.50
3. r_A vs. r_B for independent rs	0.10	0.30	0.50
4. $P = 0.5$ and the sign test	0.05	0.15	0.25
5. P_A vs. P_B for independent proportions	0.20	0.50	0.80
6. Chi-square for goodness of fit and contingency	0.10	0.30	0.50
7. One-way analysis of variance	0.10	0.25	0.40
8. Multiple and multiple partial correlation	0.02	0.15	0.35

Source: This table is derived from Cohen (1992).

Note: For formulas to create these effect sizes and effect sizes for other statistical tests, see Cohen (1988).

of the research to more easily interpret and understand the results.

The final factor to consider in a power analysis is the directionality of the statistical test, that is, whether to use a one-tailed (directional) or a two-tailed (nondirectional) test (Hurlburt, 2003). A one-tailed test is used only when the researcher is sure about how the independent variable will affect the dependent variable (Norwood, 2000). Often researchers do not know what the effect of the independent variable will be on the dependent variable, so a two-tailed test is recommended in order to detect "differences in 'both directions,' or

values both greater and less than the hypothesized value" (Norwood, 2000, p. 226).

Knowing the above factors, researchers can calculate a power analysis, but many statistics books and Web sites make it much easier by presenting a variety of "power analysis" tables for various statistical tests. Because this is not a statistics textbook, we present Tables 7.6, 7.7, and 7.8 to provide the reader with an idea of what to expect from such books.

Table 7.6 is the type of table researchers would use when conducting a descriptive survey study and trying to estimate what proportion of the

Table 7.6   Sample Sizes for Studies Describing Population Proportions When the Population Size Is Known

Population size/sample size for precision of	± 1	± 3	± 5
	95% confidence interval		
500	*	*	222
1,000	*	*	286
3,500	*	843	359
5,000	*	909	370
10,000	5,000	1,000	385
25,000	7,143	1,064	394
100,000	9,091	1,099	398
$\rightarrow \infty$	10,000	1,111	400

* = In these cases the assumption of normal approximation is poor, and the formula used to derive them does not apply.

Source: This table is derived from Yamane (1973).

Table 7.7   Sample Sizes for the One-Sample Case for the Mean

Directional ("one-tailed") test for numerical (interval or ratio) data

Effect size/power	alpha = 0.05			alpha = 0.01		
	0.75	0.80	0.90	0.75	0.80	0.90
0.20	135	155	215	226	251	326
0.50	23	27	37	39	43	55
0.80	11	12	17	17	19	23

Nondirectional ("two-tailed") test for numerical (interval or ratio) data

Effect size/power	alpha = 0.05			alpha = 0.01		
	0.75	0.80	0.90	0.75	0.80	0.90
0.20	174	197	263	265	292	372
0.50	30	34	44	46	50	63
0.80	13	15	19	20	22	27

Source: This table is derived from Hinkle, Oliver, & Hinkle (1985).

study population possesses a specific characteristic. For example, suppose a researcher is interested in surveying the members of a professional health education association to estimate the proportion of members who were in favor of the various components of a new strategic plan for the association. How many of the 10,000 members of the association would have to be sampled in order for the researcher to be 95% confident that the estimate is within ±5% of the total membership's position? As can be seen in Table 7.6, the researcher would need a sample of 385.

Table 7.7 is the type of table a researcher would use when conducting a study with a pretest–posttest no comparison group design in which the pretest score of the group is compared to its posttest score. For example, suppose a researcher is interested in studying the impact of a diabetes education program on the diabetes knowledge of individuals recently diagnosed with type II diabetes. Using a diabetes knowledge test based on a 100-point scale, how many participants would be needed to determine the

average change in knowledge from pretest to posttest with the alpha set at 0.05 (one-tailed), power at 0.80, and a medium effect size of 0.50? As can be seen in Table 7.7, the researcher would need a sample of 27.

Table 7.8 is the type of table a researcher would use when conducting a study with a pretest–posttest comparison group design in which the means of the two groups would be compared. For example, suppose a researcher wants to conduct a study to determine the impact of a posteducation telephone follow-up on the exercise behavior of participants who attend the education sessions. In this two-group study, the experimental group would get the telephone call after the education session, and those in the comparison group would not get the telephone call but rather the "usual care" of a motivating follow-up letter from the instructor of the educational sessions. How many participants would be needed in each group using an alpha of 0.05 (two-tailed), power of 0.80, and a medium effect of 0.50? As can be seen in Table 7.8, the researcher would need a sample of 62.

Table 7.8   Sample Size for Studies Comparing Means

For power = 0.80, alpha = 0.05, nondirectional ("two-tailed")

		alpha = 0.05			alpha = 0.01		
Number of comparison groups	Effect size =	0.50	0.75	1.0	0.50	0.75	1.0
2		62	29	17	93	43	25
3		78	35	20	112	52	29
4		88	40	23	124	56	32
5		96	43	25	134	60	34
6		103	47	27	144	64	36
7		110	50	29	150	68	38
8		117	52	30	156	71	40

Note: The sample size is per group.

Source: This table is derived from Hinkle & Oliver (1983).

Determining Sample Size for Qualitative Studies

Unlike determining the sample size for quantitative studies using specific procedures based, in large part, on probability theory, determining the sample size for qualitative studies is much less structured and based more upon the research approaches (Patton, 1990). In fact, "there are no rules for sample size in qualitative inquiry" (Patton, 1990, p. 184), but as when determining the sample size for quantitative studies, the researcher has to balance the need for appropriate data with the resources necessary to collect it.

As a general rule, qualitative studies typically have many fewer participants than quantitative studies. Quantitative studies typically collect a limited amount of data from a large number of participants, but qualitative studies collect much more detailed data from a small number of people. In qualitative studies, samples "are judged by the extent to which they are informationally representative rather than statistically representative" (Norwood, 2000, p. 234). Patton (1990) has indicated that the sample size in qualitative studies should depend on: (1) what the researchers want to know,

(2) the purpose of the study, (3) what is at stake based upon the outcomes of the study, (4) what will be useful data, (5) what will have credibility with others interested in the study, and (6) what can be accomplished with the available time and resources. In other words, the sample size is left to the judgment of the researcher. For example, suppose a researcher is interested in knowing why senior citizens from a specific community are not obtaining the free influenza vaccines from the county health department. It would be possible to draw a probability sample of seniors to try to get answers to the research question, if a sampling frame existed. But if a frame did not exist, a nonprobability snowball sampling method could be used to identify a small number of seniors that could lead to data to get more seniors immunized. You might be saying, "That sounds good, but still how many seniors need to be identified and interviewed?" The consensus answer seems to be the number when the data being collected reaches a point of redundancy (Lincoln & Guba, 1985) or saturation (Norwood, 2000; Sandelowski, 1996; Strauss & Corbin, 1990). In our example, that would mean the sample is large enough when the researcher collecting the data keeps hearing the

same reasons why seniors are not getting the shots or no new information is forthcoming (McMillan, 2008).

One final comment about the size of the sample in a qualitative study: Patton (1990) states that "in the end, sample size adequacy, like all aspects of research, is subject to peer review, consensual validation, and judgment. What is crucial is that the sampling procedures and decisions be fully described, explained, and justified so that the information users and peer reviewers have the appropriate context for judging the sample" (p. 186).

Summary

In this chapter we presented information on the processes used to select participants for a research project. We began the chapter by discussing how to identify the priority population and inclusion/exclusion criteria. That was followed by a discussion of whether to collect data from all (census) or some (sample) of those in the priority population. With the discussion of samples came an explanation of probability and nonprobability samples, the advantages and disadvantages associated with each, and an explanation of the various means of selecting such samples. The remaining portion of the chapter presented three theoretical considerations (central limit theorem, precision and reliability, and power analysis) for determining sample size for a quantitative study. As part of the discussion of power analysis, type I and II errors, effect size, and directionality were discussed. Finally, we presented a brief discussion on how to determine the sample size for a qualitative study.

Review Questions

1. What is meant by the terms inclusion and exclusion criteria? Give an example of each.

2. What is the difference between a census and a sample?

3. Explain the relationship among universe, population, study population, and sample.

4. What is the difference between probability and nonprobability samples?

5. Briefly explain how to select a simple random sample (SRS) using a table of random numbers.

6. Briefly describe what is meant by probability sampling and then list at least five different methods of selecting a probability sample.

7. Briefly describe what is meant by nonprobability sampling and give an example of when it would be appropriate to use a nonprobability sampling method.

8. What are the three different theoretical considerations that can be used to determine an appropriate sample size for quantitative studies?

9. What are the major factors to consider when calculating a power analysis?

10. Briefly describe the major concerns associated with determining sample size for qualitative studies.

References

Babbie, E. (1995). *The practice of social research* (7th ed.). Belmont, Calif.: Wadsworth.

Backstrom, C.H., & Hursh-Cesar, G. (1981). *Survey research* (2nd ed.). New York: Wiley.

Baumgartner, T.A., & Hensley, L.D. (2006). *Conducting and reading research in health and human performance* (4th ed.). Boston: McGraw-Hill.

Borg, W.R., & Gall, M.D. (1989). *Educational research* (5th ed.). New York: Longman.

Bowling, A. (2002). *Research methods in health: Investigating health and health services* (2nd ed.). Buckingham, UK: Open University Press.

Buhi, E. (2005). The insignificance of "significance" tests: Three recommendations for health education researchers. *American Journal of Health Education*, 36(2), 109–112.

Cohen, J. (1992). A power primer. *Psychological Bulletin,* 112(1), 155–159.

————. (1988). *Statistical power analysis for behavioral sciences* (2nd ed.). Hillsdale, N.J.: Lawrence Erlbaum Associates.

Cozby, P.C. (1985). *Methods in behavioral research* (3rd ed.). Palo Alto, Calif.: Mayfield.

Crowl, T.K. (1993). *Fundamentals of educational research.* Madison, Wis.: WCB/Brown & Benchmark.

Hinkle, D.E., & Oliver, J.D. (1983). How large should the sample be? A question with no simple answer? Or. . . . *Educational and Psychological Measurement,* 43(4), 1051–1060.

Hinkle, D.E., Oliver, J.D., & Hinkle, C.A. (1985). How large should the sample be? Part II—the one-sample case for survey research. *Educational and Psychological Measurement,* 45(2), 271–280.

Hinkle, D., Wiersma, W., & Jurs, S. (1988). *Applied statistics for the behavioral sciences* (2nd ed.). Boston: Houghton Mifflin.

Hurlburt, R.T. (2003). *Comprehending behavioral statistics* (3rd ed.). Belmont, Calif.: Wadsworth/Thomson Learning.

Isaac, S., & Michael, W.B. (1995). *Handbook in research and evaluation* (3rd ed.). San Diego, Calif.: Educational and Industrial Testing Services.

Kuzma, J.W., & Bohnenblust, S.E. (2005). *Basic statistics for the health sciences* (5th ed.). Boston: McGraw-Hill.

Leedy, P.D. (1993). *Practical research: Planning and design* (5th ed.). New York: Macmillan.

Lincoln, Y.S., & Guba, E.G. (1985). *Naturalistic inquiry.* Newbury Park, Calif.: Sage.

McDermott, R.J., & Sarvela, P.D. (1999). *Health education evaluation and measurement: A practitioner's perspective* (2nd ed.). St. Louis: WCB/McGraw-Hill.

McKenzie, J.F., Neiger, B.L., & Thackeray, R. (2009). *Planning, implementing, and evaluating health promotion programs: A primer* (5th ed.). San Francisco: Benjamin Cummings.

McMillan, J.H. (2008). *Educational research fundamentals for the consumer* (5th ed.). Boston: Pearson Education, Inc.

Neutens, J.J., & Rubinson, L. (2010). *Research techniques for the health sciences* (4th ed.). San Francisco: Benjamin Cummings.

Norwood, S.L. (2000). *Research strategies for advanced practice nurses.* Upper Saddle River, N.J.: Prentice-Hall.

Patton, M.Q. (1990). *Qualitative evaluation and research methods.* Thousand Oaks, Calif.: Sage.

Sandelowski, M. (1995). Sample size in qualitative research. *Research in nursing and health,* 18, 179–183.

Stevens, J. (2002). *Applied multivariate statistics for the social sciences* (4th ed.). Mahwah, N.J.: Lawrence Erlbaum Associates.

Strauss, A., & Corbin, J. (1990). *Basic qualitative research: Grounded theory procedures and techniques.* Newbury Park, Calif.: Sage.

Valente, T.W. (2002). *Evaluating health promotion programs.* New York: Oxford University Press.

Wang, M.Q., Fitzhugh, E., & Westerfield, R.C. (1995). Determining sample size for simple-random surveys. *Health Values,* 19(3), 53–56.

Watkins, D.C., Rivers, D., Rowell, K.L., Green, B.L., & Rivers, B. (2006). A closer look at effect sizes and their relevance to health education. *American Journal of Health Education*, 37(2), 103–108.

Windsor, R., Baranowski, T., Clark, N., & Cutter, G. (1994). *Evaluation of health promotion, health education, and disease prevention programs* (2nd ed.). Mountain View, Calif.: Mayfield.

Yamane, T. (1973). *Statistics: An introductory analysis* (3rd ed.). New York: Harper & Row.

CHAPTER 8 | **Instrumentation**

Chapter Objectives

After reading this chapter and answering the review questions, you should be able to:

1. Define measurement and measurement instrument.
2. Explain the differences between the four levels of measurement.
3. Write instrument items that create data for each of the different levels of measurement.
4. Explain what is meant by psychometric properties and why they are so important in measurement.
5. Define validity and identify at least four ways to estimate it.
6. Define reliability and identify at least four ways to estimate it.
7. Differentiate between sensitivity and specificity.
8. Provide a brief explanation of structured, unstructured, and hybrid instrument items.
9. Write instrument items that can measure knowledge, attitudes, and behavior.
10. Provide a brief explanation of Bloom's taxonomy and its use in measuring the cognitive domain.
11. Identify at least three different methods for measuring attitudes.
12. State the three primary ways of measuring skills and behavior.
13. Describe what is meant by authentic assessment.
14. Describe the steps one can follow when identifying, obtaining, and evaluating existing measurement instruments.
15. List the steps one can follow when creating a new measurement instrument.

Key Terms

authentic assessment
Bloom's taxonomy
cognitive domain
concurrent validity
construct validity
content validity
convergent validity
criterion-related validity
cultural competence
cultural sensitivity
discriminant validity
face validity
fairness
health-related quality of life (HRQoL)
hybrid items
instrumentation

internal consistency reliability
interrater reliability
interval measures
intrarater reliability
Kappa
measurement
measurement instrument
nominal measures
observation
obtrusive observation
operationalization
ordinal measures
parallel forms reliability
predictive validity
proxy (indirect observation)
psychometric properties
qualitative measures

quality of life (QoL)
quantitative measures
rater (observer) reliability
ratio measures
reliability
self-report
sensitivity
specificity
structured (or selected-response) items
test–retest (stability) reliability
unobtrusive observation
unstructured (or constructed-response) items
validity
variable

In the previous chapter, we began our discussion of the "Methods" chapter (Chapter III) of a thesis or dissertation by examining how research participants are selected and how researchers know when they have enough participants to create meaningful results. In this chapter, we are going to discuss another important aspect of the "Methods" chapter, instrumentation. More specifically, we will define instrumentation, measurement, and measurement instrument. We will also present background information on levels of measurement, psychometric properties of measurement instruments, and how to measure variables of interest. Finally, we will present step-by-step approaches for identifying, obtaining, and evaluating existing measurement instruments and explain how to create an original measurement instrument.

Measurement

Measurement has been defined as the process of assigning numbers or labels to objects, events, or people according to a particular set of rules (Kerlinger, 1986). Sometimes, the particular set of rules seems very logical and orderly, as when measuring the weight of an object in pounds. Other times, the set of rules may seem arbitrary, as when assigning the number 1 to those who have poor fitness, 2 to those with average fitness, and 3 to those with good fitness. Since there are different rules for assigning numbers or labels, the same number or label can have a different meaning, depending on the rules used to make the assignments (Grimm, 1993). Thus, researchers need to "clearly specify the objects to be measured, the numbers to use, and the rules by which the numbers are assigned to the objects" (Green & Lewis, 1986, p. 58).

In research, we are interested in measuring variables. As was noted in Chapter 5 of this book, a **variable** is defined as "a characteristic or attribute of an individual or an organization that can be measured or observed by the researcher and varies among individuals or organizations studied"

(Creswell, 2002, p. 129). Further, a variable "can take on any of several or many different values. For example, height is a variable (defined as the number of inches a person is tall). It takes on the value 70 inches when John is measured and 64 inches when Mary is measured" (Hurlburt, 2003, p. 15). Seventy and 64 inches are the results of assigning numbers according to a particular set of rules and are referred to as data (*data* is plural and *datum* is singular). (See Table 8.1 for different ways of classifying data.) The item(s) we use to measure a variable of interest (in the example above, a measuring tape calibrated in inches) is referred to as the **measurement instrument** (or tool or data collection instrument or just instrument). You may hear someone say the word "instrumentation" when referring to measurement instruments. **Instrumentation** is a collective term used to describe all measurement instruments used in a study.

Measurement instruments can take many different forms. For example, instruments could include paper–pencil or electronic questionnaires, a piece of equipment such as skinfold calipers or sphygmomanometers, or human beings as they observe the behaviors of others, such as instructors watching students perform CPR on mannequins. Other types of instruments commonly used in health education research include observation procedures, interview schedules, structured diaries, logbooks, standard forms for recording data from records (i.e., transferring data from medical records), or tests (Bowling, 2002; Isaac & Michael, 1995).

Table 8.1   Classifications of Data

Class	Descriptors
Quantitative data	Numerical in nature; amount or quantity
Qualitative data	Narrative or words; difference in quality
Primary data	Collected by the researcher
Secondary data	Available from another source
Raw data	Original; uncategorized
Categorical data	Categorized

When deciding on the measurement instrument to be used in a study, researchers need to consider the type of data that will be generated from the instrument, what exactly they want to measure, and what form the instrument will take.

Levels of Measurement

A fundamental question of measurement is deciding how something should be measured (McDermott & Sarvela, 1999). In other words, what particular set of rules will be used to describe the variable? For example, suppose researchers were interested in finding out how many pounds participants weighed. They could put the participants on a scale to measure them, they could measure and calculate their percent body fat, or they could ask the participants their weight. If they ask participants their weight, they could do so in several different ways. For example:

1. The last time you weighed yourself, how much did you weigh without your clothes on? With your clothes on?
2. Which category best describes your current weight? <100 pounds; 100 to 150 pounds; 151 to 175 pounds; 176 to 200 pounds; or >200 pounds.
3. What is your body mass index (BMI)?
4. Does your physician consider you to be overweight or obese?

Each of these questions gets at one's weight but generates a different kind of data. The type of data generated will dictate what type of statistical analysis that can be used. For example, if researchers were interested in calculating the mean weight of the research participants, this could best be accomplished by weighing each participant on a scale. But if the researchers were not really interested in the participants' average weight but rather whether the participants were overweight or obese, they could use questions 3 or 4 above.

There are four levels of measurement used to determine how something can be measured. These levels are hierarchical in nature and determine what statistical analyses can be used. They are nominal, ordinal, interval, and ratio measures.

NOMINAL MEASURES

Nominal measures, the lowest level in the measurement hierarchy, enable researchers to put data into categories. "The two requirements for nominal measures are that the categories have to be mutually exclusive so that each case fits into one of the categories, and the categories have to be exhaustive so that there is a place for every case" (Weiss, 1998, p. 116). Nominal measures do not convey any value to what is measured but rather just identify or name it (Dignan, 1995). A question that would generate nominal data is, "Is your father still living?" The possible answers include the categories of "yes," "no," and "not sure." We can then assign numbers to these categories according to a particular rule we create (e.g., 1 = yes, 2 = no, 3 = not sure) so the data could then be entered into a computer program.

When using nominal data, hypotheses and questions to be answered can be tested/answered by using the nonparametric test, chi-square, and also Fisher's exact probability test (Bowling, 2005). "The most common measure of association (correlation) for nominal data is the contingency coefficient" (Bowling, 2005, p. 10).

ORDINAL MEASURES

Ordinal measures, like nominal measures, allow researchers to put data into categories that are mutually exclusive and exhaustive, but also permit them to rank order the categories. "The different categories represent relatively more or less of something" (McKenzie, Neiger, & Thackeray, 2009, p. 114). However, the distance between categories cannot be measured. For example, the question "How would you describe your level of health? (select one) excellent, good, fair, poor" creates categories (good, fair, poor) that are mutually exclusive (the respondent cannot select two categories) and exhaustive (there is a category for all levels of health), and the categories represent more or less of something (amount of health). We cannot, however, measure the distance (or difference) between the levels of health (e.g., the difference between excellent health and fair health). Is the distance between good and fair the same as the distance between fair and poor? Ordinal data categories are not necessarily equal distance apart.

When using ordinal data, "hypotheses can be tested by using the nonparametric statistics such as correlation coefficients based on rankings (e.g., Spearman r or the Kendal r). An ordinal scale is sufficient only for answering basic questions such as 'How does X compare to Y?'" (Bowling, 2005, p. 10).

INTERVAL MEASURES

Interval (or ranking) **measures** enable researchers to put data into categories that are mutually exclusive and exhaustive and to rank order the categories. Furthermore, the widths of the categories must all be the same (Hurlburt, 2003), which allows for the distance between the categories to be measured. There is, however, no absolute zero value. Thus, interval measures assign numerical values to things according to a particular rule (Dignan, 1995). A question that generates interval data is, "What was the high temperature today?" We know that a temperature of 50°F is different from a temperature of 55°F, that 55°F is warmer than 50°F, that there is 5°F difference between the two, and if the temperature drops to 0°F there is still some heat in the air (though not much) because 0°F is warmer than −5°F. There are some standardized tests that may be used in research projects that generate ordinal data.

Because interval measures generate quantitative data, all parametric statistics (e.g., means, standard deviations, Pearson correlations, etc.) and common statistical tests of significance (*t*-test, *F*-test, etc.) can be used when testing hypotheses (Bowling, 2005). Interval scales are appropriate to answer the question "How different is X to Y?" (Bowling, 2005, p. 11).

RATIO MEASURES

Ratio measures, the highest level in the measurement hierarchy, enable researchers to do everything with data that can be done with the other three levels of measures; however, they are done using a scale with an absolute zero. Questions that generate interval data include, "What is your blood pressure?" "How much do you weigh in pounds?" and "During an average week, how many miles do you jog?" An absolute zero "point means that the thing being measured actually vanishes when the scale reads zero" (Hurlburt, 2003, p. 17). For example, when a person has a blood pressure reading of zero over zero, there is in fact no blood pressure.

Because interval and ratio data are continuous and rank-ordered values with equal distance between them, and because most statistical procedures are the same for both types of data (Valente, 2002), some researchers and statisticians have combined them into a single level of measurement and refer to the resulting data as *numerical data*. However, if given the choice, researchers should try to collect ratio data because it still provides the greatest flexibility in data analysis (McKenzie *et al.*, 2009).

When using ratio data, hypotheses can be tested with any statistical test (Bowling, 2005). Ratio data are needed to answer the question "Proportionately, how different is X to Y?" (Bowling, 2005, p. 11).

As we leave our discussion on the various levels of measurement, see Box 8.1 for an activity that will help you to better understand these levels.

Accuracy and Consistency

In order for a measurement instrument to be useful to researchers, it must produce data that are both accurate and consistent, and it must be fair to those who are assessed with it. That is, measurement instruments must be able to produce correct data each time they are used. Invalid or biased measurement instruments can lead to erroneous

---

Box 8.1   What Level of Data Is Generated by Each of the Following Questions?

---

1. In what country were you born?
2. What is your sex?
3. What was the temperature this morning when you got up?
4. How old were you in years on your last birthday?
5. Which of the following best represents your yearly income?
   a. $1–10,000   b. $10,001–30,000
   c. $30,001–50,000   d. $50,001–70,000
   e. $70,001+
6. Rank order the following health conditions from most serious to least serious: fractured arm, influenza, nonfatal heart attack, two-inch laceration.
7. Which of the following best represents your age?
   a. ≤65   b. >65
8. I would feel comfortable planning a health promotion program for a local health department. SA A N D SD
9. The air quality in my hometown is: good _____ bad.
10. The last time I exercised for at least 30 continuous minutes was: _____ .

---

conclusions, which in turn can influence future decisions (Borg & Gall, 1989). The terms used to describe the qualities of accuracy and consistency are validity and reliability, respectively, while the term fairness is used to describe an instrument's appropriateness. These qualities of fairness, validity, and reliability are referred to as an instrument's **psychometric properties**.

FAIRNESS

Fairness "deals with the question of whether the instrument is appropriate for the individuals of various ethnic groups with different backgrounds, gender, educational levels, etc." (Torabi, 1994, p. 56). Of the three psychometric properties, fair-

ness is the one that has been given the least attention. And unlike validity and reliability, researchers have not created quantitative means of measuring fairness. Nonetheless, when researchers are collecting data from diverse populations, they need to respond appropriately to the cultural differences of the research participants. In other words, they need to be culturally sensitive and culturally competent as they carry out their research projects. **Cultural sensitivity** "implies knowledge that cultural differences (as well as similarities) exist, along with the refusal to assign cultural differences of such values as better or worse, more or less intelligent, right or wrong; they are simply differences" (Anderson & Fenichel, 1989, p. 8). **Cultural competence** refers to the ability "to understand and respect values, attitudes, beliefs, and mores that differ across cultures, and to consider and respond appropriately to these differences in planning, implementing, and evaluating health education and health promotion programs and interventions" (Joint Committee, 2001, p. 99).

VALIDITY

Validity is concerned with whether the instrument "actually does measure the underlying attribute or not" (Bowling, 2005, p. 11). "In the broadest terms, validity in measurement addresses the degree to which the concept or concepts under study are accurately represented by the particular items on your questionnaire, test, self-report form, or other measuring device" (Green & Lewis, 1986, p. 102). For example, if an instrument is to measure the stress management knowledge of an individual, does the instrument include items from the full breadth of information about stress management? Using a valid instrument increases the chance that researchers are measuring what they want to measure, thus ruling out other possible explanations for their findings (McKenzie *et al.,* 2009).

There are four primary ways of establishing the validity of an instrument: criterion-related, construct, content, and face validity. **Criterion-related validity** refers to the extent to which data generated from a measurement instrument are correlated with data generated from a measure (criterion) of the phenomenon being studied, usually an individual's behavior or performance. Criterion-related validity can be divided into two subtypes: predictive and concurrent validity (McKenzie, Wood, Clark, Kotecki, & Brey, 1999). In both subtypes of criterion-related validity, the aim is to legitimize the inferences that can be made by establishing their predictive ability for a related criterion (Borg & Gall, 1989).

If the measurement used will be correlated with the same phenomenon at another time, the criterion-related validity is known as **predictive validity**. For example, SAT and ACT college entrance examinations are used to predict, at least in part, future college success. A health education example might involve an instrument designed to determine if people are ready to quit smoking and how many of those actually quit smoking in the future. **Concurrent validity** is established when a new instrument and an established valid instrument that measure the same phenomenon are administered to the same subjects, and the results of the new instrument correlate with the results of the established valid instrument (McKenzie *et al.*, 2009). For example, if researchers wanted to establish concurrent validity for their new, shorter HIV/AIDS knowledge instrument, they could administer their instrument and the established valid HIV/AIDS instrument to the same group of subjects and calculate a correlation coefficient with the resulting scores to determine if they are positively correlated. If there is a high positive correlation between the two instruments, the new instrument would be said to have concurrent validity.

Though criterion-related validity is very useful in establishing validity, there are times when there is no existing criterion from which to compare, or the phenomenon that researchers want to measure is more abstract than concrete, such as the constructs of locus of control, self-efficacy, or subjective norm. In such cases, validity can be established

via construct validity. **Construct validity** "is the degree to which a measure correlates with other measures it is theoretically expected to correlate with. Construct validity tests the theoretical framework within which the instrument is expected to perform" (Valente, 2002, p. 161). An instrument that has construct validity will possess both convergent validity and discriminant validity. **Convergent validity** "is the extent to which two measures which purport to be measuring the same topic correlate (that is, converge)" (Bowling, 2005, p. 12). For example, an instrument that purports to measure a person's self-efficacy for regular exercise should positively correlate with that person's exercise behavior. That is, a person who is self-efficacious with regard to exercise would exercise regularly regardless of the circumstances (i.e., normal day, busy day, inclement weather, vacation). **Discriminant validity** "(also known as divergent validity) requires that the construct should not correlate with dissimilar (discriminant) variables" (Bowling, 2005, p. 12). Thus, in the exercise example above, the self-efficacy instrument would not be expected to correlate positively with a person's inactivity.

Content validity refers to "the assessment of the correspondence between the items composing the instrument and the content domain from which the items were selected" (DiIorio, 2005, p. 213). For example, if an instrument is to measure nutrition knowledge of an individual, does the instrument include items from the full breadth of information about nutrition (McKenzie *et al.*, 1999)? Unlike criterion-related and construct validity, content validity is established during an instrument's early development, not after completion (Hopkins, Stanley, & Hopkins, 1990). Content validity is established by having a panel (or jury) of experts comprehensively and systematically review the content of the proposed instrument using both qualitative and quantitative methods. A step-by-step process to establish content validity has been presented by McKenzie and colleagues (1999) and includes Veneziano and Hooper's

(1997) ideas for quantifying the content validity process. Because establishing content valid for a measurement instrument is a common occurrence in health education research, the article written by McKenzie and colleagues has been reprinted in Appendix C of this book.

A measurement instrument is said to have **face validity** if, "on the face," the instrument appears to measure what it purports to measure. Face validity is established by having individuals who are familiar with the phenomenon to be measured "look over" the instrument to see if it appears to cover said phenomenon. Face validity is the weakest form of validity because it lacks some form of systematic logical analysis of content (Hopkins *et al.*, 1990). A measurement instrument may appear to be valid via a face validity process, but in fact it may be found to be invalid when one of the other three forms of validity is applied. Therefore, researchers should not use a measurement instrument that has only face validity if other means to establish validity are available. Face validity is a good first step toward creating a valid measurement instrument but is not a replacement for the other means of establishing validity.

When speaking about validity, health education researchers should also be familiar with the terms sensitivity and specificity. These are terms used in clinical settings and within epidemiology to express the validity of screening and diagnostic tests. **Sensitivity** is defined as "the ability of the test to identify correctly all screened individuals who actually have the disease" (Friis & Sellers, 2009, p. 422). It is recorded as the proportion of true positive cases correctly identified as positive on the test (Timmreck, 1997). The better the sensitivity, the fewer the false positives. **Specificity** is defined as "the ability of the test to identify only nondiseased individuals who actually do not have the disease" (Friis & Sellers, 2009, p. 424). It is recorded as the proportion of true negative cases correctly identified as negative on the test (Timmreck, 1997). The better the specificity, the fewer the number of false negatives. "An ideal screening test would be 100 per

cent sensitive and 100 per cent specific. In practice this does not occur; sensitivity and specificity are usually inversely related" (Mausner & Kramer, 1985, p. 217).

One final thought before leaving our discussion of validity: the validity of an instrument is thought to be a more important issue than reliability. If an instrument does not measure what it is supposed to, then it does not matter if it is reliable (Windsor, Clark, Boyd, & Goodman, 2004).

RELIABILITY

Reliability is the extent to which a measurement instrument will produce the same or nearly the same result (measure or score) each time it is used (McKenzie *et al.*, 2009; Windsor *et al.*, 2004). For example, when you get up in the morning and weigh yourself on a bathroom scale, if the scale is reliable it should give you the same (or nearly the same) reading if you step on and off it several different times to check your weight. However, in health education research it is rare to find an instrument that can provide perfect accuracy in measurement. Green and Lewis (1986) illustrate the theory of reliability with the following equation:

Total score (observed score)
= true score (unobservable) + error score

The total score represents the value generated by the measurement instrument. The true score represents the value generated by the measurement instrument if the instrument and all conditions under which the data were collected were perfect. The error score represents the portion of the total score that is generated from the "imprecision in measurement due to human error, uncontrollable environment occurrences, inappropriateness of measurement instruments, and other unanticipated things" (Dignan, 1995, p. 40). For example, suppose the total score of an individual on a knowledge test was 92 out of a possible 100 points. The question then becomes whether the 92% is a true indication of the person's knowledge. If the conditions under which the score was generated were perfect and the measurement instrument had perfect reliability, the error score would be zero and we could say, "yes, the 92% is a true indication of the person's knowledge." But if the conditions under which the score was generated were not perfect (e.g., the person had to take the test with music blaring in the background) and the measurement instrument did not have perfect reliability (e.g., it included several biased questions), the error score would not be zero and we would say, "no, the 92% is not a true indication of the person's knowledge. This person may really know more, or maybe less, than was indicated by the score." Thus, researchers need to strive to collect data under the best conditions with the most reliable measurement instruments possible.

There are several methods of estimating the reliability of a measurement instrument, "most of which call for computing a correlation coefficient between two sets of similar measurements" (Borg & Gall, 1989, p. 257). The two sets of similar measurements (with sources of error in parentheses) can be generated in one of the following ways:

- two separate instruments (lack of equivalence)
- two like halves of one instrument (inconsistency across matched items)
- the same instrument applied on two occasions (instability over time)
- the same instrument administered by two different persons (inconsistency across observers/scorers) (Black, 1999, p. 195)

The reliability coefficients that result from the correlations of the two sets of similar measurements will range between 0 and 1. "A reliability coefficient of 0.70 implies that 70 per cent of the measured variance is reliable and 30 per cent is owing to random error" (Bowling, 2002, p. 149). The lower the reliability coefficient, the less reliable the measure. Dignan (1995) offers the following interpretation of reliability coefficients.

> Generally speaking, correlation coefficients of less than .4 are considered not to represent any relationship between the tests. A value of .4 to .6 indicates a "slight" relationship, while a value of

.6 to .8 represents a "moderate" relationship. Values of r above .8 indicate a "substantial" correlation. In general, the closer the correlation coefficient (r) is to 1.00 the greater the reliability. (p. 55)

A variety of factors can influence the reliability coefficient. Generally speaking, the greater the number of items on an instrument, the more homogeneous the participants being assessed by the instrument, and the more clear the items and instructions are, the higher the reliability coefficient (Torabi, 1994).

The various methods for determining reliability are presented below.

Parallel Forms Reliability

Parallel forms reliability, or *equivalent forms* or *alternate-forms reliability*, focuses on whether different forms of the same measurement instrument measuring the same participants will produce similar results (means, standard deviations, and item intercorrelations). The advantage of having measurement instruments that possess parallel forms reliability is being able to test the same subjects on different occasions (e.g., using a pretest–posttest research design) without worrying that the participants will score better on the second administration (posttest) because they remember questions from the first administration (pretest) of the instrument. A good example of parallel forms reliability is found in the different versions of the standardized college entrance examinations.

Internal Consistency Reliability

Internal consistency reliability, which is one of the most commonly used method of estimating reliability (Windsor *et al.,* 2004), "refers to the intercorrelations among individual items on the instrument, that is, whether all items on the instrument are measuring part of the total area" (McKenzie *et al.,* 2009, pp. 116–117). Internal consistency reliability is calculated by determining the statistical relationship between the individual instrument items and the total score. The greater the consistency, the higher the reliability. The three methods most commonly used in health education research to calculate internal consistency reliability are Cronbach's alpha, Kuder-Richardson (KR) 20 coefficient, and the Spearman-Bowman split-half reliability procedure.

Test–Retest Reliability

Test–retest reliability, or *stability reliability*, "is used to generate evidence of stability over a period" (Torabi, 1994, p. 57) of time. To establish this type of reliability, the same instrument is used to measure the same group of people under similar or the same conditions at two different points in time, and the two sets of data generated by the measurement are used to calculate a correlation coefficient. The amount of time between the test and retest may vary from a few hours to a few weeks. A maximum amount of time should be allowed between the test and retest so that individuals are not responding on the basis of remembering responses they made the first time, but it should not be so long that other events could occur in the intervening time to influence their responses (McKenzie *et al.*, 2009).

Rater Reliability

Rater reliability, or *observer reliability*, is associated with the consistent measurement (or rating) of an observed event by different individuals (or judges or raters), or by the same individual (McDermott & Sarvela, 1999). If two or more raters are involved, the process is referred to as **interrater reliability**. If only one rater is involved, it is referred to as **intrarater reliability**. "It is an important measure in determining how well an implementation of some coding or measurement system works" (TextaSoft, 2008, ¶ 2), such as when raters are being trained to observe an event of interest. There are several different ways to calculate rater reliability. The two most common are by (1) simply calculating a percentage of agreement between/among raters or within an individual rater, or (2) using **Kappa**. Here is an

example using the "percentage of agreement" process. Suppose we are planning a study to observe for proper safety belt use that would require multiple observers (raters). After we have trained the observers in what to look for, we then would have all of them observe the same set of passing drivers and calculate the percentage of agreement among the raters. If they observed the drivers of 10 passing cars and agreed on 9 out of 10, the interrater reliability would be 90%. For an example of intrarater reliability, suppose a researcher wanted to conduct a study that involved the review of patients' medical charts to determine if the physicians were documenting (writing in the record) their patient education efforts. Using the same assessment form, the researcher would review the same 10 medical records at two different times. The percentage of agreement for the two observations determines the intrarater reliability.

The Kappa statistic has been used more in research studies than just the simple agreement of raters presented above because it also takes into account agreement occurring by chance. There are several different means (e.g., Cohen, 1960; Fleiss, 1981; Landis & Koch, 1977) of calculating a Kappa statistic. Some are to be used with two raters whereas others can be used with multiple raters. A presentation of the calculations of the Kappa statistic is beyond the scope of this book, but the resulting values, regardless of the process used, are reliability coefficients. The closer the value is to +1.0, the greater the agreement.

As we leave our discussion of validity and reliability, please refer to Figure 8.1 for a graphic summary of these concepts.

Types and Forms of Measures

At the most basic level, the data generated by measurement can be divided into two categories, depending on the method by which they are collected. **Quantitative measures** "rely on more standardized data collection and reduction techniques, using predetermined questions or observational

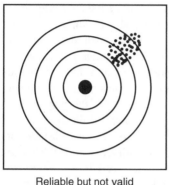 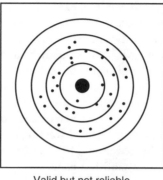 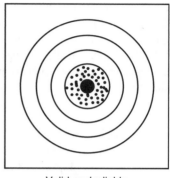

| Reliable but not valid | Valid but not reliable | Valid *and* reliable |

FIGURE 8.1
An analogy to validity and reliability.

Source: Babbie, E. (1995). *The practice of social research* (7th ed.), p. 128. Belmont, Calif.: Wadsworth. Reprinted with permission of Wadsworth, a division of Thomson Learning: www.thomsonrights.com.

indicators and established response items" (Green & Lewis, 1986, p. 151). Examples of quantitative data include the number and/or percentage of participants who lose weight and the pretest and posttest scores on a nutrition knowledge test. **Qualitative measures** "tend to produce data in the language of the subjects [participants], rarely with numerical values attached to observations" (Green & Lewis, 1986, p. 151). Qualitative data are usually assigned labels or categories (Morreale, n.d.) and often take the form of narrative (Weiss, 1998). Examples include data generated from in-depth interviews and focus groups. "Both quantitative and qualitative measures have their individual strengths and weaknesses, yet their greatest strength may come when both are used in the measurement process" (McKenzie *et al.*, 2009, p. 112).

Over the years, health education researchers have studied a wide variety of topics. Yet when it comes down to conducting the various research projects, the items of interest that are measured in most health education studies fit neatly into one of several categories. The most frequently measured items of interest in health education research studies include demographic variables (e.g., sex, age),

awareness variables (e.g., conscious of, identification of risk factors), cognitive variables (e.g., knowledge, analysis), psychosocial variables, skill variables, behavior variables, environmental variables, health status variables, and quality of life variables. A key to being able to measure these variables is being able to precisely define them. Two types of definitions are important to the measurement process—theoretical and operational definitions (DiIorio, 2005). A theoretical definition is one that uses words to explain a *concept* (a major component of a theory). As noted in Chapter 4, when a concept has been developed, created, or adopted for use with a specific theory it is called a *construct*. However, the theoretical definition does not explain the concept or construct in measureable terms and thus there is a need for an operational (or empirical) definition. The process of transforming a concept or construct into measurable terms is called **operationalization**. For example, the stage construct of the transtheoretical model has been theoretically defined as the temporal dimension of change (Prochaska, Redding, & Evers, 2008). But it has been operationally defined by the individual stages of change— precontemplation (not intending to take action in the next six months), contemplation (intending to take action within the next six months), preparation (intending to take action within the next 30 days and has taken some behavioral steps in this direction), action (overtly making the changes for less than six months), maintenance (has changed behavior for more than six months), and termination (no temptation to relapse and 100% confident). When operationalizing a concept or construct, the researcher must keep in mind the resulting level of data (nominal, ordinal, interval, ratio) and the anticipated statistical analysis. In the following sections, we will examine how these items of interest can be measured.

MEASURING DEMOGRAPHIC AND AWARENESS VARIABLES

Most often, demographic characteristics of participants (e.g., sex, race, age, income) and their awareness about something (e.g., conscious of, location of, identification of risks) are measured using some form of a self-report questionnaire (i.e., participants report about themselves). The questions used when measuring demographic characteristics and awareness can be classified into three categories: structured (or selected-response or closed or restricted) items, unstructured (or constructed-response or open or unrestricted) items, and hybrid (or combination) items, which fall somewhere in between structured and unstructured. With **structured items**, the respondents are required to choose from the possible answers provided. For example, a dichotomous structured demographic question may ask, "Are you male or female?" The advantages of using structured questions include: "(1) ease of completion for the respondent; (2) simplification of coding and analysis, particularly because the questionnaire can be precoded; (3) greater chance the respondents will answer sensitive questions (e.g., about age or income); and (4) a minimum of irrelevant responses" (Neutens & Rubinson, 2010, p. 114).

Unstructured items would be ones where the respondent is required to generate or construct the answer. For example, an unstructured awareness question may ask, "Where in the community can a smoker turn for help?" The advantages of using unstructured questions include: "(1) usable when all the response categories are unknown, (2) preferable for controversial, sensitive, and complex issues, and (3) allows for respondent creativity, clarification, and detail" (Neutens & Rubinson, 2010, p. 114).

A **hybrid item** would include elements of both a structured and an unstructured item. For example, it is common to see a demographic multiple-choice question about race have five structured responses (African American, Asian, Native Hawaiian or other Pacific Islander, Alaska Native/Native American, and Caucasian) and a sixth unstructured response that is labeled "other (please specify _____)."

MEASURING COGNITIVE VARIABLES

As we begin our discussion of measuring cognitive variables, let it be understood that we use the term in the most general way—to cover the whole cognitive domain. By **cognitive domain** we mean all mental activities related to thinking, reasoning, remembering, and so on (Black, 1999). Within the cognitive domain are several different levels. These levels, which were proposed by Bloom (1956) and are known as **Bloom's taxonomy** for the cognitive domain, are presented in a hierarchical order and require a higher level of mental functioning as one moves through the hierarchy. The levels are knowledge (remembering), comprehension (lowest level of understanding), application (using learned material), analysis (ability to analyze learned material), synthesis (creating from learned material), and evaluation (ability to judge the value).

Though different measurement instruments are used to measure the various levels in Bloom's taxonomy, "knowledge" is most often measured with achievement tests, typically administered either through a written (or "paper–pencil") test (e.g., as is used in most school settings) or online with a computer. With such tests, the total number of correct answers is typically summed to create a total score. As when measuring demographic characteristics and awareness, achievement tests also use structured, unstructured, and hybrid items. Commonly used questions for achievement tests include structured items such as true–false, multiple choice, and matching questions, and unstructured items such as completion questions (e.g., "Immunization is a good example of primary prevention because. . ."), short-answer questions (i.e., writing a sentence or paragraph as a response to a question), and essay questions (i.e., writing multiple paragraphs as a response to a question). Box 8.2 includes some examples of demographic, awareness, and knowledge questions. As you examine this box, note that the different types of questions generate various levels of data.

MEASURING PSYCHOSOCIAL VARIABLES

As has been noted elsewhere (Galli, 1976), "health education is eclectic in nature. As an applied science, it derives its body of knowledge from a variety of other disciplines" (p. 158). From the discipline of psychology come psychosocial variables such as attitude, motivation, and personality. Each of these variables is complex, abstract, and multidimensional in nature, and because of these factors, they are not easily measured. Though it is not uncommon to hear someone say that another person has a "good attitude" or "is not motivated"

Box 8.2   Sample Knowledge Questions

Structured (selected-response) items

A. True–false
   1. A risk factor for cancer is smoking.
      a. True   b. False
   2. Most people will gain weight if they consume more calories than they burn.
      a. True   b. False
B. Multiple choice
   1. The leading actual cause of death in the United States is:
      a. sedentary lifestyle
      b. use of tobacco
      c. fatty diet
      d. stress
   2. Which of the following should be written in exact measurable terms?
      a. goals
      b. objectives
      c. mission statement
C. Matching
   Match each date in the first column with a historical event in the second column.
   1. 1854   a. Passage of the Social Security Act
   2. 1965   b. J. Snow removes pump handle
   3. 1979   c. Medicare and Medicaid begin
   4. 1935   d. *Healthy People* report published

Unstructured (constructed-response) items

A. Completion questions
   1. The best way to lose weight is by . . .
   2. A person can manage stress by . . .
B. Short-answer questions
   1. Define "healthy balanced diet."
   2. Provide one reason why every health education major should seek certification after graduation.
C. Essay questions
   1. Please provide a brief summary of the development of school health education in the United States.
   2. If a friend of yours asked you how to stop smoking, what would you tell him or her?

or "has a strange personality," these variables cannot be measured directly but rather must be inferred (Torabi & Jeng, 2001).

The complex, abstract, and multidimensional nature of attitude, motivation, and personality may be in part why a number of different formats have been used to try to measure them. Most researchers have chosen to try to measure them using ordinal and interval scales. Probably the most commonly used ordinal scale in health education research is the Likert scale (McDermott & Sarvela, 1999), named after its creator Rensis Likert (1932). In this scale, items are presented and respondents are asked to indicate their agreement by selecting from the following responses: strongly agree (SA), agree (A), neutral (N), disagree (D), strongly disagree (SD). Other types of scales appearing in health education research to measure these variables include summated rating scale, value scale, cumulative scales, semantic differential scales, paired comparisons (also called forced choice), and rank order (Backstrom & Hursh-Cesar, 1981; McDermott & Sarvela, 1999; Neutens & Rubinson, 2010). Box 8.3 provides examples of each of these different types of scales and questions.

MEASURING SKILL AND BEHAVIOR VARIABLES

Skills (or capability or performance) and behaviors make up the psychomotor domain. Skill (or capability or performance) "variables represent a person's ability to perform a task" (Windsor *et al.,* 2004, p. 84). For example, a person can possess the skills to perform CPR or exercise aerobically. Behaviors are different than skills. A person may possess a skill, such as CPR, but not use it (or behave) when confronted with the opportunity to do so. Often skills are measured in a laboratory setting, but behavior is measured in a more naturalistic setting (i.e., in the field).

Perhaps the most basic aspect of measuring skills (or capability or performance) and behaviors, and what distinguishes it from measuring knowledge, attitudes, motivation, and personality traits, is that skills and behavior have to be rigidly

defined (Dignan, 1995). The key to being able to measure skills and behavior is to be able to specifically define what is to be measured. For example, take the term compliance (or adherence) as used in a health care setting. The term "is applicable to any behavior in which the outcome is dependent on that behavior occurring on a regular and specific schedule" (Patterson, 2001, p. 6). Suppose a researcher is interested in measuring the compliance of patients taking a medication that must be taken three times a day. Most, if not all, would agree that patients who take their medication without missing a dose are compliant. But if over the course of a week a patient takes 20 of the 21 required doses, is he or she noncompliant? What about the patient who forgets to take the last dose one day but takes 4 the next and thus takes all 21 for the week? At what point does a compliant patient become a noncompliant patient? This example illustrates the need for a good operational definition of the skill or behavior.

Once defined, researchers must determine the best way to measure the skill or behavior. The three most often used ways to measure skills and behavior have been having people report about their behavior when asked (i.e., self-report or self-completion), actually observing a person's skills or behavior, and using a proxy (or indirect) measure of behavior. There are advantages and disadvantages to each of these techniques of measurement. The advantages of measuring skills or behaviors by **self-report** is that it is convenient and cost-effective, data can be collected from many people in many locations, the respondents are all exposed to the same questions, and data can be collected that cannot be gathered via observation or proxy (i.e., private or personal behaviors such as sexual behavior). The obvious weakness of a self-report measure is that the respondent may not tell the truth. Other weaknesses include the respondents being unable to remember in order to repeat accurately, not understanding or misinterpreting the question, or not using the appropriate definition for the skill or behavior.

Box 8.3   Sample Attitude Scales and Questions

Summated rating scales

1. Exercise is a key to good health.
   a. Strongly agree
   b. Agree
   c. Neutral
   d. Disagree
   e. Strongly disagree
2. Abortion should be illegal no matter what the circumstances.
   a. Agree strongly
   b. Agree moderately
   c. Agree mildly
   d. Disagree mildly
   e. Disagree moderately
   f. Disagree strongly

Value scale

1. Do you think the legal age for drinking alcohol should be lowered to 18 years old?
   a. Yes
   b. No
2. Women should be able to have an abortion if they want to.
   a. Agree
   b. Disagree

Cumulative scale

1. • There should be no restrictions on the purchase of handguns.
   • A person should be able to purchase a handgun to protect oneself.
   • It should be illegal to own a handgun.
2. • It is okay not to exercise.
   • One should exercise at least three times a week.
   • One should exercise four to six times per week.
   • One should exercise most days of the week.

Semantic differential scales

1. A vegetarian diet is:
   Good _____ Bad
2. How would you rate the leadership of the current secretary of Health and Human Services?
   Strong +3 +2 +1 0 −1 −2 −3 Weak

Paired comparisons (forced-choice)

1. Which of the following best represents your view?
   a. Smokeless tobacco is okay.
   b. Smokeless tobacco should never be used.
2. Which of the following best represents your attitude toward eating?
   a. Living to eat
   b. Eating to live

Rank order

1. Rank order the following from most important to least important in your quest for good health.
   _____ a. Exercise
   _____ b. Manage stress
   _____ c. Maintain ideal body weight
   _____ d. Eat a variety of foods
2. Rank order the following from most effective to least effective in keeping young children from smoking.
   _____ a. Being around good role models
   _____ b. Increasing the cost of cigarettes
   _____ c. Removing all vending machines that contain cigarettes
   _____ d. Having an antitobacco curriculum in schools
   _____ e. Limiting the point-of-sale options

Because of some of the weaknesses inherent in measuring skills and behavior with self-report, some researchers have found direct observation of skills and behavior more useful. **Observation** has been defined as "notice taken of an indicator" (Green & Lewis, 1986, p. 363). However, researchers must be aware of several issues when using direct observation. The first is having a good definition of the skill or behavior, without which the observation cannot be valid. In other words, what exactly is the observer looking for? Second, there must be reliable observers and thus high rater reliability. Third, there is the issue of obtrusive versus unobtrusive observation. The term **obtrusive observation** "indicates that the person being studied is aware of being measured, assessed, or tested" (Windsor *et al.,* 2004, p. 111); **unobtrusive observation** means just the opposite. The issue of obtrusive versus unobtrusive observation raises concerns because some people act differently when they know they are being observed (see Chapter 9 for a discussion of the Hawthorne effect), and there are questions about the ethics of unobtrusive observation (see Chapter 6).

A **proxy** (or indirect) measure is an outcome measure that provides evidence that a behavior has occurred, or as Dignan (1995) states, "indirect measures are unmistakable signs that a specific behavior has occurred" (p. 103). Examples of proxy or indirect measures may include: (1) lower blood pressure for the behavior of medication taking, (2) body weight for the behaviors of exercise and dieting, (3) cotinine in the blood for tobacco use, (4) empty alcoholic beverage containers in the trash for consumption of alcohol, or (5) a spouse reporting on the compliance of his or her partner. Proxy or indirect measurement of skills or behavior "usually requires more resources and cooperation than self-report or direct observation" (Dignan, 1995, p. 104). The greatest concern associated with using proxy or indirect measures is making sure that the measure is both valid and reliable.

The instruments used to measure skills and behaviors include questionnaires, logs, journals, and diaries (for self-report); checklists and rubrics (for observation); and physical evidence and physiological tests (for proxy measures). Figures 8.2 and 8.3 provide examples of a self-report log and an observation checklist, respectively.

Before leaving our discussion of measuring skills and behavior, we need to mention the term **authentic assessment**. It is a term that has surfaced in the teacher education literature (but has application elsewhere) and refers to a type of performance-based assessment that more accurately measures a person's skills or ability to perform (behave). For example, having a preservice teacher take a written test on creating a lesson plan is not as good as having that same person write and share a lesson plan with others. Williams, Hetrick, and Suen (1998) report that the proponents of authentic assessment claim (1) it is a better measure of what a person should know, (2) it accentuates a higher order of cognition, and (3) it encourages active participation in the learning process; however, the critics of authentic assessment are concerned with its (1) high cost, (2) efficiency, (3) limited utility, (4) cultural sensitivity, and (5) questionable validity and reliability.

MEASURING ENVIRONMENTAL VARIABLES

In recent years, health education specialists have become more concerned with the environmental factors or conditions associated with health behavior and their impact on health (Bartholomew, Parcel, Kok, & Gottlieb, 2006; Green & Kreuter, 2005; McLeroy, Bibeau, Steckler, & Glanz, 1988). "Environmental factors are those determinants outside an individual that can be modified to support behavior, health, and the quality of life" (Green & Kreuter, 2005, p. 14). Thus health education researchers have measured the economic environment (e.g., incentives and disincentives, affordability), service environment (e.g., access to health care, equity of health care, barriers to health care), physical environment (e.g., clean air and water, proximity to facilities), social environment (e.g., social support, peer pressure), political environment (e.g., health policy), and psychological environment (e.g., emotional learning climate).

A variety of measures have been used to measure environmental factors or conditions including self-report instruments (e.g., amount of social support), checklists (e.g., barriers to health care), laboratory tests (e.g., for polluted air and water), and observation (e.g., amount of peer pressure).

MEASURING HEALTH STATUS VARIABLES

Health status is dynamic in nature and can range on a continuum from excellent to poor. Further,

Directions: Record every cigarette you smoke beginning with the first cigarette of the day and ending 24 hours later.

Need for cigarette rating scale: 1 = extreme; 2 = moderate; 3 = minimal

Cigarette	Time smoked	Rating	Location	Mood or reason	Place	With whom?
#1	___:___	1 2 3	_____	_____	_____	_____
#2	___:___	1 2 3	_____	_____	_____	_____
#3	___:___	1 2 3	_____	_____	_____	_____
#4	___:___	1 2 3	_____	_____	_____	_____
#5	___:___	1 2 3	_____	_____	_____	_____
#6	___:___	1 2 3	_____	_____	_____	_____
#7	___:___	1 2 3	_____	_____	_____	_____
#8	___:___	1 2 3	_____	_____	_____	_____
#9	___:___	1 2 3	_____	_____	_____	_____
#10	___:___	1 2 3	_____	_____	_____	_____
#11	___:___	1 2 3	_____	_____	_____	_____
#12	___:___	1 2 3	_____	_____	_____	_____
#13	___:___	1 2 3	_____	_____	_____	_____
#14	___:___	1 2 3	_____	_____	_____	_____
#15	___:___	1 2 3	_____	_____	_____	_____
#16	___:___	1 2 3	_____	_____	_____	_____
#17	___:___	1 2 3	_____	_____	_____	_____
#18	___:___	1 2 3	_____	_____	_____	_____
#19	___:___	1 2 3	_____	_____	_____	_____
#20	___:___	1 2 3	_____	_____	_____	_____

(Use the back if you need more space)

FIGURE 8.2
Self-report 24-hour cigarette count.

Adapted from McKenzie, J.F., Neiger, B.L., & Thackeray, R. (2009). *Planning, implementing, and evaluating health promotion programs: A primer* (5th ed.). San Francisco: Benjamin Cummings.

Date: _____   Time of data collection: _____

Parking lot observed: _____   Person collecting data: _____

Car#	Safety belt on		Sex of driver	
1.	Yes	No	Female	Male
2.	Yes	No	Female	Male
3.	Yes	No	Female	Male
4.	Yes	No	Female	Male
5.	Yes	No	Female	Male
6.	Yes	No	Female	Male
7.	Yes	No	Female	Male
8.	Yes	No	Female	Male
9.	Yes	No	Female	Male
10.	Yes	No	Female	Male
11.	Yes	No	Female	Male
12.	Yes	No	Female	Male
13.	Yes	No	Female	Male
14.	Yes	No	Female	Male
15.	Yes	No	Female	Male
16.	Yes	No	Female	Male
17.	Yes	No	Female	Male
18.	Yes	No	Female	Male
19.	Yes	No	Female	Male
20.	Yes	No	Female	Male

Totals: Females (yes) ___; Females (no) ___; Males (yes) ___; Males (no) ___

FIGURE 8.3
Observation checklist: safety belt use.

continued

Safety Belt Use Defined

Criteria for inclusion:

a.   Observe cars, trucks, and vans entering and exiting the university parking lots.

b.   Cars must have a university parking hangtag.

c.   Observe only drivers.

d.   Look for correctly worn shoulder harness. Assumption: if shoulder harness is in place, so is the lap belt.

e.   Driver must be wearing the safety belt the whole time he/she is in your sight to be counted as wearing the safety belt.

Criteria for exclusion:

a.   No vehicle with a visitor or handicapped hangtag should be included in the data collection.

b.   No commercial vehicle should be included in the data collection.

c.   Try your best to observe all included in the inclusion criteria; however, if you cannot see through tinted glass or the vehicle is too far off the ground to see the shoulder harness, the vehicle should not be included in the data collection.

FIGURE 8.3 *Continued*

health status is specific to any one individual. For example, a typically healthy college student who gets a cold may see him/herself as unhealthy or in poor health, but a person with a disability who requires the use of a wheelchair may see him/herself as perfectly healthy. Because of the difficulty in trying to quantify health status, most measures of health status "are expressed using health statistics based on the traditional medical model of describing ill health (injury, disease, and death) instead of well health" (Cottrell, Girvan, & McKenzie, 2009, p. 9). That is, "the higher the presence of injury, disease, and death indicators, the lower the level of health; the lower the presence of injury, disease, and death indicators, the higher the level of health" (Cottrell *et al.,* 2009, p. 9). Therefore, out of necessity, health status has been measured with just the opposite—ill health (Cohen, 1991; McKenzie, Pinger, & Kotecki, 2008).

The measures used to quantify health status have included self-report health status (i.e., excellent, good, fair, and poor), presence of risk factors (using health risk assessments), epidemiological data (e.g., birth and death rates), life expectancy based on actuarial tables, years of potential life lost (YPLL) (a measure of premature death), disability-adjusted life years (DALYs) (a measure of the loss of healthy life years), and the results of physiological screenings (e.g., blood pressure, blood glucose and blood lipid levels).

MEASURING QUALITY OF LIFE VARIABLES
Quality of life (QoL) "is a popular term that conveys an overall sense of well-being, including aspects of happiness and satisfaction with life as a whole" (Centers for Disease Control and Prevention [CDC], 2000, p. 5). There are many different domains that comprise QoL including occupation,

housing, school, neighborhoods, health, and spirituality, to name a few. Those aspects of people's QoL that can be clearly shown to affect their health, either physically or mentally, make up their **health-related quality of life (HRQoL)**. Because both QoL and HRQoL are composed of complex collections of interacting objective and subjective dimensions (Lawton, 1991) it has not been easy for researchers to create "clean" operational definitions. Therefore, a number of different scales (Bowling, 2005) have been created to measure both QoL (e.g., WHOQOL Group, 1998) and HRQoL (e.g., CDC, 2000). Most of these scales are composed of measures much like those found when measuring psychosocial variables.

Using an Existing Measurement Instrument

As you will discover in the next section of this chapter, it takes a great deal of time, energy, and resources to create a measurement instrument with good psychometric properties. Because of this, we recommend that you conduct a thorough search to try to find a measurement instrument that could be used, either in whole or in part, for your research project. Though it is indeed easier to use an existing instrument than to create a new one, the process of identifying and gaining permission to use an existing measurement instrument is not without its challenges. Following is a list of steps that can be used when identifying, obtaining, and evaluating an existing instrument.

Step 1: Identifying measurement instruments. Conducting a thorough search of the literature to see what other researchers have used to collect data on your topic is a good place to start. Be aware that seldom is an instrument included in published literature. If the instrument is not an original instrument for the study being reported on, it should provide a citation of its source. The U.S. government also develops a number of measurement instruments that are useful to health

education researchers. Conducting a search of applicable Web sites (e.g., National Center for Health Statistics, Centers for Disease Control and Prevention) can be useful. Also, be aware that some commercial companies (e.g., Psychological Assessment Resources, Inc. [PAR]) publish and sell various measurement instruments. Network with others, including your thesis/dissertation committee members, who have an interest in your research topic to see if they know of possible instruments. Finally, be aware that you may not find a measurement instrument that you can use in whole, but you may find a certain section of an instrument that could be of use to you.

Step 2: Getting your hands on the instrument. Once you have identified potential measurement instruments, you then have to acquire them. Unless an instrument is copyrighted, or there are plans to do so in the future, we have found that many researchers are more than happy to share a data collection instrument. A phone call, letter, or sometimes a "formal" e-mail requesting a copy of an instrument is all that it takes to get a copy. The biggest issue we have found when trying to track down an author to ask permission for a copy of an instrument is having outdated contact information. If you do not find contact information about the author of an instrument in the literature or if the literature may be too old to have current contact information, often the easiest way to find the author is merely to "Google" him or her (Cone & Foster, 2006). Once you have located the source of the instrument, be aware that you may have to pay for an instrument, and you may have to meet certain criteria (i.e., be a licensed psychologist) to be able to obtain and use certain measurement instruments. Also, be aware that in addition to having to pay for an instrument, the author/owner may ask you to share any data that you collect with the instrument or request coauthorship on any resulting publications or presentations.

Step 3: Is it the right instrument? With the instrument in hand, you need to make some judgments to determine if the instrument is the right one for your study. Questions you need to find answers to are: (1) Is there evidence of the psychometric properties (validity, reliability, and fairness) of the instrument? (2) Has it been used with participants similar to yours? (3) Are there standard or normative scores available for various participants? (4) Is it culturally appropriate for your participants? (5) Has the reading level for the instrument been determined? (6) Is there a cost to administer the instrument or have the instrument scored? Can you afford it? (7) Will it answer the research questions or hypotheses you posed in Chapter I?

Even if the answers to all the above questions are positive, it is still recommended that you pilot test the instrument with people as much like your participants as possible to ensure that the instrument will indeed work in your study. It is also an opportunity to check the validity and reliability of the instrument with your participants.

Step 4: Is the instrument copyright protected? If you think it is the right instrument, before proceeding make sure you have done everything necessary to be able to use the instrument. Remember that for instruments that are not in the public domain (available for anyone to use without permission), "you need the permission of the author for any use of the instrument, usually in writing, and particularly if you need to make any changes" (Dignan, 1995, p. 67). Also, you need to fulfill any conditions placed on the use of the instrument before you use it.

Step 5: Adapt an instrument with caution. There are times when researchers find an instrument that has all the necessary questions that need to be asked, but the instrument may not have been created for the research participants that are going to be studied. For example, a researcher who wants to study the osteoporosis knowledge of college-age women may find an instrument that was developed to measure osteoporosis knowledge of middle-age women. The instrument may contain all the right questions and have good psychometric properties (validity, reliability, and fairness) but uses

the term "middle-aged woman" in several different questions. Can the researcher adapt the instrument by just substituting "college-age woman" every place where the term "middle-age woman" is used? The answer is that if there are changes in the instrument, no matter how small, it is possible that the psychometric properties will also change. "Logically, the less you change an instrument, the more you should be able to assume that its properties would stay the same" (Cone & Foster, 2006, p. 179). However, if any changes are made, new data should be collected, say through a pilot study with a small group of the new research participants, to establish the psychometric properties for the "adapted" instrument (Cone & Foster, 2006).

Developing a Measurement Instrument

Only when researchers are unable to use or adapt another instrument with established validity and reliability for their research project should they undertake the process of developing their own (Janz, Champion, & Strecher, 2002). A number of authors (Backstrom & Hursh-Cesar, 1981; Dignan, 1995; Green & Lewis, 1986; McDermott & Sarvela, 1999; Neutens & Rubinson, 2010; Pealer & Weiler, 2000; Schonlau, Fricker, & Elliott, 2002; Torabi & Jeng, 2001; Williams *et al.*, 1998; Windsor *et al.*, 2004) have suggested steps to follow in creating an instrument. The steps presented below, and outlined in Box 8.4, are a combination of the work of these other authors and deal with creating an instrument appropriate for collecting data for most of the measures noted earlier in the chapter, with the exception of the physiological measures. Health education specialists typically do not have the expertise or resources to create physiological measurement instruments.

It is assumed prior to engaging in this process that the researcher is very familiar with the related literature under study. You may also want to review the work of others (e.g., Arriola *et al.*, 2009; Atkinson, 2007; Becker, Dolbier, Durham, Glass-

Box 8.4	Steps for Creating a Measurement Instrument

Step 0: Be familiar with the related literature.

Step 1: Determine the specific purpose (or goal) and the objectives of the proposed instrument.

Step 2: Determine the individuals who are to be measured.

Step 3: Identify the conceptual theory/model that will provide the foundation for the instrument.

Step 4: Create a table of specifications and specifications for the instrument.

Step 5: Identify items from other existing instruments that could be used.

Step 6: Create new instrument items.

Step 7: Create directions for completing the instrument and directions and instructions for administering the instrument.

Step 8: Establish procedures for scoring the instrument.

Step 9: Assemble an initial draft of the instrument.

Step 10: Establish face validity for the instrument.

Step 11: Check the readability of the instrument.

Step 12: Establish content validity for the instrument.

Step 13: Pilot test the instrument.

Step 14: Conduct item analysis, factor analysis, and checks of psychometric properties.

Step 15: Review, revise, and reassess.

Step 16: Conduct a second pilot test, if necessary.

Step 17: Determine a cut score, if needed.

Step 18: Refine as needed and create the final version.

coff, & Adams, 2008; Glover, Nilsson, Westin, Glover, Laflin, & Persson, 2005; Howard & Weiler, 2003; Torabi, 1989; Zullig, Huebner, Patton, & Murray, 2009) who have created an instrument to help you better understand the process. Finally, be aware that depending on the circumstances under which an instrument is created, the order of the steps may change.

Step 1: Determine the specific purpose (or goal) and the objectives of the proposed instrument (McDermott & Sarvela, 1999; O'Rourke & O'Rourke, 2002; Williams *et al.*, 1998). In other words, what exactly is to be measured? Be as specific as possible. (Note: This should be determined by your research questions and/or hypotheses.)

Step 2: Determine the individuals who are to be measured. (Torabi & Jeng, 2001). Again, be as specific as possible.

Step 3: Identify the conceptual theory/model (see Chapter 4 for commonly used theories and models) that will provide the foundation for the instrument. The constructs of the theory/model will help to identify the variables that will be measured (Windsor *et al.*, 2004).

Step 4: Create a table of specifications (Torabi & Jeng, 2001) and specifications for the instrument (McDermott & Sarvela, 1999). Using information identified in Step 3, answer the following questions: What content will be included? What question types/format(s) will be used? Approximately how many items will be on the instrument? How will the instrument be delivered? Administered? Approximately how much time will it take for participants to complete the instrument? How will the instrument be scored?

Step 5: Identify items from other existing instruments that could be used. Remember to get permission to use them, if necessary, and "adapted" items still need to be checked for psychometric properties.

Step 6: Create new instrument items. To ensure that the instrument is content valid, create a wide variety of items, and more than you think will be needed (McDermott & Sarvela, 1999). Give considerable thought to the measurement level at which the questions are written, since that will determine the statistical analysis (O'Rourke & O'Rourke, 2001, 2002). If structured questions are being used, make sure the response categories are mutually exclusive (no overlap of possible responses, e.g., 0–20, 21–40) and exhaustive (includes every possible answer) (O'Rourke & O'Rourke, 2001, 2002).

Step 7: Create directions for completing the instrument and directions and instructions for administering the instrument. Keep all the directions and instructions short and clear (O'Rourke, 2001). Make the completion and administration of the instrument as easy as possible.

Step 8: Establish procedures for scoring the instrument (McDermott & Sarvela, 1999). How many points will be awarded for each item? Will a total score for the instrument be generated?

Step 9: Assemble an initial draft of the instrument. Give the instrument a title (O'Rourke, 2001); include the directions for completion; if appropriate, consider using section headings to divide the instrument (O'Rourke, 2001); and put the instrument in a logical format (O'Rourke & O'Rourke, 2001) of how you might expect the final instrument to look. In order to build a rapport with the participants, place nonthreatening questions at the beginning and threatening, sensitive, and demographic questions at the end (O'Rourke & O'Rourke, 2001). If possible, route respondents around items they do not need to read (e.g., "if no to question #4, skip to question #8") (O'Rourke & O'Rourke, 2001). Be aware that both the format and visual appeal are important. Make sure that the instrument is neat, has plenty of "white space," and does not appear to be cluttered.

Step 10: Establish face validity for the instrument. Ask your thesis/dissertation committee members or colleagues to review the instrument and then make revisions based on their comments.

Step 11: Check the readability of the instrument. If the general public is going to be reading the instrument, try to get the reading level down to the sixth-grade level. By doing so, 75% of adult Americans will be able to read it without difficulty (Doak, Doak, & Root, 1996). There are many different readability formulas available, and most word processing programs have one included.

Step 12: Establish content validity for the instrument. It is suggested that you follow the two-step process using a jury (or panel) of experts outlined in Appendix C of this book (McKenzie *et al.,* 1999).

Step 13: Pilot test the instrument. If at all possible, use at least 30 participants (remember the central limit theorem from Chapter 7) who are as much as possible like the people who will comprise the participants in your study. Pilot testing is critical to developing a quality instrument (Daley, McDermott, McCormack Brown, & Kittleson, 2003).

Step 14: Conduct item analysis, factor analysis, and checks of psychometric properties. Determine the reliability of the instrument and, if possible, seek to determine a second type of validity (besides the content validity).

Step 15: Review, revise, and reassess. Based on the completion of Steps 13 and 14, review the comments of those in the pilot group and take the necessary steps to enhance the validity and reliability of the instrument.

Step 16: Conduct a second pilot test, if necessary. A second pilot test may be needed if significant changes have been made in the instrument or if the validity and reliability are low.

Step 17: Determine a cut score. If a criterion-referenced instrument or screening instrument is being created, a cut score will be needed (McDermott & Sarvela, 1999).

Step 18: Refine as needed and create the final version. Keep the instrument as brief as possible; do not keep any unnecessary or redundant items (O'Rourke, 2001).

Though the steps presented above are generic steps to follow in creating a measurement instrument, you may have to incorporate additional steps that may be peculiar to the instrument you are creating. Also, if you are creating an instrument that will be delivered via a computer, e-mail, or the Web, there may be other things with which you will need to be concerned. Several health education authors (Daley *et al.,* 2003; Kittleson, 2003; Pealer & Weiler, 2000) have provided lessons, suggestions, and ideas for using the Web to collect data, while Schonlau and colleagues (2002) have provided a more in-depth presentation of collecting data electronically.

Summary

A well-designed measurement instrument will produce consistent and accurate data. This chapter presented background information on levels of measurement (nominal, ordinal, interval, and ratio), psychometric properties (validity, reliability, and fairness) of measurement instruments, and how to measure various variables of interest. In addition, step-by-step approaches were presented for identifying, obtaining, and evaluating existing measurement instruments, and how to go about creating an original measurement instrument.

Review Questions

1. Define measurement and measurement instrument.
2. What are the four levels of measurement? Describe the characteristics of each.
3. Write an instrument item that creates data for each different level of measurement.
4. What is meant by the term psychometric properties?
5. Why are good psychometric properties so important in measurement?
6. Define the term validity and provide a brief explanation of the following types of validity: concurrent validity, construct validity, content validity, convergent validity, criterion-related validity, discriminant validity, face validity, and predictive validity.
7. Define the term reliability and provide a brief explanation of the following types of reliability: internal consistency reliability, parallel forms reliability, rater reliability, and test–retest (stability) reliability.
8. What is meant by the terms sensitivity and specificity? In what situations are these terms used?
9. Define and differentiate among structured, unstructured, and hybrid instrument items.
10. What is Bloom's taxonomy? How should it affect the measuring of knowledge?
11. Write three instrument items that measure attitudes. Create one using a Likert scale, a second using semantic differential, and a third using paired comparisons.
12. What are the six different "environments" that health educators measure?
13. What is the key to measurement through observation?
14. What are the three ways of measuring skills and behavior? What are the advantages and disadvantages of each?
15. What is the difference between obtrusive and unobtrusive observation?
16. What is meant by authentic assessment?
17. What are the steps one should follow when identifying, obtaining, and evaluating an existing measurement instrument?
18. What are the steps one should follow when creating a new measurement instrument?

References

Anderson, P., & Fenichel, E. (1989). *Serving culturally diverse families of infants and toddlers with disabilities.* Washington, D.C.: National Center for Clinical Infant Programs.

Arriola, K.R.J., Usdan, S., Mays, D., Weitzel, J.A., Cremeens, J., Martin, R.J. *et al.* (2009). Reliability and validity of the alcohol consequences expectations scale. *American Journal of Health Behavior*, 33(5), 504–512.

Atkinson, N.L. (2007). Developing a questionnaire to measure perceived attributes of ehealth innovations. *American Journal of Health Behavior*, 31(6), 612–621.

Babbie, E. (1995). *The practice of social research* (7th ed.). Belmont, Calif.: Wadsworth.

Backstrom, C.H., & Hursh-Cesar, G. (1981). *Survey research* (2nd ed.). New York: Wiley.

Bartholomew, L.K., Parcel, G.S., Kok, G., & Gottlieb, N.H. (2006). *Planning health promotion programs: An intervention mapping approach* (2nd ed.). San Francisco, Calif.: Jossey-Bass.

Becker, C.M., Dolbier, C.L., Durham, T., Glasscoff, M.A., & Adams, T.B. (2008). Development and preliminary evaluation of the validity and reliability of a positive health scale. *American Journal of Health Education*, 39(1), 34–41.

Black, T.R. (1999). *Doing quantitative research in the social sciences: An integrated approach to research design, measurement, and statistics*. Thousand Oaks, Calif.: Sage.

Bloom, B.S. (Ed.) (1956). *Taxonomy of educational objectives: The classification of education goals. Handbook I: Cognitive domain*. New York: David McKay.

Borg, W.R., & Gall, M.D. (1989). *Educational research* (5th ed.). New York: Longman.

Bowling, A. (2002). *Research methods in health: Investigating health and health services* (2nd ed.). Buckingham, UK: Open University Press.

Bowling, A. (2005). *Measuring health: A review of quality of life measurement scales* (3rd ed.). Berkshire, England: Open University Press.

Campinha-Bacote, J. (1994). Cultural competence in psychiatric mental health nursing: A conceptual model. *Nursing Clinics of North America,* 29, 1–8.

Centers for Disease Control and Prevention (CDC). (2000). *Measuring healthy days*. Atlanta, Ga.: Author.

Cohen, H.J. (1991). My mother said, "if you had your health you have everything." What did she mean? In M. Feinlieb (Ed.), *Vital health statistics: Proceedings of 1988 International Symposium on Data on Aging* (DHHS Pub. No. PHS-91–1482) (pp. 5–9). Washington, D.C.: U.S. Government Printing Office.

Cohen, J.A. (1960). A coefficient of agreement for nominal scales. *Educational and Psychological Measurement*, 20(1), 37–46.

Cone, J.D., & Foster, S.L. (2006). *Dissertations and theses from start-to-finish*. Washington, D.C.: American Psychological Association.

Cottrell, R.R., Girvan, J.T., & McKenzie, J.F. (2009). *Principles and foundations of health promotion and education* (4th ed.). San Francisco: Benjamin Cummings.

Creswell, J.W. (2002). *Educational research: Planning, conducting, and evaluating quantitative and qualitative research*. Upper Saddle River, N.J.: Merrill/Prentice Hall.

Daley, E.M., McDermott, R.J., McCormack Brown, K.R., & Kittleson, M.J. (2003). Conducting Web-based survey research: A lesson in Internet design. *American Journal of Health Behavior,* 27(2), 116–124.

DiIorio, C.K. (2005). *Measurement in health behavior: Methods for evaluation and research*. San Francisco, Calif.: Jossey-Bass.

Dignan, M.B. (1995). *Measurement and evaluation of health education* (3rd ed.). Springfield, Ill.: Charles C. Thomas.

Doak, C.C., Doak, L.G., & Root, J.H. (1996). *Teaching patients with low literacy skills* (2nd ed.). Philadelphia: J.B. Lippincott.

Fleiss, J.L. (1981). *Statistical methods for rates and proportions* (2nd ed.). New York: John Wiley.

Friis, R.H., & Sellers, T.A. (2009). *Epidemiology for public health practice* (4th ed.). Sudbury, Mass.: Jones and Bartlett Publishers.

Galli, N. (1976). Foundations of health education. *Journal of School Health*, 46(3), 158–165.

Glover, E.D., Nilsson, F., Westin, A., Glover, P.N., Laflin, M.T., & Persson, B. (2005). Developmental history of the Glover-Nilsson smoking behavioral questionnaire. *American Journal of Health Behavior*, 29(5), 443–455.

Green, L.W., & Kreuter, M.W. (2005). *Health promotion planning: An educational and ecological approach* (4th ed.). Boston: McGraw-Hill.

Green, L.W., & Lewis, F.M. (1986). *Measurement and evaluation in health education and health promotion*. Palo Alto, Calif.: Mayfield.

Grimm, L.G. (1993). *Statistical applications for the behavioral sciences*. New York: Wiley.

Hopkins, K.D., Stanley, J.C., & Hopkins, B.R. (1990). *Educational and psychological measurement and evaluation* (7th ed.). Englewood Cliffs, N.J.: Prentice-Hall.

Howard, E.M., & Weiler, R.M. (2003). Development of a scale to assess the appropriateness of curricula materials for diverse populations. *American Journal of Health Education,* 34(3), 141–145.

Hurlburt, R.T. (2003). *Comprehending behavioral statistics* (3rd ed.). Belmont, Calif.: Wadsworth/Thomson Learning.

Isaac, S., & Michael, W.B. (1995). *Handbook in research and evaluation* (3rd ed.). San Diego: Educational and Industrial Testing Services.

Janz, N.K., Champion, V.L., & Strecher, V.J. (2002). The health belief model. In K. Glanz, B.K. Rimer, & F.M. Lewis (Eds.), *Health behavior and health education: Theory, research, and practice* (3rd ed., pp. 45–66). San Francisco: Jossey-Bass.

Joint Committee on Terminology. (2001). Report of the 2000 Joint Committee on Health Education and Health Promotion Terminology. *American Journal of Health Education*, 32(2), 89–103.

Kerlinger, F.N. (1986). *Foundations of behavioral research* (3rd ed.). Austin, Tex.: Holt, Rinehart & Winston.

Kittleson, M.J. (2003). Suggestions for using the Web to collect data. *American Journal of Health Behavior,* 27(2), 170–172.

Landis, J.R., & Koch, G.G. (1977). The measurement of observer agreement for categorical data. *Biometrics*, 33(1), 159–174.

Lawton, M.P. (1991). Background: A multidimensional view of the quality of life in the frail elderly. In J.E. Birren, J. Lubben, J. Rowe, & D. Deutchman (Eds.), *The concept of measurement of quality of life in the frail elderly* (pp. 4–27). San Diego, Calif.: Academic Press.

Likert, R. (1932). A technique for the measurement of attitudes. *Archives of Psychology,* 21, 140.

Mausner, J.S., & Kramer, S. (1985). *Epidemiology—an introductory text* (2nd ed.). Philadelphia: W.B. Saunders.

McDermott, R.J., & Sarvela, P.D. (1999). *Health education evaluation and measurement: A practitioner's perspective* (2nd ed.). St. Louis: WCB/McGraw-Hill.

McKenzie, J.F., Pinger, R.R., & Kotecki, J.E. (2008). *An introduction to community health* (6th ed.). Sudbury, Mass.: Jones and Bartlett.

McKenzie, J.F., Neiger, B.L., & Thackeray, R. (2009). *Planning, implementing, and evaluating health promotion programs: A primer* (5th ed.). San Francisco: Benjamin Cummings.

McKenzie, J.F., Wood, M.L., Clark, J.K., Kotecki, J.E., & Brey, R.A. (1999). Establishing content validity: Using qualitative and quantitative steps. *American Journal of Health Behavior,* 23(4), 311–318.

McLeroy, K.R., Bibeau, D., Steckler, A., & Glanz, K. (1988). An ecological perspective on health promotion programs. *Health Education Quarterly,* 15, 351–377.

Morreale, M. (n.d.). *Understanding public health research: A primer for youth workers. Issue brief.* Washington, D.C.: National Network for Youth.

Neutens, J.J., & Rubinson, L. (2010). *Research techniques for the health sciences* (4th ed.). San Francisco: Benjamin Cummings.

O'Rourke, T. (2001). Techniques to improve questionnaire format. *American Journal of Health Studies,* 17(1), 36–38.

O'Rourke, T., & O'Rourke, D. (2001). The ordering and wording of questionnaire items: Part I. *American Journal of Health Studies,* 17(3), 156–159.

O'Rourke, T., & O'Rourke, D. (2002). The ordering and wording of questionnaire items: Part II. *American Journal of Health Studies,* 17(4), 208–212.

Patterson, R. (Ed.). (2001). *Changing patient behavior: Improving outcomes in health and disease management.* San Francisco: Jossey-Bass.

Pealer, L.N., & Weiler, R.M. (2000). Web-based health survey research: A primer. *American Journal of Health Behavior,* 24(1), 69–72.

Prochaska, J.O., Redding, C.A., & Evers, K.E. (2008). The transtheoretical model and the stages of change. In K. Glanz, B.K. Rimer, & K. Viswanath (Eds.), *Health behavior and health education: Theory, research and practice* (4th ed., pp. 97–121). San Francisco, Calif.: Jossey-Bass.

Schonlau, M., Fricker, R.D., & Elliott, M. (2002). *Conducting research surveys via e-mail and the web (MR-1480-RC).* Santa Monica, Calif.: RAND.

TextaSoft. (2008). *SPSS tutorials for statistical data analysis: Interrater reliability (Kappa) using SPSS.* Retrieved May 16, 2009, from http://www.stattutorials.com/SPSS/TUTORIAL-SPSS-Interrater-Reliability-Kappa.htm.

Timmreck, T.C. (1997). *Health services cyclopedic dictionary* (3rd ed.). Boston: Jones and Bartlett.

Torabi, M.R. (1994). Reliability methods and numbers of items in development of health instruments. *Health Values,* 18(6), 56–59.

Torabi, M.R. (1989). A cancer prevention knowledge test. *The Eta Sigma Gamman* 20(2), 13–15.

Torabi, M.R., & Jeng, I. (2001). Health attitude scale construction: Importance of psychometric evidence. *American Journal of Health Behavior,* 25(3), 290–298.

Valente, T.W. (2002). *Evaluating health promotion programs.* New York: Oxford University Press.

Veneziano, L., & Hooper, J. (1997). A method for quantifying content validity of health-related questionnaires. *American Journal of Health Behavior,* 21(1), 67–70.

Weiss, C.H. (1998). *Evaluation* (2nd ed.). Upper Saddle River, N.J.: Prentice-Hall.

WHOQOL Group. (1998). Development of the World Health Organization WHOQOL-BREF quality of life assessment. *Psychological Medicine,* 28, 551–558.

Williams, B.L., Hetrick, C.J., & Suen, H.K. (1998). Development of performance-based assessments. *American Journal of Health Behavior,* 22(3), 228–234.

Windsor, R., Clark, N., Boyd, N.E., & Goodman, R.M. (2004). *Evaluation of health promotion, health education, and disease prevention programs* (3rd ed.). Boston: McGraw-Hill.

Zullig, K.J., Huebner, E.S., Patton, J.M., & Murray, K.A. (2009). The brief multidimensional students' life satisfaction scale—college version. *American Journal of Health Behavior,* 33(5), 483–493.

| # Quantitative Research Methods: Experimental (Writing Chapter III)

Chapter Objectives

After reading this chapter and answering the review questions, you should be able to:

1. State the purpose of experimental research.
2. Differentiate between laboratory and field research.
3. Define internal and external validity.
4. Explain each of the potential threats to internal validity as presented in this chapter.
5. Explain each of the potential threats to external validity as presented in this chapter.
6. Discuss how threats to internal and external validity can be controlled.
7. Describe the essential components of a true experimental design.
8. Identify the statistical test that can be used to control for variations between groups.
9. Demonstrate usage of the nomenclature used to diagram research designs.
10. Present an appropriate research design given a specific research question.
11. Discuss threats to internal and external validity given a specific research design.
12. Describe criteria to be used in evaluating experimental and quasi-experimental research.

Key Terms

analysis of covariance	history treatment interaction	population
baseline	implementation effect	procedures
blind study	interaction effect	selection bias
control group	internal validity	selection maturation effect
diffusion effect	laboratory research	selection treatment interaction
double blind study	location effect	setting treatment interaction
experimental group	main effect	statistical regression
experimental research	maturation effect	study population
external validity	mortality effect	testing effect
field research	pilot studies	test-wise
Hawthorne effect	placebo	threats to internal validity
history effect	placebo effect	

In the previous two chapters of the text, we presented information on sampling and instrument development. As discussed, you will need to provide complete descriptions of both your study participants and your instrumentation in separate sections of Chapter III for a quantitative thesis or dissertation. The next section of Chapter III to be written is the "**Procedures**" or methods section. In this section you will describe in detail how you conducted the research and explain the research design. The information you will need to make decisions about research design and methodology is contained in this chapter and the following two chapters of this text. In this chapter we will provide an explanation of experimental research and what is needed to be sure that conclusions drawn from experimental research are valid. By "valid" we mean that the results are technically sound and accurate. In other words, the results represent real differences and are not due to extraneous variables, statistical manipulation, or chance.

Experimental Research

The purpose of **experimental research** is to establish cause-and-effect relationships (Gay, Mills, & Airasian, 2006; Patten, 2009). In fact, "identifying causes—figuring out why things happen—is the goal of most social science research" (Schutt, 2009, p. 190). To many researchers, experimental research is the gold standard to which all other research is compared. The value of other, non-experimental research should not, however, be diminished by this statement. There are many research questions that cannot be answered with experimental research designs. These will be discussed in the following chapter.

Experimental research that takes place in laboratory settings is often called **laboratory research**, and experimental research that takes place in more "natural" or "real-life" settings is called **field research**. Laboratory research is usually found in disciplines such as chemistry, biology, physics, and sometimes psychology. In health education, field research is much more common than laboratory research, but laboratory research is occasionally utilized as well. Health education studies that measure stress levels using biofeedback equipment might be done in a laboratory setting. Measuring fitness levels by gas analysis and treadmill testing in a laboratory could also be part of a health edu-

cation specialist's research agenda. The actual fitness testing, however, would typically be conducted by an exercise physiologist or a trained lab technician. It would be far more common for health education specialists to be studying groups such as students, patients, employees, and communities in their natural setting.

Internal and External Validity

Establishing cause-and-effect relationships with experimental research is accomplished by manipulating the independent variable and observing the effects on the dependent variable. (See Chapter 5 for a discussion of variables.) In addition, the research design must control for the possible effects of extraneous variables that could mask, enhance, or in some way alter the effect of the independent variable on the dependent variable.

A study that does a good job controlling for the possible effects of extraneous variables on the dependent variable is said to have strong **internal validity**. In other words, internal validity exists if the observed effects of the independent variable on the dependent variable are real and not caused by extraneous factors. Anytime there are alternative explanations for the effect of the independent variable on the dependent variable, internal validity is threatened. **External validity** is concerned with the ability to generalize the study results to other groups and settings beyond those in the current experiment. Research that can be generalized will typically have more practical value to the profession than research that cannot be generalized.

It is more difficult to achieve internal validity in field research studies than in laboratory research studies. This is because there are so many extraneous variables to control in field research. Laboratory research, conducted in the tightly controlled conditions of an experimental laboratory, is more likely to produce results with internal validity. A paradox of research is that the more tightly controlled a study so as to achieve internal validity, the less likely it is to resemble the conditions of the real world, and the less likely it is to have external validity (Gay *et al.*, 2006; Neutens & Rubinson, 2010). For example, consider a study that might be designed to examine weight loss. Recruited obese participants will spend three weeks in a tightly controlled laboratory-type setting where their food intake will be carefully regulated and a stringent exercise regimen will be followed (independent variables). At the end of the three weeks, the participants have lost significant amounts of body fat (dependent variable). Because this study was so well controlled, it would have high internal validity. In other words, we would be fairly sure that the participants lost body fat because of the diet and exercise program. The study would not have high external validity, however, because it would be difficult to transpose the laboratory's structured diet and monitored exercise program to the real world.

Threats to Internal Validity

Those extraneous factors that allow for alternative explanations as to what caused a given effect on the dependent variable are known as **threats to internal validity**. Some of the more common threats to internal validity will now be discussed. Strategies to control the threats to internal validity will also be presented. See Box 9.1 for a listing of some of the more common threats to internal validity.

History

A **history effect** threatens internal validity when events occur between the pretest and posttest of a research study that could affect participants in such a way as to impact the dependent variable (Creswell, 2005). Events that could affect participants might include stress, natural disasters, news events, and illness. Suppose, for example, a health educator devised a study to examine the effects of a media campaign encouraging women to have a

---

Box 9.1   Common Threats to Internal Validity

History: an event occurring between pretest and posttest other than the independent variable that could affect the dependent variable

Maturation: changes occurring in participants because of passage of time (e.g., physical, mental, etc.)

Testing: taking a pretest somehow affects the taking of the posttest

Instrumentation: instruments are not accurate/precise enough or do not measure what they are supposed to measure

Selection bias: participants selected in a non-random manner differ in some way

Selection maturation: using intact groups that vary in some element of maturity

Statistical regression: extremely high or extremely low scores regress toward mean

Mortality/attrition: participants drop out of the study or cannot be located

Hawthorne: altered behavior due to the effects of being studied and observed

Placebo: altered behavior because of expectations

Diffusion: treatment of experimental group spills over to comparison or control groups

Location: the location of program or data collection affects participant responses

Implementation: differences in persons presenting a program affect the program

---

yearly mammogram on actual mammography rates. During the course of the study, however, a prominent celebrity figure announces that she has breast cancer that was diagnosed by a mammogram. This highly visible and vocal celebrity encourages all women to have a yearly mammogram. The media campaign study results indicate that indeed there was an increase in mammography rates. Was this increase a result of the media program? the publicity generated by the celebrity? a combination of the two? Depending on how the study was designed, it might be impossible to determine what caused the increased mammography rates because of this history effect.

The best way to control for the history effect would have been to use a control group that was not exposed to the media campaign. In experimental research, a **control group** is a group of participants exactly like the treatment group in every way possible except they receive no treatment. The group receiving the treatment is often referred to as the **experimental group**. Comparisons between the experimental group and control group can be made at the end of the study. Since both the control and experimental groups would be exposed to the celebrity message, it could be assumed that any differences between the control and experimental groups would be the result of the media campaign.

Maturation

A **maturation effect** occurs when changes are seen in subjects because of the time that has elapsed since the study began and that may not be the result of any program effects (Fraenkel & Wallen, 2006). In other words, over time the participants may have become older, wiser, stronger, or more experienced. Maturation effects are most common when children are being studied, because of their rapid growth rates (Berg & Latin, 2004). For example, suppose we wanted to study the effects of a year-long "Fun and Fit" preschool exercise program on the arm and leg strength of five-year-old children. At the end of the year, the preschoolers exhibit increased strength in both their arms and legs. Was this increase in strength because of the "Fun and Fit" program? It might be, but an alternative explanation would be that five-year-olds naturally increase muscular strength as they mature over a one-year period of time. Again, a control group would eliminate this threat to internal validity. Since both the control and experimental group would be expected to grow and gain muscle strength at the same rate during the year-long program, any differences between the two groups at the end of the study would most likely be the result of the fitness program.

Testing

In many types of research it is often necessary to pretest participants before beginning a study to establish a baseline level of the dependent variable. A **baseline** is a measurement taken to obtain the status or level of a variable prior to initiating a study. The pretest or baseline measurement is usually compared to a posttest measurement to determine the effectiveness of a program. The problem, as it relates to internal validity, is that by being tested, participants may learn how to do better on the test or be **"test-wise"** the next time they take the test (Neutens & Rubinson, 2010). Any differences seen from baseline to posttest may be from a **testing effect** and not the independent variable.

Consider participants being tested for relaxation on biofeedback equipment. During the pretest, they may be nervous if they have never been hooked up to biofeedback equipment before. They do not know what will happen and what they will be asked to do. The uncertainty of the situation may affect their ability to relax. They may also have difficulty relaxing because they have never practiced the skill. Following the pretesting, participants take part in a series of relaxation classes designed to teach them relaxation skills. After the classes, participants are posttested on the same biofeedback equipment. This time they know what the biofeedback test is like. They are more calm and relaxed about the procedure and may even remember what they did in the pretest to obtain higher levels of relaxation. Any improved relaxation levels seen in the posttest could be from a testing effect and not the relaxation classes. Use of a control group that does not receive any pretesting will reduce this threat to internal validity.

Instrumentation

The instrumentation used to collect data in a study can cause threats to internal validity when measurements are not accurate or procedures are not standardized (Neutens & Rubinson, 2010). Any actual physical instruments such as blood pressure cuffs, skinfold calipers, or biofeedback equipment must be carefully calibrated to give consistent and accurate results. Further, the individual or individuals using the equipment must be well trained and must follow consistent procedures. For example, if one was taking blood pressure measurements with two different instruments, there could be differences between the two instruments that might affect internal validity. If two different individuals were taking skinfold measures and using slightly different points on the body, internal validity could be affected.

Written instruments must accurately measure what they are supposed to measure or internal validity will be threatened. An instrument designed to measure the effect of "daily hassles" on stress levels must actually measure "daily hassles" and not some other concept such as burnout or long-term stressors. In addition, items on written instruments must be carefully designed to ask the correct question. If a researcher wanted to know how much refined sugar participants eat, this information would not be obtained by asking how often one eats desserts. Refined sugar can be found in many foods other than desserts such as breakfast cereals and sodas. Poorly designed questions can also cause internal validity problems. Asking participants to respond to the question, "How many cigarettes do you smoke in 24 hours?" by choosing from a list of options that includes 1–5, 5–10, 10–15, and so forth is problematic. Participants who smoke 10 cigarettes a day, for example, might place themselves in the 10–15 category on the pretest and in the 5–10 category on the posttest without ever changing their smoking behavior.

Well-designed instruments reduce this threat to internal validity. For further information on designing instruments, see Chapter 8 of this text.

Selection Bias

Anytime individuals are selected in a nonrandom manner, **selection bias** may be present, which will reduce internal validity. Selection bias introduces the possibility that participants in experimental and control groups may have differences before the start of the study that could account for any differences found between groups during the study, instead of such differences being due to the effects of the independent variable (Gay *et al.*, 2006).

In health education many studies are conducted in the field using intact groups, such as participants in a diabetes education class at XXX Hospital, or Ms. Smith's fourth-grade class, or members of a worksite fitness facility. In addition, volunteers must often be recruited to participate in studies, because it is not possible to use random selection and require those selected to participate in a given health program. Consider, for example, a new health program being studied at a corporate site. It is not uncommon that those who choose to participate are those most interested in health and not those who may most need the program. The use of intact groups and volunteers increases the likelihood that experimental and control groups are not the same. Any differences found at the end of the study may be the result of initial differences between the groups and not the program being studied.

Although selection bias resulting from lack of randomization cannot be completely countered, there are strategies that can help. Recruiting volunteers and then randomly assigning them to groups is better than allowing the volunteers to self-select a group. Matching participants on selected characteristics and then randomly assigning them to groups can also reduce selection bias. Finally, pretesting groups on measures of the dependent variable to make sure there are no pretreatment differences between groups is another control that can be used.

Selection Maturation Effect

Another threat to internal validity that actually combines a selection bias with a maturation threat is known as the **selection maturation effect** (Gay *et al.*, 2006; Neutens & Rubinson, 2010). This occurs when using intact groups that vary in their maturation level. One group, for example, may be older, more emotionally mature, more intellectually mature, and so forth.

Consider a study designed to evaluate the impact of two different coaching styles on the self-esteem of high-level competitive youth soccer players. Further consider that the two different coaching styles are being used with the youth soccer players in two neighboring cities. Unfortunately, one city allows players to begin at a younger age and moves them to the next age level sooner than does the other city. This could present a selection maturation effect in that the youth soccer players in the one city are not as mature as the youth soccer players in the other city. Pretesting and/or prescreening groups on maturity levels is a way to avoid this threat to internal validity.

Statistical Regression

Statistical regression concerns occur when participants are selected on the basis of their extremely high or low scores (Gay *et al.*, 2006). If these same participants were administered the same instrument again, the tendency would be for those who scored extremely high on the first test to score lower on the second test and those who scored extremely low on the first administration to score higher on the second administration. Essentially, those that score the highest may have nowhere to move but down, and those that score the lowest have nowhere to move but up. This would happen with no program in effect to impact scores and is called regression to the mean.

Suppose a researcher wanted to study the health knowledge of incoming freshmen and then follow those freshmen over their college years to see if those with higher knowledge levels practiced better health behaviors than those with lower knowledge levels. To determine knowledge level, a 100-item multiple-choice test is given to all entering freshmen. Those scoring in the top 10% (the

high health knowledge group) and those in the bottom 10% (the low health knowledge group) are followed through their college years and their health behaviors compared. For this study to have internal validity, those in the high health knowledge group would have to have the highest health knowledge levels, and those in the low health knowledge group would have to have the lowest health knowledge levels. Statistical regression would cause internal validity concerns with this study.

To demonstrate this concern, imagine these freshmen knew absolutely nothing about health and guessed at every question. They should get 25% of the questions correct, assuming each question had four possible answers. Obviously, however, all of these students would not score 25% on the test. Due to luck or chance, some would score above 25% and some would score below 25%. If we took those that scored the highest and those that scored the lowest and administered the test again, those that scored highest would likely score lower and those that scored lowest would likely score higher.

Given this statistical reality, the internal validity of the college freshmen study described above would be suspect. Even though the college freshmen had some level of health knowledge, regression to the mean would occur to some extent. Those in the top 10% might not be in the top 10% if tested a second time and those in the bottom 10% might not be in the bottom 10% if tested a second time. To counter this weakness, the study could be designed to follow a random sample of freshman students representing the full range of health knowledge scores rather than placing students in high and low groups based on one testing.

Mortality/Attrition

It is common to lose participants over the course of a study. In long-term longitudinal studies, some participants may actually die or be in such a poor state of health they cannot complete the study. In addition, a number of participants will move and not provide updated contact information and will be lost to the study. More commonly, however, in any experimental study where participants are pre- and posttested, some will drop out. This attrition creates a serious **mortality effect** problem that is difficult to counter (Fraenkel & Wallen, 2006). Loss of subjects can create problems in terms of group comparisons when the number of participants in some groups falls below established guidelines for statistical analysis. Smaller numbers of participants can also make it difficult to generalize to the larger population. In addition, dropouts can introduce bias into the study. Consider the bias introduced in a study if those that drop out are those with the least motivation, leaving only the highly motivated to participate in the study. Replacing dropouts is also problematic. If dropouts are replaced by simply going to the population and drawing additional participants, the replacement participants may differ in some important way from the original participants that dropped out.

Consider a corporate health education specialist who is conducting a study of two different smoking cessation programs to determine which is most effective in helping employees at his worksite to stop smoking. He recruits individuals who want to stop smoking and randomly places them in three different groups. One group of 20 participants receives program A, a second group of 20 participants receives program B, and the final group of 20 participants is a no-program control group, but they are told they will be in the next group to receive the smoking cessation program in two months. The results find that a higher percentage of those completing program A had quit smoking than those completing program B. Unfortunately, however, there was a 50% dropout rate in program A but only 10% dropped out of program B. Because of the high mortality in program A, internal validity is threatened and it cannot be concluded that program A is better than program B.

Oversampling and using large group sizes is one way to overcome small group size after mortality has occurred, but it does not eliminate the problem that those dropping out of the study may be different from those completing the study. Using incentives to encourage participants to stay in the study may be helpful in reducing mortality. Although the effects of mortality cannot be completely eliminated, they can be documented and analyzed. Obtaining good demographic information about study participants at the beginning of the study and then determining if the group makeup has changed at the end of the study after mortality has occurred can help measure the impact of mortality on the research (Gay *et al.*, 2006).

Hawthorne Effect

When participants' attitudes toward being involved in a study affect the way they behave, a **Hawthorne effect** has occurred. This phenomenon was first observed at the Hawthorne Plant of the Western Electric Company in Chicago (Gay *et al.*, 2006; Fraenkel & Wallen, 2006). Researchers were interested in determining the effects of altered work conditions on productivity. They believed, for example, that if lighting in the plant were improved, productivity would be improved. What they found, however, was that whether lighting was improved or reduced, productivity still increased. They concluded that the observed improvements in productivity resulted from the attention being paid to the workers involved in the study and not the changes in the work environment. The implication of this finding to health education research is that anytime an experimental group receives special attention over the control group, any noted differences in the dependent variable between the two groups may simply be a result of the attention given the experimental group and not the effect of the independent variable being studied.

To control for this, the researcher may try to provide the control group with some type of special treatment that is comparable to the experimental group but would not have a direct impact on the dependent variable. Therefore, with both groups receiving special attention, any differences in the dependent variable would likely be from the intervention. Although simple in theory, it is sometimes difficult to devise a special treatment that will provide a similar amount of attention but not affect the dependent variable. Another way to try to compensate for the Hawthorne effect is to keep participants from knowing that they are taking part in a study or being observed. Often, however, because of full disclosure requirements of institutional review boards, it is not possible to conduct studies without obtaining permission of the participants.

Placebo Effect

A **placebo effect** is caused by participants' expectations rather than by any provided treatment. In some ways the placebo effect is similar to the Hawthorne effect, except that the placebo effect is caused by expectations and the Hawthorne effect is caused by being studied and observed (Gay *et al.*, 2006). When taking medications, if a patient expects a drug to work, it may actually work, not because of the drug's properties but because the patient believes the drug will work. To control for this when testing new drugs, a control group is used that receives a **placebo**. The placebo looks like the real drug but is actually an inactive substance. Measures are taken to ensure that those involved in the study do not know whether they are receiving the real drug or the placebo. This is called a **blind study**. If the researcher also does not know who is taking the real drug and who is taking the placebo, it is called a **double blind study**. By using these procedures, any differences seen between the real drug and the placebo can be attributed to the drug and not the expectations of the participants or the researcher.

Placebo effects do not occur only in pharmaceutical studies. There can be a placebo effect for any research treatment where participants have an expectation about the outcome. To control for a placebo effect in health education studies, the researcher tries to make sure that those in both the

control and experimental groups receive the same information so that both groups would have similar expectations. Another way to handle this is to give both groups as little information as possible so as to reduce any expectations. If both groups have similar expectations at the beginning of the study, any differences between groups are more likely from the treatment effects than placebo effects.

Diffusion of Treatment

A **diffusion effect** occurs when the treatment being applied to one group spills over or contaminates another group (Neutens & Rubinson, 2010). Suppose a health education specialist designs a study to test the effects of a new in-chair physical conditioning program on the mobility of persons living in a large retirement community. One group of retirees is receiving the new in-chair program and a control group is just doing normal activities. Those in the in-chair group are excited about the program and tell those in the control group about the new exercises. Some of those in the control group now start to do the in-chair exercises on their own. A diffusion of treatment has occurred. If no differences in mobility between the two groups are found at the end of the study, it could be because the in-chair exercises had no effect, or it could be because the control group increased their mobility with the in-chair exercises, thus diminishing any differences in mobility between the two groups.

Controlling for a diffusion effect can be difficult, particularly if those in the experimental and control groups live or work together. In the above situation, it would be best to use another retirement community in another part of the city or even in another city as the control group. One would want to pay careful attention to match the retirement communities in terms of age, race, gender, health condition, and so forth (see Box 9.2). If only one retirement community is available, it would be important to explain the nature of the

---

Box 9.2   Matching Groups and Subjects

Sometimes it is necessary to study and compare intact groups of participants. To do so requires that the groups be matched as closely as possible on any traits that might affect the study. For example, if using two different corporate sites in a study, one might want to make sure that the workers at each site are similar with respect to age, gender, race, job type (e.g., labor vs. management), education level, and so on. If significant differences exist between worksites on any of these characteristics, differences seen in the dependent variable could be from the characteristic differences and not the intervention program.

In some studies, individual participants may be matched on a specific trait or traits and then assigned to either the experimental or control group. For example, in a smoking cessation study, it might be important for those in the control group to be similar to those in the experimental group in terms of number of years one has smoked and number of cigarettes smoked per day. Therefore, each individual smoker might be matched with another smoker who has been smoking for the same length of time and smokes about the same number of cigarettes per day. Once the matching is complete, one person from each pair is then randomly assigned to the experimental group and the other person to the control group.

Suppose that you are going to initiate a new health education curriculum into a selected group of school districts in your state. You want to have a group of school districts to compare with your districts receiving the new program. Obviously, it would be important that the comparison districts be very similar to the experimental districts. On what factors do you think the school districts should be matched? Think of as many possible factors as possible, then read the next paragraph to see how your factors compare with those of the authors.

Some factors on which to match the districts might include district size, district cost per pupil expenditures, district location (rural, urban, suburban), district racial distribution, district graduation rates, and district teacher/pupil ratios.

---

study to participants, emphasizing the need to keep all in-chair exercises confidential until the end of the study period.

Location

Location effect occurs when there are differences in the locations where interventions take place (Fraenkel & Wallen, 2006). Suppose two different interventions to stimulate health behavior change are being compared. Each intervention is being implemented at a different corporate site to control for a possible diffusion effect. A major part of the intervention involves individual counseling sessions with employees. At corporate setting A, the room for the counseling sessions is well lit, comfortable in temperature, and aesthetically pleasing with comfortable chairs. At corporate setting B, the room for the counseling sessions is dimly lit, too warm, and has paint peeling from the walls and hard chairs. Might the location have an impact on the effectiveness of the counseling sessions? If so, a location effect has occurred. The best method to control for a location effect is to make the locations the same for all participants. If that is not feasible, the researcher should do everything possible to minimize location differences that could impact the dependent variable.

Implementation

A final threat to internal validity has been described as the **implementation effect** or threat (Fraenkel & Wallen, 2006). This involves the individual or individuals responsible for implementing the experimental treatment and the possibility that they may inadvertently introduce inequality or bias into the study. This can happen in two ways.

First, if there are multiple people providing the treatment program or intervention, they may not be equal in their knowledge levels, understanding of the program, personality traits, presentation skills, and so forth. If, for whatever reason, some people do a better job of presenting the information than others, an implementation bias has been introduced.

This type of implementation bias can be controlled by trying to make sure that all persons responsible for implementing the program are equally trained and competent, and by following a standardized protocol for implementation. This could involve providing multiple comprehensive training programs for program implementers. Although this may take considerable time, it is well worth the effort. Another strategy is to have all the individuals involved in implementation instruct or present to all groups. That way both the stronger and weaker presenters will be equally involved with all groups.

The second way implementation bias can occur is if an individual implementing the intervention inadvertently favors one group over another. For example, suppose the researcher is implementing a new smoking cessation program she has developed. She is very excited about the new program and her enthusiasm shows in the way she treats the experimental group. She is more energetic and excited when meeting with the experimental group than when meeting with the standard treatment comparison group. It is possible that any differences found between the two groups could be the result of her interaction style with the experimental group and not the superiority of the smoking cessation program.

To control for this implementation threat, whenever possible, have someone other than the program developer present the program. The person presenting should be neutral and not have a vested interest in either the new experimental program or the standard treatment program. If this is not possible, another idea is to have a neutral observer watch the presenter with specific instructions to look for ways in which the two groups are being treated differently. This neutral observer can provide feedback while the program is ongoing that can then be incorporated into presentations to reduce presenter-introduced bias.

Threats to External Validity

As discussed at the beginning of this chapter, external validity is concerned with the ability to generalize study results to other groups and settings beyond those in the current experiment. As Creswell (2005) notes, "By ruling out extraneous factors and assuming that the treatment influences an outcome, researchers make claims about the generalizability of the results" (p. 293). Generalizing is an important aspect of research. "The whole notion of science is built on the idea of generalizing. Every science seeks to find basic principles or laws that can be applied to a great variety of situations and, in the case of the social sciences, to a great many people" (Fraenkel & Wallen, 2006, p. 104).

There are threats to external validity just as there are threats to internal validity. Obviously, if any of the threats to internal validity actually influence the results, those results are not true results caused by the independent variable's impact on the dependent variable and therefore could not be generalized to any other population. If we assume that the results seen in the experiment are true, there are still threats to external validity. In summarizing the work of Cook and Campbell (1979), Creswell (2005) identifies three major threats to external validity.

Selection Treatment Interaction

The first of the three threats to external validity is **selection treatment interaction**. This threat concerns the ability of a researcher to generalize the results of a study beyond the groups involved in the study. To what extent the results of a given study can be generalized to others is an important question and one we would like to discuss in detail.

There is always the danger of overgeneralizing to groups for whom the study results might not apply. If we assume that the results of a given experiment are valid, this obviously means they hold true for the group being studied. If that group was an intact group, we should not generalize beyond them. When using intact groups, researchers have no way of knowing if they are truly representative of a larger population.

For example, suppose a health education specialist received a grant from the state department of education to study the effects of a new conflict resolution program on sixth graders. Three sixth-grade classes in one school building are selected to receive the conflict resolution program. Results one year after the program was implemented indicate that the number of disciplinary actions by principals and the number of student fights were both significantly reduced for those receiving the program. Because an intact group, sixth-grade classes in one school building, was used, these results should not be generalized to sixth-grade classes in other school buildings in the district or to sixth-grade classes in other school districts. Sixth-grade classes in other buildings or districts could vary greatly in terms of school climate, cost per pupil expenditures, socioeconomic status, race, parental support, community involvement, and so forth. Fraenkel and Wallen (2006) note that whenever intact groups are used, "generalization is made more plausible if data are presented to show that the sample is representative of the intended population on at least some relevant variables. The procedure, however, can never guarantee representativeness on all relevant variables" (p. 104).

If, on the other hand, a study uses a random sample of participants, results can legitimately be generalized to the group from which the random sample was selected. This text will refer to this group as the **study population**. Using the conflict resolution example, suppose the health education specialist selected a random sample of sixth graders (not classes) to receive the program from all sixth graders in the school district. After one year, both the number of disciplinary actions by principals

and the number of student fights were significantly reduced among those sixth graders receiving the program. It would be appropriate to generalize these findings to the study population of all sixth graders from whom the sample was drawn—sixth graders in the school district.

It would not be appropriate, however, to generalize these findings to all sixth graders in the state, which very well might be considered the **population** by the department of education who funded the research. Essentially, results can be generalized to those persons that had a chance to be randomly chosen to be a study participant (see Figure 9.1). There is always the temptation to generalize beyond the sample population to the larger population. If the department of education truly wanted to generalize findings to all sixth graders in the state, the health education specialist would probably have begun by randomly selecting an appropriate number of school districts from all school districts in the state and then randomly selecting sixth-grade classes to receive the training from those randomly selected school districts. Using this procedure, all sixth-grade students in the state would have had an equal chance of being selected for the study. All sixth-grade students in the state would now be the sample population. From a feasibility perspective, this would be a much more difficult study to conduct than using randomly selected sixth graders from one school district. In turn, using randomly selected sixth graders from one school district would be more difficult than using intact classes in one school building. In general, research sophistication and difficulty increase as one desires to generalize to larger groups.

Setting Treatment Interaction

A second threat to external validity described by Creswell (2005) is the **setting treatment interaction**. This threat concerns the extent to which the environmental conditions or setting under which an experimental study was conducted can be duplicated in other settings. An effective alcohol education program in a private high school may

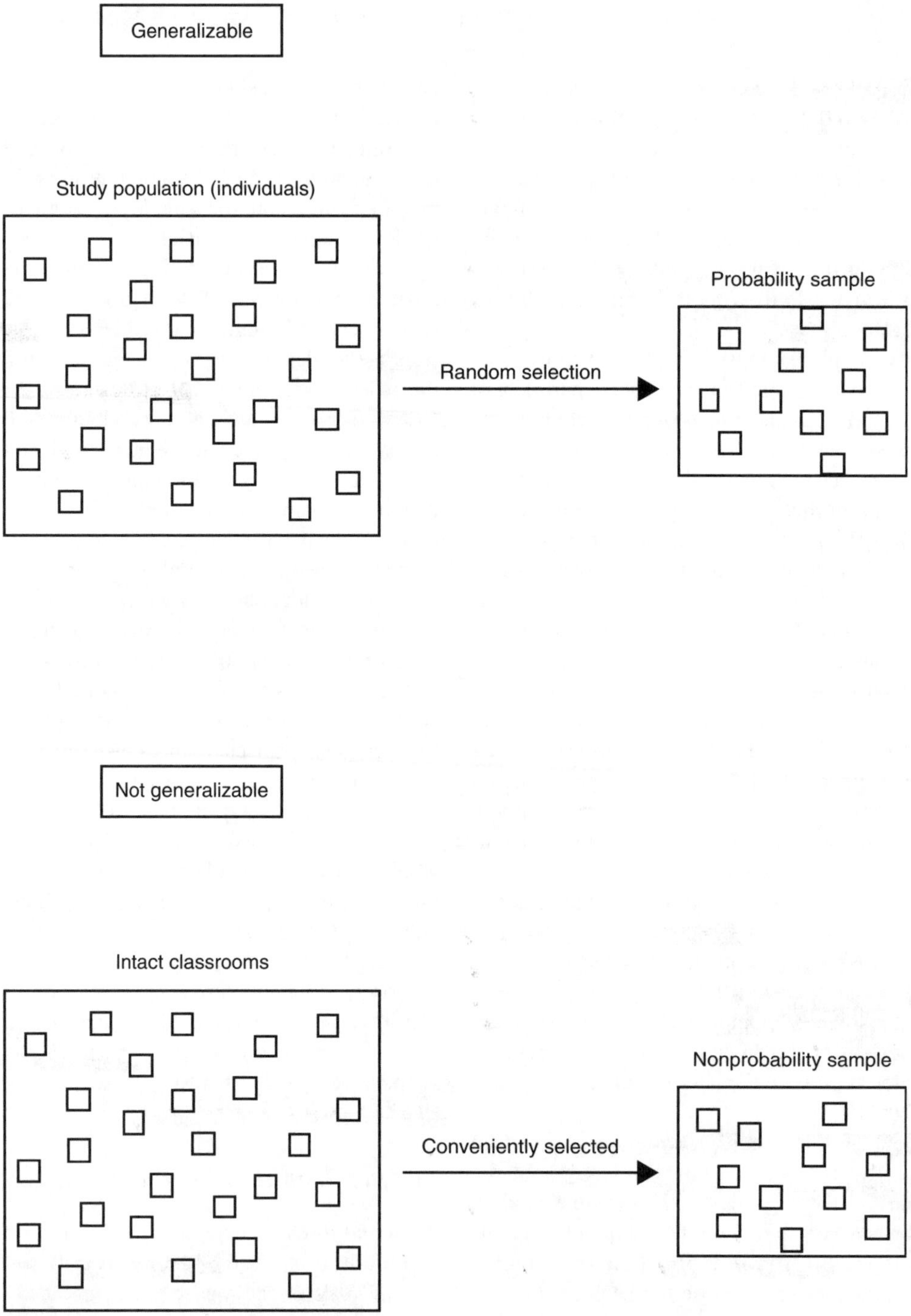

FIGURE 9.1
Generalizability.

not work when tried in a public high school. Those students attending the private high school may have more family support, higher socioeconomic status, and higher career aspirations, making them more receptive to the alcohol education program than students attending the public high school. Similarly, a mammography screening campaign that was effective at one worksite may not succeed when implemented at another corporate worksite. This could be because of differences in both the participants (e.g., knowledge, socioeconomic status, etc.) and the setting (e.g., cultural climate, previous breast cancer cases, privacy for screenings, etc.).

History Treatment Interaction

The **history treatment interaction** is the final threat to external validity described by Creswell (2005). "This threat to external validity develops when the researcher tries to generalize findings to past and future situations" (p. 294). Some experiments may be time-sensitive and may not produce similar results if conducted earlier or later. For example, a corporate fitness program offered at the lunch hour might attract many participants who make significant gains in physical fitness. The same program offered either before or after work might not attract many participants or produce gains in physical fitness. Similarly, a smoking cessation program offered in early January after community members had made their New Year's resolutions attracts many people and produces higher than expected quit rates. The same program offered in June attracts very few people and produces lower than expected quit rates.

Increasing Internal and External Validity

Having read about the potential threats to internal and external validity, one might assume that there is little need to conduct experimental research because it is impossible to obtain valid results. This

certainly is not the case. There are three important strategies that can be employed to control for most threats to internal validity. They are to randomly select participants from a well-defined study population, to randomly assign selected participants to groups, and to include non-treatment control groups in the research design. In addition to these strategies, the use of a fairly powerful statistical procedure called **analysis of covariance** or ANCOVA can be used to equalize many initial differences that might exist between groups. Your statistics course should cover this procedure in more detail.

In terms of external validity, carefully consider what groups one can legitimately generalize to, and do not generalize to other outside groups. In addition, always duplicate setting and historical factors as nearly as possible when replicating a program with a different population.

One final point needs to be emphasized before leaving internal and external validity. It should be remembered that external validity cannot exist without internal validity. That is to say, if the results of an experiment are not internally valid, there is nothing to generalize. Therefore, researchers should always be concerned about ensuring internal validity before trying to establish external validity.

Experimental Designs

The main purpose in selecting a research design is to identify and utilize the design that will control for as many extraneous variables as possible and that will still be practical and feasible to implement. In this section of the chapter we will review different research designs categorized as pre-experimental designs, true experimental designs, and quasi-experimental designs (Gay *et al.*, 2006).

The true experimental designs are the strongest designs that best control the threats to internal validity, thus creating the most confidence in any observed cause-and-effect relationships. That said, why is there a need to present pre-experimental and quasi-experimental designs in this text? Often it is neither feasible nor practical to conduct true experimental studies. Perhaps participants cannot be randomized, there are not enough potential participants to make control groups, a time factor or insufficient resources do not allow for pretesting, and so forth. Pre-experimental or quasi-experimental designs may be the only alternative. Although there may be more limitations and thus questions surrounding the results of pre-experimental and quasi-experimental studies than true experimental studies, they are nevertheless valuable. Pre-experimental and quasi-experimental studies can be replicated with similar populations or different populations. The more studies that report comparable findings, the more confident one can be that the results of pre-experimental and quasi-experimental studies are valid. In addition, results from pre-experimental and quasi-experimental studies are often considered preliminary findings. These preliminary findings may provide important justification for establishing a research agenda leading to future studies involving more sophisticated research designs.

Before beginning a discussion of research designs, it is important to understand the nomenclature or symbols used to visually represent the various aspects of a research design. This nomenclature is standardized and is utilized in numerous research texts (Fraenkel & Wallen, 2006; Gay *et al.*, 2006; Neutens & Rubinson, 2010).

X = Independent variable that is manipulated—the treatment

X_2 or Y = additional treatments

O = An observation or a measurement of the dependent variable (each observation may be numbered independently, indicating the order in which the observations occur—O_1, O_2, O_3, etc.)

R = Random assignment

Xs and Os in a given horizontal line are applied to the same group or persons

Xs and Os in a vertical line are simultaneous

Parallel rows separated by a dashed line means groups are not equivalent

Left to right indicates temporal order

Pre-experimental Designs

As we have mentioned, the pre-experimental designs are the weakest designs. They lack one or more features such as randomization, pre-/posttests, or control groups that are needed to minimize threats to internal validity. We will begin with the weakest of all pre-experimental designs.

One-Shot Case Study Design

$$X \qquad O$$

In this type of experiment, a treatment is given to one group. There is no randomization, no control group, and no pretesting. None of the threats to internal validity are controlled when using this design. Essentially, the researcher examines the results based on what he or she expected to see if no intervention had taken place. The researcher's expectations might or might not be accurate. An example of this design might involve a researcher wanting to explore the effects of a motorcycle safety pamphlet on the attitudes of motorcycle riders. After having a group of motorcyclists read the pamphlet (X), an attitude instrument is administered (O). If the attitude of the motorcyclists is fairly positive, the researcher might decide that the pamphlet is effective. In actuality, however, with no control group, no randomization, and no pretesting, there is no way of knowing if the pamphlet had any effect on attitudes. These motorcyclists may have had positive attitudes toward motorcycle safety prior to reading the pamphlet. It is possible that the pamphlet had no impact whatsoever on these motorcyclists. Still, it would be better to administer this design than to do nothing. One might find that the motorcyclists still had rather negative attitudes toward motorcycle safety after reading the pamphlet. In this case, the researcher would at least know that the pamphlet did not have the desired effect.

One-Group Pretest–Posttest Design

$$O_1 \quad X \quad O_2$$

Although this design is an improvement over the one-shot case study design, it is still weak. Using the motorcycle safety pamphlet example, this time the riders are given an attitude pretest (O_1), then they read the pamphlet (X), and then they are given an attitude posttest (O_2). If there is an improved attitude from pretest to posttest, it may mean the pamphlet is effective. The improved attitude could also be explained by a possible testing effect whereby the pretest gave the riders hints as to how they "should" answer the posttest. Another possibility is that this group of motorcyclists is very receptive to an attitude change because someone they ride with has just experienced a serious accident.

Although the one-group pretest–posttest design is weak, it is sometimes necessary in situations where it is neither permissible nor ethical to give different treatments to different groups. Schools, for example, may not allow programs where some students are treated differently—that is, one group gets the program and the other does not.

The Static-Group Comparison Design

$$X \quad O$$
$$\text{------}$$
$$O$$

This research design includes a comparison group that does not receive the treatment. Note,

however, that the participants are not randomly assigned to their respective groups, as indicated by the lack of Rs and the dashed line denoting unequal groups. Using our motorcycle pamphlet example again, in this design a group of motorcycle riders receive the pamphlet (X) and then are administered the attitude survey (O). A second group of motorcycle riders is given the attitude survey (O) but not the pamphlet. Comparisons are then made between the attitude survey scores of the two groups. Again, if differences are found, one cannot be sure that they are the result of reading the pamphlet. Because the participants in the two groups were not randomly selected, there may be differences between the two groups that could account for any observed differences in attitudes. For example, one group may be better readers or more receptive to safety tips than the other group. Since there was no pretest, the researcher does not know if there were differences in attitude prior to reading the pamphlet that may have carried over to the posttest.

Static-group comparison designs can take on slightly different forms than that seen above. In one variation, the first group still receives the experimental treatment (X_1), but the second group might receive an alternative or standard treatment (X_2) (Fraenkel & Wallen, 2006). There is still no pretesting and no randomization. The following would depict this static-group comparison design:

$$X_1 \quad O$$
$$\text{--------}$$
$$X_2 \quad O$$

The results from any pre-experimental study must be considered preliminary until they can be replicated and confirmed over time or by using a more sophisticated research design. Sometimes these studies are referred to as **pilot studies**, which means they are designed on a small scale with the intent to determine if there are any positive results that would justify further study.

True Experimental Designs

In true experimental designs, randomization, control groups, and experimental groups are included in each design. Whenever possible, true experimental designs should be selected for use in experimental research studies. These are the strongest types of designs controlling for most threats to internal validity.

Posttest-Only Control Group Design

$$R \quad X \quad O$$
$$R \quad\quad O$$

The posttest-only control group design looks similar to the static-group comparison design with one important difference, randomization. Note the presence of the Rs and the absence of the dashed line. By randomizing participants into the two groups, equivalence at the beginning of the study is assumed. This is a powerful design controlling for most threats to internal validity with the exception of mortality. Since there is no pretesting this design is especially useful if there is concern about a possible testing effect.

For example, suppose a health education specialist wanted to test a new smoking cessation program with employees of a large corporation. The health education specialist would recruit smokers who want to quit. From those recruited, two random groups would be selected (R). One of the groups would randomly be assigned the new smoking cessation program, and the other group would be told that the smoking cessation class had filled up but they would be enrolled in the next class to be offered. The experimental group would receive the smoking cessation program (X). At a specified time after the program, participants in both groups would be questioned or observed (O) related to the dependent variable. In this example, the dependent variable would probably be either cessation or number of cigarettes smoked per day or both. Comparisons could then be made between the group that had the new program and the control group that did not. Given the randomization and control group comparison inherent in the design, the researcher could conclude that any differences in the dependent variable were the result of the new smoking cessation program.

Pretest–Posttest Control Group Design

$$R \quad O_1 \quad X \quad O_2$$
$$R \quad O_1 \quad\quad O_2$$

This is a very strong design. Both groups are randomly assigned (R) and experience a pretest (O_1) and a posttest (O_2). The design controls for all threats to internal validity. It also allows for pretest comparisons to make sure there are no preintervention differences between the groups. If differences are found, the ANCOVA statistical test can be used to control them.

The only weakness of the pretest–posttest control group design is a possible pretest–intervention interaction that could limit external validity. Suppose a health education specialist was testing a new nutrition intervention program. The pretest consisted of a three-day dietary recall. Perhaps the act of recording everything one has eaten in the past three days creates an awareness that somehow enhances the effect of the new nutrition intervention. Because both groups would do the three-day dietary recall, threats to internal validity would be controlled. Let us further suppose that the results of the study indicate that the new nutrition intervention has a positive effect on nutrition behaviors. The new program, having demonstrated effectiveness, is now to be implemented with other groups. Because these new implementations with the other groups are not set up as studies, no pretest three-day dietary recall will be done. If the three-day dietary recall actually did enhance the nutrition intervention, these new groups receiving the program will not experience the same degree of success as did the original study group.

Solomon Four-Group Design

R	O	X	O
R	O		O
R		X	O
R			O

The Solomon Four-Group Design is a particularly robust and sophisticated research design. It controls for factors associated with both internal and external validity. This design allows researchers to (1) determine the effects of a treatment in relation to a control group, (2) determine any effects of a pretest on the dependent variable, and (3) explain any interactions between the pretest and the treatment. In reality it is a combination of the posttest-only control group design and the pretest–posttest control group design. By combining the two designs, the weaknesses of each are eliminated.

If the Solomon Four-Group Design is such a powerful design, why do only some researchers utilize it when conducting experimental research? The answer to this question is that it is also a difficult design to implement. In many settings, it is impossible to randomize participants into four groups as this research design requires. Many settings require intact groups to remain intact. Schools and corporations in particular are often not amenable to separating students or employees into four random groups. Even when intact groups are not necessitated by the setting, it is often not feasible to find enough subjects to make up four different randomly assigned groups. Each group must have a sufficient number of participants to allow for meaningful comparisons and statistical analysis. Time and effort are also increased with this design. The researcher must administer two pretests, two interventions, and four posttests. With all the various comparisons that can be made among the four groups, at the end of the study, data analysis is more complicated. Fortunately, with today's computers sophisticated data analysis can be accomplished with little difficulty.

Factorial or Multivariate Designs

R	O_1	X	Y_1	O_2
R	O_3		Y_1	O_4
R	O_5	X	Y_2	O_6
R	O_7		Y_2	O_8

Factorial designs are more complicated than the previously discussed designs. In all previously discussed designs, there was only one independent variable being studied in relation to a dependent variable. In factorial designs two or more independent variables are studied simultaneously to determine their independent and combined effects on the dependent variable. In the above diagram, variables X, Y_1, and Y_2 are being examined. Also in this example, the observations are numbered with subscripts. This is simply to help make comparisons easier. For example, the researcher may want to make an O_2–O_4 comparison to determine the added effect of X on Y_1.

The terminology associated with factorial designs is unique. The effect of each independent variable on the dependent variable is termed a **main effect**. The combined effect or the interaction of two or more independent variables on a dependent variable is known as an **interaction effect** (Neutens & Rubinson, 2010).

An example of a factorial design might occur in a worksite setting. The health education specialists want to know what recruitment strategy or strategies work best to encourage new memberships in the corporate health center. Variable X represents a standard e-mail message sent by the health center director to each employee. Variable Y_1 is a personalized letter from the company president encouraging employees to join the fitness center. Variable Y_2 is a personal phone call to employees from a health education specialist inviting them to join the fitness center. By utilizing a factorial design, the researcher could determine the effectiveness of each recruitment strategy and of combining recruitment strategies.

To fully test all possible permutations of the three techniques for recruitment in the previous example we could add more groups to the original four groups as follows:

R O_9 X O_{10}

R O_{11} Y_1 Y_2 O_{12}

R O_{13} X_1 Y_1 Y_2 O_{14}

Quasi-Experimental Designs

As has been mentioned, there are often situations where it is impossible to use a true experimental design. Perhaps there may not be enough available participants, randomization is not possible, and/or intact groups must be used. In these situations, using quasi-experimental designs may be the best and only alternative. Quasi-experimental designs are stronger than the pre-experimental designs but not as strong as the true experimental designs. As will be seen, they do not involve the use of randomization and control groups as in true experimental designs.

Interrupted Time Series Design

O_1, O_2, O_3, O_4 X O_5, O_6, O_7, O_8

In the interrupted time series design, there is no randomization and no control or comparison group. Essentially, a series of observations take place over a given period of time to establish a true baseline of the dependent variable. An intervention is administered followed by another series of observations. The observations from the preintervention are compared to the observations from the postintervention.

Suppose a corporate health education specialist was interested in studying job satisfaction before and after the opening of a new health center at a company. Job satisfaction scores could be obtained monthly for four months prior to the opening of the new center (O_1, O_2, O_3, O_4) and a mean job satisfaction score could be calculated. Once the center is opened and operational, job satisfaction scores could be obtained monthly for another four months (O_5, O_6, O_7, O_8) and a mean job satisfaction score could be calculated. The pre- and postopening mean job satisfaction scores could then be compared. By using the time series design, the impact of individual months where there might be an unusually high or unusually low job satisfaction score would be minimized by the utilization of the calculated mean score for the four-month time intervals. It should be noted that both the model and the example use four observations pre- and postintervention. Actually the number of observations could be either greater or less than four. There is nothing sacred about four observations.

Equivalent Time Sample Design

X_1O X_2O X_1O X_2O

The equivalent time sample design uses one group and no randomization, just like the interrupted time series design. The difference is that the intervention or interventions are initiated and withdrawn several times to determine effects. Consider a health education specialist who wants to determine if the type of morning snack provided to preschool children influences their behavior throughout the rest of the morning hours. For three weeks, the students are given donuts and a high-calorie fruit drink for their regular morning snack (X_1). The next three weeks, the students are given a bagel or muffin and milk (X_2). During the following three weeks, the donuts and fruit drinks are reintroduced (X_1). After the second round of donuts and fruit drinks, a second round of bagels or muffins and milk is initiated (X_2). At noon each day during the 12-week testing period, the preschool teachers respond to a short evaluation of their preschoolers' behavior. Mean behavior scores could be calculated for each three-week period and comparisons made. This study design would be even stronger if the teachers did not know what snacks the children were given.

Again, there is nothing sacred about introducing and reintroducing the intervention two times. We could have alternated interventions three, four, or five times just as easily. In fact, the more times the interventions are introduced and withdrawn, the more certain one can be of valid results.

The Counterbalanced Design

	Time 1	Time 2	Time 3
Group A	X_1O	X_2O	X_3O
Group B	X_2O	X_3O	X_1O
Group C	X_3O	X_1O	X_2O

A counterbalanced design is effective in comparing any number of treatments over the same number of groups if the groups cannot be randomized. Each group will receive each treatment in a different order. By rotating the order of treatments among the groups, any potential effects due to previous learning from other treatments will be minimized. The previous diagram is designed for three treatments, but it could easily be adjusted for two or four treatments. In this example, each treatment will be given to one group first, one group second, and one group third.

As an example, a hospital-based health education specialist wants to study the impact of three different relaxation techniques on the perceived relaxation levels of hospital nurses. Three intact groups of nurses are selected to participate in the study. Each group will receive all three treatments but in different orders. Treatment 1 involves neuromuscular relaxation exercises (X_1), treatment 2 involves yoga exercises (X_2), and treatment 3 involves tai chi exercises (X_3). After each treatment, participants complete a standardized instrument to

determine their perceived level of relaxation (O). To analyze the results, the health education specialist will take the perceived relaxation scores for each treatment from all three groups and average them together. The average perceived relaxation scores for neuromuscular relaxation, yoga, and tai chi can then be compared.

Nonequivalent Control Group Design

$$O_1 \quad X \quad O_2$$
$$\text{-----------}$$
$$O_1 \qquad\quad O_2$$

The nonequivalent control group design is similar to the true experimental pretest–posttest control group design but without the important element of randomization (note the absence of Rs in the design). A positive aspect of this design is that a control group is used. The nonequivalent control group design is commonly used in health education, as it is often necessary to use intact groups in health education research.

For example, a health education specialist employed at a public health department desires to determine the effectiveness of a pilot community recycling program on the recycling behaviors of community residents. The program consists of radio, TV, and newspaper promotions; free distribution of recycling bins; and free recycling pickup. A second community in another part of the state is selected as the control community. This community will receive no recycling program and was selected because it is similar in size and is outside the radio, TV, and newspaper distribution area of the experimental community. Measurements of recycling are taken in both communities before the actual recycling program is initiated (O_1). After the recycling program (X) has been in place for four months, measurements of recycling are again conducted in both communities (O_2). Comparisons are made between the recycling levels in the two communities.

There is some question about how to classify the nonequivalent control group design. Fraenkel and Wallen (2006) discuss nonequivalent control group designs in their presentation of weak or pre-experimental designs. Others consider it a quasi-experimental design (Gay *et al.*, 2006; Neutens & Rubinson, 2010; Patten, 2009). We have chosen to present it as a quasi-experimental design because we believe it to be stronger than the other designs presented as pre-experimental.

See Box 9.3 to practice selecting research designs for a given research question.

Evaluating Experimental and Quasi-Experimental Research

Earlier in this chapter it was noted that for many researchers, experimental research is the gold standard to which other research is compared. Even so, not all experimental research is good research. It is important for health education specialists to analyze and evaluate experimental and quasi-experimental research to determine its quality and practical application to the field. Creswell (2005) identified several criteria on which to evaluate experimental research. The intervention (or independent variable) used in experimental research must be carefully examined. Is the intervention robust or strong enough to create the hypothesized change in the dependent variable? In health education, we are often seeking to create a behavioral change; yet the intervention may be a one-time awareness-raising presentation or the distribution of a pamphlet. Although such interventions may enhance knowledge or awareness, it is unlikely they will lead to long-term and sustained behavior change. Such weak interventions, even when used in an experimental research design, do not make good research. Another criterion of good experimental research is that participants should gain from the intervention, and it is doubtful if such weak interventions will actually benefit the participants in terms of health behaviors.

Box 9.3   Designing Research

Below are several research questions. For each research question, design an appropriate research study to answer the question. Be realistic in designing the research, considering whether randomization is possible, intact groups must be used, human subjects approval would be granted, funding would be available, and so on. For each design, identify any threats to internal and external validity. After designing your study, compare your designs with other students in class. How do the designs differ? How are they similar?

1. Will a mandatory warm-up/stretching program reduce the frequency and severity of injury to youth soccer players in grades K–6?

2. Will there be significant differences in sexual attitudes and behaviors among high school sophomores based on their participation in an abstinence-based sexuality education course versus an abstinence-only sexuality education course?

3. Will parents be more likely to have their babies vaccinated if they are exposed to a vaccination education program while visiting their obstetrician during pregnancy, if exposed to a vaccination education program while visiting the pediatrician after pregnancy, or if exposed to no vaccination education program?

4. Will a five-year citywide effort to reduce heart disease be successful in lowering the incidence of cardiac episodes in Cincinnati?

5. Do those employees who participate in the corporate wellness program miss fewer days of work and have lower health care costs than employees who do not participate in the corporate wellness program?

The number of participants is also an important criterion when evaluating experimental research. Is there a sufficient number of participants overall and within each experimental and control group? How was the number of participants determined? There should be a systematic and rational process utilized to determine the number of participants needed for a study. (See Determining Sample Size in Chapter 7.) Even when a good experimental design is utilized, if the number of participants is not large enough, the statistical results will be questionable.

Measurement is another issue to be considered in experimental research. Any measurement of the dependent variable must be valid and reliable. Physical measurements such as weight, height, blood pressure, and body fat must be done by qualified individuals using well-calibrated and reliable instruments. Other instruments that measure knowledge, attitudes, behaviors, or various theoretical constructs must also be valid and reliable. Self-report measures of behavior, although often the only feasible way to collect data in some health education studies, are suspect and may not provide valid results. The strongest and most robust experimental research designs are worthless if the measurements being used are inaccurate.

Finally, when conducting experimental research, threats to internal and external validity must be minimized. Since the practical realities of conducting behavioral research often require health education specialists to use quasi-experimental designs, it is extremely important to understand, consider, and minimize threats to both internal and external validity. Selecting an appropriate research design, randomizing when possible, and using carefully matched control groups are the best ways to increase the credibility of experimental and quasi-experimental research.

Summary

This chapter presents essential information to help readers understand experimental research. Although not every health educator or health education student will conduct experimental research, it is important to understand this important type of research so as to critically analyze the research of others and to understand the relative strengths and weaknesses of pre-experimental, true experimental, and quasi-experimental research.

The chapter begins with a general discussion of experimental research and where it is conducted. The concepts of internal and external validity are defined, followed by a thorough discussion of those factors that can threaten the internal and/or external validity of a study. Although many factors can have a negative impact on validity, most can be controlled through the use of randomization and control groups.

Numerous research designs are presented that are categorized into pre-experimental designs, true experimental designs, and quasi-experimental designs. A diagram of each research design is presented along with a description and an example of how each design could be utilized. True experimental designs are the strongest designs and produce the highest levels of confidence in the validity of results. Nevertheless, pre-experimental and quasi-experimental designs are often utilized because there is no other practical way to conduct the research. Health education specialists are often involved in field research that involves pre-experimental or quasi-experimental designs and are seldom involved in laboratory research, which tends to use more true experimental designs.

Review Questions

1. Explain what information should be included in the "Procedures" section of a thesis or dissertation's Chapter III.
2. Define experimental research.
3. Compare and contrast field and laboratory research. Which is most common to health education? Why?
4. List and describe five potential threats to internal validity.
5. A health education specialist designs a study to compare the alcohol drinking behaviors of those students that scored highest on the alcohol knowledge assessment with the alcohol

drinking behaviors of those students that scored lowest on the alcohol knowledge assessment. What internal validity concerns might you have?

6. Describe three broad categories of threat to external validity.

7. Name and describe the following research diagram.

$$O \quad X \quad O$$
$$O \qquad O$$

8. Name and describe the following research diagram.

$$R \quad X \quad O$$
$$R \qquad O$$

9. Explain the advantages and disadvantages of using a Solomon Four-Group Design.

10. Describe a study where you might use an interrupted time series design.

11. Based on the following hypothesis, diagram and explain an appropriate research design: High-cholesterol patients who are given the *Reduce Cholesterol the Easy Way* video series will lower their cholesterol levels more than high-cholesterol patients who are given the standard written information.

References

Berg, K.E., & Latin, R.W. (2004). *Essentials of research methods in health, physical education, exercise science, and recreation*. Philadelphia: Lippincott Williams & Wilkins.

Cook, T., & Campbell, D. (1979). *Quasi-experimentation*. Boston: Houghton Mifflin.

Creswell, J.W. (2005). *Educational research: Planning, conducting, and evaluating quantitative and qualitative research*. Upper Saddle River, N.J.: Pearson Education, Inc.

Fraenkel, J.R., & Wallen, N.E. (2006). *How to design and evaluate research in education* (6th ed.). Boston: McGraw-Hill.

Gay, L.R., Mills, G.E., & Airasian, P. (2006). *Educational research: Competencies for analysis and applications*. Upper Saddle River, N.J.: Pearson Education, Inc.

Neutens, J.J., & Rubinson, L. (2010). *Research techniques for the health sciences* (4th ed.). San Francisco: Benjamin Cummings.

Patten, M.L. (2009). *Understanding research methods: An overview of the essentials*. Glendale, Calif.: Pryczak Publishing.

Schutt, R.K. (2009). *Investigating the social world: The process and practice of research*. Boston: Pine Forge Press.

CHAPTER 10 | # Quantitative Research Methods: Non-experimental (Writing Chapter III)

Chapter Objectives

After reading this chapter and answering the review questions, you should be able to:

1. State the purpose of non-experimental research.
2. Describe how non-experimental research differs from experimental research.
3. Define survey research.
4. Identify research questions that can best be answered by survey research.
5. Describe the two main types of survey research designs.
6. Explain advantages and disadvantages of mail surveys, group administered surveys, electronic questionnaires, personal interviews, and telephone surveys.
7. Identify strategies for enhancing the effectiveness of mail surveys, group administered surveys, electronic questionnaires, personal interviews, and telephone surveys.
8. Explain when to use correlational studies.

9. Explain positive relationship, negative relationship, and curvilinear relationship.
10. Discuss interpretation limitations of correlational studies.
11. Describe causal-comparative research.
12. List three techniques that can be used to improve the validity of causal-comparative research.
13. Define evaluation research.
14. Differentiate between summative and formative research.
15. Differentiate between goals and objectives.
16. Describe the multiple levels at which objectives may be written.
17. Write goals and objectives at multiple levels.
18. Explain the data collection process needed for a given evaluation study.

Key Terms

analysis of covariance	correlational study	formative evaluation
anonymous	cross-sectional study	goals
behavioral objectives	curvilinear relationship	group administration
causal-comparative research	descriptive group-comparison design	incentives
census survey	electronic questionnaire	interview
cohort study	enabling learning objectives	learning objectives
confidential	environmental objectives	linear relationship
correlation	evaluation	longitudinal study
correlation coefficient	ex post facto research	multiple regression

continued

Key Terms *continued*

non-experimental research	process evaluation	return services
objectives	process (formative) objectives	rule of sufficiency
objectives-oriented approach	program goals	summative evaluation
panel study	program objectives	survey research
passive consent	questionnaire	telephone survey
predisposing learning objectives	reinforcing learning objectives	trend study

In the previous chapter of the text we presented information on experimental research. You may recall that the purpose of experimental research is to establish cause-and-effect relationships (Leedy & Ormrod, 2010; Patten, 2009). Also in experimental research, one or more independent variables were manipulated in some way to determine their effects on a dependent variable. In this chapter we will examine non-experimental research. Keep in mind the characteristics of experimental research and note how they differ from non-experimental research as you read this chapter.

Non-experimental Research

Non-experimental research designs are typically utilized when it is not practical, possible, feasible, or desirable to manipulate an independent variable as would be necessary in experimental research. For example, it would be unethical to have someone smoke cigarettes to determine the effect of smoking on appetite. Instead, we might design a study to ask both smokers and nonsmokers about their appetites and compare their answers. Another approach might be to ask people that are trying to quit smoking about any effects they have observed on appetite. These would be non-experimental research designs.

Non-experimental research is also used to examine the knowledge, attitudes, beliefs, and behaviors of people. If, for example, health education specialists had questions concerning what nurses think about health insurance, what sexual behaviors the elderly practice, whether corporate employees would support a fitness center, or what elementary school children believe about snack foods, non-experimental research designs would be utilized to answer these questions. Relationship-type questions can also be answered by non-experimental research. To what extent is religious affiliation related to health locus of control? How are stress levels related to sexual behavior? What is the relationship between age and seat belt use?

Although there are differences between experimental and non-experimental research in the methods or strategies employed, there are similarities as well. Berg and Latin (2004) summarize non-experimental research as follows:

> Most nonexperimental studies are conducted using the basic elements of the scientific method—that is, a hypothesis is stated and tested and conclusions are made. In fact, the only distinction from experimental research in this respect is that the hypothesis is tested using nonexperimental procedures, and these methods characteristically do not have very good control over the experimental condition. Therefore it is important to emphasize that nonexperimental research is not as robust as experimentation when it comes to establishing cause and effect relationships. (p. 198)

The fact that non-experimental research is not as "robust" as experimental research does not mean it has little or no value. To the contrary, it is very important research, often answering important questions for the health education profession. For that reason, it is important for future health education professionals to know and understand non-experimental research designs. In this chapter we will present information on four different types of non-experimental research—survey research, correlational research, causal-comparative research, and evaluation research. Although there are other types of non-experimental research, the four types presented here are those most commonly utilized by health education professionals.

Survey Research

Survey research designs are among those designs most frequently seen in health science literature (Neutens & Rubinson, 2010). O'Rourke (1999) noted that "Surveys are an integral and indispensable part of health education" (p. 107). The purpose of a survey, no matter what type of survey is being used, is to gather specific information from a targeted group of people (Windsor, Clark, Boyd, & Goodman, 2004). **Survey research** involves the administration of a questionnaire to a sample or to an entire population of people in order to determine the attitudes, opinions, beliefs, values, behaviors, or characteristics of the group being studied. A **questionnaire** is a form or instrument used in survey research that contains questions that participants are asked to answer. Survey research is sometimes also called descriptive research, because survey results describe the way things are. Comparing subgroups is a common feature of survey research. For example, one may want to determine if male and female, older and younger, or urban and rural respondents differ in the way they answer questions (Gay, Mills, & Airasian, 2006).

Survey research is an excellent way to gain information about a particular group of people; therefore, surveys are frequently used in our society. Surveys can be conducted at the local, county, state, or national level. Most people are familiar with some of the larger, nationwide surveys such as the Gallup Poll, which measures national opinions on a variety of issues; the Nielson ratings, which use survey techniques to determine television viewership; and the U.S. census, which is a survey administered to all people in the United States by the federal government every 10 years and whose results are an invaluable resource frequently utilized by health education professionals. Any survey administered to an entire population, such as the U.S. census, is called a **census survey** (Patten, 2009).

On the surface, survey research seems simple. One just needs to make up some questions, get people to answer the questions, and count the responses. In reality, however, survey research techniques are very exact and must be followed closely. Leedy and Ormrod (2010) note that survey research is not "any less demanding in its design requirements or any easier for the researcher to conduct than other types of research. Quite the contrary, the survey design makes critical demands on the researcher that, if not carefully respected, may place the entire research effort in jeopardy" (p. 187).

Table 10.1 represents a sample flow plan for a survey research project. The steps in this flow plan must be closely followed if a survey is to produce accurate results. Dillman, (2007) and Salant and Dillman (1994) discuss the importance of accuracy in survey research. They note that a survey is accurate when the results represent the true opinions or values of a population. They describe four characteristics that if followed will avoid common survey errors and produce accurate results. They also note, however, that a completely accurate survey is seldom, if ever, conducted.

1. Every member of the population that the researcher is trying to describe would have an equal (or known) chance of being selected for the sample. Hence a coverage error is avoided.
2. Enough people would be sampled randomly to achieve the needed level of precision. Hence, sampling error is minimized.
3. Clear, unambiguous questions would be asked so that respondents are both capable of and

Table 10.1   Survey Flow Plan

- Clearly define the purpose and objectives of the survey.
- Conduct a thorough literature review looking for other surveys with the same population or on the same topic. See if survey instruments have already been developed to use in your study.
- Determine survey design (cross-sectional or longitudinal).
- Determine data collection procedures (mail, e-mail, telephone, group, interview).
- Identify or, if necessary, develop a questionnaire and write the cover letter.
- If necessary, determine reliability and validity of questionnaire.
- Make changes to questionnaire as indicated.
- Retest for reliability and validity if necessary.
- Pilot test procedures and questionnaire.
- Make any final changes to procedures and/or instrument.
- Identify population and obtain sample.
- Conduct the survey, including all follow-up procedures.
- Enter data and verify or clean.
- Run descriptive statistics (frequencies, percentages, means, medians, modes).
- Complete any additional data analysis.
- Report results.

motivated to answer correctly. Hence, measurement error is avoided.

4. Everyone in the sample responds to the survey, or nonrespondents are similar to respondents on characteristics of interest in the study. Hence, nonresponse error is avoided. (Salant & Dillman, 1994, p. 15)

Survey Designs

Once the purpose and objectives of a survey have been determined, it is time to consider survey design. Although survey research can be used in many different ways and for many different purposes, there are basically two survey designs: cross-sectional and longitudinal (Creswell, 2005).

Cross-sectional studies collect data at one specific point in time. They can be used to determine the current attitudes, opinions, beliefs, values, behaviors, or characteristics of a given population. For example, if a researcher wanted to determine the attitude of nurses toward certified health education specialists, a cross-sectional survey could provide that information. Essentially, the researcher would administer a questionnaire to a sample of nurses or to the entire population of nurses in a given area. The results would give the researcher a glimpse into the attitudes of nurses at that particular point in time. As time passes, the value of the cross-sectional survey results is diminished as the attitudes of nurses could change in either a positive or negative direction.

In addition to examining the attitudes of all nurses in the sample, if so desired, comparisons could be made between public health nurses and clinical nurses, between younger nurses and older nurses, between nurses who have worked closely with a health education specialist in the past and nurses who have not. It would also be possible to administer the same questionnaire with minor modifications to other health professionals such as doctors, dentists, and physical therapists to determine their attitudes toward certified health education specialists. Although Creswell (2005) considers such comparisons as cross-sectional survey research designs, Aday and Cornelius (2006) consider a cross-sectional study that compares groups within the study at the same point in time as a **descriptive group-comparison design.**

In addition to learning about a particular group of people, cross-sectional surveys are often used for other purposes in health education. They can be used to evaluate a program by asking participants questions about the program. They can also be used when conducting a community needs assessment by asking community members about their perceived needs. Occasionally, health education specialists may also need to test the market for a particular product or service by conducting a cross-sectional market survey.

Longitudinal studies collect data from the same population over time. Thus, in longitudinal studies, the population is surveyed multiple times at specified intervals. The actual individuals surveyed may be the same or different each time the survey is administered.

There are three main types of longitudinal studies (Creswell, 2005). **Trend studies** identify a population and examine changes within that population over time. Suppose a health education specialist wanted to examine the attitudes of high school seniors toward marijuana use over time to determine if any trends were apparent. The researcher might ask members of the graduating class in 2010, 2011, 2012, 2013, and 2014 to complete a questionnaire concerning marijuana use. Comparisons could then be made between the seniors in these five graduating classes to determine any trends in marijuana use attitudes among high school seniors.

A second type of longitudinal study is known as a **cohort study**. Instead of studying the changing trends in a population, the researcher may be interested in following a particular group or subgroup over time. That group or subgroup would be called the cohort. In keeping with the marijuana example, this time the researcher selects all students in the graduating class of 2010 in the state of Ohio as the cohort. A random sample of these individuals would be surveyed in 2010. The group would be followed and another random sample might be surveyed in 2012. The group would continue to be followed and still another random sample might be surveyed in 2014. Again, data could be compared from the three administrations of the questionnaire to determine if attitudes toward marijuana use held by the graduating class of 2010 in the state of Ohio changed over time.

In the third type of longitudinal study, known as a **panel study**, the researcher examines the same group of people over time. The high school seniors surveyed in 2010 will be the same group surveyed in any subsequent administration of the survey. The advantage to this type of study is that the individuals surveyed each time are the same, permitting the researcher to track changes in specific individuals over time. The disadvantage is that the participants must be tracked over time, and some participants will be lost to the study through morbidity and attrition.

Collecting Data

When conducting survey research there are essentially five different strategies for collecting data: mailed questionnaires, group administration, electronic questionnaires, personal interviews, and telephone surveys. The decision as to which strategy to employ should be made prior to sample selection and questionnaire design (Neutens & Rubinson, 2010). Both sample selection and questionnaire design are dependent on the survey research strategy selected. We will now discuss each of the five strategies.

MAILED QUESTIONNAIRES

Mailed questionnaires are an excellent way to access populations that are distributed over wide geographic areas. They are fairly inexpensive when compared with the manpower requirement of personal interviews, and they typically take less time to administer. They are easily standardized because the wording on all questionnaires is the same, and there is no chance that interviewer bias can affect the results since no interviewer is present. Mailed questionnaires are completed at the convenience of the responder, and most responders feel more anonymous when completing mailed questionnaires than when responding on the phone or in a face-to-face interview. An additional advantage is that if responders need to access their records to provide accurate responses, they have the ability to do so.

The disadvantages of a mailed questionnaire are equally important to consider. One major concern is response rate. In reviewing the literature, it is clear that there is no universally accepted response rate required of a study, as can be seen from the following statements concerning response rates from the authors of research methods texts. In his classic research text, Kerlinger (1986) said that response rates of 80–90% are required to be confident that the sample represents the population. Wiersma and Jurs (2009) say that a 70% return rate is expected when dealing with a professional population. Creswell (2005) notes that, "Many survey studies in leading educational journals report a response rate of 50% or better" (p. 367). Leedy and Ormrod (2010) state that the return rate in a questionnaire study is often 50% or less. In discussing the need for follow-up letters, Gay, Mills, and Airasian (2006) report that "first mailings will typically result in a 30–50% return rate, and a second mailing will increase the percentage by about 20%; mailings beyond a second are generally not cost-effective, in that they each increase the percentage by about 10% or less" (p. 171). In general, however, it seems something in the 50–60% range would be the minimum required of an acceptable study. Obviously, the higher the response rate the better. With a 60% response rate, for example, there are still 40% that did not respond. It is possible that the 40% not responding may differ in significant ways from the 60% that did respond. See Box 10.1 for an example of how low response rates can cause serious problems when interpreting results.

Several precautions can be taken to help improve response rates for mailed surveys (see Table 10.2). Sponsorship of the survey is important. Responses are higher when a survey is mailed by a recognized and respected institution. If Joe Schmo sends a questionnaire on plain paper, it will probably not get the same response as it would if mailed by Professor Schmo on university letterhead. Further, questionnaires should be designed for ease of completion and should not appear cluttered or use a font size or line spacing that makes the questionnaire difficult to read. A longer survey that is less cluttered will get a better response rate than a shorter survey that is more difficult to read (Neutens & Rubinson, 2010). **Return services,**

Box 10.1   Case Study: Low Response Rate

A local school district was in a controversy over the inclusion of sex education in the health education curriculum. The school board decided to conduct a survey of parents in the district concerning their attitudes toward the teaching of sex education in the schools. A questionnaire was developed and sent to every family in the district that had children in the public schools. When the survey was completed, there was a 50% response rate. The results indicated that more than half of respondents did not wish to have sex education taught in the schools. As a result, the school board decided to eliminate sex education from the curriculum. In reality, however, the 50% that responded included nearly all of the people in the district who were opposed to sex education. They felt strongly about the topic, and most returned the survey. Some of these individuals even called friends of a like mindset, encouraging them to return the survey. Of the 50% that did not respond, nearly all were in favor of sex education in the schools. The problem was that they were not as emotionally involved in the decision and were less likely to return the survey. If all parents in the district had responded, nearly 70% would have favored sex education in the schools.

How can researchers keep from making the mistake made by the above school district? There are two possible answers to this question. First, obtain a higher response rate. This may be accomplished by sending prior notice that an important questionnaire is about to be distributed, by conducting multiple follow-up mailings, and by including incentives for returning the survey. A second option is to conduct a telephone interview with a random sample of the nonrespondents to determine if they hold the same attitudes toward sex education as did the respondents.

Table 10.2   Ways to Enhance Mailed Survey Response Rates

- Obtain a well-recognized sponsor and use letterhead
- Make questionnaire easy to complete, easy to read, uncluttered, and brief
- Provide postage-paid, self-addressed return envelope
- Develop a well-written cover letter that is personally addressed and hand signed
- Conduct surveys that are of interest to the target group
- Place controversial or personal questions at the end of the questionnaire
- Prenotify participants that they will be receiving a survey in the mail
- Consider using an incentive to encourage participant response
- Conduct extensive follow-up efforts with nonresponders
- Mail questionnaires at a time when target group is most likely to respond

which would include a postage-paid, self-addressed return envelope, should be included with a mailed questionnaire.

A cover letter should always be included with a questionnaire. When participants know who is sponsoring the questionnaire and why the study is important, they are more likely to take the time to respond. Whenever possible, the cover letter should be addressed specifically to the individual being asked to respond. Every effort should be made to avoid the appearance of a form letter, and each cover letter should be hand signed by the researcher (Fraenkel & Wallen, 2003). The cover letter should introduce the researcher and any institution(s) sponsoring or supporting the survey to the participant, state the purpose of the study and why it is important, assure confidentiality or anonymity, note the importance of completing the questionnaire, indicate the approximate amount of time needed to complete the questionnaire, state a requested return date, and provide directions for returning the

completed questionnaire. To meet human subjects guidelines, it is necessary to obtain the informed consent of all participants, even in a survey study. The cover letter is typically used either to explain a separate consent form included with the questionnaire or to indicate **passive consent**. In other words, the cover letter would indicate that returning the completed questionnaire implies consent to participate in the study.

The nature of the questions and the group being surveyed will affect response rate. If those being surveyed have a strong interest in the topic of the survey, a higher response rate can be expected. The converse is also true. If the group surveyed does not have a strong interest in the topic, response rates will suffer. Content that is controversial or personal can also reduce response rate. If controversial or personal questions must be asked, ask them near the end of the questionnaire. By doing so, respondents may already have bought into the survey when they reach the difficult questions and will choose to answer them.

It is advisable to prenotify participants that they have been selected to participate in a survey (Creswell, 2005). This can be done via a note card or letter that is mailed one to two weeks ahead of mailing the actual questionnaire. This communication should describe the purpose of the study and explain the importance of returning the questionnaire once it is received. This notification can also be used to request potential participants' permission or consent to be studied.

Except in rare cases where an initial mailing of the questionnaire nets an extremely high response rate, follow-up contacts should take place. Gay and colleagues (2006) indicate that a 20% increase in response rate can be expected with one follow-up. An additional 10% can be expected with a second follow-up. One of the follow-up mailings can be a postcard reminder, but the other mailing should include a new questionnaire and return envelope in case the original mailing was lost. In some cases telephone follow-up reminders with nonresponders after the final mailing can further improve response rates. As a general rule of thumb, time between mailings should be two weeks. If following a four-mailing schedule as recommended (initial notification, first survey mailing, follow-up postcard, second survey mailing), a minimum of eight weeks would be required for data collection. This would allow for a two-week period after the final mailing to make certain all responses are in before data analysis begins.

Remember, if one is conducting an **anonymous** survey, follow-up materials will need to be sent to all participants. In an anonymous survey the respondent is unknown to the researcher. The follow-up letter to an anonymous survey should thank those who have already responded and encourage those who have not responded to do so. If the survey is **confidential**, meaning that the researcher can identify respondents but promises not to divulge or share their information, then the researcher can send follow-up mailings only to those that have failed to respond. This could be a significant cost savings if large numbers of participants are involved.

When a questionnaire is mailed can also affect response rates. No mailed surveys should be conducted during the holiday season, which would include mid-November through the first of January. If possible, it is also best to avoid the busy summer months. In general, March is considered the month with the highest return rates. This, however, would certainly not be true for tax preparation professionals. The point here is that the researcher needs to know the group being surveyed. Teachers, for example, might be best surveyed in September as the school year is just beginning. The day of the week a questionnaire arrives may also affect return rates. Surveys received later in the week are more likely to receive a quick response than those received early in the week (Neutens & Rubinson, 2010).

A final strategy to increase response rates is to use **incentives**. Incentives are nominal inducements to encourage participant response. Some incentives that have been used include small monetary gifts ($0.25–$1.00), a stick of gum or piece of candy, or the opportunity to be included in a lottery for a nice prize. Creswell (2005) states that studies on the effectiveness of incentives show mixed results; however, Fowler (2009) states that the prepayment to participants of several dollars does increase response rates, and Aday and Cornelius (2006) unequivocally state that "Methodological research has borne out the effectiveness of systematic follow-up strategies for achieving good response rates, particularly in combination with sending even a modest monetary incentive (one to two dollars) with an initial mailing or before an interview" (p. 317). A question is often raised as to whether those who respond to incentives might be different in some way from those who do not respond to incentives, thus introducing another possible point of bias. Further the U.S. Office of Management and Budget forbids the blanket offering of financial incentives to participants in federally sponsored surveys (Aday & Cornelius, 2006). Certainly more research needs to be completed on the impact of incentives.

In addition to low response rates, other disadvantages also exist with mailed surveys. Obviously, if the respondent cannot read well or does not understand the questions, the results will not be valid. When surveying young children, international populations, or people of low socioeconomic status, reading level can be a major problem. Sometimes respondents will not complete the entire questionnaire, or may leave large sections blank. The researcher must determine how and if to use these data. Also, there is no control over when and where the participant decides to respond to the questionnaire. It could be at the Laundromat while washing clothes, at home while watching TV, or with a group of friends at a party. Both location and the activity around an individual could affect how that person responds.

GROUP ADMINISTRATION

Group administration is just what it sounds like: administering a questionnaire to a large group of people at one time. For example, if a health education specialist wanted to conduct a survey of college students, one way to approach this would be to obtain a random sample of classes being taught. The health education specialist would then visit each selected class and administer the questionnaire to all those attending. Although informed consent is still needed and individual students could opt out of responding, the response rate is usually high with this approach. Within a relatively short period of time, large amounts of data can be collected using this procedure. In addition to schools, any settings where people congregate in groups on a regular basis are ideal for group administration. For example, group administration could be utilized in churches, camps, worksites, retirement centers, professional conferences, and so forth.

Although at first glance this may seem like an ideal method for data collection, there are problems. Many target groups do not meet in identifiable groups on a regular basis. In the college example, it is possible that students could be in two or more selected classes and therefore could submit more than one survey. Explicit directions must be given that if students have completed this survey in another class, they should not complete another questionnaire. Further, it can be difficult to get administrators, professors, or supervisors to grant permission to use their classes or groups for administering the questionnaire. If many groups need to be surveyed, it takes a significant amount of researcher time to administer the questionnaire to each group. If the researcher expects the professor or supervisor to administer the survey, clear and detailed instructions must be written, and even then there are concerns about how consistently the questionnaire will actually be administered. Finally, randomly selecting groups is not the same as randomly selecting individuals. When groups are selected, it is possible that certain individuals, such as those in an advanced physics class that has only one section, might have less chance of being selected than those in freshman

history classes where there are many large sections. This could create what Salant and Dillman (1994) call a coverage error.

ELECTRONIC QUESTIONNAIRES

An **electronic questionnaire** or e-mail questionnaire is nothing more than a "survey instrument for collecting data that is available on the computer" (Creswell, 2005, p. 361). With increased use of the Internet and e-mail, it is a natural extension to consider sending survey questionnaires by means of this technology. Essentially, an e-mail is sent to a prospective participant with either an attachment or a Web site address to locate and download a questionnaire. The participant completes the questionnaire and e-mails it back to the researcher or completes the questionnaire online where the survey data are collected directly on the survey Web site.

Recently, Web-based survey methods have become the method of choice for some researchers due to the advantages they have over the pencil and paper method, such as reduced response time, reduced cost of materials, ease of data collection (responses are collected directly from the Web site), flexibility in design and format of the survey, control over administration (such as creating a specific date that the e-mail invitation will arrive), and recipient familiarity with the format and technology (Granello & Wheaton, 2003). Responses received can be formatted to enter directly into Excel or a statistical package such as SPSS, thus eliminating manual data entry or scanning.

Some specific issues with electronic surveys include the fact that there are still groups of people who do not have Internet access and would not feel comfortable using a computer to access the Web and download a questionnaire even if they had access. This would certainly raise concerns that those who do complete electronic questionnaires might be very different from those who do not. Further, there may to be smaller numbers of people who actually complete electronic questionnaires as compared to mailed questionnaires. Fowler

(2009) compared two studies that used both mail and e-mail delivery. In one study among college faculty the response rate for the two delivery methods was nearly the same at 60%. In the other study, of college students, the response rate for the e-mail was only half that received by faculty in the previous study and was significantly less than for the mailed surveys among the students. Both college faculty and students have easy access to computers and are computer literate, but the response rates varied greatly. In still another study of college students, return rates were fairly good for a Web-based survey (Daley, McDermott, McCormack-Brown & Kittleson, 2003). The authors of the college student survey went on to conclude that "regarding the question of the feasibility, desirability and utility of collecting and analyzing data from an online survey directed at a college population, the answer seems to be resoundingly affirmative" (p. 123). In another study of physicians, after five rounds of electronic requests for them to respond by e-mail, two rounds of mailed questionnaires were sent. Twenty-four percent of the total responses were received via paper (Kroth *et al.*, 2009). This clearly indicates that many physicians in this group still preferred responding via paper, and that paper follow-ups can enhance the response rate of electronic surveys. Based on these few studies it would seem the response rate for electronic questionnaires may be very group dependent and difficult to predict.

Steps can be taken to improve the response rate for electronic questionnaires. "The same kinds of steps that have been found to be helpful to postal surveys are likely to help enlist cooperation for Internet surveys: identifiable sponsors, well-designed instruments, financial incentives, and repeated contacts, including trying mail or phone requests for those who do not respond to an initial email request" (Fowler, 2009, p. 61).

The technical software and hardware issues related to electronic surveys that were discussed in the first edition of this text are now less of a concern. Commercial, online survey services such as

Zoomerang and Survey Monkey allow users to design their survey, collect responses, and do some analyses in a very straightforward, user-friendly manner. Small surveys can be conducted for no charge, and researchers that conduct larger surveys pay a reasonable subscription fee.

With an electronic questionnaire, anonymity and confidentiality can be hard to guarantee, because hackers and/or program administrators can access computer files or electronic transmissions and they may be able to identify responders. An additional problem with electronic survey methods is access to the target population's e-mail addresses. Although it may be possible to conduct an electronic survey of the employees of a large company, students at a university, or the members of a professional association, where e-mail addresses are likely known, it would not be possible at this point in time to use electronic surveys for a random sample of city, county, or state residents.

Pealer and Weiler (2003) developed an eight-step approach for conducting Web-delivered surveys (see Table 10.3). Their 2003 article describes each of the eight steps in more detail and discusses practical issues researchers should consider when

Table 10.3   Steps for Conducting a Web-Delivered Survey

Step 1. Determine if a Web-delivered survey is appropriate for the population

Step 2. Determine if the questionnaire is appropriate for a Web-delivered format

Step 3. Determine if participants have access to the necessary computing infrastructure

Step 4. Determine sampling procedures

Step 5. Determine questionnaire format

Step 6. Determine if an incentive will be offered

Step 7. Determine how to obtain informed consent

Step 8. Determine questionnaire delivery protocol, including number of participant contacts and time line

From: Pealer, L., & Weiler, R.M. (2003). Guidelines for designing a Web-delivered college health risk behavior survey: Lessons learned from the University of Florida Health Behavior Survey. *Health Promotion and Practice*, 4 (2), 172. Reprinted with permission of Sage Publications, Inc.

doing Web-delivered survey research. Additionally, for an in-depth discussion of both mail and Internet surveys see Dillman (2007).

PERSONAL INTERVIEWS

"An **interview** is an oral, in-person question-and-answer session between a researcher and an individual respondent" (Gay *et al.*, 2006, p. 163). When compared to a mailed questionnaire, interviews are more expensive and time consuming. On the other hand, interviews have some distinct advantages over mailed surveys that may make them the method of choice in some situations.

Personal interviews allow the researcher to ask more complex questions and obtain more detailed information than does the usual multiple-choice–type questions seen on a mailed survey. The interviewer also has the opportunity to reword, redirect, or further probe questions to make sure the interviewee understands what is being asked and gives a full and appropriate response. The interviewer also has the ability to reorder questions and to observe both verbal and nonverbal responses of interviewees. When conducting interviews, the reading ability of the interviewee is typically not a problem, although the language used by the interviewer must be understandable to the interviewee.

On the negative side, the time commitment and cost to conduct personal interviews are high. Imagine the time and expense required to conduct 500 personal interviews versus obtaining 500 mailed responses. Further, there is a geographic limitation to most interview studies in that interviews are conducted in a limited geographic area, but mailed surveys can be nationwide. The cost and logistics involved in conducting a nationwide interview study would be insurmountable for most research projects.

Interviews also increase the probability of interviewer bias being introduced to the study. Factors such as the voice, gender, race, appearance, and mannerisms of an interviewer could influence how an interviewee may respond. Further, the way the interviewer rewords a question or probes for deeper answers can introduce variability into a study, which could affect results. The way responses are recorded by the interviewer and the interviewer's interpretation of responses can also introduce bias into a study. Both data recording and data entry are much more difficult when more complex questions are used in an interview format. Establishing rigid guidelines for the interviewer to follow can eliminate some of these problems but at the same time diminish the flexibility that is a potential advantage of interviews.

Interviewing requires a high level of communication and interpersonal relation skills (Gay *et al.*, 2006). Box 10.2 paraphrases the 10 commandments of interviewing as described by Salkind (2000). Since there is often more than one interviewer conducting the interviews, differences between interviewers can also create consistency issues. For that reason, all persons conducting interviews need to undergo extensive training. Creswell (2005) notes that this training should consist of "learning how to provide instructions during the interview, maintaining confidentiality about the interview, asking the exact questions on the interview guide, completing the interview within the time allocated, being courteous, and not interjecting personal opinions into the interview" (p. 361). Any training should require trainees to conduct mock interviews under the observation of the trainer. Until the trainer feels confident in the trainees' ability, no real interviews should be permitted.

Response rates on personal interviews are typically much higher than on mailed questionnaires. It seems more difficult for people to reject a face-to-face appeal for an interview than it is to discard a mailed survey. In addition, the interviewer tries to accommodate the interviewee's schedule while at the same time maintaining some control over the time and location of the interview. Although a mailed questionnaire can be completed at any location, with any number of distractions and with any number of people contributing to the responses, in an interview the interviewer controls the situation and prevents such occurrences.

Box 10.2   Ten Commandments of Interviewing

1. Practice your interview skills. Interviewing is a skill, and practice is needed to improve and perfect a skill.
2. Start the interview with general conversation about the weather, sports, or some current event—establish rapport with the interviewee.
3. Make interviewees feel like an important part of the project. Recognize how valuable their time is and how much you appreciate their participation.
4. Once the interview begins, stay on task using printed questions as a guide.
5. Know your questions well enough that you do not have to be reading from the guide constantly.
6. Dress appropriately to relate to the population being studied.
7. When possible, find a quiet place to conduct the interview where there will be minimal distractions.
8. If an answer is not satisfactory, re-ask the question. Rephrase the question in part or in whole until you feel you have gotten an appropriate answer.
9. If possible, use a tape recorder, but don't let the tape recorder replace the taking of notes. Always ask for permission to use the tape recorder because some people are intimidated when recorded.
10. Thank the interviewees and ask if they have any questions. Offer to provide them with a copy of the results, if appropriate. Be sure to follow through and provide results when requested.

(Paraphrased from Salkind (2000), pp. 197–198)

The safety of the interviewer is an additional concern that must be considered. When interviews are being conducted within the community at the homes of its residents, it is sometimes necessary to collect data in less safe, high-crime areas of the city. Sometimes situations like this are handled by pairing two or more interviewers together to conduct the interviews. Notifying local police when interviews will be taking place alerts them to be on the lookout for potential problems. Often, however, another design may need to be adopted, as interviewer safety should be the paramount concern (see Box 10.3 for a case study on interviewer safety).

Lack of anonymity can be an issue in interviews. By definition an interview can be confidential but never anonymous. Because of the face-to-face nature of an interview, interviewees may not feel comfortable sharing their true feelings or may be more likely to provide a socially acceptable response than they would on an anonymous mailed survey.

TELEPHONE SURVEYS

A **telephone survey** is actually a personal interview that takes place over the telephone. Telephone surveys are an important tool for collecting cross-sectional data on population characteristics; tracking trends in the prevalence of health conditions, risks, and health behaviors over time; and evaluating the impact of interventions. Their primary purpose is to collect data with which to make reliable, valid, and generalizable conclusions about the population based on the sample surveyed (Kempf & Remington, 2007).

Telephone surveys are very popular, and the techniques involved in conducting telephone surveys have been refined and improved over time. With the proper equipment and trained interviewers, telephone surveys are the fastest means of collecting data when compared to mailed questionnaires or personal interviews. They can cover broad geographic areas and cost much less than face-to-face interviews or mailed surveys (Neutens & Rubinson, 2010). They are particularly good for collecting sensitive information and for surveying hard-to-reach populations and populations with limited reading abilities. Participants tend to feel more anonymous when responding to a telephone interview than when responding to a face-to-face interview.

Survey researchers have benefited from improvements in call center technologies, such as computer-assisted telephone interviewing (CATI),

---

Box 10.3   Case Study: Interviewer Safety Concerns

Several years ago, a master's student posed a research question focusing on the residents of a city's lowest socioeconomic areas and their awareness of toxoplasmosis and how to prevent it. Toxoplasmosis is a parasitic infection that can cause severe problems for pregnant women. It is caused by accidental ingestion of contaminated cat feces. Because the residents in this section of the city had low reading levels and typically did not return surveys, the student proposed to conduct interviews in randomly selected homes. The master's committee rejected her proposal because of safety concerns for the student. The area of the city where she would be conducting interviews was also the highest crime area in the city. Instead, the committee and the student agreed on a telephone survey.

Although at first this may seem like an ideal solution, it was not. Because this area had a low socioeconomic status, some residents did not have telephones. Further, the student used a random number generator with the various telephone exchanges that served the general area of the city she was interested in studying. Many of the numbers called were businesses, were disconnected, were answered by children who could not answer the questions, or were for residents who had the same telephone exchange but lived outside the target area. In addition, many of the residents contacted were suspicious and refused to be interviewed over the phone. It was quite a job to complete the needed phone calls, and the results were probably less accurate than desired. In this situation, personal interviews would probably have been a better choice than telephone interviews for data collection, but the ideal research design had to be compromised for the safety of the student researcher.

---

call schedulers, and interactive voice response (IVR) systems (Kempf & Remington, 2007). CATI has made the process of conducting telephone interviews easier and quicker. CATI uses a software program that allows the actual questionnaire to be displayed on a computer screen. The interviewer reads the questions directly off the computer screen and records responses on the computer. Based on a given answer, the computer automatically brings up the next question. For example, if a question was asked about exercise and the respondent answers that he or she does not exercise, the computer would skip the following questions concerning the types and intensity of exercise and go directly to the next appropriate question. Another advantage to using CATI is that the data is entered into the computer as each participant is interviewed. As soon as the last interview is completed or at any time during the data collection phase, analyses can be run on the available data without the time delay usually associated with data entry.

Phone surveys also have disadvantages. Although most people in the United States have phones, there are still some that do not. Certainly those that do not have phones differ in important ways from those that do. Obtaining verified phone lists can be expensive, and such lists do not contain unlisted numbers. Those with unlisted numbers may differ from those with listed numbers. Using random digit dialing (RDD) creates problems such as calling business numbers, disconnected numbers, and unlisted numbers. Much time can be wasted making useless calls. Since it is important that any number selected for the study be contacted, callbacks to no-answers and busy signals can take considerable time. Callbacks also must occur for those persons who are too busy to respond when first called but agree to be interviewed at a later, agreed-upon time. In addition, the increase in the use of cell phones has made it difficult to use RDD for surveys where a household and not an individual is the unit of measure.

Participants in phone surveys may be less motivated than those in face-to-face interviews. If they do not like a survey topic or a particular item on the questionnaire, they can simply hang up and terminate the interview at any time. Some people asked to participate in phone surveys consider them the same as solicitation calls or hoaxes. They resent the intrusion and refuse to participate.

Advances in technology are creating challenges for survey researchers due to the use of caller ID, call blocking, answering machines, cell phones, and the portability of phone numbers (Kempf & Remington, 2007). Think for a moment about some issues that need to be considered when conducting a phone survey in today's technological world. Suppose a researcher wants to conduct a phone survey to determine the health behaviors of residents in a three-county urban area, and that the results of this survey will serve as baseline data for obtaining grant-money and evaluating the effectiveness of grant-funded behavioral interventions. Obviously this researcher wants to collect the best data possible. If the researcher uses a list of verified phone numbers from a directory or commercial provider, those residents with unlisted numbers and cell phones will be missed. If an RDD method is used, unlisted numbers will be included, but this will greatly increase the time and effort of the researcher as many disconnected, unused, and commercial numbers will be dialed. Also, the researcher would still be missing the approximately 17.5% of people living in households that have only cell phones (State Health Access Data Assistance Center, 2009). Research has shown that those without landline phones tend to be young, relatively affluent renters or poor, minority individuals who have no landline for economic reasons (Kempf & Remington, 2007). In one study comparing adults with landline phones to adults with only cell phones, those with cell phones were more likely to be smokers and uninsured and less likely to be diabetics, have a usual place for medical care, and to have received an influenza vaccination in the past year (Blumberg, Luke, & Cynamon, 2006).

So what happens if cell phone numbers are added to the sample frame? Another group of issues emerges. First, since most cell phone users also have landline phones there are duplicate numbers for some individuals in the sample frame, and these individuals will have an increased chance of being called as opposed to the landline-only or cell-only users. Second, cell phone numbers are portable, meaning they move with the individual. In one marketing survey reported by Kempf and Remington (2007), 30% of cell phone–only individuals were not living in the county indicated by their cell phone's area code. This means that the researcher will be calling people that are not in the three-county area. Further, there are individuals living in the three-county area of this study that will not be included in the study because their cell phones are from other area codes and exchanges outside the three-county area. When calling a land line number, the researcher can be fairly confident that the respondent is somewhere within the home and relatively safe, but when calling a cell phone number the researcher has no idea where the respondent is. The respondent could be at work, at church, or driving in the car. It could be inconvenient, inappropriate, or even dangerous to respond to survey questions at that time. Also, since some cell phone users pay for minutes used, it may actually cost the respondent to answer the phone and complete the survey. One final concern is that the use of auto-dialer machines is restricted when cell phone numbers are included in the study. The Consumer Protection Act of 1991 does not allow auto-dialer machines to be used to call cell phones, even for research. This means the researcher will have to manually dial all cell phone numbers included in the study.

So what should our researcher do given the above concerns? Probably the most likely action at this point in time is to use RDD and to eliminate cell phones from the study. Blumberg and colleagues (2006) stated, "As people substitute wireless telephones for landline telephones, the percentage of adults without landline telephones has increased significantly but is still low, which minimizes the bias resulting from their exclusion from telephone surveys" (p. 926). Although this recommendation may be good advice today, attention to this technology trend and its impact on reliable, valid, and generalizable survey results will need to be carefully monitored over time. As the number of cell phone–only users goes up, the potential bias from not including them in telephone surveys will also go up.

Low response rate is always a concern with survey research, and the number of non-respondents to phone surveys has been increasing in recent years (Dillman, 2007). Caller ID and answering machines have contributed to low response rates. Researchers need to carefully consider the visual message to be shown on caller ID. Using a well-known and respected name may increase response rates. For example, if a university's name appears on the caller ID instead of the name of an individual researcher or just a phone number, it may entice some individuals to pick up the phone. Also, if answering machines are encountered, they can be used to announce the purpose of the research and to advise respondents of future attempts to contact them (Kempf & Remington, 2007). See Figure 10.1 for a schematic of the steps that must occur to obtain a completed phone survey, starting with the selection of a potential participant. Each non-shaded box ends the possibility of utilizing a potential participant for this telephone survey.

As a result of the plethora of disrupting telemarketing calls people were receiving, the Federal Trade Commission was charged with developing a National Do Not Call Registry. The registry was activated in September 2003. If people place their phone numbers on this list, most telemarketers are not allowed to call them. Students often ask how this list impacts telephone surveys. Political organizations, charities, and telephone surveyors are not considered to be telemarketers. Telemarketing includes only calls that solicit sales of goods or services. The National Do Not Call Registry does not directly impact telephone surveys (Federal Trade Commission, 2004). It may indirectly have an effect in that those on the Do Not Call Registry may be unaware that telephone surveys are not covered and may be irritated and refuse to participate when they receive telephone surveys.

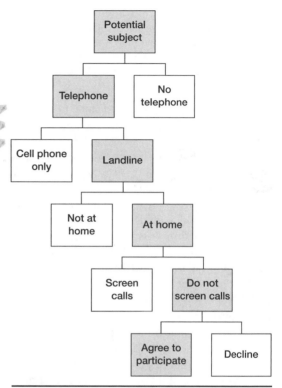

FIGURE 10.1

Steps in the selection of participants in telephone surveys.

Source: Kempf, A.M., & Remington, P.L. (2007). New challenges for telephone survey research in the twenty-first century. *Annual Review of Public Health, 28*, 115.

Multimode Surveys

With modern technology, the strategies, options, and techniques used to conduct surveys have changed greatly over the past few years, adding new complexities for the researcher to consider. Dillman (2007) notes that since writing the first edition of his survey research book in 2000,

> our ability to conduct reliable telephone surveys has declined because of lower response rates and the trend toward abandoning household telephones in favor of cellular connections. Although our ability to conduct web surveys has increased dramatically, their use remains limited by inadequate coverage of the general population. Caught

between these trends surveyors are increasingly drawn toward the conduct of mixed-mode surveys, which collect data from some respondents by one mode and use a different mode to reach other respondents, in order to preserve data quality (p. ix).

Indeed, survey response rates tend to increase with the use of multiple modes of data collection (Dillman *et al.*, 2009; Fowler, 2009). Fowler (2009) notes, "One of the best ways to minimize survey nonresponse is to use more than one mode to collect data.... Mixing modes can enable researchers to reach people who are inaccessible via a single mode. It also can allow them to collect data from less intrinsically motivated sample members" (p. 61). Multimode approaches can be particularly effective when response to the first mode tried is fairly low (Dillman *et al.*, 2009). For example, a health education specialist may begin by administering a mail survey and then follow up with non-respondents via a telephone interview, or may begin with an e-mail survey and follow up with non-respondents using a mail survey. Another possibility is to use an e-mail message to announce the pending arrival of a mail survey or a future phone interview. Sometimes it may be beneficial to initially provide respondents the choice of an e-mail or mail survey.

There are, however, potential downsides to using a multimode strategy. Dillman (2007) notes, "the design of mixed-mode surveys is itself being affected by new knowledge on the likelihood that different visual layouts for questions produce different answers from respondents" (p. ix). Fowler (2009) warns that answers to some questions may be affected by the mode of data collection, so researchers must be careful to make sure that data collected by different modes are comparable.

Conducting Survey Research

The previous six sections of this chapter have described different techniques for data collection in survey research. Once a data collection technique is chosen, the questionnaire can be developed and pilot tested. Chapter 8 of this text describes instrument development in detail. Students considering survey research should carefully read and follow the information contained in that chapter. If the questionnaire is not well designed, the results will suffer.

The next important task in survey research is to identify and obtain the survey sample. This assumes that a census approach surveying the entire population of interest will not be employed. Chapter 7 of this text describes sampling procedures. Again, students considering survey research should carefully study this chapter. A representative sample must be surveyed for the results to be valid. Access to accurate names, addresses, phone numbers, and/or e-mail addresses is critical to the success of survey research.

At this point, it is time to conduct the survey and all established follow-up procedures. Data collected then must be entered into the computer and verified for accuracy. For example, if the range of possible answers is 1 to 4 on a particular question and a frequency distribution indicates that three people responded with a 5, there is probably a data entry error. Those three surveys should be reexamined and the needed corrections made to the data set. Once the data are clean, data analysis can begin. This book will not cover statistical analysis in detail. Typically graduate students have a separate statistics course or courses that will provide this information.

The final step in conducting survey research is writing the final report. Chapter 12 of this text discusses the writing of the results chapter (Chapter V) in the thesis or dissertation. Chapter 14 of this text presents information on sharing research results through presentations at conferences and professional journal articles.

Response Rates

After reading the above sections on survey data collection, the importance of response rates should be clear. It is of utmost importance that the researcher maintain good records concerning data collection efforts and report accurate response rates along with the results of the study. Neutens and Rubinson (2010, pp. 110–111) identify four different rates that can be utilized to help readers understand the data collection process when reporting survey research results:

$$\text{response rate 1} = \frac{\text{number of completions}}{\text{number in sample}} \times 100$$

$$\text{response rate 2} = \frac{\text{number of completions}}{\begin{array}{c}\text{number in}\\\text{sample} - \\\text{(noneligible and}\\\text{nonreachable)}\end{array}} \times 100$$

$$\text{refusal rate} = \frac{\begin{array}{c}\text{number of}\\\text{respondents refused}\end{array}}{\begin{array}{c}\text{number of eligible}\\\text{respondents contacted}\end{array}} \times 100$$

$$\text{noncontact rate} = \frac{\text{total not contacted}}{\text{total known eligible}} \times 100$$

Correlational Research

"A **correlational study** examines the extent to which differences in one characteristic or variable are related to differences in one or more other characteristics or variables. A **correlation** exists if, when one variable increases, another variable either increases or decreases in a somewhat predictable fashion" (Leedy & Ormrod, 2010, p. 183). Note that in this definition we are interested in whether one variable is "related" to another, but there is no mention of cause and effect. Correlational research only identifies relationships and the degree or closeness of those relationships.

Research questions associated with correlational studies usually include the word "relationship" in them. For example, "What is the relationship between participation in sports and alcohol consumption among high school students?" "What is the relationship between scores on a hardiness scale and job satisfaction scores among employees at the county unemployment center?" "What is the relationship between religious affiliation and sexual satisfaction scores among residents of a retirement community?"

The preceding examples would all be what Fraenkel and Wallen (2003) term explanatory correlational studies; that is, they are designed to identify, clarify, and/or explain relationships between variables. The other major type of correlational study is a prediction study. "If a relationship of sufficient magnitude exists between two variables, it becomes possible to predict a score on either variable if a score on the other variable is known" (Fraenkel & Wallen, 2003, p. 340). Suppose, for example, a large city health department was concerned about the high number of teen pregnancies in the city. They would like to be able to predict which girls might be at highest risk for pregnancy so that special programs might be provided to lower their pregnancy risk. A correlational study could be completed looking for relationships between pregnancy status and a variety of other variables such as academic standing, religious affiliation, race, family characteristics, extracurricular activities, self-esteem, dating history, and so forth. Using a **multiple regression** technique, the health department could determine which of these variables when combined together could best predict pregnancy risk.

Conducting studies to answer these or other correlation-type questions requires accurate measurement of two or more variables for the same group of people. Although these measurements can take many forms, they must be quantitative. Sometimes data can be collected through observation or by examining records, but usually one or more instruments are administered to participants. These instruments must produce valid and reliable scores. Otherwise, any correlation obtained will not be an indication of the true relationship between the variables (Fraenkel & Wallen, 2003).

Sample size is an important consideration when conducting correlational research. Fraenkel and

a. Scatterplot indicating a positive relationship.

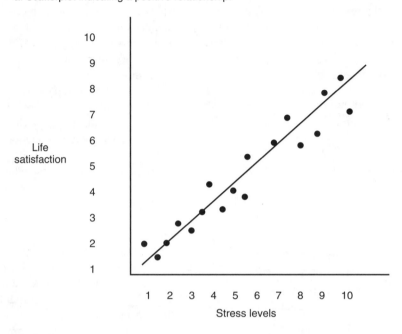

b. Scatterplot indicating a negative relationship.

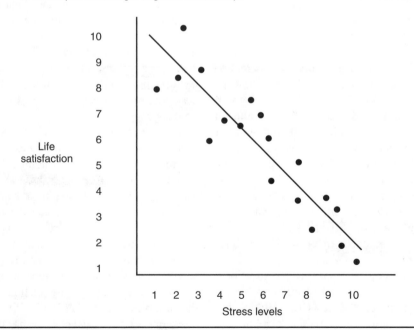

FIGURE 10.2

c. Scatterplot indicating a curvilinear relationship.

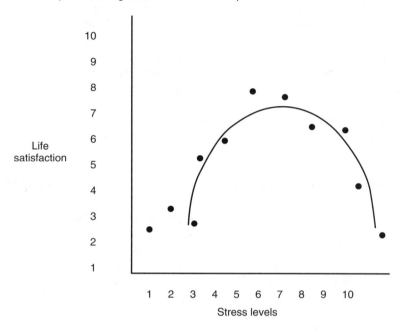

d. Scatterplot indicating no relationship.

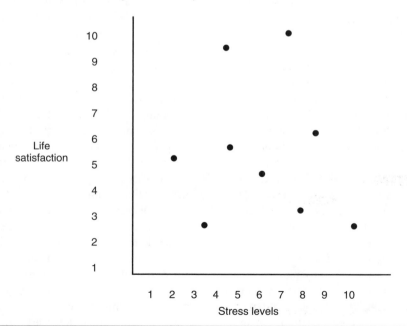

FIGURE 10.2 *Continued*

Wallen (2003) state that the minimum acceptable sample size for correlational research is 30. Smaller sample sizes may provide inaccurate estimates of potential relationships. Larger sample sizes are more likely to produce meaningful results. Stevens (2009) recommends that, "in the social sciences, approximately 15 subjects per predictor are needed to generate a reliable regression equation" (p. 120).

When examining the relationship between two variables, a **correlation coefficient**, symbolized by a lowercase r, is calculated. A perfect correlation would equal either a $+1.00$ or a -1.00. If the variables are completely unrelated, the r value would be 0.00. All correlation coefficients fall somewhere between 0.00 and either $+1.00$ or -1.00.

The positive or negative sign in front of the correlation coefficient does not indicate the strength of the relationship but rather the direction of the relationship. An r of $+0.8$ is equal in strength to an r of -0.8. When both variables move in the same direction, or one variable increases as the other increases, the relationship would be positive. When one variable moves in the opposite direction, or one variable increases as the other decreases, the relationship would be negative.

See Figure 10.2 to better clarify this point. Note in the positive relationship (Figure 10.2a) that as stress levels increase, life satisfaction increases. It would be equally appropriate to say that as life satisfaction increases, stress levels increase. In the negative relationship (Figure 10.2b), it can be seen that as stress levels increase, life satisfaction decreases. Again, it would be equally appropriate to say that as life satisfaction decreases, stress levels increase. These are both **linear relationships**. Figure 10.2c demonstrates a **curvilinear relationship**. In this example one can see that as stress increases, life satisfaction increases to a point. Beyond that point, as stress increases, life satisfaction decreases. Figure 10.2d indicates that there is no relationship between the variables.

Creswell (2005) describes a six-step process for conducting correlational studies. Step 1 is to determine if the research question can best be addressed by a correlational study; step 2 is to identify the population or sample to study; step 3 is to identify two or more specific measures to be used with each individual in the study; step 4 is to collect the data while monitoring threats to internal validity; step 5 is to analyze the data; and step 6 is to interpret the results.

Interpreting Correlational Research Results

Caution must be used in interpreting correlational research results. Remember, correlational studies only demonstrate mathematical relationships between variables, not cause-and-effect relationships (Berg & Latin, 2004). There is a tendency, however, to want to interpret correlation as cause and effect. For example, consider the relationship depicted in Figure 10.2 dealing with stress levels and life satisfaction. Wouldn't it be tempting for a health educator interested in the effects of stress to say that stress is causing the changes in life satisfaction? That would, however, be a misinterpretation of correlational research results.

To make this point more clear, consider the following example used by Vierra, Pollock, and Golez (1992). Suppose a researcher were to run a correlation on ice cream sales and deaths by drowning. (Let's not speculate on why one might choose to do this.) The researcher would find that the two are highly correlated. In other words, in months where ice cream sales go up, deaths by drowning go up and vice versa. Should the researcher interpret this finding to mean that ice cream consumption causes drownings to increase or that drownings cause surviving family and friends to eat more ice cream? Of course not. Those interpretations would be preposterous and erroneous since correlational studies do not demonstrate cause and effect. Obviously, a third factor, temperature, is related to both ice cream sales and drowning deaths. It is only because ice cream sales and drownings are both related to temperature that they appear to be related. In the stress level and life satisfaction example, there could very well be a third factor influencing both of these variables—perhaps exercise. We simply do not know; therefore, we cannot interpret the results as cause and effect.

Tests of statistical significance are used in correlational studies. What a significant correlation indicates is that an obtained correlation coefficient is really different from a correlation of zero or no correlation at all. As Gay *et al.*, (2006) note "…a significance test does not allow you to determine with perfect certainty that there is or is not a true, meaningful relationship between the variables. However, the statistical test does indicate the probability that there is or is not a significant, true relationship" (p. 195). The correlation between ice cream sales and drowning deaths would be significant but not meaningful.

Causal-Comparative Research

"In **causal-comparative research**, investigators attempt to determine the cause or consequences of differences that already exist between or among groups of individuals" (Fraenkel & Wallen, 2003, p. 368). This type of research is also called **ex post facto research** from the Latin for "after the fact."

For example, a researcher might hypothesize that participating in organized religion is a major factor that prevents high school students from experimenting with alcohol. To examine this hypothesis, the researcher might select a sample of high school students who have participated in organized religion and a group of high school students who have not participated in organized religion. The researcher would then administer a questionnaire asking students to anonymously describe their previous alcohol use behaviors. If the group that participated in organized religion has a significantly lower level of alcohol experimentation, the researcher's hypothesis would be supported, but not proven.

It is important to understand the similarities and differences among causal-comparative research,

correlational research, and experimental research. Both correlational research and causal-comparative research are descriptive in that they are attempting to describe what is. Neither approach involves any manipulation of variables or control groups. So what differentiates these two approaches? Causal-comparative studies involve comparisons between two or more groups and one independent variable, but correlational studies involve only one group that is measured on two or more variables. Correlational studies look for relationships and causal-comparative studies attempt to identify possible cause-and-effect relationships.

Since both experimental and causal-comparative studies attempt to identify cause-and-effect relationships, how are they different? In experimental studies researchers attempt to randomly select their participants, randomly divide their participants into two or more groups including a control group, randomly assign one or more treatments to the groups, and carry out the study while trying to control for as many threats to internal and external validity as possible. After the study is complete, comparisons are made between groups. In causal-comparative research, the groups already exist and the treatment has already occurred. "To put it as simply as possible, the major difference is that in experimental research the independent variable, the alleged cause, is manipulated by the researcher, whereas in causal-comparative research it is not because it has already occurred" (Gay *et al.*, 2006, p. 218).

The independent variables in causal-comparative studies are variables that cannot be manipulated (such as race), should not be manipulated (such as amount of alcohol consumed), or simply are not manipulated. Often it is less expensive and less time consuming to conduct a causal-comparative study than an experimental study, so one may choose a causal-comparative approach over an experimental design. Suppose a health education specialist who consults with several corporate clients is interested in determining which of two smoking cessation programs to recommend.

She could conduct an experimental study, which would necessitate identifying three companies to work with, recruiting volunteers to quit smoking, randomly assigning the two smoking cessation programs and a control group, conducting the cessation programs, and following up with participants for six months to a year. At the end of her study she could conclude which, if either, of the two approaches worked best. Or she could conduct a causal-comparative study. If she could locate similar companies that had already implemented the two programs and compare their past success rates, it would take far less effort and she could have results in a much shorter time.

Lack of randomization, lack of manipulation of the variables, and lack of control are all weaknesses of causal-comparative studies. Therefore, confidence in the results of causal-comparative studies is much lower than in experimental studies. Because there is a lack of randomization and control, it is possible that some other factor may account for differences found between groups. In the above smoking cessation scenario, for example, if one approach is found to be better in helping people quit smoking through a causal-comparative study, it may be because of the superiority of the approach, or perhaps the groups were not the same at the start. Perhaps the group with the better quit rate was more highly motivated, had not smoked for as long a time, smoked fewer cigarettes per day, were given incentives by the company, and so forth. As a result, even though causal-comparative studies attempt to demonstrate cause and effect, they really do not do so with the same degree of certainty as do experimental studies.

There are procedures that can be used in causal-comparative studies to control for some of the threats to internal validity. One approach is to match participants based on one or more important characteristics. Using the smoking cessation example, the researcher might individually match participants from one approach to participants in the other approach on such characteristics as years smoked and number of cigarettes smoked

per day. So someone from approach 1 who has smoked for five years or less and smokes half a pack a day would be matched with someone from approach 2 who has smoked for five years or less and smokes half a pack a day. The next match might be someone in approach 1 who has smoked a pack a day for 15–20 years with someone in approach 2 who has smoked a pack a day for 15–20 years. Only the matched pairs would be included in the study.

Another option would be to compare homogeneous groups or subgroups. The researcher might limit the study to those persons who have smoked for five years or less and smoke half a pack a day. Other smokers would not be included in the study. If the researcher does not want to limit the study to one subgroup, additional subgroups could be devised and compared.

Analysis of covariance is a statistical technique that can be used to control for initial group differences in causal-comparative studies. If the researcher in the smoking cessation study was to learn that the participants in approach 1 smoked more cigarettes per day than participants in approach 2 at the beginning of the study, it might be expected that those in approach 1 would smoke fewer cigarettes per day than participants in approach 2 at the end of the study. Analysis of covariance would mathematically adjust the number of cigarettes smoked so that the two approaches would be equal, thus removing any initial advantage those in approach 1 might have had.

Evaluation Research

In the broad sense, **evaluation** is a process to determine the effectiveness of a specific program, person, technique, strategy, or initiative. The outcome of an evaluation is then used to make decisions about the program, person, technique, strategy, or initiative in question. In the profession of health education, evaluation is of critical importance. Health education specialists must evaluate the programs they provide to demonstrate effectiveness and prevent the misuse of valuable resources. One of the seven major responsibilities of a health education specialist is to conduct evaluation and research related to health education (National Commission for Health Education Credentialing, 2009).

But is evaluation research? Does research include evaluation? Or is evaluation something completely different from research? The literature is not in agreement on the answers to these questions. Most research methods books make no mention of evaluation research (Creswell, 2005; DePoy & Gitlin, 2005; Fraenkel & Wallen, 2003; Patten, 2009; Salkind, 2000). Others briefly mention evaluation research as a type of applied research but do not provide much detail (Gay *et al.*, 2006). On the other end of the spectrum, Neutens and Rubinson (2010) dedicate a full chapter in their research methods book to discussing evaluation research, and Windsor *et al.* (2004) thoroughly discuss the need for and importance of evaluation research. See Figure 10.3 for a listing of the 10 common purposes of evaluation and note how these purposes relate to our definition of research. Both of these texts that include prominent sections on evaluation research were written for the health science or health promotion and education audience; thus,

it seems that evaluation research is more prominent in these fields.

The authors of your text believe that evaluation is an important type of research in health education and thus have chosen to cover the topic in this chapter on non-experimental research designs. However, depending on how an evaluation is designed, evaluation research could also be categorized as experimental research. Windsor, Clark, Boyd, and Goodman (2004) state that "Evaluation research attempts to produce evidence to support or reject a research hypothesis and to demonstrate a cause-effect relationship between the intervention and the impact or outcome" (p. 27). This sounds very much like a description of experimental research. Note the mention of research hypotheses and cause-and-effect relationships. Consider the program evaluation example in Box 10.4 as an example of program evaluation that is also experimental research.

Most program evaluation research conducted on health education programs, however, would not be categorized as experimental research. Often it is not possible to randomize, control groups are not utilized, and the main purpose is to determine if preestablished objectives are met. In the real world of health education practice, often it is not considered important to isolate an independent variable

1. To determine the degree of achievement of program objectives
2. To document program strengths and weaknesses in making planning decisions
3. To establish quality assurance and control methods and to monitor performance
4. To determine generalizability of a program to other populations/settings
5. To identify hypotheses about human behavior for future evaluations
6. To contribute to the science base of health education programs
7. To improve staff skills required for planning, implementation, and evaluation
8. To fulfill grant or contract requirements
9. To promote positive public relations and community awareness
10. To meet public and fiscal accountability requirements

FIGURE 10.3
Ten common purposes of evaluation, as outlined by Windsor *et al.* (2004).
Source: Windsor, Clark, Boyd, & Goodman, 2004, p. 15.

Box 10.4   Experimental Evaluation Research Case Study

Terri-Lynn is a health education specialist working in a large metropolitan hospital. As part of her job, she has been offering regular smoking cessation programs that are free to hospital staff and open to the general public for a small fee. She has been offering these classes for the past several years and has evaluated each class with a follow-up survey one year after program completion. Overall, she has achieved a 24% quit rate at one year following the program. Although 24% is an acceptable quit rate for smoking cessation programs, Terri-Lynn believes that she can do better. She designs a new smoking cessation program that incorporates several new elements she has learned about in the literature and from her own personal experience. Her objective is to obtain a one-year quit rate of 33%. Her hypothesis is that the new program will have a higher smoking cessation rate at one year than will the standard program.

To evaluate the new program, Terri-Lynn designs an evaluation research study. She recruits volunteers to participate in her next few smoking cessation programs and develops a list of potential participants. She randomly assigns the participants to one of two groups and then randomly assigns the standard program and the new program to the groups. She uses a third group that is waiting to be enrolled in future classes as a control group. All of the participants are given preprogram questionnaires to determine their current smoking status, how much they smoke, how long they have smoked, and so forth. This information is used to make sure the two groups are comparable at the outset. Terri-Lynn now offers three consecutive series of classes; in each series she teaches one standard program and one new program. At the end of each session she collects data to compare the smoking rates between the groups. One year after each series is complete, she does a follow-up interview with all participants to determine their smoking status. A saliva test is also conducted to verify participant responses.

From this evaluation, Terri-Lynn is able to compare quit rates among the standard program, the new program, and no program at one year following the smoking cessation programs. From statistical analysis, she can determine if the new program is significantly better than the standard program or no program at helping participants to quit smoking. She can also look at the overall quit rate among new program participants to determine if her objective of a 33% one-year quit rate was obtained.

Review: Although this is an experimental design, based on the information in Chapter 9, what threats still exist to internal and external validity?

---

to determine its specific effects on a dependent variable. Instead, two, three, or even more program initiatives (independent variables) are tried simultaneously to see if program objectives can be met. Although the intent is to demonstrate that the program components caused a specific response (met the objective), the rigor of the design is typically not sufficient to prove cause and effect at the expected standards of true experimental research. For that reason evaluation research is presented as non-experimental research in this text.

Can evaluation research be used to complete a project, thesis, or dissertation? Certainly, evalua-

tion research studies can be designed in such a way as to meet the rigor expected in theses or dissertations. The majority of evaluation research, however, would probably fit best as a project or perhaps a senior capstone experience. Ultimately, faculty in one's own graduate program can best answer questions concerning what can be used for a thesis or dissertation.

Types of Program Evaluation

There are many different models or approaches for conducting program evaluation. McDermott and

Sarvela (1999) discuss the transactional approach, the Context Input Process Product (CIPP) model, systems analysis, art criticism, the adversarial or quasi-legal approach, and the accreditation or professional review approach. Although all of these have value and are utilized in different settings and situations, the model most utilized by health education is the **objectives-oriented approach**. In this approach, specific objectives are stated for a health education program or initiative. Procedures are devised to collect the necessary data to determine if the stated objectives have been met. Program success is determined by the degree to which the stated program objectives were accomplished.

Objectives can be written that focus on how a program is implemented. For example, objectives could be established stating that a program is to be offered in six 90-minute sessions, all programs be administered by certified health education specialists (CHES), all participants meet specified criteria such as being in their first trimester of pregnancy, participants attend 90% of classes, and so forth. The type of evaluation that develops objectives to assess the program while it is being conducted or to assess how the program is implemented is called **formative** or **process evaluation** (McDermott & Sarvela, 1999).

Formative or process objectives essentially are written to evaluate those charged with implementing the program. The purpose of formative evaluation is to determine while the program is in progress if the program is actually being presented as designed and if changes need to be made to the program to increase the likelihood that program objectives will be accomplished. This brings up an important difference between experimental research and evaluation research (Patten, 2009). In experimental research, altering a program after it has begun would not be allowed because it would greatly diminish the validity of the study. In other words, the research design controls how the program is presented. In evaluation research, the program can be altered after it has been initiated to increase effectiveness. Evaluation research is merely a tool to evaluate a program whose main purpose is to meet stated objectives. In other words, the program is primary to the research.

Beyond formative evaluation is summative evaluation. A **summative evaluation** assesses the final effects or benefits of a program on its participants (Patten, 2009). Note that the target of summative evaluation is the program participants, but the target of process evaluation is the program providers. Summative evaluation might examine objectives related to reducing the number of teenage pregnancies, increasing condom use, improving attitudes toward condom use, increasing knowledge of condom use, or increasing the availability of condoms. Each of these objectives would actually be considered a different level or type of objective. The following section discusses goals and objectives and how they can be written at multiple levels.

Writing Goals and Objectives

One of the most important aspects of program evaluation is developing clear, concise **goals** and **objectives**. Although goals and objectives are related, they are not synonymous. Goals are broad statements of direction written in nontechnical language. Goals are less specific than objectives and are used to explain the general intent of a program to those not directly involved in the program. They are often used for public relations or promotional purposes. Objectives, on the other hand, are much more specific than goals. Objectives are written at multiple levels and serve as the guideposts on which the entire program is developed. No program initiative should be implemented unless it is designed to meet or help meet a specific objective. Objectives are the foundation of program development, implementation, and evaluation.

The development of goals and objectives needs to be accomplished early in the planning process before any program efforts are implemented. Goals and objectives should be written based on the results of a completed needs assessment and must be in agreement with the mission of the organization sponsoring the program.

Table 10.4 outlines the steps in evaluation research. Note that after conducting the needs assessment, six of the next seven steps relate to developing some type of goal or objective. For anyone conducting evaluation research in health education, the ability to write sound goals and objectives is essential. Descriptions of these various types or levels of goals and objectives will now be provided.

Program goals are broad statements of direction. Remember, goals are used primarily to explain to those outside the program what the program is designed to do in the most general of terms. Perhaps the best way to think of a goal is that it is the way you would respond to your mother or father if they asked you what you were doing at work. Your response might be, "I am working on a program to reduce the number of new HIV-positive patients in XYZ County." The program goal might actually be written as follows: "To reduce the number of new HIV-positive patients in XYZ County." Although there is usually only one program goal, it is possible that there may be more than one. For example, a complementary goal for the HIV example might be "To reduce the number of newly diagnosed sexually transmitted disease patients in XYZ County." Program initiatives to meet these two program goals would certainly be complementary.

Once a program goal has been established, the next step is to develop **program objectives**. Depending on who is doing the writing, these could also be called health objectives, outcome objectives, or long-term objectives. This level of objective usually deals with improving some health problem or health indicator. Program objectives might relate to reducing the number of fatal heart attacks, diabetic complications, sexually transmitted infections, and so forth. This level of objective can also include some long-term corporate outcomes such as reduced sick leave or lower health care costs. Using the HIV example from above, a program objective might be as follows: "At the end of the three-year HIV intervention program, there will be a 20% reduction in the number of new HIV-positive patients diagnosed per year in XYZ County."

Several points need to be made about the above program objective. First, note that the program objective is directly related to the program goal. It simply goes farther to quantify the amount of change that is expected and establishes a timeline. Second, notice the length of time that the program will be in effect (three years). Program objectives usually require a long-term effort in the two- to five-year range. Third, although we are calling this a program objective, others might label this same objective a long-term, outcome, or health objective. Terminology used when writing objectives can be confusing. Be sure you know at what level you need to write an objective, and use terminology accepted by the sponsoring agency. Finally, why was 20% selected? Essentially, specifying to what extent change will occur is the planners' best educated guess as to the amount of change they can create. The number is not just picked out of thin air. The planners should have reviewed the literature, talked to other health education specialists involved in such programs, and utilized past experience and their best professional judgment to arrive at the 20% figure. It is also important to note

Table 10.4   Steps in Evaluation Research

- Conduct needs assessment
- Develop program goal(s)
- Develop program objective(s)
- Develop behavioral objectives
- Develop learning objectives (predisposing, enabling, and reinforcing)
- Develop environmental objectives
- Develop formative/process objectives
- Develop program strategies
- Implement program and collect needed evaluation data
- Evaluate program
- Continue, modify, and/or extend program

that the planners must identify a current baseline level of HIV diagnoses to be able to determine if they have a 20% reduction in three years. This may seem simplistic, but solid baseline data are critical to program evaluation. Sometimes program planners decide to evaluate a program after it is already implemented, and no baseline data are available. In these cases a quality program evaluation cannot be accomplished. Such situations emphasize the need to consider program evaluation up front during the initial planning process.

At this point, let us examine how to write a clear, concise objective. Every objective, regardless of the level at which it is written, should contain four components: who, what, when, and how much (Windsor *et al.*, 2004). Consider the above program objective related to HIV: "At the end of the three-year HIV intervention program, there will be a 20% reduction in the number of new HIV-positive patients diagnosed per year in XYZ County."

The "who" would be XYZ County residents; the "what" would be reduction in the number of new HIV-positive diagnoses each year; the "when" would be at the end of the three-year intervention program; and "how much" would be a 20% reduction. These four components should be present in any objective written as part of a program evaluation. Check all future sample objectives written in this chapter to make certain they contain the four required components.

With the program objective or objectives now in place, the next objectives to be written are **behavioral objectives.** As the name implies, these objectives will examine the behaviors of the target population. Behavioral objectives can also be called impact objectives or intermediate objectives. Remember, the focus here is on behaviors such as number of cigarettes smoked, number of exercise sessions completed, number of fat servings consumed, fastening of seat belts, flossing teeth, and so forth. Be careful, as there is a tendency to sometimes confuse behavioral and program objectives. For example, if an objective were to specify the number of pounds an individ-

ual was to lose, would it be program or behavioral? Students often write objectives related to pounds lost as a behavioral measure, but such a statement is actually a health or program objective. The behaviors to be measured as related to weight loss might include increased exercise and following a reduced-calorie diet. In staying with the HIV example, a behavioral objective would be: "After a four-month program to encourage condom use, the self-reported condom use rate by clients at the XYZ County Health Department Clinics will increase from 62% to at least 75%." Most programs would include multiple behavioral objectives. Other objectives might focus on different populations (e.g., college students, gay alliance members) and/or on different behaviors (e.g., IV drug use, needle exchange). Essentially, a sufficient number of behavioral objectives must be written so that if each behavioral objective were met, planners would feel confident that the higher-level program objective would be met. We call this the **rule of sufficiency**. If planners do not feel there will be a sufficient amount of behavioral change created by meeting the behavioral objectives so that the desired program objectives will be met, there is no reason to offer the programs.

Writing **learning objectives** follows the development of behavioral objectives. Green and Kreuter (2004) break learning objectives into three categories: predisposing, enabling, and reinforcing. **Predisposing learning objectives** relate to the knowledge, attitudes, values, and beliefs of the target population that need to be modified for the behavioral objective to be met. For example, we would not expect people to begin using condoms if they did not have knowledge of condom use, did not have a positive attitude toward condoms, did not value their health and the health of their partners, and did not believe that condoms would help reduce the risk of HIV infection. Some sample predisposing learning objectives follow: "After reading the pamphlet on condom use, clients will be able to list three benefits of condom use." "After meeting with the street-level health department contact, clients will believe that condom use will decrease the risk of HIV infection." "After viewing the condom video, clients will demonstrate a positive attitude toward condom use." It is important to remember that any objective written must be evaluated. This means that we would need to determine if clients really can list three benefits of condom use, really believe condoms will reduce HIV risk, and really do have a positive attitude toward condom use. Further, the rule of sufficiency applies here as well. A sufficient number of predisposing factors must be changed to create the desired behavior modification.

Enabling learning objectives refer to the skills and/or resources people need to change the desired behaviors. In this case we are trying to get people to increase their condom use behaviors. A resource that is obviously necessary is the actual condom. If clients were unable to afford condoms, it would do little good to provide the information and encouragement to purchase condoms. Therefore, an enabling learning objective might be: "Beginning June 1, every client at XYZ County Health Department Clinics will be given access to free condoms." This could also be considered as process or formative evaluation, where the other levels of objectives written before this would be considered summative. Supplying free condoms by June 1 would be an objective health department personnel might set for themselves, hence, process evaluation.

Beyond access to condoms, clients need the skills to effectively use the condoms; that is, clients must be able to correctly open the condom package and apply a condom to an erect penis. A sample enabling objective might be: "After receiving instructions on condom use at XYZ County Health Department Clinics, clients will be able to demonstrate how to apply a condom to the model penis as per the instructions."

The last type of learning objective to be written is **reinforcing learning objectives.** Program planners need to determine what factors reinforce a current undesirable behavior and diminish them,

while also determining those factors that would reinforce the new desirable behavior and encourage them. In the HIV example, suppose the peer group is saying that real men do not use condoms. This would certainly not reinforce condom use. A sample objective might be: "By the end of the first year of programming, at least 50% of XYZ County Health Department Clinic clients will verbally share their opinion in group settings that it is a man's responsibility to protect himself and his partners from HIV infection." An objective to reinforce the desired behavior of coming to the clinic to obtain free condoms might read, "Men who come to the clinic during the first three months of the program to obtain condoms will be given free coffee and muffins." This latter objective would also be considered a process objective because supplying free coffee and muffins would be an objective for health department personnel.

An additional level of objective to discuss is the **environmental objective** (Green & Kreuter, 2004). Environmental objectives are developed based on an ecological approach to health promotion. The ecological approach views health "as a product of the interdependence of the individual and the subsystems of the ecosystem (such as family, community, culture, and physical and social environment)" (Green & Kreuter, 2004, p. 22). Altering the ecosystem that supports health may involve changes in the economic, political, and/or social conditions. This often necessitates changes in policies, procedures, guidelines, requirements, or laws to accomplish this task. Health education specialists need to get involved in the political systems of their organizations, cities, counties, states, and the federal government to promote needed changes. Environmental objectives could be written to place a stoplight at a dangerous intersection, initiate no-smoking policies in restaurants, or develop a new bike/jogging path. Using our HIV example, suppose the XYZ County Health Department had a policy that prevented the distribution of free condoms. If the health education specialists on the planning committee believed that distribution of free condoms was critical to bringing about the behavior changes necessary to reduce new HIV cases, they would need to work to get that policy changed. A sample environmental objective could be, "Within one year, a new XYZ County Health Department policy will be written allowing for the free distribution of condoms." This objective could be further broken down by stating, "Within six months, 7 of the 12 Health Board members will support the need for free condom distribution in XYZ County."

Process or formative evaluation also requires the development of **process** or **formative objectives**. These objectives guide the work of the program planners and/or implementors. In writing process or formative objectives, the "who" is the staff or group entrusted with instituting the program instead of the target population. In other words, it is an objective for those individuals that have to make something happen related to the program being implemented. For example, "Health educators will conduct at least 15 presentations at homeless shelters on condom use to prevent HIV within the next six months."

A few more comments about objectives are needed before we leave the topic. To plan a complete health promotion and education program, objectives should be written at all levels described above. Often, however, health education specialists may not develop a complete program. Different levels of planning can take place at different points within an organization. Consider a health education specialist working at a county-level voluntary health agency. The national level of the agency may have developed certain priority areas or goals. The state level may have developed program objectives related to the national goals. This all passes down to the county-level health education specialist, who is told to develop programs to alter certain behaviors. The county health education specialist may then develop behavioral objectives, learning objectives, and process objectives. Environmental objectives

could be written at the national, state, or local level, depending on the policies, regulations, or laws that need to be instituted or modified.

An example may help to clarify this point. The national level of the American Cancer Society may establish a goal to reduce the number of lung cancer deaths in the United States. Given this national goal, a state-level American Cancer Society office may write a program objective to reduce lung cancer deaths in their state from 24 per 100,000 to fewer than 20 per 100,000. Given this program objective, a health education specialist at the county-level American Cancer Society may develop a behavioral objective to reduce the incidence of smoking in the county by X%. The local-level health education specialist only works with behavioral and learning objectives and is not responsible for developing the program objectives and goals. Further, there may also be an environmental objective at the state level to increase by five the number of municipalities that have a ban on smoking in bars, restaurants, and entertainment centers. The county-level health education specialist may advocate for the passage of such a ban in the county.

The importance of objectives in program evaluation cannot be overstated. Without objectives there is nothing to evaluate. One of the best examples of objectives in long-term planning is the health objectives for the nation (Centers for Disease Control and Prevention, 2000). These objectives established the agenda for public health for the decade from 2000 to 2010 and served as the basis for evaluating public health efforts. An example of health objectives for the nation related to high blood pressure can be seen in Box 10.5. Note that all four components for an objective are present, but these objectives are structured in a different way than you have seen in this chapter. For the four objectives written in Box 10.5, can you identify the four essential components of an objective in each? Note that the "when" is a given because all objectives are to be completed by 2010. Can you determine at what level each objective is written?

Box 10.5 National Health Objectives: Blood Pressure

12–9. Reduce the proportion of adults with high blood pressure.
Target: 16 percent.
Baseline: 28 percent of adults aged 20 years and older had high blood pressure in 1988–1994 (age adjusted to the year 2000 standard population).

12–10. Increase the proportion of adults with high blood pressure whose blood pressure is under control.
Target: 50 percent.
Baseline: 18 percent of adults aged 18 years and older with high blood pressure had it under control in 1988–1994 (age adjusted to the year 2000 standard population).

12–11. Increase the proportion of adults with high blood pressure who are taking action (for example, losing weight, increasing physical activity, or reducing sodium intake) to help control their blood pressure.
Target: 95 percent.
Baseline: 82 percent of adults aged 18 years and older with high blood pressure were taking action to control it in 1998 (age adjusted to the year 2000 standard population).

12–12. Increase the proportion of adults who have had their blood pressure measured within the preceding 2 years and can state whether their blood pressure was normal or high.
Target: 95 percent.
Baseline: 90 percent of adults aged 18 years and older had their blood pressure measured in the past 2 years and could state whether it was normal or high in 1998 (age adjusted to the year 2000 standard population).

Source: Centers for Disease Control and Prevention. (2000). *Healthy People 2010: Focus Area 12— Heart disease and stroke.* Available at: www.healthypeople.gov.

By the time this book is published, the new objectives for the nation in 2020 should be released and available for health education professionals.

Data Collection in Evaluation Research

Data collection is a critical part of evaluation research. The appropriate data need to be collected in valid and reliable ways to determine if an objective has been met. This means that both baseline and postintervention data need to be collected in the same manner to be sure one is comparing apples with apples and not apples with oranges.

Both quantitative and qualitative data may be needed to evaluate objectives. Quantitative data might include numerical counts such as numbers of cigarettes, servings of fruits and vegetables, or reported seat belt use. Actual physical measurements can be used for some objectives such as measures of body fat or measures of physical fitness. Quantitative measurements can also include scores such as might be obtained from knowledge questions, attitudinal questions, behavioral questions, or instruments to measure such constructs as locus of control or self-concept. A variety of qualitative methods can also be used to collect data in evaluation research. McDermott and Sarvela (1999) describe the use of participant–observer studies, unobtrusive observations, interviewing, focus groups, case studies, nominal group process, and Delphi technique as possible strategies in health education evaluation.

In evaluation research, the data collected are those that are needed to evaluate the objectives. The way objectives are written should determine what data need to be collected. If a behavioral objective, for example, specified that fat intake was to be reduced to x number of grams per day, the data collection would have to measure fat intake in grams. It would not be appropriate to examine only the number of fat servings from the food pyramid, the number of meat servings, or any other indirect measure of fat.

The results of evaluation research are typically used to determine future program direction. If objectives were met, additional programs of the same type may be offered. If a program is offered multiple times with similar results, more confidence can be placed in the results. If the objectives were not met, it may mean the program was not effective. The program may need to be modified prior to offering it again. It is also possible that the objectives were not met because they were set too high. Remember that objectives are the planners' best guess as to what can be achieved. The expected level of change may need to be reassessed.

See Figure 10.4 for an example of program evaluation objectives written at all levels. These can be used as templates for developing future objectives. For students wanting to do more work in program evaluation, the Windsor *et al.* (2004) book is an excellent source. It provides a good overview of evaluation in health promotion and education, and includes three case studies of actual evaluation projects in public health.

Summary

This chapter has presented information on non-experimental research designs. Although not as robust as experimental designs, non-experimental designs are often more practical and may answer questions that cannot be answered by traditional experimental research. Non-experimental designs are frequently employed in health education.

Survey research is an important and frequently used means of collecting data in health education. Several different methods of collecting survey data were discussed, including mailed surveys, group administered surveys, electronic surveys, personal interviews, and telephone interviews. Each technique has its advantages and disadvantages. Response rate was discussed as a critical element of survey research, and several different ways of calculating response rate were presented.

Correlational research was presented as another non-experimental approach to research. In correlational research, relationships are explored but cause and effect cannot be determined. This is an important distinction that must be taken into consideration when discussing the results of correlational research.

Causal-comparative or ex post facto research seeks to determine the cause or consequences of differences that already exist between or among groups of individuals. Again, it is a type of research sometimes utilized in health education, but it is not as strong as experimental research. This type of research does attempt to establish cause-and-effect relationships, but less confidence is placed in the results than with true experimental research. This type of research can be utilized to provide justification for further research using experimental designs.

The chapter concludes with a thorough discussion of evaluation research. The need to write appropriate objectives was stressed. Different types or levels of objectives were presented and examples provided of each type. For any health education program, objectives should be written at all levels. Individual health education specialists, however, may only be responsible for a particular aspect of a program and only utilize objectives appropriate to that aspect.

Review Questions

1. Explain the difference between experimental and non-experimental research.
2. Suppose a researcher wanted to conduct a study of incoming freshmen to determine how their health behaviors change over the four years they are in college. What type of research design might this researcher use?
3. What can be done to increase the response rates of mailed surveys?
4. Explain the advantages and disadvantages to conducting a telephone survey.

Program Goal

To reduce the incidence of dental disease in children of ZZZ County.

Program (Health, Outcome, Long-Term) Objective

By 2006, there will be a 25% decrease in the number of dental caries found in third-grade children in ZZZ County.

Behavioral (Impact, Mid-Term) Objectives

In three years, 80% of ZZZ County third graders will brush their teeth at least once a day.

By the program's end, at least 50% of ZZZ County third graders will have visited a dentist for prophylactic treatment in the past year.

Learning Level (Short-Term) Objectives

*Predisposing—Knowledge
By the end of the program period, 90% of ZZZ County third graders will be able to:
A) list four health dangers associated with poor dental care.
B) describe proper dental care as per ADA guidelines.
C) identify the various professionals that care for teeth.

*Predisposing—Beliefs, Values, Attitudes
By the end of the program period, 90% of ZZZ County third graders will:
A) believe that dental caries can be prevented through proper brushing of the teeth and regular dental exams.
B) value good dental health.
C) exhibit a positive attitude toward dental professionals.

*Enabling—Skills & Resources
By the end of the program period, 90% of ZZZ County third graders will:
A) demonstrate the proper technique for brushing the teeth.
B) own a toothbrush and toothpaste.
C) have access to regular dental checkups.

*Reinforcing
After the dental program is in place:
A) all third graders who have perfect checkups will receive 20 free tokens to a video arcade.
B) all third graders who keep and submit brush/floss records will receive coupons for free pizza.
C) all third graders who bring a friend in for a checkup will receive a free sport T-shirt.

Environmental Objective

Within two years, full-service dental clinics will be available in the two elementary schools that service primarily low socioeconomic level children.

Process or Formative Objectives

A) Program staff will obtain funding for eight dental clinics within the next 12 months.
B) In the next three months, program staff will contact all ZZZ County dentists requesting contributions of time and/or money to implement the third-grade dental program.
C) By December, program staff will provide dental health presentations at 10 PTA or civic organization meetings.

FIGURE 10.4
Sample program evaluation goal and multilevel objectives.

5. How has technology impacted telephone surveys?

6. When conducting a correlational study, a researcher found that as levels of exercise went up, self-concept went up. What type of relationship is this? Explain what these results mean.

7. A researcher found a correlation between the average daily outside temperature from January 2009 to May 2009 and the number of newly diagnosed swine flu cases. The results demonstrated that as outside temperature increased, the number of swine flu cases increased. The researcher concluded that temperature increases caused increases in swine flu cases. What do you think of the researcher's findings? How would you interpret these results?

8. How do causal-comparative studies differ from correlational studies? Why might it be said that causal-comparative studies are not as robust as experimental studies?

9. Is program evaluation really research? Can a research study be used to evaluate a program?

10. Describe the difference between a goal and an objective.

11. What four components should be present in any written objective?

12. At what level is the following objective written: "Within five years, the number of gonorrhea cases in XXX County will be decreased by 20%."

13. A county health department learns that its county has a higher than expected incidence of falls resulting in hip fractures among the elderly. The health education specialist at the department develops a new program initiative with the goal to reduce the number of hip fractures in persons over 60 years of age in XXX County. Write a program objective, behavioral objective, environmental objective, three learning objectives, and a process objective related to the program goal.

References

Aday, L.A., & Cornelius, L.J. (2006). *Designing and conducting health surveys: A comprehensive guide*. San Francisco: Jossey-Bass.

Berg, K.E., & Latin, R.W. (2004). *Essentials of research methods in health, physical education, exercise science, and recreation* (2nd ed.). Philadelphia: Lippincott Williams & Wilkins.

Blumberg, S.J., Luke, J.V., & Cynamon, M.L. (2006). Telephone coverage and health survey estimates: Evaluating the need for concern about wireless substitution. *American Journal of Public Health*, 96(5), 926–931.

Centers for Disease Control and Prevention (CDC). (2000). Healthy people 2010: Focus area 12—heart disease and stroke. Available at: www.healthypeople.gov.

Creswell, J.W. (2005). *Educational research: Planning, conducting, and evaluating quantitative and qualitative research* (2nd ed). Upper Saddle River, N.J.: Pearson Education, Inc..

Daley, E.M., McDermott, R.J., McCormack-Brown, K.R., & Kittleson, M.J. (2003). Conducting Web-based survey research: A lesson in Internet designs. *American Journal of Health Behavior,* 27(2), 116–124.

DePoy, E., & Gitlin, L.N. (2005). *Introduction to research: Understanding and applying multiple strategies* (3rd ed.). St. Louis: Elsevier/Mosby.

Dillman, D.A. (2007). *Mail and Internet surveys: The tailored design method* (2nd ed.). Hoboken, N.J.: John Wiley & Sons.

Dillman, D.A., Phelps, G., Tortora, R., Swift, K., Kohrell, J., Berck, J., & Messer, B.L. (2009). Response rate and measurement differences in mixed-mode surveys using mail, telephone, interactive voice response (IVR) and the Internet. *Social Science Research,* 38, 1–18.

Federal Trade Commission. (2004). FTC consumer alert Q&A: The National Do Not Call Registry. Available at: www.ftc.gov/bcp/conline/pubs/alerts/dncalrt.htm.

Fowler, F.J. (2009). *Survey research methods* (4th ed.). Los Angeles: Sage Publications.

Fraenkel, J.R., & Wallen, N.E. (2003). *How to design and evaluate research in education.* (5th ed.) Boston: McGraw-Hill.

Gay, L.R., Mills, G.E., & Airasian, P. (2006). *Educational research: Competencies for analysis and applications.* Upper Saddle River, N.J.: Pearson Education, Inc.

Granello, D., & Wheaton, J. (2003). *Using Web-based surveys to conduct counseling research.* (ERIC Document Reproduction Service No. ED481144). Retrieved May 8, 2009, from ERIC database.

Green, L.W., & Kreuter, M.W. (2004). *Health program planning: An educational and ecological approach* (4th ed.). Mountain View, Calif.: Mayfield.

Kempf, A.M., & Remington, P.L. (2007). New challenges for telephone survey research in the twenty-first century. *Annual Review of Public Health*, 28, 113–126.

Kerlinger, F.N. (1986). *Foundations of behavioral research* (3rd ed.). Austin, Tex.: Holt, Rinehart & Winston.

Kroth, P.J., McPherson, L., Leverence, R., Pace, W., Daniels, E., Rhyne, R.L., & Williams, R.L. (2009). Combining Web-based and mail surveys improves response rates: A PBRN study from PRIME Net. *Annals of Family Medicine*, 7(3), 245–248.

Leedy, P.D., & Ormrod, J.E. (2010). *Practical research: Planning and design* (9th ed.). Upper Saddle River, N.J.: Pearson Education, Inc.

McDermott, R.J., & Sarvela, P.D. (1999). *Health education evaluation and measurement: A practitioner's perspective* (2nd ed.). St. Louis: WCB/ McGraw-Hill.

National Commission for Health Education Credentialing. (2009). Responsibilities and competencies of health educators. Available at www.nchec.org/credentialing/responsibilities/.

Neutens, J.J., & Rubinson, L. (2010). *Research techniques for the health sciences* (4th ed.). San Francisco: Benjamin Cummings.

O'Rourke, T.W. (1999). The importance of an adequate survey response rate and ways to improve it. *American Journal of Health Studies,* 15(2), 107–109.

Patten, M.L. (2009). *Understanding research methods* (7th ed.). Glendale, Calif: Pryczak Publishing.

Pealer, L., & Weiler, R.M. (2003). Guidelines for designing a Web-delivered college health risk behavior survey: Lessons learned from the University of Florida Health Behavior Survey. *Health Promotion and Practice,* 4(2), 171–179.

Salant, P., & Dillman, D.A. (1994). *How to conduct your own survey.* New York: Wiley.

Salkind, N.J. (2000). *Exploring research* (4th ed.). Upper Saddle River, N.J.: Prentice-Hall.

State Health Access Data Assistance Center. (2009). *The impact of wireless-only households on state surveys of health insurance coverage.* Issue Brief #15. Minneapolis, Minn.: University of Minnesota.

Stevens, J.P. (2009). *Applied multivariate statistics for the social sciences* (5th ed.). New York: Routledge.

Vierra, A., Pollock, J., & Golez, F. (1992). *Reading educational research* (3rd ed.). Upper Saddle River, N.J.: Merrill/Prentice Hall.

Wiersma, W., & Jurs, S.G. (2009). *Research methods in education: An introduction.* Boston: Pearson Education, Inc.

Windsor, R., Clark, N., Boyd, N.R., & Goodman, R.M. (2004). *Evaluation of health promotion, health education and disease prevention programs* (3rd ed.). New York: McGraw-Hill.

CHAPTER 11

Qualitative Research Methods (Writing Chapter III)

Kelli McCormack Brown

Chapter Objectives

After reading this chapter and answering the review questions, you should be able to:

1. Describe when qualitative research methods should be used.
2. Compare and contrast the five qualitative research approaches.
3. Describe the premise of biographical research.
4. Describe the premise of case study methodology.
5. Identify and discuss three types of case studies.
6. Describe the premise of ethnographic research.
7. Describe the premise of grounded theory.
8. Describe the process of data analysis when using grounded theory.
9. Describe the premise of phenomenological research.
10. Describe how to determine the sample size in qualitative research.
11. Describe the advantages and disadvantages of in-depth interviews, focus groups, and observation.
12. Describe when to use in-depth interviews as a data collection method.
13. Describe when to use focus groups as a data collection method.
14. Identify and describe the five characteristics of focus groups.
15. Identify when to use participant observation.
16. Describe the process of content analysis.
17. Identify key factors in ensuring quality in qualitative research.
18. Describe why mixed methods may be best to answer health education's complex research questions.

Key Terms

autobiographic study	codebook	ethnography
axial coding	collective case study	etic
biographic study	concepts	fieldwork
bounded system	conditional matrix	focus group
bracketing	credibility	grounded theory
case study	culture	homogeneity
categories	emic	in-depth interview

continued

Key Terms *continued*

instrumental case study	participant observation	rigor
intrinsic case study	phenomenological study	saturation
life history	propositions	selective coding
open coding	qualitative research	triangulation
oral history	reflexivity	

In Chapter 1, qualitative research was defined and compared to quantitative research, which you have recently reviewed in detail in the last three chapters. As an overview, qualitative research is designed to answer complex questions with the purpose of describing, explaining, and understanding the phenomena being researched. Qualitative researchers use inductive reasoning to understand the "how" and "what" of a particular research question better.

As is the case when conducting quantitative research, qualitative research should be carefully planned with a well-written description of sound research principles that tie methodological strategies to research goals (Belgrave, Zablotsky, & Guadagno, 2002). Qualitative researchers often identify approaches to or traditions in qualitative inquiry. The three approaches most often discussed are grounded theory, ethnography, and phenomenology (Avis, 2003). However, others are also recognized. This chapter provides an overview of qualitative research and describes five approaches to qualitative inquiry (Creswell, 1998, 2003): biography, case study, ethnography, grounded theory, and phenomenology. This chapter also reviews sampling procedures, common data collection methods, and qualities of a qualitative researcher.

Overview

As described in Chapter 1, **qualitative research** is one of two "different paradigms" of research. Table 11.1 compares qualitative research to its counterpart, quantitative research. Qualitative research uses words to describe meaning, to discover things, and to understand phenomena. It is a subjective approach to research that considers the whole as greater than the sum of its parts. Although it uses research questions, it is less concerned with sample size than its quantitative counterpart. It uses inductive reasoning and strives for uniqueness rather than generalization. With qualitative research, the researcher is engaged in part of the investigative process. Qualitative research has been defined in several ways. It is sometimes defined by its source of information: "a situated activity that locates the observer in the world" (Denzin & Lincoln, 2000, p. 3). The qualitative researcher studies "things in their natural settings, attempting to make sense of, or to interpret, phenomena in terms of the meanings people bring to them" (Denzin & Lincoln, 2000,

Table 11.1   Qualitative vs. Quantitative Methods

Qualitative	Quantitative
Provides depth of understanding	Measures level of occurrence
Asks "why?"	Asks "how often?" and "how many?"
Studies motivations	Studies actions
Is subjective	Is objective
Enables discovery	Provides proof
Is exploratory	Is definitive
Allows insights into behavior, trends, and so on	Measures level of actions, trends, and so on
Interprets	Describes

Source: Debus, M. (1988). *Handbook for excellence on focus group research.* Washington, D.C.: Academy for Educational Development.

p. 3). Creswell (1998) defines qualitative research less by its sources of information than as "an inquiry process of understanding based on distinct methodological traditions of inquiry that explore a special or human problem. The researcher builds a complex, holistic picture; analyzes words; reports detailed views of informants; and conducts the study in a natural setting" (p. 15). Patton (2002) distinguishes qualitative theoretical perspectives by their foundational questions. Although Patton does not wish to oversimplify qualitative research to a foundational question, he focuses on "distinguishing foundational questions as a basis for understanding and contrasting longstanding and emergent qualitative inquiry approaches" (2002, p. 80).

For example, health educators wanting to understand bullying among adolescents could benefit from observing and interviewing adolescents in schools, community parks, local youth organizations, or other venues where youth hang out. Using field notes, conversations, and interviews, the researcher would begin to interpret the phenomenon of bullying among adolescents. Although this approach may seem random, qualitative research, as with quantitative research, is systematic and employs rigorous data collection procedures.

A fundamental question a researcher should ask is, "When should qualitative research methods be used?" Creswell (1998) identifies eight reasons for conducting qualitative research (see Table 11.2).

Table 11.2   When to Conduct Qualitative Research

1. Nature of research question
2. Topic needs to be explored
3. A detailed view of topic is needed
4. To study participants in a natural setting
5. Interest in writing in a literary style
6. Have sufficient time and resources
7. Audience is receptive to qualitative research
8. Emphasize researcher's role as an active learner

Source: Creswell, J.W. (1998). *Qualitative inquiry and research design: Choosing among five traditions.* Thousand Oaks, Calif.: Sage. Reprinted with permission of Sage Publications, Inc.

First, what is the research question? Based on the nature of the inquiry, the researcher determines the most appropriate approach and then the most appropriate research method(s) to use to answer the research question. If the researcher is asking "why" and has comparison groups, then qualitative research methods may not be appropriate. (See Box 11.1 for some sample research questions in which qualitative research may or may not be appropriate.) Second, does the topic need to be explored? If theories or variables have not been identified to explain or understand the phenomena under study, then qualitative research methods

---

Box 11.1   Qualitative or Quantitative Research Methods: How Would You Answer These Questions?

For the following research questions, determine whether quantitative or qualitative research methods are most appropriate to answer the research question, and explain why.

1. Are there differences in types of bullying or victimization as a function of school, gender, ethnicity, or grade?
2. To understand the meaning of cancer, cervical cancer, and cervical cancer screening constructed by Panamanian women, how do women think about cervical cancer screening?
3. To what extent is parenting style associated with healthy eating among college freshmen?
4. How do school personnel construct their perceptions of school refusal?
5. What factors motivate California school board members and superintendents to develop and/or implement healthy food choice policies in their school districts?
6. To understand the process that leads to Indian women defining marital abuse, how do women evaluate their own experiences of abuse?
7. What are the independent effects of individual, family, peer, school, and religious influences on the transition of adolescent alcohol nonuse to first use in 7th–8th grade and 9th–10th grade students?

may be valuable. Third, is the problem understood in global or specific terms? If all that is available are panoramic views of the problem, then a qualitative approach is appropriate. Fourth, is it best to study the participants in their natural setting? If yes, a qualitative approach may bring greater range, depth, and richness. Fifth, if writing in a literary style is comfortable, then qualitative research that employs the pronoun "I," storytelling, or other narrative forms is a good fit. Sixth, are there enough resources and time to employ qualitative methods? To carry out qualitative research properly requires the investment of considerable time, effort, and other resources (Morse, 2002). Seventh, are audiences receptive to qualitative research? If you are a student, is your advisor or committee amenable to qualitative research? If your study is receiving financial support, will a qualitative approach satisfy the funder? Is there a publication outlet for your qualitative research? Because not all researchers or research journals subscribe to qualitative approaches or understand the richness they can bring to the investigative setting, there may be a negative publication bias. Thus, other approaches may provide you with better options. Finally, if you are willing to be an active learner and tell the story from the participant's viewpoint, then qualitative methods are not only appropriate, but also interesting and dynamic ways to convey meaning.

Qualitative research is used by many disciplines, including health education, and has no theory that is distinctly its own. Qualitative research is sometimes said to be multimethod, as it draws upon many approaches to foster understanding of phenomena. Some of these approaches are presented in the following paragraphs.

Qualitative Research Approaches

Biography

"A biographical study is the study of an individual and her or his experiences as told to the researcher or found in documents and archival material" (Creswell, 1998, p. 47). A biographic approach to qualitative research allows the researcher to understand an individual's life better through four types of inquiry: (1) biographic, (2) autobiographic, (3) life history, and (4) oral history. Biographic research is nontraditional among health education researchers, but as a form of qualitative inquiry, it may be a promising avenue of research in the future. Someone other than the individual who is the subject of study uses interviews with that person as well as other documents to write a **biographic study**, whereas an **autobiographic study** is a first-person account of one's own life. A **life history** is based not only on interviews with the person, but also on analysis of the economic, historical, political, and social contexts of the individual's life. An **oral history** has the researcher collecting information from an individual or individuals about specific events and their causes and effects.

Biographic inquiry often takes place in the form of stories. Stories can be collected through interviews with the individuals or with others and from archived documents (e.g., newspaper stories). These stories can be organized chronologically (childhood, adolescence, early adulthood, old age), through experiences (education, marriage, employment), or around special events in the individual's life. The researcher seeks to understand the meaning of these stories through discussions with the individual, as well as by analyzing the context of the individual's life. One example of a health education biographic study is "Delbert Oberteuffer: His Professional Activities and Contributions to the Fields of Health and Physical Education" (Grosshans, 1975). Biographies of prominent health education specialists help us understand not only the individual, but also the health education profession itself (Calitri, 1998; Eberst, 1998; Goldsmith, 1997; Morrow, 1998). In the stories of prominent health education specialists we read about opportunities, challenges, influential mentors, and pivotal events. At the same time our understanding of the historical context of these events within their lives becomes enhanced. Although these interviews may be only "brief biographies," they do provide a glimpse into biographic inquiry.

Case Study

Sociologists and anthropologists have traditionally used case studies. However, recently other disciplines such as health education have come to embrace this qualitative approach to understanding a problem. For example, Kegler and Wyatt (2003) used a multiple case study approach to identify successful mobilization characteristics of five neighborhood teen pregnancy prevention programs. Data collection methods included observation, review of existing documents, and individual interviews. A **case study** "is an exploration of a bounded system or a case (or multiple cases) over time through detailed, in-depth data collection involving multiple sources of information" (Creswell, 1998, p. 61). A **bounded system** is one that is bound by time and place, for example, an HIV program for youth at a particular location and for a delineated period of time.

Most often a case study is defined by what is being studied (e.g., individual, family, program, event) (Stake, 2000) rather than as a method of research (Creswell, 1998). Case studies are the preferred qualitative method when "how" or "why" questions are asked, when the researcher has little or no control over events, when a holistic understanding of a problem is required, and when there is a contemporary focus within a real-life context. Research questions are limited in number and are tied to specific events and their interrelationships.

Rather than studying the effect of an intervention or treatment in a single-subject case experiment, the researcher in a case study observes and records the subject's reaction to a naturally occurring event. Take, for instance, a school counseling intervention. In a single-subject case experiment the researcher would determine the impact of the intervention on the subject (i.e., a student). Using the case study approach, the researcher would seek to understand *why* the student is doing (or not doing) a particular behavior and *how* the behavior changes as the student adapts to his or her environment (i.e., classroom, fellow students, teacher). One of the greatest advantages of a case study is the depth of information it provides. In this example, the researcher would attempt to understand the whole student in the context of the student's environment. A researcher does not merely record the behavior of the student within the environment but tries to understand *why* the behavior occurs within the context of the case (i.e., physical, social, historical, or economic context).

A health education example of case study research might involve studying a single client who is trying to lose weight. The health education specialist may want to more fully understand all of the factors that affect the success or lack of success that the client experiences. The researcher may wish to delve more deeply into the emotional and mental strain of following a diet and exercise program.

Stake (2000) identifies three types of case studies: intrinsic, instrumental, and collective (see Table 11.3). In an **intrinsic case study** the case

Table 11.3   Types of Case Studies

Coordinated school health program	
Type	**Illustrative example**
Intrinsic case study	A researcher examines one successful coordinated school health program to gain a better understanding of *how* and *why* the program succeeds.
Instrumental case study	A researcher examines a successful coordinated school health program to understand qualities of school staff within this program (i.e., case).
Collective case study	A researcher examines five different coordinated school health programs (i.e., five cases) to better understand *how* and *why* the programs succeed or fail.

itself is of interest. The researcher wants a better understanding of this one particular case. An **instrumental case study** is when the case itself is of secondary interest, and the primary purpose is to provide insight into an issue. **Collective case studies** are more than one instrumental case study. Studying multiple cases can lead to a better understanding of the issue under consideration.

Case study data can be collected through a review of documents and records, interviews, observation, audiovisual materials, and other artifacts. As an example, to understand the process of the development and sustainability of a coordinated school health program (case) better, portfolios that included documents, records, and artifacts, as well as key informant interviews, can be used (data collection methods) (McCormack Brown *et al.*, 2004). Regardless of the method used to generate a case study, the researcher needs to describe the meaning of the case clearly. Often a narrative accomplishes this task, offering a rich description for the reader that integrates and summarizes key information.

Case study research is not unlike other qualitative research approaches in that it requires the researcher to spend considerable time, be onsite, be personally involved with activities of the case, and reflect and revise meanings of what is occurring.

Ethnography

Ethnography comes from the Greek words *ethnos* and *graphos,* for "groups of people" and "writings about." Creswell (1998) defines ethnography as a "description and interpretation of a cultural or social group or system" (p. 58), whereas Chambers (2000) defines it as "those varieties of inquiry that aim to describe or interpret the pace of culture in human affairs" (p. 852). Creswell's definition suggests that ethnography is defined by its subject matter (i.e., culture), not by its method. Ethnography also may be a product of research (i.e., book) as well as a process (i.e., prolonged observation). Regardless of which definition is used, anthropolo-

gists traditionally have used ethnography to assist them in understanding and describing cultures. Ethnography is being used by many other disciplines today, including education and public health. For example, ethnographic research can provide a better understanding of participation in breast cancer support groups. Using an ethnographic approach, Coreil, Wilke, and Pintado (2004) focused on the perceived role of support groups in shaping how women participating in breast cancer support groups viewed breast cancer and recovery.

To understand qualitative research better, it is helpful to become familiar with several terms. **Culture** is defined as "the patterned ways of thought and behavior that characterize a social group, which are learned through socialization processes and persist through time" (Coreil, Bryant & Henderson, 2001, p. 29). Culture is evolving and changes over time. Culture is reflected in the way people view the world and events happening around them. Culture can be viewed differently by those within the culture and those outside the culture. An **emic** perspective is referred to as an insider's perspective, whereas an **etic** perspective is an outsider's perspective. Health education researchers need to be aware of these emic and etic perspectives to facilitate meaning and understanding across culture and language and to avoid drawing culturally bound interpretations (Pasick, D'Onofrio, & Otero-Sabogal, 1996; Pasick, Sabogal, *et al.*, 1996). When using ethnography (or any qualitative approach, for that matter) the researcher should provide a clear understanding of how the research was or could have been affected by what the researcher brings. This is known as **reflexivity**. This is accomplished through the use of field notes during the research. Being reflexive reminds researchers to observe themselves and to acknowledge the biases and limitations they bring to the study. Preconceptions are not biases unless the researcher fails to mention them; personal issues can be valuable sources for relevant and specific research, as can be changes in the researcher's position and perspectives throughout the study (Grbich, 1999; Malterud, 2001).

Some ethnographic research relies on **participant observation**, a process by which the researcher integrates with and participates in the day-to-day activities of the group being studied. This day-to-day engagement is known as **fieldwork** and allows the researcher to obtain information through observations and interviews. Interviews can take place with gatekeepers as well as key informants, allowing the researcher to observe things that most members of the group would take for granted and to ask questions to foster better understanding. Ethnographic research, like other qualitative research methods, allows for what is often referred to as "thick descriptions" of events, rituals, and customs (Geertz, 1973). Suppose, for example, that a health education specialist wanted to study the health-related problems of the homeless. The health education specialist might integrate into the homeless community and experience what life as a homeless person is like. The health education specialist might learn about the opinions, attitudes, beliefs, and behaviors of homeless people related to a variety of health topics such as nutrition, dental health, foot care, sexuality, drug/alcohol use, and so forth. An actual example of ethnographic research is the work by Cunningham and others (1999) looking at the experiences of individuals with serious mental illness and using this research to develop a manual for an educational program.

Grounded Theory

Grounded theory, first introduced in the 1960s and having roots in sociology, involves the use of systematic inductive guidelines for collecting and analyzing data to generate theory (Charmaz, 2000). The pioneering authors of grounded theory, Glaser and Strauss, believed that theories should not to be created a priori but rather be grounded in field-derived data (Creswell, 1998). The goal of grounded theory is to develop theory to aid in understanding phenomena. Wilson, Hutchinson,

and Holzemer (2002) used grounded theory to explain how diverse men and women living with HIV manage their symptoms and medication side effects and how they decide which treatments to follow or not follow (adherence). Grounded theory was used to "generate a dense conceptual explanation of the interplay between symptom management and medication adherence" (p. 1312). Their data suggest that adherence or nonadherence is much more complex than medication being too expensive or unavailable or people forgetting or being too busy. The data provide a rich, contextual description of how patients make medication adherence decisions and the why behind these decisions.

Grounded theory has three basic elements: concepts, categories, and propositions (or hypotheses) (Strauss & Corbin, 1990). **Concepts** are the basic units from which the theory is developed. Concepts are grouped into **categories**, which become the cornerstones of theory development. **Propositions** are the relationships between a category and its concepts.

The application of grounded theory may be illustrated in the following way. Suppose a researcher conducts 20 or more interviews with participants until no new information is being obtained (i.e., until saturation is reached). **Saturation** is a term used to describe when a researcher is no longer hearing new information (Krueger & Casey, 2008) and is also referred to as "sufficient redundancy." Interviews are transcribed verbatim. Unlike quantitative data analysis, data are analyzed as they are collected. Coding begins early and defines the concepts and categories that are used in the chain of theory development (Charmaz, 2000). It is through systematic coding that the inductive process begins as concepts and categories are defined and explored. As the interviews are being read and systematically coded, it is not uncommon to decide that more information is needed and to engage more participants for that purpose. In grounded theory research a standard process is used in data analysis. This process includes open coding, axial coding, selective coding, and conditional matrix preparation.

The **open coding** process is the part of the analysis when the researchers read each line, sentence, and paragraph attempting to answer the question, "What is this about?" As researchers carry out this step they develop a **codebook**, which includes a detailed description of the code, inclusion and exclusion criteria, and examples of real text for the concept or category (Ryan & Bernard, 2000).

After open coding, the researcher reassembles the data in new ways through axial coding (see Table 11.4). **Axial coding** is the process of drawing a relationship between a category and its subcategories. In this process the researcher uses a coding paradigm to develop a framework of relationships. This framework includes six elements: central phenomena, causal conditions, strategies, context, intervening conditions, and consequences (Creswell, 1998). With grounded theory the researcher looks for causal relationships and uses this framework to understand the phenomenon better.

Table 11.4   Axial Coding Basic Framework

Element	Description
Central phenomenon	The central category about the phenomenon
Causal conditions	Events or variables that influence the phenomenon
Strategies	Activities or actions that result from the central phenomenon
Context	Conditions or variables (such as values and beliefs) in which the phenomenon is taking place; difficult to distinguish between causal conditions and intervening conditions
Intervening conditions	Narrow and broad conditions that influence the phenomenon and strategies
Consequences	The outcomes of the strategies, intended and unintended

Using **selective coding** researchers use initial codes that reappear frequently to sort large amounts of data. This type of coding is more direct than line-by-line coding and provides more precise categorization (Charmaz, 2000). Selective coding allows the researcher to develop a single storyline around which grouping of related data and themes follows.

Formation of a **conditional matrix** allows researchers to depict the range of conditions and consequences visually as they are related to the phenomenon of interest. It is suggested that "such matrices can sharpen the researchers' explanations of and predictions about the studied phenomenon" (Charmaz, 2000, p. 516). However, Creswell (1998) notes that the use of conditional matrices is infrequently found in grounded theory work.

The result of this systematic data collection allows researchers to develop a theory to explain a phenomenon. As with all theories, the theory must undergo further testing. However, the outcome of grounded theory has been accomplished—that is, the generation of a theory based on the systematic collection and analysis of data.

Phenomenology

Earlier, biography was described as the study of an individual. In a **phenomenological study** "the meanings of lived experiences for several individuals about a concept or phenomenon" are conveyed (Creswell, 1998, p. 51). Researchers using phenomenology search for the central underlying meaning of an experience or phenomenon. Phenomenology has been used in a variety of disciplines, including education and health sciences. To be open to the phenomenon, researchers need to set aside all preconceived notions, personal beliefs, feelings, and perceptions (a process known as **bracketing**). Hycner (1985) describes phenomenology as an approach or an attitude and encourages researchers not to take a cookbook approach to phenomenology.

Hycner (1985) describes the approach he takes to analyzing phenomenological data. Typically, data are collected through in-depth interviews with the persons who have experienced the phenomenon of interest. If researchers were examining the phenomenon of being a victim of bullying, they would need to interview individuals who had been bullied. If the researchers themselves had experienced bullying, they would need to bracket their own personal experiences. Finding individuals who have experienced the phenomenon being investigated and bracketing one's personal experiences can be challenging.

Phenomenological studies are not frequently found in the health education literature; however, the use of phenomenology in understanding a particular heath issue is often used. For example, to better understand how people living with AIDS view their disease, Anderson and Spencer (2002) interviewed 58 men and women with AIDS to describe their cognitive representations of their illness.

Qualitative Data Collection Methods

As with quantitative research methods, some qualitative data collection methods are more popular or used more frequently than others. Once the researcher has selected the theoretical framework and qualitative research approach, sample selection and data collection strategies follow. Creswell (1998) provides a concise overview of data collection activities for the five approaches to qualitative research previously described. Common data collection methods include in-depth one-on-one interviews, focus group interviews, and direct observation (see Table 11.5). Other data collection methods include content analysis.

Sampling

Understanding how to select a sample for qualitative research is just as important as in quantitative research. There are two distinct categories of sampling procedures: probability and nonprobability

samples (see Chapter 7). A basic principle of probability sampling is that the sample is representative of the population. Because of this basic premise, qualitative researchers do not use probability samples (Luborsky & Rubinstein, 1995). Qualitative researchers use nonprobability samples, taking advantage of those who are available and accessible to the researcher (McDermott & Sarvela, 1999; Sandelowski, 1995). Five major types of nonprobability sampling techniques used by qualitative researchers are identified by Luborsky and Rubinstein (1995): (1) case study, (2) convenience (or opportunistic) sampling, (3) purposive sampling, (4) snowball sampling, and (5) quota sampling. Samples of convenience often allow the researcher to take advantage of an existing group. For example, to better understand how women perceive breast cancer, a researcher may interview women who visit the doctor's office. Purposive sampling is analogous to stratified sampling in probability-based approaches. Purposive sampling is used when subjects are intentionally selected to represent a predefined characteristic or trait. For instance, to understand bullying among adolescents, the researcher would purposefully select adolescents who had bullied and those who had been bullied.

Snowball or word-of-mouth techniques locate subjects through a referral process. This process is useful when there are no lists of people available. Consider a health education specialist who wants to study some aspect of gay men and lesbians who are "in the closet." A snowball technique might involve interviewing a few individuals known to the researcher and then seeking referrals from those individuals for other "in the closet" homosexuals.

Quota sampling is used to select subjects based on characteristics being studied. Quota sampling assures inclusion of people who may be underrepresented by convenience or purposive sampling. For example, if in a particular health education study design it was considered important to interview Asians from specific countries, a quota sampling technique might be employed.

Table 11.5   Common Data Collection Methods

Method	Appropriate use	Inappropriate use	Advantages	Disadvantage
In-depth interviews	Complex subject matter Knowledgeable respondents Need to understand individual experiences and decision making	Highly sensitive topics Geographically dispersed respondents Topic influenced by peer pressure/ social desirability	Generates more depth and detail Easier to set up than focus groups Less expensive than focus groups Unit of analysis is individual	Interviewer must be familiar with topic/content area Respondents dispersed over a large geographical area
Focus groups	Relatively small numbers needed (5–10) Generates breadth of responses Can conduct several groups in a short period of time for initial exploration	Cannot use to make reliable quantitative estimates	Able to observe how people are influenced by others Less threatening to some vs. individual interview Unit of analysis is group	Highly dependent on the skill of the moderator Requires skills in interpreting data
Observation	Generates understanding of the cultural context in which health behavior/beliefs occur	When observer's presence would be an intrusion When situation is completely hidden from public	Can identify differences between real and verbal behaviors Can understand how the setting affects behavior	Can be time consuming

The key question to sampling in qualitative research is always, "How many subjects?" There are no computations, power analyses, or "gold standards" to determine the minimum number needed (Luborsky & Rubinstein, 1995; Sandelowski, 1995). Rough "rules of thumb" do exist (Sandelowski, 1995), however, for different qualitative methods. For example, six participants are needed for phenomenological research, whereas grounded theory and ethnographies require about 30 to 50 interviews (Sandelowksi, 1995). Determining adequate sample size is ultimately a matter of judgment and experience. "A good principle to follow is: An adequate sample size in qualitative research is one that permits—by virtue of not being too large—the deep, case-oriented analysis that is a hallmark of all qualitative inquiry, and that results in—by virtue of not being too small—a new and richly textured understanding of experience" (Sandelowski, 1995, p. 183).

In-Depth Interviews

Seidman (1998) states that at "the root of in-depth interviewing is an interest in understanding the experience of other people and the meaning they make of that experience" (p. 3). **In-depth interviews** are used to uncover feelings and attitudes an individual has regarding a specific experience. Open-ended questions are asked, ranging from broad and general ones to highly specific ones. For example, when interviewing school board members regarding school nutrition policies, researchers started with "Please talk about how long you have been a school board member" (McCormack Brown, Henry, & Pitt, 2001). Subsequently, they proceeded to more focused items about nutrition policies. The best time to use in-depth interviews is when the topic is complex, the respondents are knowledgeable, and understanding of individual experiences is needed. Appendix 11-A provides an example of an interview guide used with a topic that is relatively complex (school policymaking), when the individual is knowledgeable (all participants were school board members, superintendents, or principals), and the researchers sought to better understand how decisions were made regarding school nutrition policymaking. In-depth interviews can occur face to face, over the telephone, or via Internet chat sessions (U.S. Department of Health and Human Services, 2002).

Focus Group Interviews

Krueger and Casey (2008) describe a **focus group** as not just a group of people convened but

> a special type of group in terms of purpose, size, composition, and procedures. The purpose of a focus group is to listen and gather information. It is a way to better understand how people feel or think about an issue, product, or service. Participants are selected because they have certain characteristics in common that relate to the topic of the focus group (p. 4).

There are five characteristics of the focus group interview (Krueger & Casey, 2008). First, the typical focus group size is 5 to 10 people, but depending on the topic and other arrangements, it can be as many as 12 people. Second, the focus group participants possess similar characteristics deemed important by research (**homogeneity**). This homogeneity is determined by the purpose of the study. For example, characteristics can be as broad as school board members or as narrow as 10- to 13-year-old youth who participate in physical activity three days a week outside of school. Third,

focus groups provide qualitative data. Focus group data allow researchers to understand a phenomenon from the discussion that ensues. Fourth, focus groups are indeed a "focused discussion." The moderator's guide is carefully crafted to answer the research questions. Lastly, focus groups assist the researcher in understanding a topic in detail. Health education specialists might use focus groups to determine safety concerns of the elderly living in a high crime neighborhood, the opinions of adolescents concerning marijuana use, the beliefs of health education college students concerning future career opportunities, or the attitudes of corporate executives toward health promotion programs.

Determining when to use an in-depth interview versus a focus group interview can be challenging. Debus (1988) lists 11 issues to consider when making such a decision (see Table 11.6). Although in-depth interviews and focus group interviews are selected for different reasons, the process for developing an interview/focus group guide can be similar (see Appendix 11-B). For more examples and development guidelines, go to the National Cancer Institute's book titled *Making Health Communication Programs Work* (http://cancer.gov/pinkbook).

Observation

As with other qualitative data collection methods, observing a setting, person, or group requires research skills to ensure observer validity and reliability, to facilitate meaning and understanding across culture and language, and to avoid drawing culturally bound interpretations (Pasick, D'Onofrio, & Otero-Sabogal, 1996; Pasick, Sabogal, *et al.*, 1996). Observational data collection can include unobtrusive measures such as the number of items removed (e.g., health education brochures), thrown away (e.g., health education brochures discarded after meeting with a health education specialist), or used (Bernard, 2000). Bernard suggests that participant observation

Table 11.6   Which to Use: Focus Groups or In-Depth Individual Interviews

Issue to consider	Use focus groups when . . .	Use in-depth interviews when . . .
Group interaction	Interaction of respondents may stimulate a richer response or new and valuable thoughts.	Group interaction is likely to be limited or nonproductive.
Group/peer pressure	Group/peer pressure will be valuable in challenging their thinking of respondents and illuminating conflicting opinions.	Group/peer pressure would inhibit responses and cloud the meaning of results.
Sensitivity of subject matter	Subject matter is not so sensitive that respondents will temper responses or withhold information.	Subject is so sensitive that respondents would be unwilling to talk openly in groups.
Depth of individual responses	The topic is such that most respondents can say all that is relevant or all that they know in less than 10 minutes.	The topic is such that a greater depth of response per individual is desirable, as with complex subject matter and very knowledgeable respondents.
Interviewer fatigue	It is desirable to have one interviewer conduct the research; several groups will not create interviewer fatigue or boredom.	It is desirable to have numerous interviews on the project. One interviewer would become fatigued or bored conducting the interviews.
Stimulus materials	The volume of stimulus material is not extensive.	A larger amount of stimulus material must be evaluated.
Continuity of information	A single subject area is being examined in depth and strings of behaviors are less relevant.	It is necessary to understand how attitudes and behaviors link together on an individual pattern basis.
Experimentation with interview guide	Enough is known to establish a meaningful topic guide.	It may be necessary to develop the interview guide by altering it after each of the initial interviews.
Observation	It is possible and desirable for key decision makers to observe "first-hand" consumer information.	"First-hand" consumer information is not critical or observation is not logistically possible.
Logistics	An acceptable number of target respondents can be assembled in one location.	Respondents are geographically dispersed or not easily assembled for other reasons.
Cost and timing	Quick turnaround is critical, and funds are limited.	Quick turnaround is not critical and budget will permit higher cost.

Source: Debus, M. (1988). *Handbook for excellence on focus group research,* p. 10. Washington, D.C.: Academy for Educational Development.

places "you where the action is and lets you collect data—any kind you want, qualitative or quantitative, narrative or numbers" (p. 318). Participant observation generally includes direct observation but can also include videotaping.

Participant observation is appropriate when seeking an understanding of the cultural context in which health behaviors occur and when the activities within the setting give meaning to those behaviors. Advantages of participant observation include: (1) identifying differences between real and verbal behavior; (2) determining the language of subjects to address issues that are unfolding, rather than relying on questions previously constructed; (3) identifying the sequence and connectedness of events that contribute to that behavior; and (4) identifying how the setting affects the behavior (Parsons & McCormack Brown, 2004). There are instances when participant observation is not appropriate (Bryant, 2003). An example would be condom usage between partners. In this situation the observer's presence would be an intrusion. Another inappropriate situation would be when those being observed have significantly different views from the observer.

Kinnison, Cottrell, and King (2004) used observation to collect data on hand-washing behaviors in public restrooms. In this study, the researcher and a trained observer pretended to be using the restroom facilities while actually observing hand-washing behavior. By utilizing observation, accurate data concerning hand washing were obtained that probably could not have been obtained through any other data collection method.

Creswell (1998) suggests a series of steps in using observation as a data collection method: (1) select site to be observed; (2) identify who or what to observe, when, and for how long; (3) determine initially the role of the observer; (4) design an observation protocol for recording notes; (5) record the physical setting, particular events and activities, and observer reactions; (6) be introduced as an outsider; and (7) slowly withdraw from the site upon concluding the observation. Box 11.2 contains an example of an observation protocol.

Content Analysis

Content analysis, although most popular in communication and behavioral sciences, has been effectively used in health education with a variety of health topics (see Table 11.7). A Kaiser Family Foundation report, *Here's Looking at You, Kid,* used content analysis to determine how often and in what ways the media convey information about substances and substance use and, when conveyed, whether substances were reported positively or negatively (Roberts & Christenson, 2000).

Content analysis has been defined in numerous ways. Holsti (1969) defines content analysis as "any technique for making inferences by objectively and systematically identifying characteristics

---

Box 11.2   Participation Observation Protocol Example

Consider the following during participant observation:

Setting
What is the physical environment?
What is the context?
What kind of behavior does the setting encourage, permit, discourage, or prevent?

Participants
Who is in the scene?
How many people are there?
What are the roles of the people present?
What brings these people together?
Who is allowed here?

Activities and Interactions
What is going on?
Is there a definable sequence of activities?
How do the people interact with the activities and one another?
How are people and activities connected or interrelated?

Frequency and Duration
When did the situation begin?
How long does it last?
Is it a recurring type of situation or unique?
If the situation recurs, how frequently?
What are the occasions that led to it?
How typical does this situation appear to be?

Subtle Factors
Informal activities
Unplanned activities
Nonverbal communication (dress, physical space, facial expressions)
What does not happen? (especially if it was expected)

Source: Torrens Salemi, A. (2004). The social construction of school refusal: An exploratory study of school personnel's perceptions. Unpublished doctoral dissertation, University of South Florida.

Table 11.7   Selected Content Analysis Projects

Topic	Author(s) and year
Frequency of health-related topics in select Sunday comic strips	Sofalvi, 1985
Content of school worksite wellness conferences	Fetro & Drolet, 1991
Content of the first year of HEDIR List	Welle, Kittleson, & Olgetree, 1995
Content of tobacco industry smokers' rights publications	Cardador, Hazan, & Glantz, 1995
Spiritual health coverage in college health textbooks	Allen, 1998
Content and accessibility of sex education information on the Internet	Smith, Gertz, Alvarrez, & Lurie, 2000
Content of worksite health promotion college courses	Glew, 2000
Newspaper coverage of tobacco farming and diversification	Smith, Altman, & Strunk, 2000
Teaching strategies published in two health education journals	Johnson & Kittleson, 2000
Content of Web sites promoting smoking culture and lifestyle	Ribisl, Lee, Henriksen, & Haladjian, 2003
Health-related infomercials	Hill, Lindsay, Thomsen, & Olsen, 2003
Content of patient education college courses	Heitzer, 2004

of messages" (p. 14). Kerlinger (1973) defines content analysis as a means of analyzing all documents in a "systematic, objective, and quantitative" way (p. 256). Holsti (1969) also suggests that content analysis can use both quantitative and qualitative research methods. Regardless of the definition or the data collection methods, "content analysis is an established research tool" (Nandy & Sarvela, 1997).

Duncan (1989) describes a step-by-step process for content analysis that includes nine steps (see Box 11.3). With regards to determining the unit of analysis, in content analysis the unit is the document of some element of communication. For example, in Johnson and Kittleson's (2000) content analysis the units of analysis were phrases that describe the health education topic, teaching strategies/ideas, target groups, teaching strategy objectives, article length, and information about the author. A key step within content analysis is establishing coding categories. As part of the Sarasota County Demonstration Project (SCDP) of the Florida Prevention Research Center (FPRC),

a content analysis was conducted to assess changes in the quantity, content, theme, space, and placement of articles related to tobacco and alcohol use included in the major local newspaper over

---

Box 11.3   Step-By-Step Process for Content Analysis

Step 1	Define the units of analysis
Step 2	Establish the coding categories
Step 3	Pretest the coding on a sample of the documents
Step 4	Assess the reliability of the coding
Step 5	Revise the coding categories if necessary and return to Step 3
Step 6	Draw the sample of documents
Step 7	Code all the units of analysis
Step 8	Assess the achieved reliability of coding
Step 9	Tabulate the categories

Source: Duncan, D.F. (1989). Content analysis in health education research: An introduction to purposes and methods. *Health Education*, 20(7), 27–31. Used with permission.

the project period (Zapata *et al.*, 2003). Selection criteria were developed to capture articles related to (1) tobacco, alcohol, and drug use; (2) adolescent health; and (3) community capacity.

Sampling procedures in content analysis are similar to those in survey research. Like survey research, the sample must be representative of the universe from which it is drawn, and it must be large enough to allow for reliable analysis (Duncan, 1989). For example, Johnson and Kittleson (2000) studied two health education journals (*Journal of Health Education* and *Journal of School Health*) from 1970 to 1998. Reliability is critical to content analysis and is computed by determining the agreement between inter- and intracoder reliability tests (Nandy & Sarvela, 1997). The Nandy and Sarvela (1997) article provides an example of a content analysis coding and theme generation sheet.

Computer Software

Various software packages are available to aid in the management of qualitative data analysis. The first and most popular was **Ethnograph**, which allowed the researcher to organize, code, and search for data using computer technology instead of the old "cut and paste" paper-based technology. Today, there are several computer software packages available (see Box 11.4). A computer software analysis package can store and manage data, search and retrieve data, code and recode data,

develop and test theory, and write reports (Lacey & Luff, 2007). Computer software analysis packages are a tool; they do not replace the researcher. "Computer-aided analysis can be deceptively easy—coding and searching, for instance is quick and satisfying"; however, "at the end of the day, there are no short cuts to the demanding process of reading and re-reading the data, sorting, categorizing and analyzing the data and building and testing theories" (Lacey & Luff, 2007, p. 35).

Ensuring Quality in Qualitative Research

In qualitative research, emphasis is placed on quality and credibility. Lincoln and Guba (1985) suggest that credibility, dependability, and transferability can be combined to increase the quality of qualitative research. Credibility depends on: (1) rigorous methods, (2) the credibility of the researcher, and (3) philosophical belief in the value of qualitative research (Patton, 2002). **Rigor** in qualitative research refers to employing a systematic approach to research design, careful data collection and analysis, and effective communication (Mays & Pope, 1995; Patton, 1999). **Credibility** of the researcher is reflected in the person's training, experience, and presentation of credentials (Patton, 2002). Credibility is considered qualitative research's analog to quantitative research's concept of internal validity. Validity refers to the appropriateness, meaningfulness, and usefulness of the measure and the extent to which something measures what it purports to measure (McDermott & Sarvela, 1999). Validity in qualitative research lies in the reader being convinced that the researcher has accessed and accurately represented the data. Various methods can be used to increase credibility, including rigorous data collection and analysis; prolonged engagement; persistent observation; rich, thick description; triangulation; peer review or debriefing; reflexivity (clarifying researcher bias); member checks;

Box 11.4	**Qualitative Research Software Packages**
ATLAS.ti	www.atlasti.com
HyperRESEARCH	www.researchware.com
MAXQDA	www.maxqda.com
NVivo	www.qsrinternational.com
QDA Miner	www.provalisresearch.com
Qualrus	www.qualrus.com
Transana	www.transana.org

and external audits (Creswell, 1998; Patton, 2002; Tashakkori & Teddlie, 1998). The degree or level of truth of participant responses also increases the validity of the study. Developing trust and building rapport between the researcher and research participants can accomplish this element.

Triangulation is based on the premise that no single method can adequately answer a research question; therefore, multiple methods of data collection and analysis are ideal (Patton, 1999). A myth regarding triangulation is that it uses different data sources to find the *same* result. The key to triangulation is to look for consistency rather than identical results. Patton (1999) describes four kinds of triangulation that validate qualitative research: (1) triangulation of methods, (2) triangulation of sources, (3) triangulation of analysis, and (4) triangulation of theory.

Dependability is similar to reliability. Reliability in quantitative research is the extent to which the research results are consistent, dependable, and stable (McDermott & Sarvela, 1999). In qualitative research, dependability focuses on whether the results found are consistent with the data collected (Patton, 2002).

Transferability is related to external validity (i.e., generalizability). External validity is the ability to generalize the results of a particular study to other persons, settings, and times (McDermott & Sarvela, 1999). In general, qualitative research is not obviously generalizable. However, Malterud (2001) proposes that findings from qualitative research can be transferable to other populations in similar situations. Qualitative research offers the researcher thick, rich, descriptive findings that can sometimes be transferred to other persons, settings, and times and even other types of phenomena. Therefore, what is true of people in one situation may be true of other people in a similar situation (Grbich, 1999). Nevertheless, caution should be used in generalizing qualitative research findings as it is typically better to err on the conservative side.

Evaluating Qualitative Research Articles

Qualitative research needs to be read with the same eye for rigor as with quantitative research. Several evaluation tools have been developed for qualitative research (Law *et al.*, 1998) including the Evaluation Tool for Qualitative Studies (www.fhsc.salford.ac.uk/hcprdu/qualitative.htm). This tool has six sections that cover the overview, phenomenon studied and context, data collection, data analysis and researcher bias, policy and practice implications, and other comments. Each section contains a series of questions for the reader to consider when determining the quality of the research.

Rolfe (2006) argues that rather than develop a set of criteria to determine the validity of qualitative research, we should acknowledge that there are multiple qualitative paradigms and that each requires a different qualitative approach to determine validity. Therefore, "each research methodology (and perhaps each individual study) must be appraised on its own merits" (p. 310). Despite Rolfe's compelling argument, there are common questions one should pose when reading a qualitative research article to determine its quality. Greenhalgh and Taylor (1997) have developed a set of nine questions to guide the reader in assessing quality qualitative research. First, did the article describe an important health problem addressed via a clearly formulated question? Answering this first question is no different than assessing the quality of a quantitative research article. Regardless of research method, the article must clearly state the need and the research question should be based upon need. Second, was the qualitative approach appropriate? Answering this question goes back to the basic understanding of qualitative research. If the researcher was interested in understanding the incidence and prevalence of dental decay among older adults, qualitative research would not be appropriate. However, if the researcher knew the incidence and prevalence of dental decay among older adults, but wanted to have a better understanding of *how* older adults perceived oral care within the context of their living environment, then a qualitative approach would be appropriate. The third question to ask is how were the setting and the subjects selected. Unlike quantitative research, a random sample of subjects is not appropriate. Qualitative researchers use sampling techniques that allow them to intentionally seek individuals for their research (e.g., snowball technique). For example, older adults who have experienced dental decay in recent years are asked whether they know other people their age who have also experienced dental decay.

Question four gets to an issue that is not often a concern of quantitative research: What was the researcher's perspective and was it taken into account? Unlike quantitative research, qualitative research uses words to study issues in their natural setting in an attempt to make sense of a phenomenon. Because of this, understanding the researcher's potential biases are important. If the researcher's parents lost all their teeth at an early age due to dental neglect this may impact how he or she approaches understanding older adults' perceptions. The researcher must understand his or her potential bias so they can ask the right questions and interpret the data accurately.

The fifth question to ask is whether the data collection methods are sufficiently explained. There are no set guidelines for determining this, but as the reader you need to ask yourself, "Are these methods adequate to answer the research question?" and "Have I been given enough information to feel confident in the data collected?"

As a reader of qualitative research, the sixth question you ask yourself is about the methods used in analyzing the data and what quality control measures were taken. The researcher must describe the systematic means by which the data were analyzed and provide examples from the transcripts that support or contradict the existing literature. The article must also describe how quality control was handled. Some, if not all, of the data must be analyzed by another researcher who assigns the same or similar meaning to the words.

As mentioned earlier in the chapter, credibility of the results is important; therefore, question seven is: Are the results credible? One means of determining this is whether the authors cite actual data in their article. The authors may state that "many older adults have many other health problems and therefore do not pay attention to their oral health until it is too late." This general statement becomes more credible if the authors cite actual quotes from the study that corraborate this statement.

The eighth question to ask yourself is whether the conclusions stated are justified by the results. In qualitative research the discussion and results sections often become blurred as the results are an interpretation of the data. In determining whether the conclusions are valid, ask the following: "1) How well does the analysis explain why people behave the way they do? 2) How comprehensive would this explanation be to a thoughtful participant in the setting? and 3) How well does the explanation cohere with what we already know?" (Greenhalgh & Taylor, 1997, p. 742). The final question to ask is: Are the study's findings transferrable? If the researchers used appropriate theoretical sampling the results should be transferrable.

Role of Mixed Methods in Health Education Research

Some researchers use an either-or approach to health education research: either qualitative or quantitative methods or what is referred to as a mono-method design. However, to answer the complex health questions being asked today, mixed-method designs are preferred and are growing in acceptance (Creswell, 2003; Forthofer, 2003; Tashakkorri & Teddlie, 1998). Frequently a mixed-method approach begins with qualitative research (interviews, focus groups) to develop a preliminary understanding of the health problem (Forthofer, 2003). The results from qualitative research are used to develop more standardized methods, usually quantitative methods such as surveys. Often, quantitative research is followed by more qualitative research to aid interpretation of findings. This process allows for an optimal qualitative–quantitative–qualitative sequence.

An illustration of this process is the research on the determinants of breast and cervical cancer screening among underserved women in Florida (Bryant et al., 2000; Forthofer, 2003). The research included three phases. The first phase was qualitative research in which focus groups and in-depth interviews were conducted with these underserved women. Using this information, a standardized survey was developed (phase 2) and used in phase 3 to interview women face to face. Following the face-to-face interviews, in-depth individual interviews were conducted to clarify findings from the survey research. Using a mixed-method approach not only allowed the researchers to understand how many women had sought breast cancer screening, but also provided insight into why they had or had not taken advantage of the screening services in their area. The use of mixed methods also provided confidence in both the internal and external validity of the studies' findings (Forthofer, 2003). Parsons and McCormack Brown (2004) provide another example of mixed-method research to answer research questions regarding tobacco and alcohol use among middle school–age youth.

Summary

Qualitative research provides a level of understanding that is not available through quantitative research methods. In trying to understand the complexities of health education and promotion, Morse (2004) states,

the level of detail in qualitative analysis provides insights into problems that have stymied policy people and health providers, and even uncovers problems that appear inconceivable. It [qualitative research] is essential for health promotion research, with its ability to expose mechanisms of causation, to provide insights into complexities that underlie seemingly simple surveys (p. 4).

The bottom line is that the qualitative approach, alone or in combination with quantitative methods, enriches the research tools that the health education specialist has available to understand the phenomena about which decisions must be made in everyday practice.

Review Questions

1. Describe when qualitative research methods should be used.
2. Describe the five qualitative research approaches and when you would use each.
3. Explain when it is best to use in-depth interviews as a data collection method.
4. Describe the focus group data collection process.
5. Describe the content analysis process.
6. Describe the factors that ensure quality qualitative research.
7. Using a topic of interest, develop an in-depth interview guide or focus group guide (see Appendices A and B).

References

Allen, D. (1998). Spiritual health coverage in college health textbooks. *The Health Educator,* 30(1), 3–10.

Anderson, E.H., & Spencer, M.H. (2002). Cognitive representations of AIDS: A phenomenological study. *Qualitative Health Research,* 12(10), 1338–1352.

Avis, M. (2003). Do we need methodological theory to do qualitative research? *Qualitative Health Research,* 13, 995–1004.

Belgrave, L.L., Zablotsky, D., & Guadagno, M.A. (2002). How do we talk to each other? Writing qualitative research for quantitative readers. *Qualitative Health Research,* 12, 1427–1439.

Bernard, H.R. (2000). Participant observation. In H.R. Bernard, *Social research methods: Qualitative and quantitative approaches* (2nd ed., pp. 317–374). Thousand Oaks, Calif.: Sage.

Bryant, C.A. (2003). Formative research. Paper presented at the 13th annual Social Marketing in Public Health conference, Clearwater Beach, Florida. Tampa, Fl.: Florida Prevention Research Center.

Bryant, C.A., Forthofer, M.S., McCormack Brown, K.R., Alfonso, M.L., & Quinn, G. (2000). A social marketing approach to increasing breast cancer screening. *Journal of Health Education,* 31(6), 320–328.

Calitri, D.L. (1998). An interview with Carl J. Peter, MPH, PhD, CHES. *International Electronic Journal of Health Education,* 3, 182–199.

Cardador, M.T., Hazan, A.R., & Glantz, S.A. (1995). Tobacco industry smokers' rights publications: A content analysis. *American Journal of Public Health,* 85(9), 1212–1217.

Chambers, E. (2000). Applied ethnography. In N.K. Denzin & Y.S. Lincoln (Eds.), *Handbook of qualitative research* (2nd ed.). Thousand Oaks, Calif.: Sage.

Charmaz, K. (2000). Grounded theory: Obstructionist and constructivist methods. In N.K. Denzin & Y.S. Lincoln (Eds.), *Handbook of qualitative research* (2nd ed.). Thousand Oaks, Calif.: Sage.

Coreil, J., Bryant, C.A., & Henderson, J.N. (2001). *Social and behavioral foundations of public health.* Thousand Oaks, Calif.: Sage.

Coreil, J., Wilke, J., & Pintado, I. (2004). Cultural models of illness and recovery in breast cancer support groups. *Qualitative Health Research,* 15(70), 905–923.

Creswell, J.W. (1998). *Qualitative inquiry and research design: Choosing among five traditions.* Thousand Oaks, Calif.: Sage.

Creswell, J.W. (2003). Research design: Qualitative, quantitative, and mixed methods approaches (2nd ed.). Thousand Oaks, Calif.: Sage.

Cunningham, K., Gieszer, M., Bullard, M., Castlen, C., Dumont, D., & Zeoli, J. (1999). Ethnographic research and programmatic outcomes: Empowering families of individuals with serious mental illness. *Practicing Anthropology,* 21, 13–17.

Debus, M. (1988). *Handbook for excellence on focus group research.* Washington, D.C.: Academy for Educational Development.

Denzin, N.K., & Lincoln, Y.S. (2000). Introduction: The discipline and practice of qualitative research. In N.K. Denzin & Y.S. Lincoln (Eds.), *Handbook of qualitative research* (2nd ed.). Thousand Oaks, Calif.: Sage.

Duncan, D.F. (1989). Content analysis in health education research: An introduction to purposes and methods. *Health Education,* 20(7), 27–31.

Eberst, R.M. (1998). An interview with Dr. Peter Cortese. *International Electronic Journal of Health Education,* 1, 112–134.

Fetro, J.V., & Drolet, J.C. (1991). State conferences for school worksite wellness: A content analysis of conference components. *Journal of Health Education,* 22(2), 80–94.

Forthofer, M.S. (2003). Status of mixed methods in the health sciences. In A. Tashakkori & C. Teddlie (Eds.), *Handbook of mixed methods in social and behavioral research* (pp. 527–540). Thousand Oaks, Calif.: Sage.

Geertz, C. (1973). Thick description: Toward an interpretive theory of culture. In C. Geertz, *The interpretation of cultures: Selected essays* (pp. 3–32). New York: Basic Books.

Glew, A.M. (2000). A descriptive analysis of worksite health promotion courses in undergraduate health education programs. Unpublished master's thesis, Ball State University.

Goldsmith, M.D. (1997). An interview with Robert Russell, Emeritus Professor. *International Electronic Journal of Health Education,* 1, 60–71.

Grbich, C. (1999). *Qualitative research in health.* Thousand Oaks, Calif.: Sage.

Greenhalgh, T., & Taylor, R. (1997). How to read a paper: Papers that go beyond numbers (qualitative research). *British Medical Journal,* 315, 740–743.

Grosshans, I.R. (1975). Delbert Oberteuffer: His professional activities and contributions to the fields of health and physical education. Unpublished doctoral dissertation, Indiana University.

Heitzer, J. (2004). A descriptive analysis of patient education courses in undergraduate and graduate health education programs. Unpublished master's thesis, Ball State University.

Hill, S.C., Lindsay, G.B., Thomsen, S.R., & Olsen, A.M. (2003). A descriptive analysis of health related infomercials: Implications for health education and media literacy. *American Journal of Health Education,* 34(1), 9–16.

Holsti, O. (1969). *Content analysis for social sciences and humanities.* Reading, Mass.: Addison-Wesley.

Hycner, R.H. (1985). Some guidelines for the phenomenological analysis of interview data. *Human Studies,* 8, 279–303.

Johnson, P.H., & Kittleson, M.J. (2000). A content analysis of health education teaching strategy/idea articles: 1970–1998. *Journal of Health Education,* 31(5), 292–298.

Kegler, M.C., & Wyatt, V.H. (2003). A multiple case study of neighborhood partnerships for positive youth development. *American Journal of Health Behavior,* 27, 156–169.

Kerlinger, F.N. (1973). *Foundations of behavioral research* (2nd ed.). New York: Holt, Rinehart & Winston.

Kinnison, A., Cottrell, R.R., & King, K.A. (2004). Proper hand-washing techniques in public restrooms: Differences in gender, race, signage and time of day. *American Journal of Health Education,* 35(2), 86–89.

Krueger, R.A., & Casey, A. (2008). *Focus groups: A practical guide for applied research.* Thousand Oaks, Calif.: Sage.

Lacey, A., & Luff, D. (2007). Qualitative research analysis. Trent RDSU. Available at: www.trentrdsu .org.uk.

Law, M., Stewart, D., Letts, L., Pollock, N., Bosch, J., & Westmorland, M. (1998). Guidelines for critical review of qualitative studies. Available at: www.fhs .mcmaster.ca/rehab/ebp/pdf/qualreview.pdf.

Lincoln, Y.S., & Guba, E.G. (1985). *Naturalistic inquiry.* Newbury Park, Calif.: Sage.

Luborsky, M.R., & Rubinstein, R.L. (1995). Sampling in qualitative research: Rationale, issues, and methods. *Research on Aging,* 17(1), 89–113.

Malterud, K. (2001). Qualitative research: Standards, challenges, and guidelines. *The Lancet,* 358(28), 483.

Mays, N., & Pope, C. (1995). Qualitative research: Rigour and qualitative research. *British Medical Journal,* 311, 109–112.

McCormack Brown, K.R., Henry, T., & Pitt, S. (January 2001). *Formative research: Key informant interviews for the examination of communication factors affecting policymakers.* University of South Florida, Florida Prevention Research Center. Report to the Public Health Institute and the California Department of Health Services.

McCormack Brown, K., Akintobi, T.H., Pitts, S., Berends, V., McDermott, R., Agron, P., & Purcell, A. (2004). School board members' perceptions of factors influencing school nutrition policy decision-making. *Journal of School Health,* 74(2), 52–58.

McDermott, R.J., & Sarvela, P.D. (1999). Health education evaluation and measurement: A practitioner's perspective (2nd ed.). Madison, Wis.: WCB/McGraw-Hill.

Morrow, M.J. (1998). An interview with Ann E. Nolte, Ph.S., CHES, FASHA. *International Electronic Journal of Health Education,* 1, 222–234.

Morse, J.M. (2002). Myth #53: Qualitative research is cheap (editorial). *Qualitative Health Research,* 12, 1307–1308.

Morse, J.M. (2004). The complexities of health promotion (editorial). *Qualitative Health Research,* 14(1), 3–4.

Nandy, B.R., & Sarvela, P.D. (1997). Content analysis reexamined: A relevant research method for health education. *American Journal of Health Behavior,* 21(3), 222–234.

Parsons, N.P., & McCormack Brown, K. (2004). Formative research: The bedrock of social marketing. *The Health Education Monograph Series,* 21(1), 1–5.

Pasick, R.J., D'Onofrio, C.N., & Otero-Sabogal, R. (1996). Similarities and differences across cultures: Questions to inform a third generation of health promotion research. *Health Education Quarterly,* 23(Suppl.), S142–S161.

Pasick, R.J., Sabogal, F., Bird, J.A., D'Onofrio, C.N., Jenkins, C.N.H., Lee, M., *et al.* (1996). Problems and progress in translation of health survey questions: The *Pathways* experience. *Health Education Quarterly,* 23(Suppl.), S28–S40.

Patton, M.Q. (1999). Enhancing the quality and credibility of qualitative analysis. *Health Services Research,* 34(5), 1189–1193.

Patton, M.Q. (2002). Variety of qualitative inquiry: Theoretical orientations. In *Qualitative research and evaluation methods* (3rd ed.). Thousand Oaks, Calif.: Sage.

Ribisl, K.M., Lee, R.E., Henriksen, L., & Haladjian, H.H. (2003). A content of Web sites promoting smoking culture and lifestyle. *Health Education and Behavior,* 30(1), 64–78.

Roberts, D.F., & Christenson, P.G. (2000). *Here's looking at you, kid.* Menlo Park, Calif.: Kaiser Family Foundation.

Rolfe, G. (2006). Validity, trustworthiness and rigour: Quality and the idea of qualitative research. *Journal of Advanced Nursing*, 53(3), 304–310.

Ryan, G.W., & Bernard, H.R. (2000). Data management and analysis methods. In N.K. Denzin & Y.S. Lincoln (Eds.), *Handbook of qualitative research* (2nd ed.). Thousand Oaks, Calif.: Sage.

Sandelowski, M. (1995). Sample size in qualitative research. *Research in Nursing and Health,* 18, 179–183.

Seidman, I. (1998). *Interviewing as qualitative research: A guide for researchers in education and the social sciences* (2nd ed.). New York: Teachers College, Columbia University.

Smith, M., Gertz, E., Alvarrez, S., & Lurie, P. (2000). The content and accessibility of sex education information on the Internet. *Health Education and Behavior,* 27(6), 684–694.

Smith, M.H., Altman, D.G., & Strunk, B. (2000). Readiness to change: Newspaper coverage of tobacco farming and diversification. *Health Education and Behavior,* 27(6), 708–724.

Sofalvi, A.J. (1985). An analysis of health-related content of Sunday comic strips in selected years from 1950–1984. Unpublished master's thesis, Southern Illinois University.

Stake, R.E. (2000). Case studies. In N.K. Denzin & Y.S. Lincoln (Eds.), *Handbook of qualitative research* (2nd ed.). Thousand Oaks, Calif.: Sage.

Strauss, A., & Corbin, J. (1990). *Basics of qualitative research: Grounded theory procedures and techniques.* Newbury Park, Calif.: Sage.

Tashakkori, A., & Teddlie, C. (1998). Research design issues for mixed method and mixed model studies. In A. Tashakkori & C. Teddlie (Eds.), *Applied social research methods series: Vol. 46. Mixed methodology: Combining qualitative and quantitative approaches* (pp. 40–58). Thousand Oaks, Calif.: Sage.

Torrens Salemi, A. (2004). The social construction of school refusal: An exploratory study of school personnel's perceptions. Unpublished doctoral dissertation, University of South Florida.

U.S. Department of Health and Human Services. (2002). *Making health communication programs work.* Public Health Service, National Cancer Institute. NIH publication No. 02–5145. Washington, D.C.: U.S. Government Printing Office.

Welle, H.M., Kittleson, M.J., & Olgetree, R.J. (1995). A content analysis of the first year of HEDIR List: Implications for the future. *Journal of Health Education,* 26(6), 366–371.

Wilson, H.S., Hutchinson, S.A., & Holzemer, W.L. (2002). Reconciling incompatibilities: A grounded theory of HIV medication adherence and symptom management. *Qualitative Health Research,* 12(12), 1309–1322.

Zapata, L., Forthofer, M.S., Bell, B., Bryant, R.L., McCormack Brown, K.R., Bryant, C., & McDermott, R.J. (2003). Content analysis of tobacco and alcohol related articles in the newspaper: Utility for evaluating interventions to prevent youth smoking and drinking in the community. Presentation at the 3rd Annual Scientific Meeting of the American Academy of Health Behavior, St. Augustine, Florida.

Appendix 11-A
In-Depth Interview Guide

Healthy Food Choices and School Policies:
Key Opinion Leaders

Name: _____   Date: _____

Project LEAN Region: _____   Interviewer: _____

Statements in bold are instructions or comments that the interviewer should provide to the key informant (KI).

[OTHER INSTRUCTIONS AND COMMENTS INTENDED ONLY FOR THE INTERVIEWER ARE PROVIDED IN BRACKETS AND CAPS AND SHOULD NOT BE READ TO THE KI]

Introduction

Thank you for agreeing to be interviewed.

Your assistance and comments are valuable and important.

This interview is informal, like a conversation.

Purpose

Discuss how school health policies are determined, in particular, what influences school board members (like yourself, if appropriate) in their school health policy decision-making process.

I am doing this interview as part of a collaborative process between Project LEAN and the University of South Florida (Tampa).

I am very interested in all of your ideas, comments, and suggestions.

There are no right or wrong answers: I want both positive and negative comments.

Results from this interview will be combined with other interviews to assist in developing a survey for school board members.

Procedure

This interview will last about 30–45 minutes.

I will be audiotaping this interview as well as taking notes.

This interview is confidential. You may stop the interview at any time.

As indicated on the phone, I will need you to read and sign this informed consent form. [GIVE TO THEM, HAVE THEM READ AND SIGN, YOU THEN SIGN. OFFER THEM A COPY IF THEY WANT.]

We have a lot to cover so I might change the subject or move ahead, but let me know if you want to add something. Don't let me cut you off.

1. Please talk about how long you have been a school board member, principal, superintendent, etc.

   PROBE: How long have you lived in this school district? _____

   Have you held more than one term on the school board?

   [   ] Yes   [   ] No

   If YES, how many terms have you held?

   _____

2. To help us better understand how school policies are made, can you explain to me generally how a policy is brought forward to the school board and then acted on?

3. As a school board member/principal/superintendent, what do you consider to be important issues concerning schools today?

   PROBE: pouring/contract rights, busing, academic achievement, testing, fast food, etc.

   [AFTER THEY HAVE TOLD YOU THE ISSUES THEY THINK ARE IMPORTANT, ASK THEM TO RATE HOW IMPORTANT THE ISSUE IS: VERY IMPORTANT (1), IMPORTANT (2), SOMEWHAT IMPORTANT (3)]

4. Of the above issues you mentioned, which issues are being addressed by your school board this year?

   PROBE: How did these issues become issues that the school board decided to address?

PROBE: With these issues you mentioned [YOU MAY WANT TO NAME EACH SEPARATELY] how did they become an agenda item?

[WHO BROUGHT THE ISSUE TO THE TABLE? A SCHOOL BOARD MEMBER, PTA/PTO, PRINCIPAL, SUPERINTENDENT?]

5. Of the issues that you deem important and not addressed this year, why do you believe they are not being considered?

6. Who in the past has approached you regarding school health policies/issues (i.e., parent, teacher, PTA/PTO)?

   PROBE: Were they seeking support for a policy or requesting that a new policy be developed? What was the outcome?

7. When making a decision about a school health policy, who do you seek advice from?

   PROBE: Are any of these more influential than others?

   PROBE: Do you look to other school districts or CSBA for sample policies?

8. What type of support do you need from community members (e.g., parents, business leaders) to bring forth a school health policy OR to support a school health policy?

9. What do you need to know about a specific school health policy (e.g., healthy food choice, pouring contracts) in order to bring it to the board's attention for discussion?

10. If a parent/community member brought to your attention a school issue (e.g., fast food, soda machines in the school), what is the process that takes place to have this issue placed on the school board agenda?

11. Where do you get your information regarding school issues (e.g., TV, newspaper, radio, professional organizations)?

12. Where do you get your information regarding community issues (e.g., TV, newspaper, radio, professional organizations)?

13. What have you found to be the major pitfall with regard to implementing school [health] policy?

14. Thinking about all the things we have talked about today, which of these things is most influential for you when making a decision about school health policies in your school district?

15. Does personal experience play a role in your decision-making process?

    If so, please explain how.

16. We have covered a lot. Is there anything else you believe I should know to help us better understand what influences how decisions are made?

I have just a few final demographic questions.

Gender: [   ] Female
        [   ] Male

Age: _____

Ethnicity: [   ] African American
           [   ] Alaskan Native
           [   ] Asian/Pacific Islander
           [   ] American Indian or Native American
           [   ] Other {specify}: _____

Do you consider yourself:
           [   ] Hispanic OR
           [   ] Non-Hispanic

Do you have any school-age children?
           [   ] Yes   [   ] No

If YES,   How many? _____

           What grades? _____

           Are they enrolled in public school?
           [   ] Yes   [   ] No

THANK YOU FOR YOUR TIME!
[GIVE THEM COOKBOOK]

Source: McCormack Brown, K.R., Henry, T., & Pitt, S. (January 2001). *Formative research: Key informant interviews for the examination of communication factors affecting policymakers.* University of South Florida, Florida Prevention Research Center. Report to the Public Health Institute and the California Department of Health Services.

Appendix 11-B
Interview Guide Development Tips

Writing Good Questions

- Match to research objectives
- Use open-ended questions
- Consider order of questions
- Review question types/techniques to find creative approaches

Good Questions . . .

- Explore feelings and aspirations
- Focus on reasons or motives
- Avoid beginning with "Why"
- Are specific
- Do not lead or introduce

Avoid . . .

- Subtly leading
  - What do you like? vs. How do you feel about . . . ?
- Double barreled
  - What do you like and dislike?
- Unnecessary, nice-to-know information
- Loaded terms (e.g., disappointed)
- Questions that make respondents feel bad

Common Problems to Avoid

- Covering too much
- Closed-ended questions
- Eliciting long stories
- Asking everyone the same thing each time
- Using the same guide for all types of groups (users vs. nonusers)

Sample Guide

- Introduction
- Warm-up or opening question
  - Easy and quick to answer; puts participants at ease
- Introductory question
  - Focus on general topic
  - Top of the mind, first impressions, general comments
- Transitional statements and questions
  - Announce shift and move toward key questions
  - Focus on participants
- Key questions
- Closing questions
  - Opportunity to reflect on everything discussed
  - Select most important issues
  - Solidify opinion or view
- Wrap and summary
  - Participants have opportunity to comment on summary

Logistical Concerns

Location

- Will respondents have privacy?
- Can respondents see and hear each other well?
- Will tape be clear? Background noise?
- Is the location easy to find? Safe?
- Will respondents feel comfortable in that setting?

Select Facilitator/Moderator

- Physical and social attributes
- Abilities
  - Put participants at ease
  - Listen attentively
  - Convey warmth and empathy
  - Control nonverbal reactions
  - Conceptualize and think through contingencies
  - Withhold own comments and views

Moderator Responsibilities

- Set the tone
- Make sure every participant is heard

- Get full answers
- Monitor time closely
- Keep discussion on track
- Head off damaging exchanges and conflicts

Role of the Co-moderator (with focus groups)

- Help handle distractions
- Take notes
- Set up and monitor the tape recorder
- Greet guests or help with refreshments
- Interview "extras"
- Do not participate unless invited
- Closing
- Pay respondents

Source: Florida Prevention Research Center. (2003). *Interview Guide Development Tips.* Tampa: Florida Prevention Research Center, University of South Florida.

CHAPTER 12 | Data Analysis and Reporting the Findings (Writing Chapters III and IV)

Chapter Objectives

After reading this chapter and answering the review questions, you should be able to:

1. Write Chapter III of a thesis or dissertation.
2. State what needs to be completed prior to a proposal hearing/presentation.
3. Explain who is invited or attends a proposal hearing/presentation.
4. Explain what typically happens in a proposal hearing/presentation.
5. Describe the various sections included in Chapter IV.
6. Describe the three areas to cover in the "Participants" section of Chapter IV.
7. Explain the process for data entry and the importance of cleaning data.

8. Identify nominal, ordinal, interval, and ratio data.
9. Select appropriate statistics to analyze data collected.
10. Report results related to a specific research question, hypothesis, or objective in concise, straightforward terms.
11. Summarize or recap research findings in a narrative, nonstatistical manner.
12. Write a discussion, summary, or conclusion section to Chapter IV as prescribed by one's program.

Key Terms

descriptive statistics	ordinal data	proposal hearing
inferential statistics	*p* value	ratio data
interval data	practical significance	statistical significance
missing data	proposal	tests of significance
nominal data		

In the beginning of Chapter 7 of this text, we discussed what would be included in the writing of a thesis or dissertation's Chapter III, which is usually titled "Methods" or "Procedures." It was noted that writing Chapter III requires such a significant amount of information about research design that the needed information would be contained in the next five chapters of the text (Chapters 7–11). If you have been reading this book in the order it was written, you have now studied those five chapters and should be able to complete writing Chapter III, with the exception of the last section on data analysis. Basic information on data analysis will be included in this chapter of the text along with information for writing Chapter IV of a thesis or dissertation.

To review, Chapter III of a thesis or dissertation should begin with a brief introduction that restates the purpose of the study exactly as it was written in Chapter I. In addition, Chapter III should contain detailed sections describing the study participants (see Chapter 7) and instrumentation (see Chapter 8) used in the study. Following these two sections, a section on the procedures or methods (see Chapters 9, 10, and 11) to be utilized in the study is written. The section on procedures must be detailed enough that someone reading your study could repeat it exactly as you conducted it from the information you include in this section of the thesis or dissertation. The procedures section of Chapter III is sometimes written in the future tense, but in many programs past tense is used in all sections of the thesis/dissertation document (Manning, Algozzine, & Antonak, 2003). Remember that when the final consumer reads your research it will already be completed and thus is in the past.

After draft versions of Chapters I, II, and III are written to the satisfaction of the committee chair and all committee members, the thesis or dissertation **proposal** is complete. Although there are no guidelines as to the length of proposals, many are in the 30–40 page range, but others are much longer or shorter. Qualitative proposals are typically longer than quantitative proposals (Manning *et al.*, 2003).

Proposal Hearings/Presentations

The fact that a student has a completed draft of a proposal does not mean that additional changes will not be made. At this point most graduate programs require students to hold a formal **proposal hearing** or presentation. A proposal hearing

includes the committee chair, all committee members, and any invited guests. Most proposal hearings are open to the entire university community, so other graduate students or faculty may attend as well. It is a good idea to attend several proposal hearings prior to your own hearing to see how they flow and what is expected.

The format of proposal hearings/presentations may differ from university to university, but they usually contain most of the following elements. The hearing begins with the student making an oral presentation of the proposal. This is for the benefit of invited guests and others attending the proposal hearing who have not read the actual proposal. It also helps committee members to determine how well students can articulate the research they are proposing. After the oral presentation, the committee may ask a variety of conceptual and/or theoretical questions about the research. These are to help committee members determine if the student fully understands the work being proposed. Next, the questions get more specific concerning the actual proposal. The committee may want to move chapter by chapter or even page by page through the proposal document, which would include a thorough review of any instruments developed for the study. Throughout this process, suggestions for changes to the proposal document may be made. After all questions have been asked by the committee, others attending the proposal hearing are typically given the opportunity to ask any questions they may have.

At the completion of this process, the committee deliberates and makes a decision as to whether the student is ready to move forward. If the student has worked diligently in preparing the proposal, has kept the committee informed, and has incorporated the feedback of the committee chair and committee members, the proposal is usually accepted. Very few students have proposals rejected at the proposal hearing stage. Most students, however, will make changes to their proposal as a result of the proposal hearing. These changes can be fairly minor or extensive, in which case another proposal hearing may be required.

In lieu of a formal proposal hearing, some universities hold a private committee meeting with only the committee members and student present. It is at this meeting where a proposal is actually approved. Following the committee meeting, the student makes a formal, public presentation of the proposal. Changes to a proposal can still be made at the formal presentation if necessary.

Successfully proposing or presenting one's research marks an important step in the thesis/dissertation process. An approved proposal means that if the student follows through with the research as stated in the proposal, the committee agrees that this work can be used to meet the thesis or dissertation requirement.

Once the proposal has been approved and any additional modifications made, the student can seek IRB approval and then actually conduct the research and collect data. As Blaxter, Hughes, and Tight (2002) note, "The process of collecting data may be quite a lengthy and demanding part of your research project. It may be a part which you particularly enjoy, or you may dislike it intensely" (p. 185). Either way, it must be done, and it must be done well if your research is to produce meaningful results. Although data collection is one of the most important aspects of research, we will not spend much time discussing it. The procedures for collecting data vary greatly from one study to another. In the thesis/dissertation process the procedures for conducting this work must be spelled out in Chapter III and agreed upon by your committee.

Even though data collection is usually completed by students with little committee oversight, students are encouraged to stay in close contact with their committee chair while involved in this phase of the research. If problems arise, students should keep their committee chair informed. Students cannot alter their data collection procedures without approval of the committee chair, committee members, and the human subjects committee.

Before Writing Chapter IV

Data Entry

At this point, we will assume that you have conducted your research as proposed and have your data collected. If the study is a quantitative study, the next step is to enter the data into the computer. If the data were collected on scan sheets or with a software system such as SurveyMonkey or the computer-assisted telephone interviewing (CATI), the data entry phase can be relatively quick and easy. Quantitative data collected on questionnaires or data sheets that needs to be entered by hand into the computer will be more time consuming and more prone to errors. If the study is qualitative, the task of summarizing and analyzing the field notes or other collected data begins. Software programs such as NUDIST are available that can help with this task. Types of qualitative studies and the data they generate were discussed in Chapter 11 of this text.

For most graduate students doing quantitative research, data need to be entered by hand into a spreadsheet program or directly into a statistical analysis program, such as SPSS. A system to code the data needs to be developed prior to beginning this process. A coding system is simply a way of transferring participant responses on the questionnaire to the computer. For example, if a participant marks that he is a male, males may be coded as the number "1" when entered into the computer. A female may be coded as the number "2." The coding system also establishes rules for dealing with problem situations. For example, if a participant circles two answers or places a mark between two answers or leaves one or more items blank, how will this be handled? This scenario should be discussed with and approved by your committee chair both before coding begins and during the coding process as problems arise.

Once data are entered, regardless of whether by hand or computer system, they must be cleaned.

This means that frequency distributions are run for the data set so that outliers can be identified and corrected. For example, if the possible range of answers for a particular question is 1–5 and the frequency distribution identifies some 6's, those questionnaires with the 6's must be identified and checked to determine if the responder made an error or if there was an error made by the person doing the data entry. If there was a data entry error, it should be corrected. If the responder made an error, it would be treated as no response to that question or as **missing data**. There are special rules for handling missing data that should be discussed in one's statistics course or in a data analysis course. It is always a good idea to discuss the treatment of missing data with one's committee chair prior to initiating data analysis.

Data Analysis

The purpose of our discussion of data analysis here is to provide broad conceptual understandings of statistical analysis, not to provide detailed information on specific statistical applications. Most students will have taken one or more statistics courses prior to reaching this point in the thesis or dissertation process and should have at least a basic understanding of statistical methods.

We will begin by examining the two major branches of statistics: descriptive and inferential. **Descriptive statistics** are used to summarize data about a given population or variable so they can be easily comprehended. Suppose, for example, we had administered a 20-question diabetes knowledge assessment instrument to a group of 466 worksite employees. A listing of all 466 scores would not be of much help in trying to describe how well informed the group was about diabetes. Instead, by using descriptive statistics, a frequency table such as that seen in Table 12.1 might be developed. Simply by examining the table, it is possible to determine which scores were obtained most often. Fifteen was the score most often obtained, followed by scores of 14 and 16. With some sim-

Table 12.1   Sample Frequency Distribution Table

Score	Frequency	Percentage
20	15	3.2
19	19	4.1
18	38	8.2
17	45	9.7
16	71	15.2
15	109	23.4
14	78	16.7
13	37	7.9
12	33	7.1
11	21	4.5
Total	**466**	**100%**

ple calculations the mean (15.2), median (15), and mode (15) can be determined, which are all measures of central tendency. In other words, they indicate where the middle of the distribution is.

Now suppose that the 466 employees tested were a random sample of the 4,000 people employed by the company. If all 4,000 had been tested, would the results be exactly the same? Probably not; there would be some chance differences between the population and the sample. These differences between the true responses of the population and those of the sample are known as sampling errors (see Chapter 7). **Inferential statistics** can be used to help us draw inferences about the effects of sampling error on our results (Patten, 2009). In other words, inferential statistics can tell us the probability that the results found in the sample represent the results that would have been found if the entire 4,000 had been tested. Further, if we wanted to determine whether male employees scored differently than female employees, inferential statistics would be used to help make that determination as well.

An important element of inferential statistics involves **tests of significance**. Tests of significance help determine if observed differences are real differences or simply the result of chance. If in the above example the mean female score on the diabetes knowledge test was 15.8 and the mean male score on the diabetes knowledge test was 15.1, would this mean that the females had a better knowledge of diabetes, or would this difference be the result of chance? By applying an appropriate statistical test, in this case a t-test, one could determine the probability that these two scores are significantly different.

To actually test whether the 0.7 difference in mean diabetes knowledge test scores is a real difference, a null hypothesis would be developed stating that there is no difference between male and female mean diabetes knowledge assessment scores. As a general rule, if the probability, or **p value**, calculated from the t-test is less than 0.05, then we would consider the difference to be a real or significant difference and would reject the null hypothesis. In other words, we would be 95% sure that the observed differences in diabetes knowledge assessment scores were real differences. On the other hand, if the p value calculated from the t-test was greater than 0.05, we would not reject the null hypothesis and would assume that the observed differences in mean diabetes knowledge assessment scores between males and females was the result of chance. Researchers must always state in any research reports what probability level they used to determine if results were significant or not. Although 0.05 is the most common level utilized, other levels such as 0.1, 0.01, and 0.001 are also sometimes seen in research.

Does **statistical significance** always equal **practical significance**? The answer to this question is "no." Remember that statistical significance is indicating that the differences noted are real differences and are not the result of chance. This does not mean, however, that there are any practical significance or real-world applications to these findings. Take the above diabetes knowledge assessment, for example. Suppose that the difference in males' ($x = 15.1$) and females' ($x = 15.8$) mean knowledge scores was significant ($p < 0.05$). What does this mean in terms of real-world or practical significance? Does it mean that programs need to be initiated for males so that their mean

diabetes knowledge can be brought up to that of females? Probably not. Even though real differences (statistical significance) exist between males and females in mean diabetes knowledge scores, the difference is small (practical significance). It would probably not be a wise use of time or money to initiate diabetes information programs specifically for males based on the results of this study.

Sometimes it may be more difficult to determine practical significance. Stevens (2009) suggests using the confidence interval as one way of evaluating practical significance. He uses the following example:

> Suppose you are comparing two teaching methods and decide ahead of time that the achievement for one method must be at least 5 points higher on average for practical significance. The results are significant, but the 95% confidence interval for the difference in the population means is (1.61, 9.45). You do not have practical significance because, although the difference could be as large as 9 or more, it could also be less than 2 (p. 8).

Note that in this case, determining the amount of difference needed for practical significance ahead of the study and considering the lower end of the confidence interval were important elements in determining practical significance.

Selecting Statistical Tests

Determining which statistical procedure to use is dependent on two factors: the level of measurement and the type of research question or hypothesis being addressed. Wiersma and Jurs (2009) define measurement as "a process of assigning numerals according to rules. The numerals are assigned to events or objects, such as responses to items or to certain observed behaviors" (p. 353). A number is a symbol with no meaning until a rule is created that provides meaning.

There are four scales or levels at which we measure. The lowest level of measurement is the **nominal** scale. This is essentially just categorizing or naming a variable. When a question is asked that will produce nominal data, the answer is usually in words, not numbers. For example, we may ask a group of health education professionals if they are certified health education specialists. They would answer either "yes" or "no." This is a nominal level of measurement. When we enter this into the computer, we may record the "yes" answer as a 1 and the "no" answer as a 2. These numbers, however, have no mathematical meaning. In data analysis the numbers are simply counted to indicate the number of people responding 1 (yes) or 2 (no). Other examples of nominal data would include gender, race, marital status, religion, and so forth.

The next level of measurement is **ordinal**. At this level data are rank ordered from high to low. Beyond simply naming objects as in a nominal scale, an ordinal scale identifies relative position. To be reliable, ordinal scales must include objective criteria for ordering objects. For example, in health education we might want to examine the variable of socioeconomic status. Based on predetermined criteria to separate people based on socioeconomic status, we might place people into the high, middle, or low category. Note that we could have many more categories, such as upper middle or lower middle, if the criteria would allow for such discrimination. Each category would be assigned a number, so high might be a 3, middle might be a 2, and low might be a 1. Although the numbers do represent relative position, so that a 3 has a higher socioeconomic status than a 2, there is no mathematical relationship between the numbers. In other words, we could not say that a 2 has double the socioeconomic status of a 1. Therefore, statistical methods for use with ordinal data are limited to those not assuming equal interval measurement between scale positions such as median and rank correlations (Schloss & Smith, 1999). Other examples of ordinal scales may include wealth, exercise level, satisfaction, health status, and so forth.

Interval scales are the next highest level of measurement. As the name implies, there are equal intervals between numbers on the scale. If a scale with equal intervals also has a true zero point, then it is a **ratio** scale, which is "the highest and most complete form of measurement" (Schloss & Smith, 1999, p. 146). Zero is an arbitrary point on the scale. In some of the physical measurements used by health education specialists, there is a true zero point and thus a ratio scale. Height, weight, and blood pressure are examples of ratio scales because they have a true zero point; test scores would be another example. Ratio scales are not common in social and behavioral sciences, because the scales we devise and use to measure such constructs as locus of control, self-concept, stress, and so forth do not have a true zero point. In other words, there is no true zero amount of locus of control, self-concept, or stress. See Box 12.1 to test your understanding of measurement levels.

Although categorization of items into the proper scale seems clear, there can be confusion with differences between the ordinal and interval scale. In health education research, Likert scales are used, particularly in measuring items within a concept. For example, 10 items (statements) may be measuring self-efficacy using a five-point Likert scale from strongly agree to strongly disagree. It is a common practice to score each item from 1 to 5 and then to total the 10 items so the higher score shows more self-efficacy and the lower score shows less self-efficacy. The difficulty arises in the debate over whether there is equal distance between the points on the scale, making it either ordinal (no equal distance) or interval (equal distance) (Wiersma & Jurs, 2009).

A final step, which helps with clarification of the variables, is to operationally define the measurement. This means to clearly and concisely define how the variable is being measured in a particular study. For example, self-efficacy might be defined as the score on a 10-item self-efficacy scale developed specifically for the research study (Wiersma & Jurs, 2009).

Once level of measurement has been determined, the type of research question or hypothesis

---

Box 12.1   Levels of Measurement

Consider the following items that might be from a health behavior instrument. At what measurement level is each of these items?
1. How old are you in years? _____
2. Do you visit a dentist every six months for preventive treatments?
   1) yes
   2) no
3. How often do you eat high-sugar foods?
   1) hourly
   2) daily
   3) weekly
   4) never

Answers:
1. The number participants write on this line would provide ratio data. The spacing between numbers is equal and there is a true zero point. If the actual number written on the line was entered into the computer for data analysis, the data would be ratio data. What if the researcher decided to classify participants as being young, middle-aged, or elderly and entered only these three categories into the computer? The researcher would have changed the data from ratio to ordinal. As a general rule, data should be kept at the highest level of measurement possible when entered into the computer. It is always possible to regroup data once it is entered.
2. This would be nominal level. We are simply labeling people as yes's or no's.
3. Although numeric values with equal interval spacing are used to differentiate the possible answers, it is clear that equal spacing does not exist for the categories. There is, however, an order from high to low. Therefore, this is ordinal measurement.

---

education specialists support initiating a new profession-wide system of program accreditation?" Part of the response to this question might be, "Eighty percent of college health education specialists surveyed believe a new profession-wide system of program accreditation is needed." Obviously, there may be more questions related to this research question and the responses would be expanded beyond the one sentence above.

Descriptive statistics are also used to report on meeting stated objectives when objectives are written instead of research questions. A particular health education program, for example, might establish an objective that 70% of its graduating students would take and pass the CHES exam by the end of the year. Reporting this result is simple: the percentage of students taking and passing the CHES exam by the stated time would be presented. For example, "54% of graduating students took and passed the CHES exam by the end of the year." Although stating the percentage to meet the objective is straightforward, there may need to be much more discussion about why the objective was or was not met.

If a research question asks about relationships between variables, then correlation coefficients will be used in the data analysis. A research question of this type might read, "What is the relationship between income and health status?" This could also be written as a hypothesis: "There will be a positive relationship between income and health status among the study population." If the words "relationship" or "related" appear in the research question, correlations are called for.

As you may remember from Chapter 10, a correlation coefficient explains the degree of relationship between two variables and is expressed as a numerical value between $+1$ and -1. The closer a correlation coefficient is to either $+1$ or -1, the stronger the relationship. A zero would indicate no relationship. Tests of statistical significance are used to determine the probability that a given correlation is actually different from a correlation of zero. A possible response to the above hypothesis

to be addressed must be considered. If a research question simply asks to what extent something is occurring, then simple descriptive statistics, such as frequencies, and measures of central tendency can be used. An example of such a question might be, "To what extent do college health

related to income and health status might read, "In analyzing the data on health status and income using the Pearson product moment statistic, a moderate correlation of + 0.63 was found. This correlation was significant at the 0.05 alpha level ($p = 0.001$). The null hypothesis, which stated that there would be no relationship between health status and income, was rejected. It was concluded that there is a moderate positive relationship between health status and income. As income increases, health status increases."

Any hypothesis that seeks to determine if there are differences between groups on one or more variables will require a test of statistical significance. For example, a hypothesis that states, "While driving a car, college females are more likely to fasten their seat belts than are college males" might use a chi square statistic to determine if there actually was a difference between college females and males in seat belt use.

It is beyond the scope of this text to provide a complete discussion of all the possible statistical tests that could be used to analyze data for a thesis or dissertation. Table 12.2 provides an overview of commonly used statistical tests, the purpose for which they are used, and the type of data collected. The point we wish to make in this text is that based on the research questions or hypotheses asked and the type of data collected, students should be able to make decisions on the appropriate statistical tools to be utilized in the data analysis phase of a thesis or dissertation. Students should be very thorough when conducting their statistical analysis. Data should be carefully entered into the computer and checked to eliminate errors. All appropriate statistical tests should be completed and results reported exactly as received.

Writing Chapter IV

Pryczak and Bruce (2007) have developed practical guidelines to follow when writing results and analysis. These can be seen in Box 12.2. Following these guidelines will help students stay on track while writing Chapter IV. We will now discuss in detail the three main sections in Chapter IV: "Participants," "Results," and "Discussion."

Participants

Chapter IV should begin as previous chapters with a brief introduction that restates the purpose of the study exactly as it was written in Chapter I. A section that thoroughly describes the participants in the study follows the introduction. This section is typically titled "Subjects" or "Participants" and should do three things: (1) thoroughly describe how the participants were selected and all information pertaining to their selection and decision to participate; (2) thoroughly describe the demographic characteristics of the participants (gender, age, race, occupation, etc.); and (3) thoroughly describe the subjects based on specific characteristics related to the study (knowledge level, attitude scores, behavioral scores, stage of change, height, body fat, cholesterol level, etc.).

In describing how the participants were selected and all information pertaining to their selection, the researcher should note whether a census or a sample was used. Next, the procedures for selecting and contacting participants should be described. It is very important to describe how potential and actual participants responded when contacted. In a mailed survey, for example, information needs to be provided concerning how the sample frame was selected, how many questionnaires were mailed out, how many were returned undeliverable, how many were returned complete and usable, and how many were returned incomplete and unusable. Appropriate return rates need to be calculated and reported in this section of Chapter IV. (See Chapter 10 for information on calculating return rates.) In a telephone survey, the researcher needs to report how the sample frame was established, how many calls were made, how many numbers were disconnected, how many were no answers or busy signals, how many callbacks were successful, how

Table 12.2   Commonly Used Significance Tests

Test name	Test statistic	Purpose	Variable 1 (independent)	Variable 2 (dependent)
t-test for independent samples	t	Test the difference between means of two groups	Nominal	Interval or ratio
t-test for dependent samples	t	Test differences between means of two dependent groups	Nominal	Interval or ratio
Analysis of variance (ANOVA)	F	Test the difference among three or more independent groups	Nominal	Interval or ratio
Pearson product correlation	r	Test whether a correlation is different from zero (a relationship exists)	Interval or ratio	Interval or ratio
Chi square test	x^2	Test the difference in proportions in two or more groups	Nominal	Nominal
Median test	x^2	Test the difference of the medians of two independent groups	Nominal	Ordinal
Mann-Whitney *U* test	U	Test the difference of the medians of two independent groups	Nominal	Ordinal
Wilcoxon signed rank test	Z	Test the difference in the ranks of two related groups	Nominal	Ordinal
Kruskal-Wallis test	H	Test the difference in the ranks of three or more independent groups	Nominal	Ordinal
Friedman test	x	Test the difference in the ranks of three or more dependent groups	Nominal	Ordinal
Spearman rho	ρ	Test whether a correlation is different from zero	Ordinal	Ordinal

Based on a table in Gay, L.R., Mills, G.E., & Airasian, P. (2006). *Educational research: Competencies for analysis and applications* (8th ed., p. 378). Upper Saddle River, N.J.: Pearson Education, Inc.

many refused to respond, and how many actually were reached and responded to the questions.

Obviously, it is extremely important to know what response data need to be reported in this section of Chapter IV prior to beginning data collection. Once the data have been collected, it is too late to go back and make these determinations. Failure to maintain accurate information concerning response rates may mean that one's results will be questioned and may not be accepted for publication in professional journals.

Demographic information is important to report because it helps readers understand who was being studied. Even if there is no research question or

---

Box 12.2   Guidelines for Writing Results Section and Analysis

1. Organize the analysis and results section around the research hypotheses, purposes, or questions stated in the introduction.
2. Standard statistical procedures need only be named; you do not need to show formulas or calculations.
3. The scores of individual participants usually are not shown; instead, statistics based on the scores should be reported.
4. Present descriptive statistics first.
5. Organize large numbers of statistics in tables, and give each table a number and descriptive title (i.e., caption).
6. When describing the statistics presented in a table, point out the highlights for the reader.
7. Statistical figures (i.e., drawings such as bar graphs) are best used to present important data, especially striking data that might be otherwise overlooked in a table of statistical values. Use these sparingly.
8. Statistical symbols (i.e., t, df, and p) should be italicized.
9. Use proper case for each statistical symbol. For example, a lowercase *"f"* stands for frequency, but an uppercase *"F"* is an inferential statistic.
10. Follow rules and be consistent in deciding when to use numerals and when to spell out numbers. Spell out numbers that start sentences.
11. Qualitative results should be organized and the organization made clear to the reader.

Source: "Guidelines for Writing Results Section and Analysis" adapted from *Writing Empirical Research Reports: A Basic Guide for Students of the Social and Behavioral Sciences*, 3rd ed by F. Pyrczak and R.R. Bruce, 2003, pp. 85–90.

Finally, the participants should be described in terms of any specific variables of interest in the study. For example, if a knowledge test were administered, minimum and maximum scores along with the mean score should be reported for the group as a whole. If body fat analyses were being conducted, then it would be appropriate to describe the mean body fat levels of the group along with minimum and maximum body fat levels. If subgroup comparisons are being made, between genders, for example, the mean scores for each subgroup can be reported either in this section or in the "Results" section of Chapter IV as the specific research questions and hypotheses are being presented.

Results

As the name implies, the "Results" section is where the actual results of the research study are presented. This section should be organized based on the research questions and/or hypotheses that were specified in Chapter I. Essentially, all research questions and hypotheses from Chapter I must be addressed in Chapter IV. Conversely, if there is no research question or hypothesis on a topic in Chapter I, it should not be discussed in Chapter IV.

From a format perspective, each research question and hypothesis or null hypothesis is repeated, and then information pertaining to that specific research question or hypothesis is presented. Descriptive statistics such as percentages, means, medians, modes, standard deviations, and ranges may be sufficient to answer some research questions. When hypotheses have been developed, inferential statistics must be presented along with the descriptive statistics. According to the American Psychological Association (APA) (2010), "When reporting inferential statistics (e.g., t tests, F tests, x^2, and associated effect sizes and confidence intervals), include sufficient information to allow the reader to fully understand the analyses conducted. The data supplied, preferably in the text

hypothesis that pertains to demographic information, it still needs to be reported. When there is a long list of demographic information, it can usually be included in a table (see Table 12.3). Even so, it still must be highlighted in the text.

Table 12.3   Sample Demographic Table

Summary of the Demographic Characteristics of the Sample of Asian Indian Students ($n = 185$)

Variable	Frequency (*n*)	Percent
Gender		
1. Male	114	61.6
2. Female	71	38.4
Educational status		
1. Undergraduate	14	7.6
2. Graduate	77	41.6
3. Doctoral	91	49.2
4. Post-doctoral	3	1.6
Parent institution		
1. University of Cincinnati	74	40.0
2. Ohio State University	111	60.0
Have you ever consulted a health care provider for psychological (mental and/or emotional) issues?		
1. Yes	21	11.4
2. No	164	88.6
Have you ever consulted a health care provider for psychological (mental and/or emotional) issues in the past one year?		
1. Yes	9	4.9
2. No	176	95.1

Source: Atri, A. (2007). Role of social support, hardiness, and acculturation as predictors of mental health among international students of Asian Indian origin in Ohio. Unpublished master's thesis, University of Cincinnati. Reprinted with permission.

but possibly in an online supplemental archive depending on the magnitude of the data arrays, should allow the reader to confirm the basic reported analyses (e.g., cell means, standard deviations, sample sizes, and correlations) and should enable the interested reader to construct some effect-size estimates and confidence intervals beyond those supplied in the paper per se" (p. 116). It is important to completely and thoroughly present this information even if no significant effect is being reported. See Box 12.3 for a list of what should be included when reporting the results related to a research question or hypothesis in Chapter IV.

Once a format is established, it is essentially repeated for each question, objective, and/or hypothesis. The writing for this section is very precise but also somewhat rote. In most theses and dis-

sertations this section contains only results with no interpretation or discussion from the researcher. In writing about the "Results" section of Chapter IV, Manning and colleagues (2003) describe it as "A straight forward presentation of outcomes; nothing should be 'read into the data,' and no interpretations of meaning should be forwarded here" (p. 24). Interpretation and discussion are included in the next section of Chapter IV or in Chapter V. Some academic programs, however, combine the writing of the results with discussion. Students should be sure to determine their program's preferred method of writing before beginning this section.

Tables are usually included in Chapter IV to fully explain data and relationships of interest. Tables provide exact numerical data and are organized in columns and rows so that data can be

> **Box 12.3   Outline for Reporting Findings Related to a Hypothesis**
>
> - Repeat hypothesis or null hypothesis (usually not both)
> - Report relevant data related to variables identified in hypothesis
> - Identify statistical test and report its outcome (use publication style manual to determine format)
> - Include any relevant tables or figures
> - State the decision to reject or not reject the null hypothesis
> - Based on null hypothesis decision, state findings or conclusion(s)

quickly and easily comprehended. Typically, it is more efficient to use tables than to present large amounts of data in the narrative. Students should use caution, however, and not include too many tables. When an excessive number of tables are included, readers may find it difficult to follow the narrative without losing track of the message. In addition, layout may be difficult as text is constantly being broken by tables, and tables are more expensive to publish. For that reason, reserve tables for crucial data that are directly related to the study's content and for simplifying text that otherwise would be dense with numbers (APA, 2010). Also, when developing tables, be sure to follow formatting requirements for the specific publication manual guidelines approved by your program.

Let us now consider a few examples of research questions and hypotheses and how results might be presented in Chapter IV. Remember that these are just examples; different programs might have slight variations in the way they wish results to be presented. As always, it is a good idea to seek the input of your committee chair before progressing too far with writing results to make sure your approach is acceptable to the program.

RESEARCH QUESTIONS WITHOUT HYPOTHESES

First, let us examine a sample research question that does not require hypotheses. A research question,

for example, might ask, "How are health promotion and education programs offered through faith-based communities coordinated or managed?" Notice that the question is *not* asking about relationships or differences between groups; therefore, only descriptive statistics are needed to answer this question. The results written for this research question might look something like the following:

> Based on data collected in this study 167 (57%) of faith communities indicated there was a coordinator for their health promotion and education programs. As a whole, clergy ($n = 102$, 35%) were most likely to coordinate health promotion and education programs followed by 59 (20%) listed as other, 33 (11%) parish nurses, 25 (9%) health committees, 11 (4%) health educators and 5 (2%) health ministers. Of those who indicated "other" coordinators, those mentioned were secretaries, wedding coordinators, church members, officers, deacons, retired nurses, wellness coordinators or directors, members with degrees in health care or counseling, or the responsibility fell to another type of church committee such as athletics, senior ministry, or compassionate ministry. (Walter, 2007)

Now go back and reread the research question. Does this response answer that question? Do you now know who tends to coordinate or manage health promotion and education programs in faith-based communities responding to this survey?

HYPOTHESIS WITH SIGNIFICANT FINDINGS

For this example, suppose a researcher was trying to determine if participating in relaxation activities prior to taking final exams increased final exam grades. The researcher might state the hypothesis as follows: "Those students participating in relaxation activities prior to taking their final exam will score higher on the exam than will those students not participating in relaxation activities prior to taking their final exam."

The results related to this hypothesis might read as follows:

> Those students participating in relaxation activities scored an average of 86.8% on the final exam, and those students not participating in relaxation

activities scored an average of 82%. Using a *t*-test, this difference of 4.8 percentage points was determined to be significant ($t\{3\} = 3.11$, $p = 0.02$ {one-tailed}). Based on the results of this study, Null Hypothesis #1, which stated that there will be no difference in final exam grades between those students participating in relaxation activities prior to taking their final exam and those students not participating in relaxation activities prior to taking their final exam, was rejected. It was therefore concluded that differences in final exam scores do exist between those students participating in relaxation activities prior to taking their final exam and those students not participating in relaxation activities prior to taking their final exam. Students participating in relaxation activities prior to taking their final exam scored better on the final exam than students not participating in relaxation activities prior to taking the final exam.

Note in the above example that the reporting of results began by providing descriptive statistics (mean test scores) for both groups. Next the statistical test was identified (*t*-test), and the specific results of the test were provided ($t\{3\} = 3.11$, $p = 0.02$ {one-tailed}). At this point, the meaning of the statistical test in terms of the null hypothesis is provided. Finally, conclusions are specifically stated related to the final exam scores for the two groups of students.

HYPOTHESIS WITHOUT SIGNIFICANT FINDINGS

For this example, let us consider the same hypothesis as stated above: "Those students participating in relaxation activities prior to taking their final exam will score higher on the exam than will those students not participating in relaxation activities prior to taking their final exam." In this example, however, we will present the results as if there are no significant findings.

The description of the results for this hypothesis might be written as follows:

Those students participating in relaxation activities scored an average of 86.8% on the final exam, and those students not participating in relaxation activities scored an average of 85.8%. Using a *t*-test, this difference of one percentage

point was determined not to be significant ($t\{3\} = 1.11$, $p = 0.42$ {one-tailed}). Based on the results of this study, Null Hypothesis #1, which stated that there will be no difference in final exam grades between those students participating in relaxation activities prior to taking their final exam and those students not participating in relaxation activities prior to taking their final exam, was not rejected. Based on these data, it was concluded that there were no differences in final exam scores between those students participating in relaxation activities prior to taking their final exam and those students not participating in relaxation activities prior to taking their final exam. Students participating in relaxation activities prior to taking their final exam scored about the same on the final exam as did students not participating in relaxation activities prior to taking the final exam.

CORRELATIONAL STUDY

In this example the researcher is trying to determine if there is a relationship between skin cancer knowledge and reported sun protection behaviors of state-employed lifeguards. Because the hypothesis is seeking to determine if a relationship exists between two variables, this would be a correlational study. The research question might be written as follows: "To what extent is knowledge of skin cancer related to sun protection behaviors among state-employed lifeguards?" A hypothesis related to this research question might predict that "There will be a positive relationship between skin cancer knowledge and sun protection behaviors among state-employed lifeguards." Notice that this is a directional hypothesis. By taking out the word "positive," the hypothesis could have been nondirectional.

The description of the results for this particular research question and hypothesis may look like the following:

The mean skin cancer knowledge score for this population of state-employed lifeguards was 15.2 on a scale of 20, with 20 indicating a perfect score. Sun protection behaviors were rated on a scale from 0 to 10, with 10 indicating someone who was practicing all sun protection behaviors.

For this population the mean sun protection score was 7.1. A Pearson product correlation was calculated on the two variables of skin cancer knowledge and sun protection behavior. The calculated r value was 0.58 with a p value of 0.001. The null hypothesis, which stated that there would be no relationship between skin cancer knowledge and sun protection behaviors among state-employed lifeguards, was rejected. These results indicate that there is a moderately strong positive correlation between skin cancer knowledge and sun protection behaviors and that this correlation is significantly different from a correlation of zero. In summary, as either skin cancer knowledge or sun protection behavior scores increase, the other variable tends to increase as well.

Box 12.4 provides several opportunities for students to practice reporting research results. Work through these four scenarios using the above examples as templates.

Discussion, Conclusions, and/or Summary

The final section of Chapter IV is sometimes called "Discussion" but may also be called "Conclusions" or "Summary." Essentially, the purpose of this section is to recap the findings from the "Results" section in a more concise form without repeating specific statistical information. Someone without a

---

Box 12.4   Writing Research Results

Scenario #1

Research Question: What factors contribute to parental use of child seat belts?

Hypothesis 1: Female parent child seat belt attitude scores will be higher than male parent child seat belt attitude scores.

Results:

87 = Female parent mean child seat belt attitude score

85 = Male parent mean child seat belt attitude score

$t = 1.87$ $df = 22$ $p = 0.765$

Write a one- to two-paragraph report to fully explain these results using the examples in the text as templates.

Scenario #2

What if instead of the above results, the following results were obtained? Write a one- to two-paragraph report to fully explain these results.

Results:

88 = Female parent mean child seat belt attitude score

75 = Male parent mean child seat belt attitude score

$t = 4.02$ $df = 22$ $p = 0.023$

Scenario #3: Stretch Yourself

This example uses a statistic not discussed in this text but that should be covered in your statistics course. If you have completed statistics, write these results as you think they should be written.

Research Question: What factors contribute to parental use of child seat belts?

Hypothesis 2: There will be differences in parental child seat belt attitude scores based on socioeconomic status.

Results:

99 = High SES

88 = Moderate SES

77 = Low SES

ANOVA $p = 0.037$

Tukey test results

High vs. Moderate = 0.462

High vs. Low = 0.009

Low vs. Moderate = 0.033

Scenario #4

Suppose we wanted to look at gender (male, female) and socioeconomic status (high, moderate, low) with regard to parental child seat belt attitude scores. Develop a table with the appropriate headings to present these results visually.

strong statistical background might better understand the findings of the study by reading this condensed section of results than by reading the complete "Results" section. When writing the "Results" section of Chapter IV, the researcher provided a straightforward presentation of the data and analysis with no interpretation of their meaning. Nothing should be written that cannot be supported by the data. In this final section of Chapter IV, the researcher may sometimes add interpretation. Some academic programs encourage interpretation and discussion at this point, but others prefer this section to be more of a summary, leaving all the interpretation and discussion to Chapter V. Because programs do differ in how the last section of Chapter IV should be written, it is a good idea to read several completed theses or dissertations from your program to observe how your program prefers this section to be written. Of course, your committee chair should also be consulted. An example of a Chapter IV "Discussion" section that provides a fairly straightforward recap of findings can be seen in Box 12.5.

Summary

In this chapter we reviewed the development of a thesis or dissertation's Chapter III. With the preliminary drafts of Chapters I, II, and III completed along with a near complete draft of any instrumentation to be utilized in the study, the thesis or dissertation proposal is complete and ready for presentation at a formal proposal hearing/presentation. This is, of course, if the committee chair and committee members feel the student is ready to propose. Information was presented on formal proposal hearings and presentations and what to expect in this process.

In the next section of this chapter, we discussed what needs to be done before one can begin to write Chapter IV of the thesis or dissertation. Information is included on data entry, data cleaning, data analysis, and selecting the appropriate statistical

test(s). This section is intentionally brief as it is assumed that students will obtain most of their statistical information in other classes.

Writing Chapter IV of a thesis or dissertation is the next major section of this chapter. This section lists the information to be included related to study participants. Essentially, three things must be included in this section: (1) a description of how the participants were selected and all information pertaining to their selection and decision to participate; (2) a description of the demographic characteristics of the participants (gender, age, race, occupation, etc.); and (3) a description of the subjects based on specific characteristics related to the study (knowledge level, attitude scores, behavioral scores, stage of change, height, body fat, cholesterol level, etc.).

Following the section on study participants, the actual results of the study are presented. This section should be organized around the research questions, hypotheses, and/or objectives written in Chapter I. This is usually a very straightforward presentation of results with no interpretation or discussion. Several sample write-ups of results are included as examples for students to follow.

The final section of this chapter provided a brief overview of the discussion, summary, or conclusion section of Chapter IV. Different academic programs may have varying expectations for this section of the chapter, so students are encouraged to follow the guidelines established by their respective programs.

Review Questions

1. List the major section headings that would be included in Chapter III of a thesis or dissertation.
2. Discuss why it is important to include so much detail in the procedures section of Chapter III.
3. What is a proposal? What is a proposal hearing? Who is invited or may attend a proposal hearing? What is discussed in a proposal hearing?

Box 12.5   Sample Discussion Section

Based on data collected in this study, the majority (95%) of faith communities in the Greater Cincinnati Consolidated Metropolitan Statistical Area (GCCMSA) offered at least one health promotion and education program within the past two years and most offered between 2 and 19 different programs. Faith communities with higher attitude scores toward health promotion and education tended to offer a larger number of health promotion and education programs when compared to those with lower attitude scores. Faith communities that were Catholic, larger in size, non-Caucasian, had a program coordinator, had higher attitude scores, had larger annual health budgets, had more members with greater than a high school education, and had a younger congregation with a higher mean number of different programs. Faith community clergy coordinated programs mainly for their members using a variety of resources. Programs most likely to be offered were spiritual health programs, blood pressure screenings, aerobics classes, basketball, and food and clothing pantries.

When health promotion and education programs were not offered in faith communities, the most common barriers reported included lack of money, lack of time, and a lack of priority for faith community leadership.

Most faith communities partnered to offer health promotion and education programs. Faith communities with a coordinator, high attitude score, non-Caucasian congregation, and a larger annual health budget were most likely to collaborate with others. Collaborations occurred with faith communities of the same or different denominations as well as with community agencies. Faith communities with a coordinator, that had a high attitude score, that were larger in size, that were non-Caucasian, and that had an annual health budget greater than $500 were more likely to collaborate with other community agencies.

Most of the respondents perceived health problems and detrimental health behaviors as more serious within the community than within their congregations. Detrimental health behaviors most often reported in faith communities were alcohol abuse, drug abuse, and stress. The majority of respondents agreed that physical and spiritual health were closely related and that the prevention of health problems was the faith community's responsibility. The majority of respondents also felt that detrimental health behaviors impacted spiritual health, that it was the responsibility of the faith community to take an active role to improve the health behaviors of members, and that God desired for the faith community to take a more active role in preventing health problems. Most faith community leaders felt they had expertise to initiate health promotion and education programs for their congregation and that there were lay leaders available to organize and lead health promotion and education programs for the congregation.

In contrast, some respondents believed faith communities should only be concerned about the spiritual health of their congregation and not about the physical health. Many felt there were plenty of community resources available to improve the health behaviors of their congregation without involving faith communities.

Respondents felt religious faith was an important element to help congregation members change unhealthy behaviors, but they were unsure if prevention programs were more effective when presented in the faith community than when presented at other community agencies. Respondents also had no opinion of whether health behavior would best be impacted when initiated within the faith community.

Source: Walter, Julia L. (2007). Determining attitude toward and level of involvement in health promotion and education programs in faith communities in the Greater Cincinnati Consolidated Metropolitan Statistical Area. Unpublished master's thesis, University of Cincinnati.

How does a proposal hearing differ from a committee meeting and formal presentation?

4. Describe what is meant by "cleaning the data."

5. Explain the four different levels of measurement.

6. What factors help one to determine which statistical applications are most appropriate?

7. If we wanted to compare the mean sleep satisfaction scores of employees depending on whether they work days, evenings, or nights, what statistical test might we use? Why?

8. A hypothesis for a study reads, "There will be a relationship between self-concept scores (interval data) and health behavior scores (interval data) among high school females." What statistical procedure might be used to test this hypothesis? Why?

9. Explain what needs to be included when reporting inferential statistics.

References

American Psychological Association (APA). (2010). *Publication manual* (6th ed.). Washington, D.C.: American Psychological Association.

Atri, A. (2007). Role of social support, hardiness, and acculturation as predictors of mental health among international students of Asian Indian origin in Ohio. Unpublished master's thesis, University of Cincinnati.

Blaxter, L., Hughes, C., & Tight, M. (2002). *How to research* (2nd ed.). Philadelphia: Open University Press.

Gay, L.R., Mills, G.E., & Airasian, P. (2006). *Educational research: Competencies for analysis and applications*. Upper Saddle River, N.J.: Pearson Education, Inc.

Manning, T., Algozzine, B., & Antonak, R. (2003). *Guide for preparing a thesis or dissertation*. Morgantown, W.Va.: PNG Publications.

Patten, M.L. (2009). *Understanding research methods* (7th ed.). Glendale, Calif: Pryczak Publishing.

Pryczak, F., & Bruce, R.R. (2007). *Writing empirical research reports: A basic guide for students of the social and behavioral sciences* (7th ed.). Glendale, Calif. Pryczak Publishing.

Schloss, P.J., & Smith, M.A. (1999). *Conducting research*. Upper Saddle River, N.J.: Merrill/Prentice Hall.

Stevens, J.P. (2009). *Applied multivariate statistics for the social sciences* (5th ed.). New York: Routledge.

Walter, J.L. (2007). Determining attitude toward and level of involvement in health promotion and education programs in faith communities in the Greater Cincinnati Consolidated Metropolitan Statistical Area. Unpublished master's thesis, University of Cincinnati.

Wiersma, W., & Jurs, S.G. (2009). *Research methods in education: An introduction*. Boston, Mass: Pearson/Allyn and Bacon.

CHAPTER 13 | Conclusions, Discussion, and Recommendations (Writing Chapter V)

Chapter Objectives

After reading this chapter and answering the review questions, you should be able to:

1. Discuss the importance of the research findings.
2. Place the research findings in the context of current literature.
3. Discuss the implications of the research findings for health education practice.
4. Compare and contrast the research findings with other relevant research.
5. Identify the strengths and weaknesses of the research study.
6. Make recommendations to improve the research.
7. Make recommendations for future research stemming from the research study.

Key Terms

abstract	bibliography of related readings	discussion
acknowledgments	conclusions	recommendations
appendices	defense hearing	

At this point you have collected your data, conducted your data analysis, and written your results in Chapter IV of your thesis or dissertation. Writing the results in Chapter IV is fairly prescriptive. In other words, your results have been reported in a straightforward manner that is acceptable to your committee and conforms to style manual guidelines. In Chapter V, which is typically titled "Summary, Conclusions, and Recommendations," or just "Conclusions and Recommendations," you will do a more in-depth analysis of the results. Your own ideas, interpretations, and explanations of the results can now be shared with the reader, but remember, anything said should be supported by the data. As Leedy and Ormrod (2010) note,

All too frequently, researchers believe that, having once presented the facts and figures, they have done all that needs to be done. To display the data is certainly important, but as we have said so many times before, the *interpretation of the data* is the essence of research. Without inquiring into the intrinsic meaning of the data, no resolution of the research problem or its subproblems is possible (p. 295).

The purpose of Chapter V is to provide the reader with a thorough understanding of what the results really mean to professional practice and to the field as a whole. In the process, you will critique your own research, identifying its strengths and weaknesses, and make suggestions for future research in the area you studied.

Hittleman and Simon (2002) have identified questions that readers should be able to answer after reading the discussion section of a research article. These same questions (with minor modifications) would apply to Chapter V of a thesis or dissertation. They are:

1) What were the researchers' purposes for the study?
2) What were the researchers' major results?
3) How did researchers interpret their results?
4) What recommendations did the researchers make for applying the results to practice situations or for future research projects?
5) Are the researchers' issues and concerns relevant to me as a professional or to my practice setting? (Hittleman and Simon, 2002, p. 228)

In discussing how to evaluate the final chapter of a thesis or dissertation, Gay, Mills, and Airasian (2006) recommend using the following guidelines:

- Is each result discussed in terms of the original hypothesis or topic to which it relates?
- Is each result discussed in terms of its agreement or disagreement with previous results obtained by other researchers in other studies?
- Are generalizations consistent with the results?
- Are the possible effects of uncontrolled variables on the results discussed?
- Are theoretical and practical implications of the findings discussed?
- Are recommendations for future action made?
- Are suggestions for future action based on practical significance or on statistical significance only (i.e., has the author avoided confusing practical and statistical significance)? (p. 544)

When writing Chapter V of a thesis or dissertation, it is a good idea to refer back to these questions and guidelines to see how one's own work measures up.

Interpreting and Analyzing Research Results

Interpreting and analyzing research results is an important skill. Not only is it important in evaluating your own research in Chapter V, but it is also important in reading and critiquing the research

---

Box 13.1   Erroneous Interpretation of Findings

The following findings are related to bread consumption:

1. More than 98% of convicted felons are bread eaters.
2. Fully half of all children who grow up in bread-consuming households score below average on statistical tests.
3. In the 18th century, when virtually all bread was baked in the home, the average life expectancy was less than 50 years; infant mortality rates were unacceptably high; many women died in childbirth; and diseases such as typhoid, yellow fever, and influenza ravaged whole nations.
4. More than 90% of violent crimes in the U.S. are committed within 24 hours of eating bread.
5. Bread is made from a substance called "dough." It has been proven that as little as one pound of dough can be used to suffocate a mouse. The average person eats more bread than that in one month.
6. Bread has been proven to be addictive. Subjects deprived of bread and given only water begged for bread after only two days.

As a result of these findings, the following restrictions on bread are proposed:

1. No sale of bread to minors.
2. No advertising of bread within 1,000 feet of a school.
3. A 300% federal tax on all bread to pay for all the societal ills associated with bread.
4. No animal or human images, nor any primary colors (which may appeal to children), may be used to promote bread usage.
5. A $40.2 billion fine on the three biggest bread manufacturers.

—Author unknown

of others throughout your career (Hittleman and Simon, 2002; McMillan & Wergin, 2002). If a researcher were to take legitimate research results and either interpret them incorrectly or overstate the importance of the research, the value of the entire study would be diminished or completely lost. Consider the tongue-in-cheek example seen in Box 13.1. In reality, the findings stated in the first six points related to bread consumption are probably true. The author, however, interprets the findings incorrectly and believes them to be more important than they really are. As a result, the author proposes restrictions on bread that are preposterous. Although this example is certainly fictitious, it points out how research results can be misinterpreted and how these fallacious results can even be used to establish policy. See Boxes 13.2 and 13.3 for additional examples of erroneous conclusions. Although these are extreme examples, researchers should be aware of misinterpreting or overstating the importance of findings as they write Chapter V. New researchers in particular often have a tendency to overstate their findings.

Box 13.2   Erroneous Conclusions

The mad scientist

There once was a scientist doing an experiment on the reactions of fleas. He had trained a flea to jump on command. The scientist would command the flea, "Jump, flea!" and the flea would jump. Then the scientist would proceed to pull off one of the flea's legs with a pair of tweezers and write a comment in his notebook.

The scientist did this many times until the flea had only one leg left. The scientist said, "Jump, flea!" and the flea made its best effort to jump, which the scientist recorded in his notebook.

After he pulled off its last leg, the scientist again commanded the flea to jump, and after repeating the command many times without the flea responding, he jotted down in his notebook, "After the flea loses all its legs, it becomes completely deaf."

—Author unknown

Box 13.3   The Final Word on Nutrition and Health

The Japanese eat little fat and suffer fewer heart attacks than the British or Americans.

The French eat a lot of fat and also suffer fewer heart attacks than the British or Americans.

The Chinese drink very little red wine and suffer fewer heart attacks than the British or Americans.

The Italians drink excessive amounts of red wine and also suffer fewer heart attacks than the British or Americans.

The Germans drink lots of beer and eat lots of sausages and fat and suffer fewer heart attacks than the British or Americans.

Conclusion: Eat and drink what you like. Speaking English is apparently what kills you!

—Author unknown

Chapter V of a thesis or dissertation typically consists of four sections: introduction, conclusions, discussion, and recommendations. Each of these four sections will now be discussed.

Introduction

The introduction to Chapter V should be somewhat longer than the introduction to previous chapters. This is because the introduction to Chapter V usually provides the reader with a brief summary of the previous four chapters. That way, if readers are trying to obtain a quick understanding of the thesis or dissertation, they can accomplish this by perusing Chapter V and will not need to hunt through all five chapters to find the basic information they need. As in previous chapters, the introduction to Chapter V should contain a repeat of the problem or purpose statement worded exactly as it appeared in Chapter I. Remember, the first four chapters are already completed, so the introduction to Chapter V should be written in past tense.

Conclusions

The **"Conclusions"** section of Chapter V should briefly restate the results as stated in Chapter IV. If a summary was included in Chapter IV, it can often be used with some modifications and enhancements as the "Conclusions" section of Chapter V. The purpose of repeating the conclusions is to give readers an idea of what was presented in Chapter IV without having them read that entire chapter. There is no need to present the specific data again or to include tables or figures in the "Conclusions" section of Chapter V. If readers wish this level of detail, they can always refer back to Chapter IV. The "Conclusions" section of Chapter V should be written in a fairly straightforward manner with little or no interpretation or explanation by the researcher. Again, because these results have

already been obtained, they should be presented in past tense.

Discussion

In the **"Discussion"** section of Chapter V (or at the end of Chapter IV), you can finally analyze your findings or lack of findings. Why do you think your results turned out the way they did? Were your results what you predicted? Possible explanations should be proposed for the results you obtained. Be sure to link your results to any theoretical framework you used to develop your research questions and hypotheses. If theory was used in developing your research proposal, then your research results must be discussed in relation to that theory. As Dorsten (1996) notes, "A well-prepared, deduc-

---

Box 13.4   Theory-Based Discussion

Given that younger women are not usually diagnosed with breast cancer, it is likely that they would not feel susceptible to the disease and thus would be less likely to engage in breast self-examination. Inasmuch, participants in this study who strongly agreed with statements about susceptibility to breast cancer on the Health Belief Model (HBM) questionnaire also reported a higher stage of readiness to perform breast self-examination (BSE).

Confidence in performing BSE was another HBM variable also related to higher stage readiness to perform BSE in this study. Participants who reported that they felt confident they could find breast lumps with BSE; could follow the correct steps for doing BSE; and knew how to use the correct part of their fingers when examining the breasts, tended to be in a higher stage of change. In fact, confidence in performing BSE was the HBM variable with the strongest relationship to stage of change. This finding was supported by previous studies that found associations between confidence in performing BSE and increased performance of BSE in college-aged women (Hailey, Lalor, Byrne, & Starling, 1992; Ronis & Kaiser, 1989).

Other HBM variables were also found to be associated with a higher stage of change. These additional variables included benefits and general health motivation. More specifically, participants who believed BSE would allow them to find breast cancer early, cause them to feel good about themselves, and cause them to worry less about breast cancer tended to be in a higher stage of change, as did participants who were mindful about their general health by exercising, eating balanced meals, and seeking out new health information.

Champion (1994) found similar findings in a study on HBM variables and compliance with mammography screening guidelines. Women who complied with mammography screening guidelines had higher HBM scores on seriousness, benefits, and health motivation....

Source: Collins, C. (2005). Correlates of breast self-examination: Application of the Transtheoretical Model of Change and the Health Belief Model. Unpublished master's thesis, University of Cincinnati.

tive research report also describes how the theory (and hypothesis) assists in the interpretation of the study findings, and whether the findings support or refute the theory" (p. 177). See Box 13.4 for an excerpt from Chapter V of a thesis dealing with breast self-examination that was based on the health belief model and the Transtheoretical Model of behavior change.

Next, the findings of your study need to be placed in perspective with other studies on the same or closely related topics in the literature. Comparisons and contrasts should be made with other studies on the topic. How are your results similar to or different from those of other studies? Based on the literature, are your results what might be expected? In addition to examining similarities and differences, you should also provide plausible explanations of why your results might differ from other studies (see Box 13.5 for an example). Any studies used to compare and contrast with your research should always be cited using the guidelines of your program's approved style manual.

Writing the "Discussion" section involves some in-depth thinking and contemplation. Look for differences in research methodology and/or populations studied to pose and answer questions about your research. To write this section well, students must fully understand the results of their own research and the literature related to their research. With this level of understanding, a thorough and thought-provoking discussion of one's research can be presented.

Box 13.5   Comparing and Contrasting Studies

The data demonstrated that there was no clear relationship between the type of sexuality education students in junior and senior high school received and their sexual knowledge, attitudes, and behaviors by the time they were college age. As was demonstrated by the overall low sexual knowledge scores, students who participated in either abstinence-focused sexuality education or comprehensive sexuality education appeared to be unprepared overall regarding their knowledge of contraception and STIs.

The attitudes and behaviors of students in both groups tended to be very similar. Assertions by those favoring abstinence-focused education that students in these classes would have a more positive attitude toward sexuality (Cook, 1994) were not confirmed. Assertions by those favoring abstinence-focused sexuality education that comprehensive sexuality education promotes sexual behavior (Thomas, 2000) were not confirmed.

French and Dishion (2003) confirmed the findings of other researchers that the median age of first intercourse was 13.9 for boys and 14.25 for girls. They also found that prior to first sexual intercourse many adolescents were engaging in other forms of sexual activity. Many adolescents engaged in sexual behavior with more than one partner, which significantly increased their risk for unplanned pregnancy and STIs. The data collected in this study demonstrated similar results: the mean age for initial sexual experience for students who participated in abstinence-focused sexuality education was 15.47 and the mean age for initial sexual experience for students who participated in comprehensive sexuality education was 14.25. The difference in ages of initial sexual experience between the two groups was 1.2 years, which, while not statistically significant, did approach significance and would seem to support earlier findings (Barnett & Hurst, 2003; Lonczak et al., 2002; Thomas, 2000; Wiley, 2002) of an increase in the age of initial sexual experience in students who participated in abstinence-focused sexuality education. Although there may be an initial delay in sexual activity among those in the abstinence-based programs, there is no evidence to support the contention that these students are waiting until marriage to initiate sexual activity or that their sexual behaviors differ from those receiving comprehensive sexuality education by the time they are in college.

Source: Browder, M.E.W. (2008). Sexuality education curriculum in secondary schools and its relationship to sexual knowledge, attitudes and behaviors of college students. Unpublished master's thesis, University of Cincinnati.

Recommendations

In this, the final section of Chapter V, the student gives **recommendations** to readers that are based on the thesis or dissertation work. It is often divided into three subsections: (1) recommendations for practice or implementation, (2) recommendations for improving the research, and (3) recommendations for future research. Sometimes the second and third subsections are combined. We, however, will treat them as two different subsections in this book.

Recommendations for Practice or Implementation

In the first subsection, recommendations for practice or implementation, you have the opportunity to tell readers how you feel this research contributes to the profession. In other words, how can practitioners working in schools, public health departments, voluntary agencies, corporate wellness centers, hospitals, and/or clinics benefit from and use the results of this study? For example, study results may indicate the need for more programs, question the need for existing programs, identify more effective programs, indicate a need to do better needs assessments, identify specific issues related to populations of interest, point to a new target population, indicate the need to develop innovative new approaches to a problem, and so forth.

Any recommendations for practice, however, must be firmly based on the findings from the literature review in combination with the findings of your study. It goes without saying that the study results must be true and accurate if practice is to be affected. Think of the possible implications if inaccurate study results or an inaccurate interpretation of study results were to affect professional practice in a negative way.

Remember, too, the concept of external validity. In other words, study results can only be generalized to those persons in the study population or to those persons very nearly like those in the study population (Berg & Latin, 2004). Suppose your study found a 13% reduction in cholesterol levels among men in their 50s and 60s with cholesterol levels above 300 mg who ate oatmeal on a daily basis for six months. You could not recommend oatmeal to women in their 40s with cholesterol levels in the 220 mg range. Nor could you make broad statements indicating that oatmeal consumption reduces cholesterol levels.

In addition to affecting the day-to-day practice of health education specialists, the results of some studies may suggest the need for policy changes (Manning, Algozzine, & Antonak, 2003). For example, this might include suggesting changes to the school health education requirements, company smoking policies, the selection of foods sold in vending machines, or the marketing of cancer prevention programs to senior citizens. Further, research can indicate the need for new or modified laws at the local, county, state, or national level. Perhaps new nonsmoking legislation or stiffer penalties for failing to wear seat belts are indicated.

Often, particularly in master's theses, the limited scope of the work can make it difficult to offer extensive recommendations for practice. The evidence is simply not strong enough or convincing enough for such recommendations to make sense. If this is the case, the researcher may choose to present preliminary recommendations while also being careful to note that these preliminary recommendations are based only on the results of this research. The researcher must then go on to explicitly note limitations such as scope, sample size, and return rates, and clearly state that further research needs to be completed or that this study needs to be replicated with larger samples before the preliminary recommendations can be fully accepted. In doing this, researchers are demonstrating that they have thought through the potential implications of their research and are noting how their findings could affect the profession. Yet they are also noting that these results need to be substantiated through further research before the findings can be fully accepted and the recommendations fully implemented.

It is also important to remember that study results that are not significant still can be important to the practitioner and to the profession (Manning *et al.*, 2003; Price & Murnan, 2003). The fact that an independent variable did not affect a dependent variable or that two variables are not related may be critical to future health education practice. In a very real sense, nonsignificant findings are often as important as or more important than significant findings. For this reason, students should discuss the implications of nonsignificant findings as well as significant findings.

Do not be superficial in making these recommendations. In addition to simply stating, for example, that programs should be initiated, you should, if possible, identify types of programs and ways of implementing the programs. Extend your thinking and be creative in presenting possible solutions to problems or program ideas related to professional practice. Talk about your findings with others. Brainstorm ideas with fellow students, your committee chair, and actual practitioners. See what other groups have posed as possible solutions and, if appropriate, restate their ideas. See Figure 13.1 for a sample implications section that does a thorough job of presenting possible solutions to an identified problem or need.

The following is the actual "Implications for Practice" section from a research article focusing on gender differences in sunscreen use:

These findings are suggestive of several strategies for the design of future intervention studies, many of which were used in the CDC's educational efforts and "Choose Your Cover" campaign. Although males and females overlap in salient beliefs about sunscreen use, several salient beliefs appear to be gender specific. Interventions geared at increasing current levels of sunscreen use may therefore benefit from gender-specific strategies.

For men, one strategy might seek to simply correct the belief that sunscreen comes only in fragrant and greasy formulas by educating people about the existence of brands that do not have these characteristics. A more long-term extension of this strategy might set out to convince the sunscreen industry to offer more sunscreen products tailored to the tastes and needs of men, as few such products currently exist. Another strategy might seek to change the male belief that sunscreen use is at odds with male gender roles. Such a strategy might be achieved by providing role models of strong, athletic men who use sunscreen in the company of other men. However, given deeply rooted norms against male to male body contact, it might be advisable to recommend that men rely on sunscreen for parts of the body where sunscreen can be self-applied and rely on other forms of sun protection such as a shirt for hard-to-reach parts such as the back.

Strategies to increase male sunscreen use might also be aimed at male normative beliefs. Normative strategies might seek to encourage girlfriends to encourage their male friends or boyfriends to use sunscreen. Mothers might also be encouraged to remind their sons to use sunscreen, much the same way mothers were reported to have done with their daughters.

For women, an effective strategy could play up appearance-related reasons for sunscreen use, such as preventing wrinkles, freckles, and sunspots. Such a strategy might also remind women that sunscreen is available in non–pore-clogging formulas, as this was a concern for women. This recommendation needs to come with a caveat. Using appearance to motivate women to use sunscreen, however, may have a potentially harmful unintended effect—it may encourage or reinforce face-only protection. Women who reported using makeup with sunscreen often did not report protecting other parts of their body. Therefore, any message that emphasizes appearance-related reasons for sunscreen use needs to be careful to remind women to protect the rest of their bodies as well. A normative strategy aimed at women might encourage peers, male or female, to encourage their female friends to use sunscreen.

FIGURE 13.1
Sample "Implications for Practice" section.

Source: Abroms, L., Jorgensen, C.M., Southwell, B.G., Geller, A.C., & Emmons, K.M. (2003). Gender differences in young adults' beliefs about sunscreen use. *Health Education and Behavior,* 30(1), 29–43. Reprinted with permission of Sage Publications, Inc.

Recommendations for Improving the Research

As one conducts thesis or dissertation research, there will inevitably be some things identified that could have been done better. Sometimes these are seen as weaknesses of a study and can have a significant impact on the interpretation of study results. For example, it might be that the instrument did not work as expected, the return rates were not as high as expected, or the population being studied was not cooperative. It might be that additional questions were needed on the instrument or that the instrument was too long and cumbersome. Perhaps the data collection process needs to be streamlined or the inclusion or exclusion criteria need to be modified. See Box 13.6 for an example of recommendations for improving the research.

It is important for the researcher to identify for readers any weaknesses in the study for three reasons. First, identifying weaknesses in a study and ways to improve the weaknesses demonstrates the researcher's understanding and mastery of research methodology. When weaknesses are not specifically identified and discussed in a study, it may be assumed that the researcher did not recognize the weaknesses, which could reflect poorly on the reputation of that researcher. Second, it is unethical to provide results without noting weaknesses that could have affected those results. Third, if the study were to be replicated, it prevents those replicating the study from making the same mistakes the original researcher made. In the long run, identifying

---

Box 13.6   Recommendations to Improve Study

To improve the quality of this research, a larger response rate is needed. The governing bodies of each denomination should be contacted regarding the survey and asked to officially support the research effort. A letter with the denominational endorsement could accompany each survey. The envelope could also be addressed to the clergy or person responsible for health ministries. Although not cost effective, bulk mail should be avoided since many faith communities reported throwing away these mailings without even opening them. Many faith communities reported they would prefer to be contacted by email so an online survey might yield a better response rate. Follow-up efforts could be improved by using a team of volunteers to help make the reminder phone calls in a timelier manner. The response rate may also be improved by shortening the length of the survey. Lastly, the study could be designed as either a personal or telephone interview. This would allow in-depth information to be obtained. Pastors seemed very receptive to talking about health promotion and education in relationship to their congregations and community despite their busy schedules. This relational approach may be most effective with them.

The survey instrument could be improved in several areas. When asked to identify the health promotion and education programs offered in the last two years, respondents should not be asked to identify the number of times these programs were offered. This required too much time and most respondents did not indicate the number of times, but just that they offered the programs. A standard like the O'Donnell model (Storlie et al., 1992) would be useful in categorizing the programs. The member age question should be divided into standard age groups as used in most research. It would also be helpful to find a similar standard for measuring perceived health status and attitude. If a health issue was perceived as serious, follow up to see if the faith community addressed that health concern by offering a health education program.

Source: Walter, J.L. (2007). Determining attitude toward and level of involvement in health promotion and education programs in faith communities in the Greater Cincinnati Consolidated Metropolitan Statistical Area. Unpublished master's thesis, University of Cincinnati.

those things that could have been done better in a study can serve to improve future research efforts.

Recommendations for Future Research

The final section of Chapter V presents recommendations for future research in the area being studied. Given the work that has been completed, what new questions have been generated? For example, suppose the researcher did not find significant results but was very close to obtaining significance. The researcher might recommend repeating the study using a larger sample size. Or suppose the researcher found significant results using a population of middle-class Caucasians. The researcher might suggest repeating the research with other population groups such as African Americans, Hispanics, or Caucasians in lower socioeconomic groups. If the researcher was looking at relationships between several variables and exercise status, through the process of completing the study the researcher might have identified additional variables that could be examined related to exercise status. Think of suggesting changes to the demographic variables, population groups, independent variables, dependent variables, instrumentation, and methodology when writing this section of the thesis/dissertation. See Box 13.7 for a sample of recommendations for future research.

"Recommendations for Future Research" is an important section because it often helps guide other researchers interested in your topic as well as future graduate students searching for their own study topic. In essence, you are the expert in this area. Who better than you to recommend the direction of future research in your area of expertise?

References

Following Chapter V is a listing of all citations used in writing the thesis/dissertation. Most of the citations will be in the literature review chapter

---

Box 13.7   Future Research Example

The need exists for conducting future studies exploring the relationships between social support, acculturation, and hardiness with mental health. Future studies should attempt to increase the sample size and incorporate more universities. Moreover, attempts should be made to replicate this study and compare the data within public funded and private owned institutions. Studies focusing solely on the significant predictor constructs, namely commitment and control in the case of hardiness, belonging in the case of social support, and perceived prejudice in the case of acculturation, should be conducted in order to further strengthen the results obtained from this study. Studies also need to be done on other Asian student populations like Chinese, Korean, and so on....

Mental health can be approached from multiple angles and directions and there remain a large number of possible variables that were not explored in this study. Religiosity, physical functioning, work environment, affectivity, sense of coherence, coping, and mastery had all been defined as predictors of mental health at some point in time (Hooker, Monahan, Bowman, Frazier, & Shifren, 1998; Parks, 1990; Vega & Rumbaut, 1991). It would be worthwhile for future studies in this field to explore the relationships between these variables and mental health.

Source: Atri, A. (2007). Role of social support, hardiness and acculturation as predictors of mental health among the international students of Asian Indian origin in Ohio. Unpublished master's thesis, University of Cincinnati.

(Chapter II), but there may be additional citations found in the other chapters. If you have kept a running list of citations throughout the writing process, as was suggested in Chapter 3 of this book, it is now very easy to place a heading on that list and insert it into the thesis/dissertation. Even so, you will still want to check the reference list for accuracy. Leaf through the thesis or dissertation page by page, marking off each citation in the reference list as it appears in the text. Remember, only those sources that are actually cited in the thesis/dissertation are listed as references. Some programs may require students to include a **bibliography of related readings** as well as a reference list of citations in the thesis/dissertation (Manning *et al.,* 2003). This would include everything the student read in preparing the thesis/dissertation, whether or not it was cited in the work.

Appendices

Following the reference list are any **appendices** that need to be included with the thesis or dissertation. Any materials relevant to replication of the study should be appended (Manning *et al.,* 2003). "A rule of thumb is that *the material appearing in the appendix enables the reader to go further in understanding the method and or results if so desired.* For instance an appendix may include informed consent letters, questionnaires, and other measurement instruments, response sheets, field notes, statistical computations or extensive data tables" (Leedy & Ormrod, 2010, p. 302). Remember that all appendices should be referenced within the text of the thesis/dissertation and are presented in the order in which they are mentioned.

Frontmatter

At this point you should go back and add to the front of the thesis or dissertation any additional required materials that could not be developed until the remainder of the document was written. This would include an abstract, a table of contents, a list of tables, a list of figures, and perhaps an acknowledgments page.

An **abstract** is a summary of the thesis or dissertation that is usually placed on a separate page following the title page. Abstracts of dissertations and theses are usually 350 words or less. Abstracts for journal articles are even shorter, with most journals restricting the abstract to 100–200 words. The abstract should contain a brief statement of the purpose of the research and perhaps the hypotheses, a brief description of the methodology and population being studied, and highlights of the results. If theory is used in the study, the theory should also be mentioned (Pryczak & Bruce, 2007). Abstracts are often one of the last items written for a thesis or dissertation, but also one of the more important items. "Remember, the abstract you write is likely to be included in one or more abstract collections (e.g., *Dissertation Abstracts International* and/or published collections of abstracts specific to your academic discipline) that then become available at many research libraries around the world. It is essential, therefore, that you take seriously the task of writing the abstract and describe your project as clearly, precisely, and succinctly as possible" (Leedy & Ormrod, 2010, p. 299) (see Box 13.8).

The **acknowledgments** page allows students to recognize and thank those people who have been most helpful with the thesis or dissertation process. Typically this is an optional page that students can choose to include if they wish. Most students that develop an acknowledgments page recognize the committee chair and committee members for their assistance, any funding agents or sponsors of the research, colleagues or fellow researchers that helped along the way, and secretaries or typists. It is also common for spouses or other family members and friends who provided support and encouragement to be mentioned. Be careful, however, not to make the acknowledgments list too long. Remember that this is for those persons who provided the most direct assistance and support for the thesis/dissertation, not for Aunt Tilly who read books to you when you were four years old. Listing too many people in the acknowledgments section can tend to diminish the importance of being recognized for those that actually contributed to your thesis or dissertation.

The table of contents is essentially an outline of all the headings and subheadings used in the thesis or dissertation with the associated page num-

Box 13.8   Sample Abstract

The purpose of this pilot study was to compare internal and chance health locus of control and God locus of health control scores between mainstream Evangelical and nondenominational Charismatic Christians attending churches in Southwest Ohio. For this study, the United Methodist Church was used to represent mainstream Evangelical Christians. A comparison between African Americans and European Americans within the same populations was also made. The Multidimensional Health Locus of Control and God Locus of Health Control Scales were integrated into one survey for use in this study. Using stratified random sampling eight churches (four United Methodist and four nondenominational Charismatic) were selected. Two of the four in each of the two groups were predominantly African American and two were predominantly European American. Convenience sampling was used to survey adult church members before and after Sunday worship services. A total of 318 surveys (125 from United Methodist Churches and 193 from nondenominational Charismatic Churches) were obtained. Using the *t*-test, mean scores from each of the locus of control scales were compared between subgroups. Results indicated that nondenominational Charismatic Christians had a stronger belief in God locus of health control than United Methodist Christians. It also indicated that European American United Methodists had a stronger belief in chance locus of health control than African American United Methodists; however, African American United Methodists had a stronger belief in God locus of health control. Results support the significance of locus of control within the religious community and warrant consideration when developing faith or church-based health ministries or health programs. Further research of other religious groups was recommended.

Source: Williams, P.B. (2004). A pilot study comparing Health Locus of Control and God Locus of Health Control scores between African American and European American Christians attending mainstream evangelical and non-denominational charismatic churches in Southwest Ohio. Unpublished master's thesis, University of Cincinnati.

ber where that section is located. For each chapter, all headings and subheadings are listed. Obviously, the table of contents is the last page to be completed when writing a thesis/dissertation. All other pages with page numbers must be in place before the table of contents can be developed. A last check of the table of contents should always be completed prior to submitting the final thesis/dissertation document.

The list of tables and the list of figures are separate pages listing all tables and figures with their respective page numbers. If there are either no figures or no tables in a particular thesis or dissertation, these pages would be omitted.

Defense Hearing

After the thesis or dissertation is completely written and preliminary approval has been obtained

from the committee chair and committee members, a formal **defense hearing** is usually required. The defense hearing is just as the name implies: an opportunity for the student to defend the thesis or dissertation before a final decision is made by the committee to accept the work. Defense hearings are typically open to fellow students and other university faculty and administrators. In addition, family and friends can usually be invited if the student wishes to do so.

Prior to the defense hearing, the committee chair and all committee members should be provided a copy of the final document that will be used at the defense hearing. This should be given to the chair and committee members one to two weeks prior to the defense hearing so as to give them adequate time to thoroughly review the document and prepare their questions and comments for the defense.

In a defense hearing, the student usually begins by giving an overview of the thesis or dissertation, including a thorough reporting of results, conclusions, implications, and recommendations. The committee chair and committee members then question the student about the work. Students should be prepared to answer theoretical, philosophical, methodological, and statistical questions pertinent to their study. The committee may brainstorm with the student to expand on the implications and recommendations or pose alternative explanations of findings. Typically, any guests at the defense hearing are given the opportunity to ask questions after the committee has completed their questioning.

Depending on the institution, defense hearings can be very formal or fairly informal. Sometimes even at the same institution, different committee chairs may run defense hearings in different ways. Sometimes defense hearings take the form of a discussion among learned colleagues, but other defense hearings have a definite question-and-answer format. Students are encouraged to discuss the format of the defense hearing with their committee chair and former students prior to the actual hearing. It would also be a good idea to attend several defense hearings as a guest to see how they are handled at your institution and by your committee chair.

Following the questioning and discussion, the student and guests are often asked to leave the hearing room so that the committee can deliberate. In most cases a decision is reached and the students are notified at the end of the defense if they have passed.

Passing the defense does not mean that the work is completed. As a result of the questioning and discussions at the defense hearing, additional information and/or citations may need to be added to the thesis or dissertation, and portions of the document may need to be modified or rewritten. Any editorial changes or correction of errors noted by the committee members must also be completed before the final copy can be printed. The final version of the thesis or dissertation should be as near perfect as possible.

Document Preparation

Be sure to check with your program and/or the graduate school office concerning the requirements for preparing and submitting the final document. Most colleges and universities require that the final document be printed on special paper that resists fading and color changes. Multiple copies may need to be made for the university, library, college, department, and committee members. Remember, they also make great holiday gifts for family and friends (until her death, my mom still had my doctoral dissertation sitting out for all her friends at the retirement community to see).

Some colleges and universities now require an electronic submission of the thesis or dissertation either in addition to the hard copy or in place of the hard copy. Electronic submissions are typically submitted in a PDF format and can be placed on the Web for easy access. In the future, electronic submissions may eliminate the need for special paper and printing and would make completed theses and dissertations more available to other researchers and the general public. Several repositories for digital theses and dissertations exist including the Networked Digital Library of Theses and Dissertations (NDLTD) (www.ndltd.org), ProQuest (www.proquest.com/en-US), and Ohio-LINK Electronics Theses and Dissertations Center (www.ohiolink.edu/etd/).

Summary

In this chapter, we have explained in detail the writing of Chapter V of a thesis or dissertation. Information was presented on what makes a good Chapter V as well as the importance of interpreting and analyzing research results. Each section of Chapter V was then discussed in detail with samples of several important sections included as figures. The references and appendices that follow Chapter V in a thesis or dissertation were also discussed, as was the frontmatter. The chapter ended by presenting information on defense hearings and the final submission of the thesis or dissertation.

Review Questions

1. Why is interpreting and analyzing research results considered such an important skill?
2. What four sections are typically found in Chapter V?
3. Why is the introduction to Chapter V typically longer than that of other chapters?
4. Suppose you used the theory of planned behavior as the basis for your thesis or dissertation. In what section of Chapter V would you discuss your findings in relation to this theory?
5. What are the different subsections under the "Recommendations" section of Chapter V?
6. Why is it important to identify weaknesses in your research and to make recommendations to improve your research?
7. What types of materials should be included as appendices to a thesis or dissertation?
8. Explain what typically happens in a defense hearing.
9. What advantages might there be to posting electronic versions of theses or dissertations on the Web instead of printing hard copies?

References

Abroms, L., Jorgensen, C.M., Southwell, B.G., Gellar, A.C., & Emmons, K.M. (2003). Gender differences in young adults' beliefs about sunscreen use. *Health Education and Behavior,* 30(1), 29–43.

Atri, A. (2007). Role of social support, hardiness and acculturation as predictors of mental health among the international students of Asian Indian origin in Ohio. Unpublished master's thesis, University of Cincinnati.

Berg, K.E., & Latin, R.W. (2004). *Research methods in health, physical education, exercise science, and recreation.* Philadelphia: Lippincott Williams & Wilkins.

Browder, M.E.W. (2008). Sexuality education curriculum in secondary schools and its relationship to sexual knowledge, attitudes and behaviors of college students. Unpublished master's thesis, University of Cincinnati.

Collins, C. (2005). Correlates of breast self-examination: Application of the Transtheoretical Model of Change and the Health Belief Model. Unpublished master's thesis, University of Cincinnati.

Dorsten, L.E. (1996). *Interpreting social and behavioral research.* Los Angeles: Pryczak Publishing.

Gay, L.R., Mills, G.E., & Airasian, P. (2006). *Educational research: Competencies for analysis and applications.* Upper Saddle River, N.J.: Pearson Education, Inc.

Hittleman, D.R., & Simon, A.J. (2002). *Interpreting educational research: An introduction for consumers of research* (3rd ed.). Upper Saddle River, N.J.: Merrill/Prentice Hall.

Leedy, P.D., & Ormrod, J.E. (2010). *Practical research* (9th ed.). Upper Saddle River, N.J.: Pearson Education, Inc.

Manning, T., Algozzine, B., & Antonak, R. (2003). *Guide for preparing a thesis or dissertation.* Morgantown, W.Va.: PNG Publications.

McMillan, J.H., & Wergin, J.F. (2002). *Understanding and evaluating educational research* (2nd ed.). Upper Saddle River, N.J.: Merrill/Prentice Hall.

Price, J.H., & Murnan, J. (2003). The publication of negative findings—myth versus reality. *American Journal of Health Education,* 34(1), 2, 8.

Pryczak, F., & Bruce, R.R. (2007). *Writing empirical research reports: A basic guide for students of the social and behavioral sciences* (6th ed.). Los Angeles: Pryczak Publishing.

Walter, J.L. (2007). Determining attitude toward and level of involvement in health promotion and education programs in faith communities in the Greater Cincinnati Consolidated Metropolitan Statistical Area. Unpublished master's thesis, University of Cincinnati.

Williams, P.B. (2004). A pilot study comparing Health Locus of Control and God Locus of Health Control scores between African American and European American Christians attending mainstream evangelical and nondenominational charismatic churches in Southwest Ohio. Unpublished master's thesis, University of Cincinnati.

CHAPTER 14 | Sharing Your Findings (Writing Beyond Chapter V)

Chapter Objectives

After reading this chapter and answering the review questions, you should be able to:

1. Describe the importance of sharing research findings with other health education professionals.
2. Identify several different avenues for sharing one's research with other health education professionals.
3. Explain the excitement and the frustrations involved in publishing.
4. Obtain publication guidelines for a given journal.
5. Explain the importance of conducting a local review prior to submitting a manuscript for publication.
6. Describe the process a manuscript goes through once submitted to a refereed journal.
7. Develop a quantitative research article that includes the following sections: abstract, introduction, literature review, methods, results, discussion, and conclusions.
8. Explain the process one goes through to give an oral research presentation at a professional conference or meeting.
9. Discuss considerations involved in determining authorship of a research article or presentation.

Key Terms

call for papers	local review	refereed peer-reviewed journal
galley proofs	poster session	seminal works

When your thesis or dissertation is completed, it is time to disseminate the results of your work more widely so that others in the profession can share in your findings. This is a very important step in the process. Consider that if you do nothing else to present your findings after completing an unpublished thesis or dissertation, only a small handful of people will ever read and be exposed to your work (Leedy & Ormrod, 2010). All of the time and effort that went into the thesis or dissertation will essen-tially be lost. DePoy and Gitlin (2005) contend that sharing research knowledge is an essential part of research. They emphasize that, "Unless you report and disseminate, you have not completed the research process" (p. 265). Blaxter, Hughes, and Tight (2001) note that "Research without writing is of little purpose" (p. 227). What is the value of doing research if the results of that research are not distributed to the wider community of health edu-cation researchers and practitioners?

Beyond the writing of a thesis or dissertation, there are several possible options for sharing your research results. The most widely regarded, efficient, and lasting way to inform others of your research is through journal articles. Once your research is published in a journal, almost anyone in any part of the world can read about it at a library, through an interlibrary loan program, by purchasing printed copies of the article, or through electronic full-text options. The Internet, through its various search engines and databases, has increased the access to literature for academics and has become a main avenue for seeking and publishing current, relevant information (Hartley, 2008). There are approximately 25,000 peer-reviewed journals, of which nearly 90% are available online. By publishing, not only can current researchers read about your work, but future researchers can read your work as long as back issues of a journal are available or it is stored in an accessible electronic format.

Oral presentation of your research is another option for dissemination. Most professional organizations hold conferences or professional meetings at state, regional, and/or national levels. These forums offer the opportunity to present your research in person to fellow professionals. According to Lucas and Murry (2007), presenting your research at a conference allows you to have a practice session prior to publishing. Then edits and fine tuning can be done in preparation for submission to a journal. Brown (2005) suggests that papers presented at conferences have a higher chance of getting accepted for publication and have more impact as a result (as cited in Hartley, 2008). Another oral presentation option when research results have strong applicability to professional practice is to develop continuing education or in-service programs that can be delivered to groups of practitioners.

When one's research is of interest or has applicability to the general public, it is sometimes possible to disseminate information through various media outlets. Newspapers, television and radio news reports, and talk shows are often interested in health-related topics and are willing to share your results. Most universities hire public relations professionals whose job it is to find and promote university news stories. These individuals are eager to learn about your research and, when appropriate, promote it to the media.

Journal Publishing

Journal publishing can be both exciting and frustrating. It is exciting from the perspective that you get to share the results of all your hard work with the profession and see your name in print. It is frustrating from the perspective that it is difficult to condense a thesis or dissertation to a 12- to 20-page journal manuscript, and after you finally submit the manuscript it may be rejected.

It is often difficult for students to condense their thesis or dissertation to the size requirements of most journals. To the student, everything in the thesis or dissertation is important. The average journal reader, however, just wants to obtain the essence of the work. Following the guidelines in this chapter and working closely with the committee chair should help students develop appropriate manuscripts. See Box 14.1 for hints to help condense one's writing.

Rejection of one's work is difficult for anyone to accept, not just students. After putting one's "heart and soul" into a research project over an extended period of time, one expects other professionals and journal editors to recognize its significance and want to publish its findings. Remember, however, that most professional journals get far more manuscripts than they can ever publish. In health promotion and education, for example, only about 20–40% of submitted manuscripts to any given journal get published (Ogletree, Glover, & Hu, 1997). That does not mean that all rejected manuscripts are bad manuscripts or that they do not merit publication. Manuscripts are often rejected because they do not fit well with the purpose of

---

Box 14.1   How to Condense Your Writing

- Greatly condense your literature review.
- Do not include lengthy lists of citations (three maximum for any point).
- Summarize the purpose of your research in a couple sentences or a paragraph.
- Remove unnecessary, qualifying, or repetitive words, and perhaps clauses, from sentences.
- Summarize two or more sentences, perhaps whole paragraphs, in one sentence.
- Delete references and quotations that are not essential to your discussion.
- Replace lengthy descriptions with tables or charts where possible.
- Eliminate unnecessary tables or charts.
- Remove whole sections where these are not central to your argument.
- Include only the most important discussion and implications for research and practice.

Modified from Blaxter *et al.* (2001).

---

smoking cessation is not effective, publishing such information may save other health education professionals the time, effort, and cost of implementing that same ineffective smoking cessation program.

Price and Murnan (2003) surveyed the journal editors of five widely recognized health education journals regarding the publishing of negative findings. All five editors reported that they would send a manuscript reporting negative findings out for review. Three editors reported they would definitely publish, one would probably publish, and the fifth was uncertain if he or she would publish a manuscript with negative findings that was recommended by reviewers for publication. In addition, four of the five editors said they either definitely would, probably would, or were uncertain as to whether they would override reviewers' decisions not to publish if those decisions were based solely on negative findings in a manuscript. Price and Murnan (2003) conclude that "rigorous research, that results in negative findings, should not be left to languish on a researcher's desk. A well-written manuscript regarding negative findings with adequate rationale for those findings is likely to be as publishable as other manuscripts" (p. 8).

Selecting the Appropriate Journal

The first step in publishing is to select a journal that is appropriate for the topic and type of manuscript you are submitting. Although several journals may seem appropriate, professional ethics require that you only submit your manuscript to one journal at a time; that is, it is unethical to submit a manuscript simultaneously to different journals. Before publishing your article, most journals will require you to sign a form or state in your cover letter that the manuscript is not being reviewed or published by another journal.

We are fortunate in health education to have a wide variety of journals to which work may be sent. Some are more scholarly and research oriented and others are less scholarly and more practitioner

the journal or meet the needs of journal readership. Other manuscripts are rejected because of writing or style issues that can be corrected. Still others may be rejected because the manuscript does not contain anything new or because articles on similar topics have been recently published. Unless the research design or data collection was so severely flawed that the results are questionable, many rejected manuscripts can be rewritten and resubmitted to other journals. A rejection often provides valuable feedback that can be incorporated into a manuscript revision so that the next submission is stronger than the previous submission.

Students sometimes believe that manuscripts presenting negative findings or nonsignificant findings will automatically be rejected. This is not true. In fact, as noted earlier in this text, negative findings or nonsignificant results are often as important or more important to the profession than positive findings or significant results. If, for example, it is found that a particular approach to

oriented. Several of the journals are owned by professional associations and tend to attract readership from specific practice settings. Therefore, manuscripts related to community or public health might be submitted to the *American Journal of Public Health* or *Public Health Reports*, manuscripts on school health issues might be submitted to the *Journal of School Health*, and those manuscripts related to college or university health issues might be submitted to the *Journal of American College Health*. Some journals in health education are broader in nature and publish across all practice settings. This would include the *American Journal of Health Education, Health Education and Behavior, The American Journal of Health Promotion, The Health Educator, The American Journal of Health Behavior,* and *The American Journal of Health Studies.* If your research might have international appeal, *Health Promotion International* and *Health Education Research* are official journals of the International Union for Health Promotion and Education. In addition, *The International Electronic Journal of Health Education* publishes research of an international nature in an electronic format. For articles that are more practical in nature, *Health Promotion Practice* might be a good journal choice (Cottrell, Girvan, & McKenzie, 2009).

Considering the characteristics of a particular journal is an important step in deciding where to submit the manuscript. Some characteristics to consider are the target popular of the journal (practitioners versus researchers), articles typically found in the journal (empirical, theory, reviews, research summary, new practices, etc.), competitiveness (will determine publication lag time), typical length of the articles, and number and breadth of the subscriptions (Pollard, 2005).

In addition to selecting the appropriate journal, sometimes it is important to submit to the appropriate column in a journal. Some journals, such as the *American Journal of Health Education,* have regular columns on specific topics such as "Teaching Ideas" or "Community Learning Ideas and Procedures" (CLIPs). These special columns may have their own publication guidelines and submission directions for prospective authors to follow. Although most research-based articles stemming from a thesis or dissertation would not be appropriate for publication in these columns, some work related to a master's project might be. These columns afford the opportunity to publish non–research-based work that may be of real value to health education practitioners.

Publication Guidelines

Once a decision has been made to submit a manuscript to a particular journal, the publication guidelines for that journal should be obtained. Most scholarly and professional journals publish these guidelines at least two times a year within the journal (DePoy & Gitlin, 2005). Other journals have their author guidelines available online. Always be sure to obtain the most up-to-date guidelines as they sometimes change. The guidelines contain important information about manuscript length, format, style, referencing, tables, and figures. In addition, they provide information on how and to whom the manuscript is to be submitted. Make a copy of these guidelines and read over them several times, highlighting the important information. Adhering closely to the guidelines is an important first step to having a manuscript accepted for publication. Many journal editors will not review a manuscript unless it follows the guidelines point by point. The last thing one should do prior to submitting the manuscript is to reread the publication guidelines to make sure they have been met. (See Figure 14.1 for a sample publication guidelines document.)

Local Review

After a near-completed draft of a manuscript has been developed and edited by all authors (more detail will be provided on manuscript development later in this chapter), it is a good idea to conduct a **local review**. This means that you give the

HEALTH EDUCATION & BEHAVIOR
Instructions for Authors

Manuscripts should be submitted through the Web-based tracking system http://heb.edmgr.com. The site contains detailed instructions on how to submit the manuscript and track the progression of the review process. All manuscripts will be assigned a manuscript number, and authors will receive email confirmation acknowledging receipt of submission. Authors are asked not to send hard copies of their manuscripts to the journal office. Inquiries with regard to the journal should be directed to tvogel@umich.edu.

The manuscript, including captions, footnotes, tables, and references, must be typed double-spaced with 1-inch margins in a 12-point font and are typically no longer than 20–30 pages in length. Footnotes to the text should be avoided where possible and no appendices included. All manuscripts should be submitted in English. An abstract of 100–150 words, followed by 3 or more keywords, must accompany each submission.

Health Education & Behavior is interested in articles directed toward researchers and/or practitioners in health behavior and health education. Empirical research, case studies, program evaluation, literature reviews, and articles discussing theories are regularly published in the journal. Each manuscript submitted is expected to include a section discussing implications for practitioners in the reported work. If a study assesses an intervention, a description of the intervention should be included in the paper.

Authors are asked not to use the term *subjects* when referring to research participants. Alternative terms such as *respondents, research participants*, or some other more specific designation (e.g., youths, females, residents) should be used.

All literature references should be done in American Psychological Association (APA) style with reference list organized in alphabetical order by author. Please see the *Publication Manual of the American Psychological Association* (5th ed.) for specific instructions. References to unpublished material are discouraged.

All tables should be cited sequentially in text, numbered, and supplied with explanatory captions. Table columns should have explanatory headings. Tables can be included at the end of the document or uploaded as separate documents during the submission process. Tables and figures should never be typed within the body of the manuscript. All figures must be cited in the text, numbered, and supplied with a caption.

Proofs will be supplied to authors to check the accuracy of typesetting and copyediting. Authors may be charged for excessive alterations to the proofs.

A reprint order form will be sent to the author after the issue containing his or her work is published, along with tearsheets of the article. Two complimentary copies of the entire issue will be sent to single authors; for articles with more than one author, each author will receive one copy.

Since a new U.S. copyright law became effective in January 1978, the transfer of copyright from author to publisher, heretofore implicit in the submission of a manuscript, must now be explicitly transferred to enable the publisher to ensure maximum dissemination of the author's work. A copy of the agreement executed and signed by each author is required with each manuscript submission. The agreement can be found on the Web site. (If the article is a "work for hire, "the agreement must be signed by the employer.) No manuscript can be considered accepted unless a signed copyright transfer agreement exists. It is the author's responsibility to obtain written permission and defray all fees for the use of any quotes over 300 words from previously published academic material; nonoriginal photographs, figures, or tables or any portion thereof, exclusive of data; and quotes of any length from newspapers, magazines, poems, songs, and anything broadcast over radio or television. Without a copy of written permission on file with the publisher, the quote cannot be used. Original photographs require signed releases from those photographed.

FIGURE 14.1
Sample publication guidelines.

Source: *Health Education & Behavior*. Used with permission.

manuscript to others at the local level to review and critique it prior to submitting it to a journal. These local individuals can be students, professors, professional colleagues, or even practitioners in the field. Usually such individuals are willing to read through a manuscript and provide feedback so long as you are willing to repay the favor for them. These local reviewers may catch errors that went unnoticed by the authors. Sometimes authors get so close to a manuscript and have read it so many times that they read over grammar, spelling, or syntax errors. They may think that their writing is clear when it is actually confusing to others. Catching these errors through a local review can increase the likelihood of publication.

Submitting a Manuscript

After making any changes following a local review and doing a final proofread, the manuscript is ready to be submitted. It is a good idea to include a cover letter, stating that the manuscript represents original work not submitted elsewhere and that it complies with appropriate regulations concerning human subjects. Again, it is extremely important to follow exactly the publication guidelines for the journal to which you are submitting. Most journals will require you to submit multiple copies of the manuscript. Some copies of the manuscript may need to be stripped of any authorship information to accommodate a blind review process. More and more journals are requiring that the manuscript be submitted electronically.

Most journals associated with professional associations and all the health education journals we listed in this chapter are **refereed peer-reviewed journals**. This means that when a manuscript is received by the editor for publication consideration, it is sent out to several peer reviewers or referees, each of whom will read the manuscript, critique it, and make a recommendation concerning publication. The editor of the journal then uses these reviews to make a final decision about publication. This process may take up to six

months or longer depending on the journal (DePoy & Gitlin, 2005). The authors of this text have personally published articles that took well over a year from submission to publication.

Eventually you should receive a decision concerning the disposition of your manuscript. Typically, there are four possible responses: (1) reject, which means the article is not suitable for publication in the journal; (2) reject, but with an invitation to revise the manuscript and resubmit it; (3) accept, but contingent upon the author making certain specified and required revisions; or (4) accept as submitted. It is rare for an article to be accepted exactly as submitted (DePoy & Gitlin, 2005).

Students often ask how to proceed when they receive either an acceptance with required revisions or a rejection with an invitation to resubmit from an editor. Henson (2005) makes the point that unless the revisions would depart from the main purpose or content of the manuscript, most authors are typically happy to make the necessary changes, because this option represents less time than preparing the manuscript for another journal. Each comment made by the reviewers should be addressed in the rewrite. A summary page that describes how each comment was addressed is helpful to reviewers and editors. If you disagree with a reviewer comment, you should note this on the summary page and justify your reason for not making a requested modification. (See Box 14.2.) In some cases it might also be helpful to call the editor to discuss major differences of opinion.

Once a manuscript is accepted for publication, some journals will send galley proofs to be reviewed. **Galley proofs** are typeset versions of your work and are exactly as the article will appear in the journal. It is the author's task to carefully review the galleys to make certain that no mistakes or errors were introduced during the typesetting process. Once the galleys are reviewed and returned, just sit back and wait to celebrate your work in print.

If your manuscript was rejected, once the original disappointment wears off, carefully read all

Box 14.2   Summary Sheet

This summary sheet should be sent to the editor with the revised manuscript that was accepted with revisions.

Reviewer 1

Reviewer Comment 1: The literature review section should be written all in past tense as you are reporting on work already completed.

Author Response: Done

Reviewer Comment 2: A seminal article by Gates, Bennett, Rottenberger, and Harkness (2008) is missing from the literature review.

Author Response: The article was located and a paragraph on this article is included on page 2 of the manuscript.

Comment 3: The purpose statement needs to be written more succinctly. You do not need a half page to state your purpose.

Author Response: See page 3—The purpose statement has been rewritten.

Comment 4: Your description of the program participants is too lengthy with too many numbers. This information could be better presented in a table.

Author Response: See new Table 1.

Comment 5: You discuss the implications of your findings to health education specialists, but you should also discuss the potential implications for doctors, nurses, and physical therapists.

Author Response: While I agree that this would be valuable, it is beyond the scope of this paper. This paper is specifically to address health education specialists and it is already at the maximum number of pages allowed. To add the requested discussion would necessitate removing other valuable information from the manuscript.

Reviewer 2

Reviewer Comment 1: State the time period between the initial test and retest of your instrument.

Author Response: The time period was 2 weeks and that information has been added to the discussion of stability reliability.

review comments provided by the editor. Use this feedback to rewrite and refine your manuscript. Significant improvements can often be made to a manuscript by following reviewer suggestions. Again, remember that a rejected manuscript does not necessarily mean bad research or bad writing. Unless major flaws in the research design were noted that cannot be modified, submission to another journal should be considered.

Manuscript Development

Writing a manuscript for publication in a journal is different from writing your thesis or dissertation. While writing your thesis or dissertation you had to be careful to make sure the literature review was complete and to include as much detail as possible concerning the methodology and results. Now you must decide what is the most important information to include so as to explain your research in a limited number of pages. Where before you were probably told to expand on your work, now you need to condense your work.

Quantitative research articles usually contain seven sections, which are ordered as follows:

- Abstract
- Introduction
- Review of the literature/background
- Methods
- Findings/Results
- Discussion (including recommendations, implications, and limitations
- Conclusions

Although writers will sometimes deviate from this order or combine sections, these seven sections are usually contained in any quantitative research article (DePoy & Gitlin, 2005; Price & Murnan, 2003). You will notice that these seven sections were also included in your thesis or dissertation. Information for these sections of a quantitative research article can be pulled directly from the thesis or dissertation, but you will need to be very selective in what information you include. You will also need to balance the coverage given to each section so that the article covers all topics without providing too much detail in one section, thus shorting another section. Glatthorn (2002) made general recommendations concerning the percentage of a manuscript that should be allocated to each section. He suggests that 5% should be abstract, 10% introduction, 15% review of the literature, 20% methods, 25% findings/results, and 25% for the discussion and conclusions.

Abstract

The abstract is placed at the front of a research article and briefly summarizes the information contained in the various article sections. It should include the purpose statement, an overview of methods, a brief statement of results, and a sentence or two on implications. Make sure to read the author guidelines closely because some journals are very prescriptive of what to include in the abstract. Most journals specify an acceptable length or word count for an abstract, some allowing as few as 100 words. The abstract for a research article is usually shorter than the abstract used for the thesis or dissertation. Most word processing programs have a word count function that can be used to make sure the abstract does not exceed length requirements.

Introduction

The introduction presents the problem or purpose statement, research questions, and/or hypotheses that were set forth in the study. The authors may also want to discuss the importance of the research or why this research is needed at this point in the article. Sometimes the introduction follows the literature review, and sometimes the two sections are combined.

Review of the Literature

The literature review in a quantitative study provides the foundation and establishes the impor-

tance of the research. In other words, it reports on those studies, theories, or models on which the current work is based. In essence, it provides a critical review or summary of the literature as a whole and usually does not provide in-depth information on each source in the literature. Guide questions for developing a literature review can be seen in Box 14.3.

In writing the thesis or dissertation, students are typically told to identify and report on all the literature that directly or indirectly relates to the topic. In a journal article, the author must report on only the most important or **seminal works** (DePoy & Gitlin, 2005). Obviously the literature review in a journal article must be much shorter than the literature review in a thesis or dissertation. Although the literature review in the thesis or dissertation may have been 10 to 30 pages in length, McMillan and Wergin (2002) state that the literature review in a research article is usually "one to several paragraphs" (p. 7) in length. They go on to state that the author of a research article should "use as many current articles as possible, but relevance is more important than recency" (p. 8) in selecting articles to cite.

The literature review in a qualitative research article is different from the literature review in a

---

Box 14.3   Writing the Literature Review: Questions

- Does the review contain up-to-date, relevant studies?
- Is there an emphasis on primary sources (i.e., actual studies), rather than other review articles?
- Is there a critical review or a summary of findings?
- Is the review well organized?
- Does the review clearly relate previous studies to the current research problem?
- Does the review help establish the importance of the research?

quantitative research article. McMillan and Wergin (2002) note that "while in quantitative studies a clear literature review section almost always precedes the methodology, in qualitative studies the review is interspersed throughout the document" (p. 8).

Methods

The methods section of a journal article may be one large section or include several subsections. In either case, the study population and sampling procedures should be explained, a description of all instrumentation, including specific information on validity and reliability, should be included, and a thorough description of the procedures used to conduct the study should be contained in this section, as well as the specific data analysis strategies employed. The challenge here is to provide enough information on all subtopics without including the entire Chapter III from a thesis or dissertation. Remember that reviewers and readers need to have enough information to determine if the study has internal and/or external validity and if the findings can be trusted. They do not need to have the level of detail necessary to replicate your study. If they desire this level of detail, they can access the original thesis or dissertation.

Findings or Results

In this section of a quantitative research article, the analyzed data are presented. Usually authors begin by presenting descriptive statistics on their sample population. After presenting the descriptive statistics, inferential and associational statistics are reported. Data may be presented in narrative, table, and/or graph form. A rationale for each statistical procedure used is typically presented and the findings are explained. Interpretation of the data, however, is not included until the next section of the article. If the thesis or dissertation produced a large amount of data, an article may need to be limited to that which is most important or to some subsection

of data that is logical to present. Sometimes it is appropriate to write two or more articles from one research study. Ethically, however, the same data should never be presented in two different journal articles.

Discussion

Just as the discussion section was the most creative part of the thesis or dissertation, it is also the most creative part of a journal article. In this section the researcher explains the meanings and implications of the results, poses alternative explanations for the results, relates the findings to the published literature, and suggests practical uses for the study findings. It is also common to identify any limitations of the study in this section.

Fraenkel and Wallen (2006) make a strong case for separating the discussion section from the results and conclusions. They note that "A discussion section will typically go considerably beyond the data in attempting to place the findings in a broader perspective. It is important that the reader not be misled into thinking that the investigator has obtained evidence for something that is only speculation" (p. 605).

Conclusions

The conclusion section of a quantitative research article is a short summary of important study findings. It may also include statements about future directions for research or health education practices.

After writing the conclusions, the manuscript should be complete and ready for the local review. Before sending the final draft of your manuscript to the publisher, review the final submission checklist as seen in Table 14.1.

As you prepare your manuscript for publication, it is not only helpful to know what to include but also why manuscripts are typically rejected. Table 14.2 lists the 10 most common reasons manuscripts are rejected by the *American Journal of Health*

Table 14.1   Guide Questions for Publishing Journal Articles

Have you selected an appropriate journal for your work?

Have you followed precisely the journal's publication guidelines?

Is your article written in the same style as other articles typically found in the journal?

Have you included all seven components of a quantitative research article?

Have you discussed the reliability and validity of your instrumentation?

Do your conclusions accurately reflect the results of your research without overgeneralizing your findings?

Is your writing free of grammatical, punctuation, and spelling errors?

Have you removed any sexist or other discriminatory language?

Are all tables, diagrams, and graphs presented in accordance with style manual requirements and the journal's publication guidelines?

Have you checked all citations and references for accuracy and format?

Have you included a cover letter?

Have you included the appropriate number of copies or submitted electronically as requested by the journal?

Table 14.2   Ten Most Common Reasons for Manuscript Rejection

Author does not follow guidelines for authors.

Manuscript is sent to the wrong journal.

Content does not significantly contribute to the professional literature.

The manuscript is poorly written with grammatical and spelling errors.

The study is poorly designed, poorly executed, and/or poorly analyzed.

The study is too narrow, reports on a single class, or appeals to a very narrow audience.

The study did not adequately review the literature (e.g., wrong or insufficient review) and did not put the findings in context.

The topic studied was irrelevant or insignificant, even though the study may have been adequately conducted.

The study is too old and may no longer represent the current condition.

Author is selectively reporting the literature and/or reporting on a biased design to prove a personal perspective.

Education (Price & Murnan, 2004). Obviously, it is important to avoid making these mistakes.

Oral Presentations

The process of giving an oral presentation of research results usually begins when a professional organization or any sponsoring organization for a conference puts out a **call for papers**. This is an invitation for individuals or groups to submit proposals or abstracts of their work to be considered for presentation. The call for papers will usually include specific information on how the proposal or abstract is to be prepared, how long it can be, and a deadline for submission. Typically, a call for papers occurs nine months to a year ahead of the actual conference or meeting.

Preparing a proposal for an oral presentation is much easier and less time consuming than developing a manuscript for publication. Most proposals are fairly short and prescriptive. Although different organizations may require different information or different formatting of information, an abstract of the research will usually be required. In general, the abstract for a publication as described earlier in this chapter can often be easily modified for use as a presentation proposal or abstract. Typically, a presentation abstract will include the purpose statement, an overview of methods, a brief statement of results, and a sentence or two on implications. Because abstracts are sometimes published in a conference proceedings publication, they may have to be precisely formatted to fit given specified dimensions.

Presentation proposals received by sponsoring organizations are usually sent out to planning committee members or independent reviewers. These individuals rank the proposals and make recommendations to accept or reject. Criteria for accepting proposals are typically based on such factors as the perceived quality of the research, the relevancy of the topic to conference attendees, the relevancy of the topic to any conference goals or theme, how new or unique the topic is, and how many other proposals have been submitted on the same topic (Cottrell & Moore, 2003).

There are several different formats for an oral presentation. Some research studies may lend themselves to a full program session. These are usually 45–90 minutes in length and allow the researchers to fully present a study in detail and discuss the results. More often, research presentations are grouped together by topic, and several individuals will present their research results within one given session. For example, there might be four proposals that relate to aging and health, so they would be grouped together and each of the four researchers would be given an equal amount of the session time to present his or her study results. Individuals presenting in such a combined session usually have 10 to 20 minutes to present their study. It is critical to stay within the allocated time when presenting in combined sessions. If one presenter goes over the time allocation, another presenter's time will be shortened. The moderator or presider of the session should closely monitor time, but good presenters will make sure they are within the time allocation.

Poster Sessions

Another type of oral presentation is a **poster session**. If presenting a poster session, the researcher will visually depict the study in a poster format and hang it on a 4×8 poster board provided at the conference or professional meeting site. There may be 10 to 30 posters presented in one time slot side by side. Presenters typically stand by their poster during the poster session to answer questions and discuss results with conference participants attending the session. At smaller conferences posters are sometimes left up throughout the meeting.

Developing a quality poster takes some time and effort. A good poster should be neat, accurate, and professional. All posters should be easy to read from a comfortable distance as people will be standing a few feet away while reviewing the poster's content. If you see people having to move up close to read any portion of your poster, the print is probably too small. Poster materials should be organized on the poster from left to right and top to bottom so that the reader is led through important points in a logical manner. Essentially the flow should be from top left to bottom right (see Figure 14.2). A good poster will have a mix of text, graphics, and possibly photographs. A common mistake is to include too much text and too much detail. Readers only need to get a flavor of your research from the poster. If they need more detail, they can ask you questions or request access to a more comprehensive document describing your work (Figure 14.3). Sometimes posters are judged in a competition. In this case judges often ask questions of you about your poster and part of your score may also be based on your knowledge, understanding, and ability to explain your poster.

Sharing Authorship

Whether you are presenting a paper at a conference or submitting a manuscript for publication, you must decide if you will be the sole author or if you will share authorship. Determining authorship is an important decision and one that should be discussed early in a research project. Feelings can be easily hurt and relationships ruined by authorship decisions. The order of authors on an article or presentation is also important. The order of authorship is generally recognized as reflecting the relative contribution to the project. Those listed first contributed most and those listed last contributed less.

Conference poster presentation

Karen Travis, MD
Department of Neurology, University of Cincinnati

Introduction

Volutpat mos at neque nulls lobortis.

Nulla arcu dolor, rutrum quis congue eget, egestas ut libero. Cum sociis natoque penatibus et magnis dis parturient montes, nascetur ridiculus mus. Maecenas sed purus in magna fermentum pellentesque. Cras condimentum mattis tellus, ut augue consequat tortor mattis et.

Nulla vestibulum nisl eget elit placerat bibendum. Proin at eleifend justo. Etiam malesuada fringilla pellentesque.

Methods

Etiam semper ligula a lorem auctor ut elementum risus bibendum. Curabitur et diam eget sem consectetur commodo vel at metus. Sed luctus imperdiet orci, quis aliquet magna viverra sit amet. Nulla in lorem lorem. Suspendisse mollis quam quis felis tincidunt sit amet dignissim leo tristique.

Results

Fusce non pretium libero. Fusce imperdiet purus ut nisi faucibus tempor eget et ipsum. Mauris faucibus accumsan sem ac semper.

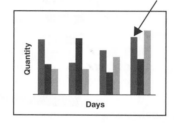

Conclusions

Praesent vulputate, sem quis vehicula interdum, velit nulla fermentum felis, ac suscipit risus mauris mattis enim. Sed tempus turpis et magna ultricies ornare.

Sed tempus turpis et magna ultricies ornare. Sed sem odio, elementum ac tempus sit amet, cursus nec nisl. Etiam blandit imperdiet metus, nec fringilla erat tempor et. Proin at magna massa, sit amet convallis arcu. Curabitur et diam eget sem consectetur commodo vel at metus.

References

Mauris nec ligula quis felis commodo lacinia non a lorem. Sed tincidunt laoreet molestie. In ultricies, dui sed interdum facilisis, dui tortor rhoncus neque, quis pulvinar sem lacus imperdiet nunc. Quisque in sapien risus. Nam laoreet dictum dolor, sed sollicitudin neque facilisis.

FIGURE 14.2

Sample poster presentation layout.

Source: Meredith Orlowski, Donald C. Harrison Health Sciences Library Poster Class, University of Cincinnati, 2009.

Students completing a thesis or dissertation often share authorship with their major advisor and perhaps one or more committee members. Some programs leave the decision to publish totally up to students, but other programs have specific policies regarding authorship and publication of theses and dissertations. For example, in the University of Cincinnati's Health Promotion and Education Program, students are given three months after submitting a completed thesis to develop the first draft of a manuscript for publication. If they develop this first draft, they are then listed as first author on any ensuing publication. The committee chair will serve as second author and assist with editing and preparing the manuscript for submission. Students may add other committee members to the author list if they wish to do so. If students do not develop a first draft within the three-month time limit, the committee chair can develop the first draft and will be listed as first author. The student then becomes second author and may assist with editing and manuscript preparation. This policy reflects the program's philosophy that the committee chair always makes a significant contribution to a thesis or dissertation and should share authorship. It further reflects their belief that research should be published and shared with the professional community. See Appendix B for another example of a university's publication guidelines.

In the absence of specific policies, there are guidelines that can be used to help make author-

FIGURE 14.3
Poster session.

ship decisions. Leedy and Ormrod (2010) note that as a general rule of thumb, "Individuals who have made significant intellectual contributions to the work should share in its authorship" (p. 310). Determining what significant intellectual contributions are to a work can be difficult and is certainly not black and white. If others have been actively involved in the conception, design, execution, analysis, and/or writing of the manuscript, they should probably be considered for authorship. Those that may have only helped with mailings, coding, data entry, computer programming, typing, and editing are usually not listed as authors. On the one hand, it is unethical to leave someone off of a publication's author list if that person really did contribute to the research, but on the other hand, it is also unethical to include persons in the author list who did not contribute. In essence, it becomes a professional judgment of the lead author as to who, if anyone, should be listed as coauthors.

One last point concerns the number of authors included on a manuscript. In recent years the number of authors has been increasing (Louis, Holdsworth, Anderson, & Campbell, 2008). This probably reflects an added emphasis on publishing for promotion and tenure and an increased interest in collaboration in grant proposals and resulting research projects. Including a large number of authors on a manuscript can raise integrity questions and can create added tensions regarding who qualifies for inclusion in an article and authorship order. Some journals have instituted policies that require authors to indicate how they have contributed to the paper. This may be an issue that health education professional associations will need to examine in the future.

Summary

In this chapter the need to present research findings beyond the writing of the thesis or dissertation is discussed. Both the joys and frustrations associated with publishing in a journal are presented. Information is provided to help readers select an appropriate journal, obtain publication guidelines, conduct a local review, and submit a completed manuscript to a refereed journal. Further, each section of a quantitative research article is discussed in detail.

Oral presentation is another way to share research findings. Information on how and when to submit proposals for oral presentations is included. A specific type of oral presentation often seen at health education professional meetings, the poster session, is also discussed. The chapter ends with a discussion of sharing authorship of research and presents some guidelines to consider when making this important decision.

Review Questions

1. Why is it important to share one's results beyond the writing of a thesis or dissertation?
2. Name three different outlets for sharing the results of one's research.
3. Discuss what is meant by "local review." Why is this important?
4. Explain the process a manuscript goes through prior to being published in a refereed journal.
5. List the seven sections typically found in a quantitative research article.
6. What is a "call for papers"? When is one likely to see a call for papers?
7. What is a "poster session"?
8. After completing your graduate program, you and several colleagues have been working on a research project. What considerations should be made as to who will be listed as authors and in what order they will be listed on an article stemming from this research project?

References

Blaxter, L., Hughes, C., & Tight, M. (2001). *How to research* (2nd ed.). Philadelphia: Open University Press.

Brown, L.D. (2005). The importance of circulating and presenting manuscripts: Evidence from the accounting literature. *The Accounting Review*, 80(1), 55–83.

Cottrell, R.R., Girvan, J.T., & McKenzie, J.F. (2009). *Principles and foundations of health promotion and education* (4th ed.). San Francisco: Pearson Benjamin Cummings.

Cottrell, R.R., & Moore, L. (2003). Presenting at AAHE National Convention. *HExtra,* 28(3), 3, 6.

DePoy, E., & Gitlin, L.N. (2005). *Introduction to research: Understanding and applying multiple strategies* (3rd ed.). Philadelphia: Elsevier Mosby.

Fraenkel, J.R., & Wallen, N.E. (2006). *How to design and evaluate research in education* (6th ed.). Boston: McGraw-Hill.

Glatthorn, A.A. (2002). *Publish or perish: The educator's imperative. Strategies for writing effectively for your profession and your school.* Thousand Oaks, Calif: Sage Publications.

Hartley, J. (2008). *Academic writing and publishing: A practical handbook.* New York: Routledge.

Henson, K.T. (2005). *Writing for publication: Road to academic advancement.* Boston: Pearson/Allyn and Bacon.

Leedy, P.D., & Ormrod, J.E. (2010). *Practical research: Planning and design.* Upper Saddle River, N.J.: Pearson Education, Inc.

Louis, K.S., Holdsworth, J.M., Anderson, M.S., & Campbell, E.G. (2008). Everyday ethics in research: Translating authorship guidelines into practice in bench sciences. *Journal of Higher Education*, 79(1), 88–112.

Lucas, C.J., & Murry, J.W. (2007). *New faculty: A practical guide for academic beginners.* New York: Palgrave MacMillan.

McMillan, J.H., & Wergin, J.F. (2002). *Understanding and evaluating educational research* (2nd ed.). Upper Saddle River, N.J.: Merrill/Prentice Hall.

Ogletree, R.J., Glover, R.B., & Hu, P. (1997). Characteristics of selected health education journals. *Journal of Health Education,* 28(4), 224–229.

Pollard Jr., R. (2005). From dissertation to journal article: A useful method for planning and writing any manuscript. *Internet Journal of Mental Health*, 2(2), 4-4, 1p. Retrieved June 17, 2009, from Academic Search Complete database.

Price, J.H., & Murnan, J. (2003). The publication of negative findings—myth versus reality. *American Journal of Health Education,* 34(1), 2, 8.

———. (2004). Strategies for getting published in the *American Journal of Health Education. American Journal of Health Education,* 35(4), 194–197.

APPENDIX A | Development of a Unified Code of Ethics for the Health Education Profession*

The earliest code of ethics for health educators appears to be the 1976 SOPHE Code of Ethics, developed to guide professional behaviors toward the highest standards of practice for the profession. Following member input, Ethics Committee Chair, Elizabeth Bernheimer and Paul Mico refined the Code in 1978. Between 1980 and 1983 renewed attention to the code of ethics resulted in a revision that was to be reviewed by SOPHE Chapters and, if accepted, then submitted to other health education professional associations to serve as a guide for the profession (Bloom, 1999). The 1983 SOPHE Code of Ethics was a combination of standards and principles but no specific rules of conduct at that time (Taub *et al.*, 1987).

Following the earlier recommendation of SOPHE President, Lawrence Green, that SOPHE, AAHE and the Public Health Education section of APHA consider appointing joint committees, a SOPHE-AAHE Joint Committee was appointed by then AAHE President, Peter Cortese and then SOPHE President Ruth Richards in 1984. This committee was charged with developing a profession-wide code of ethics (Bloom, 1999). Between August 1984 and November 1985 the Committee, chaired by Alyson Taub, carried out its charge to (1) identify and use all existing health education ethics statements, (2) determine the appropriate relationship between the code of ethics and the Role Delineation guidelines, including rec-

ommendations for enforcement, and (3) to prepare an ethics document for approval as a profession-wide code of ethics. The Joint Committee found that the only health education organization to work on ethics, other than SOPHE, was the American College Health Association which included a section on ethics in their *Recommended Standards and Practices for a College Health Education Program*. The Committee concluded that it was premature to describe how the Code might relate to the Role Delineation guidelines and further recommended that individual responsibility for adhering to the Code of Ethics be the method of enforcement. Finally, the Joint Committee recommended that in the absence of resources to retain expert consultation in development of ethical codes of conduct, the 1983 SOPHE Code of Ethics be adopted profession-wide and serve as a basis for the next step involving development of rules of conduct (Taub *et al.*, 1987). While SOPHE accepted the Joint Committee's recommendation, there was no similar action by AAHE (Bloom, 1999). The AAHE Board chose not to accept the suggestion of adopting the SOPHE Code on behalf of the profession because they realized that the membership of AAHE needed to be more completely involved in discussing and formulating a Code of Ethics before the AAHE Board could adequately represent the interests and needs of AAHE members in collaborative work on ethics with other professional societies.

In September of 1991, an ad hoc AAHE Ethics Committee, Chaired by Janet Shirreffs,

*Source: Coalition of National Health Education Organizations. Used with permission.

301

was charged by President Thomas O'Rourke to develop a code of ethics that represented the professional needs of the variety of health education professionals in the membership of AAHE. They were to review the literature including other professional codes of ethics, and conduct in-depth surveys of AAHE members. For the next two years, the AAHE Ethics Committee executed its charge through a variety of venues including correspondence; surveys; face-to-face meetings; presentations and discussion sessions at the national conventions of AAHE, ASHA, and APHA and through conducting focus group sessions at strategic locations around the country. Based upon the work of this committee, an AAHE Code of Ethics was adopted by the AAHE Board of Directors in April, 1993 (AAHE, 1994). Subsequently, both AAHE and SOPHE continued to focus on ethical issues. SOPHE has promoted programming in Ethics through its annual and midyear meetings. In December, 1992 a summary of the 1983 SOPHE Code of Ethics was prepared by Sarah Olson and distributed as a promotional piece. The SOPHE Board of Trustees supported the summary Code of Ethics in 1994. Since 1993, AAHE has had a standing committee on Ethics that recently proposed convention programming and publications in the area of Ethics. Recognizing the need to work with other organizations toward a profession-wide Code of Ethics, the SOPHE Board requested that the Coalition of National Health Education Organizations (CNHEO) propose a strategy for accomplishing this goal. In July, 1994, The Board adopted a motion that SOPHE support a profession-wide Code of Ethics based on ethical principles and that AAHE should be contacted for support in the effort (Bloom, 1999).

In 1995, the National Commission for Health Education Credentialing, Inc. (NCHEC) and CNHEO co-sponsored a conference, The Health Education Profession in the Twenty-First Century: Setting the Stage (Brown *et al.,* 1996). During that conference, it was recommended that efforts be expanded to develop a profession-wide Code of Ethics.

Shortly thereafter, delegates to the Coalition of National Health Education Organizations pledged to work toward development of a profession-wide Code of Ethics using the existing SOPHE and AAHE Codes as a starting point (Bloom, 1999). A National Ethics Task Force was subsequently developed, with representatives from the various organizations represented on the Coalition. It was decided that the Coalition Delegates would not be the Task Force. As a result, the various member organizations of the Coalition were asked to recommend individuals for inclusion on this important Task Force.

During the November, 1996 APHA meeting, Larry Olsen who was the Coordinator of the Coalition of National Health Education Organizations and delegate to the Coalition from ASHA, William Livingood (SOPHE), and Beverly Mahoney (AAHE) led a session on ethics sponsored by the CNHEO. At that meeting, the basic conceptual plan that had been developed by the Coalition's Ethics Task Force was presented. Those attending the session were asked to provide input, both for the process and the content of the "new" Code of Ethics. Those in attendance were strong in their support for the importance of having a Code of Ethics for the profession that would provide an ethical framework for health educators, regardless of the setting in which health education was practiced.

The Ethics Task Force of the Coalition reviewed the two existing Codes (SOPHE and AAHE) along with the supporting documents for both, and decided that they would enlist the support of a consultant to assist in the unification process. Claire Stiles of Eckerd College was subsequently retained to offer comments about the proposals of the Task Force, as well as the various drafts that would be developed.

A presentation on behalf of the Ethics Task Force was made in November, 1997 at the national APHA meeting in Indianapolis, and the first draft of the "Unified Code of Ethics" was presented. Attendees were asked to comment about the draft document and were asked to take copies of the draft document to distribute among their constituencies. Comments from professionals in the field were returned to and considered by the Task Force.

A second (revised) draft of the Unified Code was presented during the March, 1998 AAHE meeting in Reno. Comments received from the APHA Indianapolis meeting and field distribution had been incorporated into the document. In addition, the AAHE Ethics Committee had the opportunity to comment about the "new" document. During the presentation in Reno, participants were put into small groups to discuss and comment on each of the Articles included in the draft document. These comments were subsequently incorporated into the document and the stage was set for a series of meetings designed to elicit commentary from professionals in the field, as well as those who attended the meetings of national professional health education organizations.

Following yet another revision of the emerging Code, presentations on behalf of the Task Force were made in San Antonio in May, 1998 at the joint SOPHE/ASTDHPPHE meeting; in San Diego in June, 1998 at the national meeting of ACHA; and in Colorado Springs in October, 1998 at the national meeting of ASHA. Throughout this process, comments and suggestions about the code were received and examined by the Task Force. Throughout this process of revision and refinement, care was taken to retain the context and concepts present in the "parent" SOPHE and AAHE documents.

The "first final draft" of the Unified Code of Ethics was presented in Washington, D.C., at the November, 1998 meeting of the APHA. The Coalition also met in conjunction with APHA and it was decided that the final draft of the Unified Code would be prepared for presentation to the field in 1999.

In April, 1999, the Unified Code of Ethics was presented in Boston at the national AAHE meeting. During that meeting the Coalition also met and it was decided that all delegates to the Coalition, as well as the Ethics Task Force members would

examine closely the work that had been done, and offer comments and suggestions. It was further decided that Coalition delegates would be sent a copy of the entire document (both the long and short forms), so that the documents could be discussed during the Coalition's May, 1999 conference call. During that conference call, the delegates voted to present the Code of Ethics to their respective organizations, for ratification during the remainder of 1999.

On November 8, 1999, the Coalition Delegates met in Chicago in conjunction with the American Public Health Association's annual meeting. At that meeting, the Code of Ethics was a topic of discussion. Letters had been received from all the delegate organizations indicating that they had approved the document. It was moved and seconded that the Code of Ethics be approved and distributed to the profession. There being no further comments by the CNHEO delegates, the Code of Ethics was approved, unanimously, as a Code of Ethics for the profession of Health Education.

The Code of Ethics that has evolved from this long and arduous process is not seen as a completed project. Rather, it is envisioned as a living document that will continue to evolve as the practice of Health Education changes to meet the challenges of the new millennium.

References Cited

Association for the Advancement of Health Education. (1994). Code of ethics for health educators, *Journal of Health Education, 25*(4), 197–200.

Bloom, F.K. (1999). The Society for Public Health Education: Its development and contributions: 1976–1996. Unpublished doctoral dissertation, Columbia University.

Brown, K.M., Cissell, W., DuShaw, M., Goodhart, F., McDermott, R., Middleton, K., Tappe, M., & Welsh, V. (1996). The health education profession in the twenty-first century: Setting the stage. *Journal of Health Education, 27*(6), 357–364.

Taub, A., Kreuter, M., Parcel, G., & Vitello, E. (1987). Report from the AAHE/SOPHE Joint Committee on Ethics. *Health Education Quarterly,* 14(1), 79–90.

Members of the Ethics Task Force:
Mal Goldsmith (ASHA)
June Gorski (SOPHE)
Wanda Jubb (SSDHPER)
Ken McLeroy (PHEHP Section, APHA)
Larry K. Olsen (ASHA), Committee Chair
Alyson Taub (SHES Section, APHA)

This introduction was prepared through the joint efforts of Ellen Capwell (SOPHE), Becky Smith (AAHE), Janet Shirreffs (AAHE), and Larry K. Olsen (ASHA).
Prepared 11/14/99

Long Version

Code of Ethics for the Health Education Profession

Preamble

The health education profession is dedicated to excellence in the practice of promoting individual, family, organizational, and community health. Guided by common ideals, health educators are responsible for upholding the integrity and ethics of the profession as they face the daily challenges of making decisions. By acknowledging the value of diversity in society and embracing a cross-cultural approach, health educators support the worth, dignity, potential, and uniqueness of all people.

The Code of Ethics provides a framework of shared values within which health education is practiced. The Code of Ethics is grounded in fundamental ethical principles that underlie all health care services: respect for autonomy, promotion of social justice, active promotion of good, and avoidance of harm. The responsibility of each health educator is to aspire to the highest possible standards of conduct and to encourage the ethical behavior of all those with whom they work.

Regardless of job title, professional affiliation, work setting, or population served, health educators abide by these guidelines when making professional decisions.

Article I: Responsibility to the Public

A health educator's ultimate responsibility is to educate people for the purpose of promoting, maintaining, and improving individual, family, and community health. When a conflict of issues arises among individuals, groups, organizations, agencies, or institutions, health educators must consider all issues and give priority to those that promote wellness and quality of living through principles of self-determination and freedom of choice for the individual.

Section 1: Health educators support the right of individuals to make informed decisions regarding health, as long as such decisions pose no threat to the health of others.

Section 2: Health educators encourage actions and social policies that support and facilitate the best balance of benefits over harm for all affected parties.

Section 3: Health educators accurately communicate the potential benefits and consequences of the services and programs with which they are associated.

Section 4: Health educators accept the responsibility to act on issues that can adversely affect the health of individuals, families, and communities.

Section 5: Health educators are truthful about their qualifications and the limitations of their expertise and provide services consistent with their competencies.

Section 6: Health educators protect the privacy and dignity of individuals.

Section 7: Health educators actively involve individuals, groups, and communities in the entire educational process so that all aspects of the process are clearly understood by those who may be affected.

Section 8: Health educators respect and acknowledge the rights of others to hold diverse values, attitudes, and opinions.

Section 9: Health educators provide services equitably to all people.

Article II: Responsibility to the Profession

Health educators are responsible for their professional behavior, for the reputation of their profession, and for promoting ethical conduct among their colleagues.

Section 1: Health educators maintain, improve, and expand their professional competence through continued study and education; membership, participation, and leadership in professional organizations; and involvement in issues related to the health of the public.

Section 2: Health educators model and encourage nondiscriminatory standards of behavior in their interactions with others.

Section 3: Health educators encourage and accept responsible critical discourse to protect and enhance the profession.

Section 4: Health educators contribute to the development of the profession by sharing the processes and outcomes of their work.

Section 5: Health educators are aware of possible professional conflicts of interest, exercise integrity in conflict situations, and do not manipulate or violate the rights of others.

Section 6: Health educators give appropriate recognition to others for their professional contributions and achievements

Article III: Responsibility to Employers

Health educators recognize the boundaries of their professional competence and are accountable for their professional activities and actions.

Section 1: Health educators accurately represent their qualifications and the qualifications of others whom they recommend.

Section 2: Health educators use appropriate standards, theories, and guidelines as criteria when carrying out their professional responsibilities.

Section 3: Health educators accurately represent potential service and program outcomes to employers.

Section 4: Health educators anticipate and disclose competing commitments, conflicts of interest, and endorsement of products.

Section 5: Health educators openly communicate to employers, expectations of job-related assignments that conflict with their professional ethics.

Section 6: Health educators maintain competence in their areas of professional practice.

Article IV: Responsibility in the Delivery of Health Education

Health educators promote integrity in the delivery of health education. They respect the rights, dignity, confidentiality, and worth of all people by adapting strategies and methods to meet the needs of diverse populations and communities.

Section 1: Health educators are sensitive to social and cultural diversity and are in accord with the law, when planning and implementing programs.

Section 2: Health educators are informed of the latest advances in theory, research, and practice, and use strategies and methods that are grounded in and contribute to development of professional standards, theories, guidelines, statistics, and experience.

Section 3: Health educators are committed to rigorous evaluation of both program effectiveness and the methods used to achieve results.

Section 4: Health educators empower individuals to adopt healthy lifestyles through informed choice rather than by coercion or intimidation.

Section 5: Health educators communicate the potential outcomes of proposed services, strategies, and pending decisions to all individuals who will be affected.

Article V: Responsibility in Research and Evaluation

Health educators contribute to the health of the population and to the profession through research and evaluation activities. When planning and conducting research or evaluation, health educators do so in accordance with federal and state laws and regulations, organizational and institutional policies, and professional standards.

Section 1: Health educators support principles and practices of research and evaluation that do no harm to individuals, groups, society, or the environment.

Section 2: Health educators ensure that participation in research is voluntary and is based upon the informed consent of the participants.

Section 3: Health educators respect the privacy, rights, and dignity of research participants, and honor commitments made to those participants.

Section 4: Health educators treat all information obtained from participants as confidential unless otherwise required by law.

Section 5: Health educators take credit, including authorship, only for work they have actually performed and give credit to the contributions of others.

Section 6: Health educators who serve as research or evaluation consultants discuss their results only with those to whom they are providing service, unless maintaining such confidentiality would jeopardize the health or safety of others.

Section 7: Health educators report the results of their research and evaluation objectively, accurately, and in a timely fashion.

Article VI: Responsibility in Professional Preparation

Those involved in the preparation and training of health educators have an obligation to accord learners the same respect and treatment given other groups by providing quality education that benefits the profession and the public.

Section 1: Health educators select students for professional preparation programs based upon equal opportunity for all, and the individual's academic performance, abilities, and potential contribution to the profession and the public's health.

Section 2: Health educators strive to make the educational environment and culture conducive to the health of all involved, and free from sexual harassment and all forms of discrimination.

Section 3: Health educators involved in professional preparation and professional development engage in careful preparation; present material that is accurate, up-to-date, and timely; provide reasonable and timely feedback; state clear and reasonable expectations; and conduct fair assessments and evaluations of learners.

Section 4: Health educators provide objective and accurate counseling to learners about career opportunities, development, and advancement, and assist learners to secure professional employment.

Section 5: Health educators provide adequate supervision and meaningful opportunities for the professional development of learners.

Approved: Coalition of National Health Education Organizations, November 8, 1999, Chicago, IL. Used with the permission of the Coalition of National Health Education Organizations.

Short Version

Code of Ethics for the Health Education Profession

Preamble

The health education profession is dedicated to excellence in the practice of promoting individual, family, organizational, and community health. The Code of Ethics provides a framework of shared values within which health education is practiced. The responsibility of each health educator is to aspire to the highest possible standards of conduct and to encourage the ethical behavior of all those with whom they work.

Article I: Responsibility to the Public

A health educator's ultimate responsibility is to educate people for the purpose of promoting, maintaining, and improving individual, family, and community health. When a conflict of issues arises among individuals, groups, organizations, agencies, or institutions, health educators must consider all issues and give priority to those that promote wellness and quality of living through principles of self-determination and freedom of choice for the individual.

Article II: Responsibility to the Profession

Health educators are responsible for their professional behavior, for the reputation of their profession, and for promoting ethical conduct among their colleagues.

Article III: Responsibility to Employers

Health educators recognize the boundaries of their professional competence and are accountable for their professional activities and actions.

Article IV: Responsibility in the Delivery of Health Education

Health educators promote integrity in the delivery of health education. They respect the rights, dignity, confidentiality, and worth of all people by adapting strategies and methods to meet the needs of diverse populations and communities.

Article V: Responsibility in Research and Evaluation

Health educators contribute to the health of the population and to the profession through research and evaluation activities. When planning and conducting research or evaluation, health educators do so in accordance with federal and state laws and regulations, organizational and institutional policies, and professional standards.

Article VI: Responsibility in Professional Preparation

Those involved in the preparation and training of health educators have an obligation to accord learners the same respect and treatment given other groups by providing quality education that benefits the profession and the public.

Approved: Coalition of National Health Education Organizations, November 8, 1999, Chicago, IL. Used with the permission of the Coalition of National Health Education Organizations.

APPENDIX B | Guidelines for Faculty–Student Collaboration Department of Health Science Education University of Florida

These guidelines (1) facilitate professional dissemination of results from faculty–student collaborative work, primarily through presentations at professional meetings and publications in professional journals; (2) develop a process to ensure fair and equitable acknowledgment of contributions made by project participants; and (3) accomplish this goal through professional ethical principles. These guidelines pertain to situations in which students work under faculty supervision within courses for which they receive credit (i.e., independent study, supervised research, and thesis and dissertation research) as well as to projects on which faculty and students collaborate voluntarily outside of formal coursework.

1. Students retain primary ownership of work for which they bear primary responsibility. Primary responsibility for a project generally results when one initiates, plans, conducts, and writes the report of project results.

2. As primary authors of project results:
   a. students' names should be listed first on disseminated reports, such as professional presentations and publications.
   b. with advice from their supervisor, students should determine whether, and the order in which, faculty collaborators are listed in disseminated reports to reflect all project contributors in a just manner. Determinations should be based on significance of the contribution faculty make to the project including, but not limited to, their role in its design, completion, and writing. The faculty role should involve a substantive effort, beyond simple editorial comments and minor changes.

3. Even when students retain primary ownership, faculty retain the option to publish or present the students' work (with the student still listed first) if: (a) the student takes no action within a reasonable time period (approximately six months), and (b) the student gives written approval to the faculty member.

4. All parties to a collaborative project should sign a "memorandum of understanding" reflecting their agreement based on these guidelines. The memorandum should delineate terms under which the faculty member may initiate presentation and/or publication of the project (see #3).

5. In case of a dispute between or among any participants in a collaborative project concerning any aspect of dissemination of results, the matter should be presented to the Graduate Advisory Committee for resolution, and if not resolved, to the Department Chair.

(Approved October 29, 1993)

309

Memorandum of Understanding
Department of Health Science Education
University of Florida

(Sample Outline)

This document describes terms under which Student X and Faculty Y agree to work collaboratively on the project described below. A signature and date indicate voluntary acceptance of the following terms.

1. Project participants include Student X (SSN 000-00-0000) and Faculty Y.
2. The collaboration shall occur in the context of "HSC 7904—Advanced Readings in Health Science Education." Student X shall enroll in HSC 7904, Section 0000, for 3 semester hours of credit, Fall Semester 20XX.
3. Under the direction of Faculty Y, Student X shall conduct a literature review and related research to: (1) identify existing K–12 violence prevention curricula; (2) prepare a written report in journal article format of at least XXXX words describing, comparing, and contrasting the curricula; (3) compile a listing of resources for information and assistance on violence prevention.
4. Project results shall be submitted for presentation at (Conference) and for publication in (Journal).
5. Student X accepts responsibility for successful completion of the project as described in #3 above, including submission of the work for presentation and publication as described in #4 above. Faculty Y accepts responsibility for providing guidance to Student X throughout the planning, conduct, and successful completion of the project. Student X shall prepare and sub-

mit the presentation proposal, with assistance from Faculty Y. If accepted, Student X shall deliver the presentation if circumstances and funding permit. If not, Faculty Y retains the option to present. Student X shall prepare and submit the article manuscript, with assistance from Faculty Y.

6. Student X shall be listed as first presenter and first author. Faculty Y shall be listed as second presenter and second author. If student X does not submit a presentation proposal and/or an article manuscript by (date), Faculty Y retains the option to prepare and submit a presentation proposal and/or article manuscript. If Faculty Y exercises this option, Student X still shall be listed as first presenter and first author. This signed memorandum constitutes written approval from Student X, should Faculty Y elect to exercise the option.

Accepted:

_____

Signature/Date

_____

Signature/Date

Acknowledgment: These guidelines were created by Barbara A. Rienzo, PhD, and R. Morgan Pigg, Jr., HSD, MPH, faculty members in the Department of Health Education and Behavior (formerly Department of Health Science Education), University of Florida, Gainesville, FL, based upon the article: Rienzo, B.A. (1994). Guidelines for ethical faculty/student collaboration in health science education. In R.M. Pigg, Jr. (Ed.), *The Eta Sigma Gamma Monograph Series: Ethical Issues of Scientific Inquiry in Health Science Education* (pp. 18–30). Muncie, IN: Eta Sigma Gamma. They are used here with the permission of the authors and Eta Sigma Gamma.

APPENDIX C | Establishing Content Validity: Using Qualitative and Quantitative Steps*

James F. McKenzie, PhD, MPH
Martin L. Wood, PhD
Jerome E. Kotecki, HSD
Jeffrey K. Clark, HSD
Rebecca A. Brey, PhD

The necessity for and ability of health educators to collect valid and reliable data have been noted in *A Competency-Based Framework for Professional Development of Certified Health Education Specialists.*[1] Within the framework, two specific responsibilities—Number I, Assessing Individual and Community Needs for Health Education, and Number IV, Evaluating Effectiveness of Health Education Programs—rely heavily on health educators' ability to determine if they are collecting data with a valid and reliable instrument, if they are using data that were collected with such an instrument, or both. The importance of collecting and using valid and reliable data has been well documented.[2-6] Torabi[5] discussed the importance of using data-collection instruments that possessed good psychometric qualities. The absence of good psychometric qualities "results in a lack of confidence in findings and recommendations of

research papers."[5] Torabi went on to explain appropriate methods for establishing the reliability of a data-collection instrument. Similarly, the methods for establishing the validity of a data-collection instrument have also been presented in the literature. Depending on the type of validity to be established, some methods are established via an objective or quantitative means, whereas others are more subjective or qualitative in nature. One type of validity, content validity, is best established by using both processes. However, to date, there has not been a step-by-step process presented in the literature. Therefore, the purpose of this project was to provide a comprehensive procedure for the establishment of content validity by using both the quantitative and qualitative processes.

Validity and Data Collection Instruments

Validity has been defined as the degree to which an instrument measures what it purports to measure.[7] "In the broadest terms, validity in measurement

*Source: American Journal of Health Behavior, by James F. McKenzie et al., Volume 23, No. 4, pp. 311–318. Copyright © 1999 by PNG Publications. Reprinted with permission of PNG Publications in the format textbook via Copyright Clearance Center.

addresses the degree to which the concept or concepts under study are accurately represented by the particular items on your questionnaire, test, self-report form, or other measuring device."[8] Validity has often been thought to be a more important issue than reliability. If an instrument does not measure what [it] is supposed to, then it does not matter if it is reliable.[9] Invalid or biased data-collection instruments can lead to erroneous conclusions, which, in turn, can influence future decisions.[7]

There are three primary means of establishing validity. They include criterion-related, construct, and content validity. Criterion-related validity actually refers to a general category of evidence of the extent to which scores on a data-collection instrument are correlated with some measure of an individual's behavior or performance. The two subtypes of criterion-related validity are predictive and concurrent. The degree to which test scores are confirmed by later subject behavior is a statement of the instrument's predictive validity. In this case, the behavioral measure used is called the criterion. In concurrent validity, the criterion measure is obtained at the same time as that the instrument being developed is administered, rather than some weeks or months later, as is the case with predictive validity. In both varieties of criterion-related validity, the aim is to legitimize the inferences we make by establishing their predictive ability for a related criterion.[7] Criterion validity is established via quantitative means.

Occasionally it is more difficult to identify behavioral criteria that will directly validate our measure. In this case, one may consider how our measured variable might be theoretically related to other variables. Construct validity has been defined as the extent to which the measure of concern correlates with these other measures, among which a logical relationship can be construed to exist.[9,10] This form of validity is often used when trying to measure a theoretical construct (e.g., locus of control, self-efficacy, or perceived barriers) for which a clear-cut behavioral equivalent

does not exist. Construct validity is also established via quantitative means.

Finally, content validity refers to the degree to which the items of the data-collection instrument "are a representative sample of the universe of content and/or behavior of the domain being addressed."[11] For example, if an instrument is to measure AIDS knowledge of an individual, does the instrument include items from the full breadth of information about AIDS? Furthermore, "content validity should not be confused with 'face' validity, which lacks the systematic logical analysis required by content validation."[11] Unlike criterion and construct validity, content validity is judged during an instrument's early development, not after completion.[8] In the practice of health education, more often than not, the standard means for establishing content validity has been through subjective or qualitative processes. However, a quantitative process for establishing content validity has been available for a number of years.[3,12] More recently, the work of Lawshe has been expanded by Veneziano and Hooper[6] to include the concept of statistical significance. Even though Lawshe and Veneziano and Hooper have cited the need to use both quantitative and qualitative processes when calculating content validity, neither has presented a detailed step-by-step process to do so.

Methods

Instrumentation

Table of specifications. Before this project was undertaken, there had not been a comprehensive listing of the necessary components needed to create a content-valid data-collection instrument using both qualitative and quantitative procedures. Therefore, it was necessary to develop a table of specifications to determine what should be included. After a thorough review of the literature, a table of specifications was created (Table 1).

Table 1   Table of Specifications

I. Establishment of a jury (panel) of jurors (experts)
   A. Create criteria for selection
   B. Identify potential jurors
   C. Select jurors
   D. Create directions for the work of jurors
II. Qualitative review of instrument components
   A. Appropriateness of instrument title
   B. Appropriateness of the directions for the instrument
      1. Concise
      2. Clarity
      3. Complete
   C. Content areas covered
      1. Appropriate
      2. Complete
   D. Instrument items
      1. Appropriateness
      2. Clarity
      3. Adequacy of response options for items
   E. Opportunity for revision of items
   F. Opportunity to recommend deleting an item
   G. Opportunity to add additional items to the instrument
   H. Opportunity for additional comments
III. Quantitative review of instrument components
   A. Determine rating scale
   B. Combine jurors'/panelists' ratings
   C. Eliminate those items that are not content valid

Creating a procedure to establish content validity. Using the table of specifications and guidelines identified by others,[13] the authors prepared a list of steps to follow in order to establish content validity (Table 2).

Discussion

The procedure identified in Table 2 comprises four major tasks: (a) creating the initial draft of the instrument, (b) establishing a jury of experts, (c) completing a qualitative review, and (d) completing a quantitative review.

Creating the Initial Draft of the Instrument

A critical first step in the creation of a new instrument is clearly defining the concept to be measured and establishing the objectives outlining the purpose of the instrument. For example, if diabetes knowledge is being measured, then what is meant by this term? In whose knowledge are we interested? In what context? If a needs assessment instrument is to collect data on the health needs of a target population, what is meant by "health needs"? Who specifically is included in the target population? What type of data is needed? In what form? Many data-collection instruments that purport to measure a specific topic are theoretically ambiguous because of failure to clearly establish the conceptual framework for the instrument. McDowell and Newell stressed that "the conceptual definition of an index justifies its content and relates it to a broader body of theory, showing how the results obtained may be interpreted in light of that theory."[14] In other words, clearly defining what is to be measured significantly limits the universe of possible items and makes the selection of possible items much easier. The creation of such a definition and objectives will provide the creator with an outline (i.e., table of specifications) of what should be included in the instrument. The very act of creating a new instrument presupposes that the one creating the instrument has sufficiently reviewed the related literature in order to make judgment that an appropriate instrument does not already exist.

The review of the literature should investigate professional journals and related publications, books, government publications, or unpublished research in progress. Those creating the new instrument may also need to contact public or private funding agencies that have supported research in the relevant areas.[2] The review should establish

Table 2   Steps to Follow When Establishing Content Validity

1. Clearly define the concept to be measured and establish the objectives outlining the purpose of the instrument.
2. Create a draft of the instrument complete with title, directions, items, and data-recording procedures.
3. Create criteria for selection of jurors to serve on the jury.
4. Identify individuals who meet the selection criteria for the jury.
5. Invite those individuals identified in Step #3 to serve on the jury.
6. Select the jurors.
7. Create detailed instructions outlining the jurors' task for the qualitative review.
8. Distribute draft of the instrument and instructions to jurors for qualitative review.
9. Collect jurors' qualitative responses.
10. Analyze jurors' qualitative responses and incorporate into instrument.
11. Create a revised draft of the instrument.
12. Create detailed instructions outlining the jurors' task for the quantitative review.
13. Distribute draft of the instrument and instructions to jurors for quantitative review.
14. Collect jurors' quantitative responses.
15. Analyze jurors' quantitative responses; eliminate those items with an insufficient content validity ratio for significance at $p < .05$.
16. Calculate overall instrument content validity by determining the mean content validity ratio.
17. Create a revised draft of the instrument.
18. Send thank you letters to the jurors.

the breadth and depth of the topic of investigation and identify the most important information needed to establish the necessary content of the instrument. The review should also uncover useable questions from other selected instruments. It may be admirable, but it is also foolish to "recreate the wheel." Many well-accepted health data-collection instruments are hybrids of preexisting tools; it is perfectly permissible to adapt instruments that are not "just right" for a situation as long as appropriate permission is received from the original author(s). There are a number of reasons for using items from other instruments, not the least important of which is that it saves work and time. Items from other instruments have been used repeatedly and proven themselves to be psychometrically sound.[15]

Having exhausted the repertoire of established instruments, and having combed the literature for theoretical statements that readily translate into items, one may also consult, say via focus groups

or key informants, the anticipated target group to generate instrument items.[15] Their discussion may provide general themes from which items may be developed or may even result in clear, unambiguous items that one may be assured are at least understandable by the target group. With a good number of instrument items and a well-polished draft in hand, the instrument creator is ready to establish the instrument validity.

Establishing a Jury of Experts

The jury of experts, or panel of experts as it is sometimes called, is the initial and a critical step in establishing content validity. This process begins with the identification of criteria to be used to select the experts/jurors. Commonly used criteria include position/job, experience, knowledge, and availability. For example, Stacer[16] used the following criteria to select jurors for the creation of a diabetes knowledge test:

1. Be either a health care professional who works with people with diabetes, a diabetes educator, or be skilled in instrument creation and design.
2. Be willing to serve on the jury.
3. Be able to complete the task in the time frame provided by the researcher.

Once the criteria are established, an invitation to serve on the jury is extended to those who meet them. The method used to invite the jurors is usually determined by their proximity to those creating the instrument. It can be done face to face, via the telephone, or by letter. (See Table 3 for an example of a written invitation.) As a part of the invitation, jurors are informed of the tasks to be completed, the time frame, and the estimated amount of time to complete the tasks. If the invitation is offered via a letter, jurors are often asked to indicate their willingness to serve by either calling or returning an accompanying postcard.

Finally, when deciding on the number of jurors to invite for the review, it is important to consider the number required to meet the various minimum content validity ratio (CVR) values that satisfy the five percent probability level for statistical significance (Table 4). The greater the number of jurors who participate in the analysis of the instrument items, the lower the minimum CVR required to meet the $p < .05$ level.

Completing the Qualitative Review

With the jury selection complete, the qualitative or subjective review of the instrument can be completed. This process begins by providing the jurors

Table 3 Example of a Letter Inviting People to Serve as Jurors

Date

Name
Address
Institution
City, State, ZIP Code

Dear _____:

I am writing to request your assistance as a juror in validating an instrument I am developing to collect data on (insert topic of instrument here). I am inviting you to participate in this process because of your work, knowledge, and interest in (insert topic here). Participation in this process will include two reviews (one qualitative and one quantitative) of my draft instrument. I would estimate that each review would take you approximately (insert number of minutes) minutes to complete. Should you accept my invitation to serve as juror, in the next few weeks you will receive a packet of materials including a copy of the draft instrument and instructions for completing the reviews.

Thank you for considering this request. Please contact me via e-mail, telephone, or FAX by (insert date) to let me know of your decision. I look forward to hearing from you soon.

Sincerely,

Author's name
Title
Phone number
FAX number
e-mail address

Table 4   Minimum Values of the Content Validity Ratio for Significance at p < .05 (one-tailed test)

Number panelists	Minimum value
5	.99
6	.99
7	.99
8	.78
9	.75
10	.62
11	.59
12	.56
13	.54
14	.51
15	.49
20	.42
25	.37
30	.33
35	.31
40	.29

Taken from: Veneziano L, Hooper J. A method for quantifying content validity of health-related questionnaires. *Am J Health Behav* 1997;21(1):67-70.

with a packet of materials comprising the following: a cover letter explaining their tasks, thanking them for their participation, and establishing a due date for their work (Table 5); a copy of the draft instrument; a list of questions to answer (Created from Item II in Table 1); the objectives of the instrument; and a self-addressed, stamped return envelope.

Upon receipt of the jurors' work, the instrument creator analyzes each component of the instrument in light of the jurors' responses. In this step, the creator is normally looking for consensus among the jurors' ideas. Such consensus is the indicator that a change should be made. However, it is not uncommon for the instrument creator to receive a very good idea/comment/etc. from one juror and none of the others. If in the eye of the creator this is an idea that needs to be included, it should be, even though there is not a consensus. In the qualitative review of the instrument, it is the creator's "call" as to what is to be included in the instrument.

Completing the Quantitative Review

After the instrument creator has incorporated the jurors' qualitative review suggestions, he or she is ready to begin the quantitative review. In a similar manner as the qualitative review, the creator provides the jurors with a packet very similar to the one provided for the qualitative review; however, they will be receiving a revised instrument that includes the changes from the qualitative review.

This portion of the validating process should be patterned after the process initially described by Lawshe[3,12] and later expanded by Veneziano and Hooper.[6] This is completed by asking the jurors to rate the appropriateness of each item by stating if each item is

- essential,
- useful but not essential, or
- not necessary.

Upon receipt of each juror's rating, the instrument creator sums the responses for each item and calculates the content validity ratio (CVR) (Figure 1). The calculated CVRs are then compared to the levels necessary (Table 4) for statistical significance at $p < .05$. Because the binomial distribution was used to determine the probability values for item acceptance, the greater the number of jurors employed, the lower the minimal CVR value required for acceptance at the five percent level of chance. In concept, if the CVRs do not reach the minimal levels noted for the appropriate number of jurors, the item should then be dropped from the instrument. However, it should be noted that the use of the CVR to reject items should not prevent the use of other traditional item-analysis procedures from being employed for further determining the retention of items in the final form of the instrument.[3] When this portion of the validating process is complete, the instrument is ready to be pilot tested.

Some might ask why the qualitative and quantitative reviews should be conducted as separate reviews. We would agree that many, if not most,

Table 5   A Sample Cover Letter to Jurors

Date

Name
Address
Institution
City, State, ZIP Code

Dear _____:

   Thank you for agreeing to serve on the jury of experts for the development of the data collection instrument I am developing on (insert topic of instrument here). Your input and feedback are very important to establish the validity of the instrument. As noted in earlier correspondence, I estimate that each of your two reviews of this (insert number of items) item instrument will take approximately (insert number of minutes) minutes.
   Enclosed you will find a copy of the draft instrument to be reviewed, specific directions to follow while completing your review, and a self-addressed stamped return envelope in which to return your work. Please feel free to write your comments on the instrument or use additional paper as needed. Return the instrument with your comments in the envelope so that it will reach me no later than (insert date). If you have any questions, please feel free to contact me. Please accept my thanks in advance for your help and advice in the development of this instrument.

Sincerely,

Author's name
Title
Phone number
FAX number
e-mail address

Encl: Instrument, directions, return envelope

---

instrument creators *do* carry out these processes at the same time. However, when the two reviews are carried out simultaneously, qualitative suggestions or changes provided by any one juror cannot be reviewed quantitatively by all jurors. Thus, we feel the two reviews should be completed separately with the qualitative review occurring first.

Conclusion

The establishment of the validity of an instrument is critical in the future acceptability of its use and the practical application of findings that result

from it. In behavioral science research, particularly in the measurement of such abstract constructs as attitudes, beliefs, and values, it is imperative to attend to validity in its several forms. Content validity can be distinguished from the less rigorous "face" validity in its reliance on a systematic and logical process of analysis of individual items.[11] Clearly, quantitative research in health education continues using instruments for which evidence of content validity is limited at best. As already noted, we should be cautious in portraying these researchers as sloppy or unprepared; until now, a detailed, step-by-step protocol that incorporates both qualitative and quantitative reviews

$$CVR = \frac{n_e - N/2}{N/2}$$

where:

CVR = content validiity ratio

n_e = number of panelists (jurors)

N = total number of panelists (jurors)

FIGURE 1
Formula for calculating a content validity ratio (CVR)
Taken from: Lawshe CH. A quantitative approach to content validity. *Personnel Psy* 1975;28:563-575.

of prospective items has not been described. The procedure described herein provides just such a systematic and logical approach to demonstrating the content validity of an instrument, and results in both qualitative and quantitative evidence.

[Note: This two-step process for developing content validity has been used by several master's degree students at Ball State University, Muncie, IN. For abstracts of their work, contact the corresponding author.]

References

1. The National Commission for Health Education Credentialing, Inc. (NCHEC). A Compentency-Based Framework for Professional Development of Certified Health Education Specialists. Allentown, PA, NCHEC, 1996.
2. Aday, LA. Designing and Conducting Health Surveys: A Comprehensive Guide (2nd ed.). San Francisco, CA: Jossey-Bass, Inc., 1996.
3. Lawshe CH. A quantitative approach to content validity. *Personnel Psy* 1975;28:563–575.
4. Stacy RD. Instrument evaluation guides for survey research in health education and health promotion. *Health Education* 1987;18(5):65–67.
5. Torabi MR. Reliability methods and numbers of items in development of health instruments. *Health Values* 1994;18(6):56–59.
6. Veneziano L, Hooper J. A method for quantifying content validity of health-related questionnaires. *American Journal of Health Behavior* 1997;21(1): 67–70.
7. Borg WR, Gall MD. Educational Research: An Introduction. New York: Longman, 1989.
8. Green LW, Lewis FM. Measurement and Evaluation in Health Education and Health Promotion. Palo Alto, CA: Mayfield Publishing Company, 1986.
9. Windsor R, Baranowski T, Clark N, Cutter G. Evaluation of Health Promotion, Health Education, and Disease Prevention Programs. Mountain View, CA: Mayfield Publishing Company, 1994.
10. Babbie ER. The Practice of Social Research. (6th ed.) Belmont, CA: Wadsworth Publishing Company, 1992.
11. Hopkins KD, Stanley JC, Hopkins BR. Educational and Psychological Measurement and Evaluation (7th ed.). Englewood Cliffs, NJ: Prentice Hall, Inc., 1990.
12. Lawshe CH. Inferences from personnel tests and their validities. *J Applied Psy* 1985;70:237–238.
13. Sarvela PD, McDermott RJ. Health Education Evaluation and Measurement: A Practitioner's Perspective. Madison, WI: WCB Brown & Benchmark Publishers, 1993.
14. McDowell I, Newell C. Measuring Health: A Guide to Rating Scales and Questionnaires. (2nd ed.). New York: Oxford University Press, 1996.
15. Streiner DL, Norman GR. Health Measurement Scales: A Practical Guide to Their Development and Use. (2nd ed.). Oxford: Oxford University Press, 1995.
16. Stacer AM. Creation of a Diabetes Knowledge Test. Unpublished master's thesis, Ball State University, Muncie, IN, 1997.

GLOSSARY

abstract brief summary of the thesis or dissertation that is usually placed on a separate page following the title page

acknowledgments a separate page following the abstract that allows students to recognize and thank those people that have been most helpful with the thesis or dissertation process

active deception also called deception by commission; occurs when researchers deliberately mislead the research participants about some aspect of the study (Kimmel, 2007, Chapter 6)

analysis of covariance a statistical technique that can be used to control for initial group differences

anonymity exists when there is no link between personal information and the research participant's identity (McKenzie *et al.*, 2009, Chapter 6)

anonymous the respondent is unknown to the researcher

appendices materials following the reference list in a thesis or dissertation that provide additional detail and support future replication of the study

applied research research done with a specific question or application in mind (Leedy & Ormrod, 2010, Chapter 1) such as determining if one smoking cessation program is better than another

assent the "willingness to participate in research by persons who are by definition too young to give informed consent but who are old enough to understand the proposed research in general, its expected risks and possible benefits, and the activities expected of them as subjects" (NIH, 2000, para 2, Chapter 6)

assumption "a condition that is taken for granted and without which the research effort would be impossible" (Neutens & Rubinson, 2010, p. 19, Chapter 5)

authentic assessment a type of performance-based assessment that more accurately measures a person's skills or ability to perform (behave)

autobiographic study a personal account of one's life

axial coding the process of drawing a relationship between a category and its subcategories

baseline a measurement taken to obtain the status or level of a variable prior to initiating a study

basic research also called pure research; research with no immediate application (Salkind, 2000, Chapter 1)

behavioral objectives also called impact or midterm objectives; they examine the actions or behaviors of the priority population

Belmont Report released by the National Commission for the Protection of Human Subjects of Biomedical and Behavioral Research in 1979; identified the three fundamental ethical principles that are relevant to all research involving human subjects (respect for persons, beneficence, and justice)

best practices "recommendations for an intervention, based on critical review of multiple research and evaluation studies that substantiate the efficacy of the intervention in the populations and circumstances in which the studies were done, if not its effectiveness in other populations and situations where it might be implemented" (Green & Kreuter, 2005, p. G-1, Chapter 4)

bibliography or bibliography of related readings lists all sources read whether or not they are cited in a document

biographic study conducted by someone other than the individual who is the subject of study and may use interviews with that person as well as other documents to obtain the needed information

319

blind study those involved in the study do not know whether they are receiving the treatment or the placebo

Bloom's taxonomy a categorization of educational objectives useful in conceptualizing the way people learn and assimilate information

Boolean operators syntax terms used in the search line that help the computer to identify more precisely the articles of value to a specific search

bounded system one that is bound by time and place

bracketing the process of setting aside all preconceived notions, personal beliefs, feelings, and perceptions

call for papers an invitation for individuals or groups to submit proposals or abstracts of their work to be considered for presentation

capstone experience a major project designed as the culmination of an undergraduate program

case studies involve the in-depth study of one individual, program, community, setting, or event for a defined period of time

categories groups of concepts that become the cornerstones of theory development

causal-comparative research "attempt to determine the cause or consequences of differences that already exist between or among groups of individuals" (Fraenkel & Wallen, 2003, p. 368, Chapter 10)

census all the potential participants

census survey a survey administered to an entire population

central limit theorem (CLT) "states that the distribution of means of samples taken from any population will tend towards the normal distribution as the size of the sample increases" (Bowling, 2002, p. 179, Chapter 7)

citations brief references occurring directly in the text that provide the author(s) and date of a publication if using APA style

cluster (or area) sampling a type of probability sampling in which the sampling unit is composed of groups (or clusters or areas), not individuals

codebook a detailed description of the code, inclusion and exclusion criteria, and examples of real text for the concept or category

code of ethics a document created by professionals that outlines the norms of expected ethical behavior for the members of that profession

Code of Ethics for the Health Education Profession the code created and approved in 1999 by the Coalition of National Health Education Organizations (CNHEO)

coercion those acts that include the use of threats, force, or undue influence to get people to participate

cognitive domain all mental activities related to thinking, reasoning, remembering, etc. (Black, 1999, Chapter 8)

cohort study a type of longitudinal study that follows a particular group or subgroup (called a cohort) over time, but not necessarily the same individuals

collective case study more than one instrumental case study

committee chair faculty member who serves as the primary advisor for a thesis or dissertation

community-based participatory research ". . . a collaborative approach to research that combines methods of inquiry with community capacity-building strategies to bridge the gap between knowledge produced through research and what is practiced in communities to improve health" (Viswanathan *et al.*, 2004, Chapter 1)

comprehensive exams a culminating test designed to assess a student's understanding of the responsibilities, competencies, and subcompetencies of a health education specialist as well as any content information the program deems important

computerized searches   also called electronic literature searches; utilize computer technology to identify relevant sources and are often less time consuming and more accurate than traditional manual searches

concepts   major components of the theories and models

conclusions   a section in Chapter V that briefly restates the findings reported in Chapter IV but does not include the detailed statistical information

concurrent validity   a type of criterion-related validity in which a new instrument and an established valid instrument that measure the same phenomenon are administered to the same subjects, and the results from the new instrument correlate with the results of the established valid instrument

conditional matrix   a process of data analysis used in grounded theory research that allows researchers to depict the range of conditions and consequences visually as they relate to the phenomenon of interest

confidence interval (CI)   "the range of values which contains the true population value with the probability specified" (Bowling, 2002, p. 180, Chapter 7)

confidential/confidentiality   exists when there is a link between personal information and the research participant's identity, but that information is protected from others (McKenzie *et al.*, 2009, Chapter 6)

construct   a concept that has been developed, created, or adopted for use with a specific theory

construct validity   "the degree to which a measure correlates with other measures it is theoretically expected to correlate with. Construct validity tests the theoretical framework within which the instrument is expected to perform" (Valente, 2002, p. 161, Chapter 8)

content validity   "the assessment of the correspondence between the items composing the instrument and the content domain from which the items were selected" (DiIorio, 2005, p. 213, Chapter 8)

control group   in experimental research, a group of participants exactly like the treatment group in every way possible except they receive no treatment

control variable   a variable that has the potential to affect the dependent variable as well as the independent variable, but its effects are removed or controlled by research design or statistical manipulation

convenience sampling   a type of nonprobability sampling in which participants are selected based on certain inclusion criteria (usually few in number) and their accessibility and proximity to the researcher

convergent validity   "the extent to which two measures that purport to be measuring the same topic correlate (that is, converge)" (Bowling, 2005, p. 12, Chapter 8)

correlation   "when one variable increases, another variable either increases or decreases in a somewhat predictable fashion" (Leedy & Ormrod, 2010, p. 183, Chapter 10)

correlation coefficient   symbolized by a lower-case r, and ranges between 0.00 and either $+1.00$ or -1.00; a perfect correlation would equal either a $+1.00$ or a -1.00; if variables are completely unrelated, the r value would be 0.00

correlational research   non-experimental research that examines relationships between or among variables

correlational study   "examines the extent to which differences in one characteristic or variable are related to differences in one or more other characteristics or variables" (Leedy & Ormrod, 2010, p. 183, Chapter 10)

correlative hypothesis   predicts that there will be a relationship between variables, but does not specify the exact nature of that relationship

corresponding author   the person who takes responsibility for putting the materials together to submit the work for publication

credibility   qualitative research's analog to quantitative research's concept of internal validity

criterion-related validity   the extent to which data generated from a measurement instrument are correlated with data generated from a measure (criterion) of the phenomenon being studied, usually an individual's behavior or performance

cross-sectional study   a study that compares individuals or groups at a given point in time

culturally competent   the ability "to understand and respect values, attitudes, beliefs, and mores that differ across cultures, and to consider and respond appropriately to these differences in planning, implementing, and evaluating health education and health promotion programs and interventions" (Joint Committee, 2001, p. 99, Chapter 8)

cultural sensitivity   "implies knowledge that cultural differences (as well as similarities) exist, along with the refusal to assign cultural differences of such values as better or worse, more or less intelligent, right or wrong; they are simply differences" (Anderson & Fenichel, 1989, p. 8, Chapter 8)

culture   "the patterned ways of thought and behavior that characterize a social group, which are learned through socialization processes and persist through time" (Coreil, Bryant, & Henderson, 2001, p. 29, Chapter 11)

curvilinear relationship   as one variable increases a second variable increases, to a point beyond which the second variable decreases

debriefing   "a procedure by which any relevant information about the project that has been withheld or misrepresented is made known to the participants" (Dane, 1990, p. 49, Chapter 6)

deception   "the deliberate withholding of, or misinforming about, important information" (Kimmel, 1988, p. 34, Chapter 6) associated with the research

deductive reasoning   involves the forming of conclusions based on gathered data by applying the rules of logic to a premise

defense hearing   an opportunity to defend the thesis or dissertation before a final decision is made by the committee as to whether to accept the work

delimitations   parameters or boundaries placed on a study by the researcher

dependent variable   the measured or observed variable

descriptive group-comparison designs   used to determine differences between groups of people

descriptive research   studies designed to describe, through the use of numbers, percentages, and averages, characteristics of a group of people or some other phenomena

descriptive statistics   summarized data about a given population or variable so they can be easily comprehended

descriptors   key terms or words under which articles are cataloged in a given database

diffusion effect   occurs when the treatment being applied to one group spills over to or contaminates another group

directional hypothesis   predicts a difference between groups but also goes farther to predict the nature of that difference

discriminant validity   "(also known as divergent validity) requires that the construct should not correlate with dissimilar (discriminant) variables" (Bowling, 2005, p. 12, Chapter 8)

discussion   a section found in a research article or in Chapter V of a thesis or dissertation where the writer analyzes the findings or lack of findings

doctoral dissertation   a complex research project conducted by a doctoral student after being declared a candidate for the degree

double blind study   neither the researcher nor the participants know who is receiving the real treatment and who is receiving a placebo

duplication   "submitting the same manuscript or its essence to two or more journals for simultaneous consideration, or submitting a previously published paper or its essence for consideration by another journal without disclosing the prior publication" (Pigg, 1994, pp. 31–32, Chapter 6)

effect size (ES)   the magnitude of a difference between groups or between the sample and the population

electronic questionnaire   also called e-mail questionnaire; a "survey instrument for collecting data that is available on the computer" (Creswell, 2005, p. 361, Chapter 10)

electronic searches   also called computerized literature searches; utilize computer technology to identify relevant sources and are often less time consuming and more accurate than traditional manual searches

emic   an insider's perspective

enabling learning objectives   refer to the skills and/or resources people need to change the desired behaviors

environmental objectives   involve changes in the economic, political, and/or social conditions that necessitate changes in policies, procedures, guidelines, requirements, or laws

ethical issues   situations where there are competing values at play and the researcher needs to make a judgment about what is the most appropriate course of action

ethics   the study of moral behavior (Morrison, 2006, Chapter 6)

ethnographic studies   involve direct engagement of the researcher with the participants in their environment to obtain in-depth understanding of their behaviors and situations

ethnography   "description and interpretation of a cultural or social group or system" (Creswell, 1998, p. 58, Chapter 11)

etic   an outsider's perspective

evaluation   a process to determine the effectiveness of a specific program, person, technique, strategy, or initiative

evaluation research   a type of study to determine the effectiveness of a program, usually by determining if the program's objectives have been achieved

evidence   "a body of data that can be used to make decisions about planning" (McKenzie *et al.*, 2009, p. 413, Chapter 4)

evidence-based health education practice   the process of systematically finding, appraising, and using contemporaneous quantitative and qualitative research findings as the basis for decisions in the practice of health education

evidence-based interventions   those based on theory and shown to be effective through empirical study

exclusion criteria   those that exclude participants

exempt from review   a type of IRB review based on the assumption that there is no risk to the research participants

expedited review   a type of IRB review based on the assumption that the risk to research participants is minimal

experimental group   the group receiving the treatment

experimental research   designed to establish a true cause-and-effect relationship (Salkind, 2000, Chapter 1)

explanatory mixed method design qualitative data are collected after initially collecting quantitative data, and the qualitative data are used to help explain the quantitative results (Creswell, 2005)

exploratory mixed method design qualitative data are collected first, and based on these findings quantitative data are collected to answer research questions that arose from the initial qualitative findings (Creswell, 2005)

ex post facto research examines a phenomenon that has already occurred and attempts to infer cause-and-effect relationships

external validity involves the ability to generalize study results to other groups and settings beyond those in the current study

extraneous variable one that has an unpredictable or unexpected impact on the dependent variable; Extraneous variables "make possible an alternative explanation of results; an uncontrolled variable" (Fraenkel & Wallen, 2006, p. G-3, Chapter 5)

face validity upon quick review, the instrument appears to measure what it purports to measure

fairness "deals with the question of whether the instrument is appropriate for the individual of various ethnic groups with different backgrounds, gender, educational levels, etc." (Torabi, 1994, p. 56, Chapter 8)

field research conducted where people actually live, work, and play in the real world of classrooms, worksites, and communities

fieldwork the researcher in qualitative studies integrates with and participates in the day-to-day activities of the group being studied, thus allowing the researcher to obtain information through observations and interviews

fishbowl sampling also called out of a hat sampling; a type of probability sampling similar to simple random sampling but not as precise

focus group a group of people specifically brought together because of common characteristics to provide information about a health issue, product, or service

formative evaluation determines while a program is being planned and in progress if the program is really being presented as designed and if changes need to be made to increase the likelihood that program objectives will be accomplished

fragmentation "the preparation of multiple manuscripts regarding a topic that could be reported in one paper" (Pigg, 1994, p. 32, Chapter 6)

frame also called sampling frame; a list or quasi-list of all the sampling units in the study population

full review a type of IRB review required when research participants will be exposed to more than minimal risk and the research does not fall into the expedited review category

galley proofs typeset versions of manuscripts sent by publishers for author review and approval

goals broad statements of direction written in nontechnical language that are less specific than objectives and are used to explain the general intent of a program to those not directly involved in the program

grab sampling also called chunk sampling; a type of nonprobability sampling in which the participants include whomever researchers can access through direct contact (McDermott & Sarvela, 1999, Chapter 7)

grounded theory use of systematic inductive guidelines for collecting and analyzing data to generate theory

grounded theory research aims to discover or generate theory related to a specific phenomenon based on systematically collected data

group administration administering a questionnaire to a large group of people at one time

Hawthorne effect occurs when participants' attitudes toward being involved in a study affects the way they behave

health belief model a classic health education model that helps explain why people do or do not adopt health behaviors

health education research a systematic investigation involving the analysis of collected information or data that ultimately is used to enhance health education knowledge or practice and answers one or more questions about a health-related theory, behavior, or phenomenon

Health Insurance Portability and Accountability Act of 1996 (Public Law 104-191) sets national standards that health plans, health care clearinghouses, and health care providers who conduct certain health care transactions electronically must implement to protect and guard against the misuse of individually identifiable health information.

health-related quality of life (HRQoL) composed of those aspects of people's quality of life that can be clearly shown to affect their health, either physically or mentally

Helsinki Declaration guidelines, created in 1964 by the World Medical Association and updated in 2000, that compel "government officials who administer research funds to monitor the manner in which research is conducted" (Norwood, 2000, p. 58, Chapter 6)

history effect when events occur outside of a research study between the pretest and posttest that could affect participants in such a way as to have an impact on the dependent variable

history treatment interaction a threat to external validity that develops "when the researcher tries to generalize findings to past and future situations" (Creswell, 2005, p. 294, Chapter 9)

homogeneity in research using focus groups, refers to selecting participants that possess similar characteristics deemed important by the researcher

homogeneous sampling a type of nonprobability sampling in which a very specific group of individuals are selected because they possess a unique trait or factor

honorary authorship making a person a coauthor for contributing (or supporting) in less than a meaningful or substantial way

honors thesis usually completed by outstanding undergraduate students as either a capstone experience or an elective course

human subject also called research participant; "a living individual about whom an investigator obtains either (1) data through interaction or intervention with the individual, or (2) identifiable private information" (NIH, 2004, p. 4, Chapter 6)

human subjects committee approves research proposals utilizing human subjects before research can begin

hybrid items instrument items that include elements of both a structured and an unstructured item

hypothesis a formal statement that predicts a single research outcome; in essence, an educated guess made by the researcher that predicts the results of the research findings

implementation effect a threat to internal validity that occurs when those responsible for implementing the experimental treatment inadvertently introduce inequality or bias into the study

implied consent a type of consent that relies on the inference by a research participant's actions that consent is given to participate in a study even though a consent statement form is not signed

incentives nominal inducements to encourage participant response

inclusion criteria those that include participants

independent variable the variable being examined or tested; often the variable of most interest in a study

in-depth interviews   used to uncover feelings and attitudes an individual has regarding a specific experience

index   a listing of all articles published in those journals cataloged within the index

inductive reasoning   to develop truths or produce universal claims or principles based on feelings, insights, ideas, or awareness derived from the information collected

inferential statistics   used to draw inferences about the effects of sampling error on results (Patten, 2009); also used to determine if differences between groups are real differences or the result of chance

informed consent   "the voluntary agreement of an individual, or his or her authorized representative, who has the legal capacity to give consent, and who exercises free power of choice, without undue inducement or any other form of constraint or coercion to participate in research. The individual must have sufficient knowledge and understanding of the nature of the proposed research, the anticipated risks and potential benefits, and the requirements of the research to be able to make an informed decision" (Levine, 1988, as stated in NIH, 2000, para 1, Chapter 6)

institutional review board (IRB)   a group that reviews and approves, requires modifications (to secure approval), or disapproves research protocols relevant to the policy "to protect the rights and well-being of subjects asked to participate" (Torabi, 1994, p. 8, Chapter 6)

instrumental case study   the case itself is of secondary interest, and the primary purpose is to provide insight into an issue

instrumentation   a collective term that describes all measurement instruments used in a study

interaction effect   the combined effect, or the interaction, of two or more independent variables on a dependent variable

internal consistency reliability   "refers to the intercorrelations among individual items on the instrument, that is, whether all items on the instrument are measuring part of the total area" (McKenzie *et al.,* 2009, pp. 116–117, Chapter 8)

internal validity   the extent to which the observed effects of the independent variable on the dependent variable are real and not caused by extraneous factors

intrarater reliability   a type of rater reliability that uses a single rater

interrater reliability   a type of rater reliability that uses two or more raters

interval measures/scales/data   puts data into categories that are mutually exclusive and exhaustive, rank orders the categories, and allows for the distance between the categories to be equal; in addition, there is no absolute zero value

interview   "an oral, in-person question and answer session between a researcher and an individual respondent" (Gay, Mills, & Airasian, 2006, p. 163)

intrinsic case study   the case itself is of interest

judgmental sampling   also called purposive sampling; a type of nonprobability sampling in which researchers select participants that they judge to be "typical" of individuals possessing a given trait (McDermott & Sarvela, 1999, Chapter 7)

Kappa   a statistic to calculate rater reliability

laboratory research   conducted in the tightly structured conditions of a lab

learning objective   follows the development of behavioral objectives and subdivided into three categories: predisposing, enabling, and reinforcing

library catalog   lists books, reports, and other nonjournal resources in a library's collection by author, title, call number, or subject

life history   based not only on interviews with the person but also an analysis of the economic, historical, political, and social contexts of the individual's life

limitation   parameters or boundary of the research established by factors or people other than the researcher

linear relationship   as one variable increases, a second variable either increases or decreases at some level of predictability

literature review   "a synthesis of the literature on a topic" (Pan, 2008, p. 1.); Creswell (2005) goes into more detail in noting that a literature review involves, "locating summaries, books, journals, and indexed publications on a topic, selectively choosing which literature to include in your review, and then summarizing the literature in a written report" (p. 9)

literature search   identifying and obtaining relevant resources to include in a literature review

local review   giving a manuscript to others at the local level to review and critique prior to submitting it to a journal

location effect   occurs when there are differences in the locations where interventions take place

longitudinal study   a study that follows individuals or groups over long periods of time to determine changes

main effect   the effect of each independent variable on the dependent variable

master's project   involves program development, research, or evaluation that is usually specific to a work setting or agency and produces results that may not be generalizable or of interest to others outside of the specific setting in which the work takes place

master's thesis   a detailed, well-designed study specific to graduate schools that is typically written in five chapters; will produce results of interest to others in the profession and, therefore, should be published

matrix sampling   a type of probability sampling in which the participants need to respond to a large number of items; instead of responding to all items, several randomly selected participants' responses to different items are combined to form the response of one

maturation effect   changes seen in subjects are a result of the time that has elapsed since the study began and not any program effects

measurement   the process of assigning numbers or labels to objects, events, or people according to a particular set of rules (Kerlinger, 1986, Chapter 8)

measurement instrument   also called tool or data collection instrument or instrument; item(s) used to measure a variable of interest

mentee   usually a younger, less experienced individual who seeks the advice and support of an older, more experienced individual or mentor

mentor   usually an older, more experienced individual who provides advice and support to foster the progress of a younger, less experienced person or mentee.

missing data   data not available because of an error or skipped question that must be accounted for in data analysis

mixed method study   both quantitative and qualitative approaches to research are utilized in the same study (Creswell, 2005)

models   "generalized, hypothetical descriptions, often based on an analogy, used to analyze or explain something" (Glanz & Rimer, 1995, p. 11, Chapter 4)

modified replication   utilizing the same study design as someone else but making changes to some aspect of the original study, such as the population being studied or the instrument used

mortality effect   a threat to validity from an attrition of study participants

multiple regression a statistical technique to determine a correlation between a criterion variable and two or more predictor variables

multistage cluster sampling also called area sampling; a combination of cluster sampling and simple random sampling techniques "in which a series of random selections is made from units of progressively smaller size" (Crowl, 1993, p. 285, Chapter 7)

National Research Act of 1974 (Public Law 93-348) passed by Congress in 1974; required the Department of Health, Education, and Welfare (HEW) (renamed the Department of Health and Human Services [HHS] in 1981) to codify its policy for the protection of human subjects into federal regulations

nominal measures/scales/data the lowest level in the measurement hierarchy; puts data into categories that are mutually exclusive and exhaustive

nondirectional hypothesis predicts a difference between groups but does not specify what that difference might be

non-experimental research any quantitative research that does not look for cause-and-effect relationships; utilized when it is not practical, possible, feasible, or desirable to manipulate an independent variable as would be necessary in experimental research

nonprobability sampling all individuals in the study population do not have an equal chance and a known probability of being selected to participate in the study

nonproportional stratified random sample one generated by a type of stratified sampling in which the sampling units are not selected in the proportion to which the strata are represented in the study population

null hypothesis states that there will be no difference or relationship between groups

Nuremberg Code created in 1947; put forth 10 conditions to outline permissible guidelines for medical experimentation

objectives written at multiple levels and serve as the guideposts on which a program is developed; the foundation of program evaluation

objectives-oriented approach specific objectives are stated, procedures are devised to collect data to determine if stated objectives have been met, and program success is determined by the degree to which stated program objectives were accomplished

observation "notice taken of an indicator" (Green & Lewis, 1986, p. 363, Chapter 8)

obtrusive observation "indicates that the person being studied is aware of being measured, assessed, or tested" (Windsor *et al.,* 2004, p. 111, Chapter 8)

open coding part of the analysis in qualitative research when the researchers read each line, sentence, and paragraph attempting to answer the question "what is this about?"

operationalization the process of transforming a concept or construct into measurable terms

operational definition unique to one's own study; typically terms that need to be operationally defined are found as variables in the purpose statement, research questions, or hypotheses

oral history researcher collects information from an individual or individuals about specific events and their causes and effects

ordinal measures/scales/data put data into categories that are mutually exclusive and exhaustive, but also permit them to be rank ordered

***p* value** probability that an observed difference is the result of chance

panel study a type of longitudinal study that examines the exact same individuals from a given group over time

parallel forms reliability also called equivalent forms or alternate forms reliability; focuses on whether different forms of the same instrument will produce similar results when measuring the same subjects (means, standard deviations, and item intercorrelations).

parameters limits or boundaries of the study

participant observation researcher collects data while serving as a study participant

participatory action research has been used in educational settings and is focused on improving the quality of people's organizations, communities, and family lives (Creswell, 2005)

passive consent returning the completed questionnaire implies consent to participate in the study

passive deception also called deception by omission; the researchers purposely withhold relevant information from the participants (Kimmel, 2007, Chapter 6)

peer-reviewed journals also called **refereed journals**; only publish articles that have been reviewed and accepted by an independent panel of reviewers or referees made up of individuals in the same or a closely related profession

phenomenological study qualitative research designed to understand a small, selected group of people's perceptions, understandings, and beliefs concerning a particular situation or life event

pilot studies small-scale studies intended to determine if there are positive results that would justify further study

placebo something that looks like the actual treatment, but in reality has no effect; often used in drug studies

placebo effect differences caused by participants' expectations instead of any provided treatment

plagiarism "involves the inappropriate and unauthorized use of the 'intellectual property' of others" (Pigg, 1994, p. 33, Chapter 6)

planning models those that are used for planning, implementing, and evaluating health education/promotion programs.

population those individuals in the universe that are specified by time and place

poster session type of research presentation where the researcher visually depicts the study in a poster format and displays it on a poster board at a conference or professional meeting

power the probability of rejecting the null hypothesis when it is actually false (Isaac & Michael, 1995, Chapter 7)

power analysis a procedure that "enables a researcher to determine, based on the assumption that the research hypothesis is true, the number of subjects needed to give the hypothesis a chance of being accepted" (Norwood, 2000, p. 224, Chapter 7)

practical significance refers to how those actually practicing in the profession will benefit from a given work; a study may produce statistically significant results but lack practical significance

PRECEDE-PROCEED Model classic health planning model

predictive validity a type of criterion-related validity in which a measurement used will be correlated with a future measurement of the same phenomenon

predisposing learning objectives relate to the knowledge, attitudes, values, and beliefs of the priority population that need to be modified for the behavioral objective to be met

primary source reported or written by the person or persons who actually conducted the research

privacy "the claim of individuals, groups, or institutions to determine for themselves when, how, and to what extent information about them is communicated to others" (Westin, 1968, p. 7, Chapter 6)

probability sampling   uses random selection of participants and ensures that each person in the study population has an equal chance and known probability of being selected

problem statement   see **purpose statement**

procedures   also called methods; is the section in a thesis or article that describes in detail how the research was conducted and explains the research design

process evaluation   also called formative evaluation; develops objectives to assess the program while it is being conducted or assess how the program is implemented

process objectives   also called formative objectives; used to evaluate those charged with implementing the program

professional ethics   outline the role of the profession and what the conduct of professionals should be (Bayles, 1989, Chapter 6)

program goals   broad statements of direction used primarily to explain to those outside the program what the program is designed to do

program objectives   also called health objectives, outcome objectives, or long-term objectives; deal with improving some health problem or health indicator

proportional stratified random sample   one generated by a type of stratified sampling in which the sampling units are selected in the proportion to which the strata are represented in the study population

proposal   Chapters I, II, and III of a thesis or dissertation

proposal hearing   formal presentation of the proposal to one's committee chair, all committee members, and any guests

propositions   the relationships between a category and its concepts

proxy (indirect observation)   an outcome measure that provides evidence that a behavior has occurred

psychometric properties   an instrument's validity, reliability, and fairness

purpose statement   also called problem statement; a declarative statement that clearly and succinctly describes the overall direction or focus of the research

purposive sampling   see **judgmental sampling**

qualitative measures   "tend to produce data in the language of the subjects [participants], rarely with numerical values attached to observations" (Green & Lewis, 1986, p. 151, Chapter 8)

qualitative research   designed to answer questions about the complex nature of phenomena with the purpose of describing, explaining, and understanding the phenomena being researched

quality of life (QoL)   "term that conveys an overall sense of well-being, including aspects of happiness and satisfaction with life as a whole" (CDC, 2000, p. 5, Chapter 8)

quantitative measures   "rely on more standardized data collection and reduction techniques, using predetermined questions or observational indicators and established response items" (Green & Lewis, 1986, p. 151, Chapter 8)

quantitative research   the more traditional form of research used to answer questions about relationships among measurable variables while utilizing the time-honored procedures of the scientific method

quasi-experimental research   attempts to control and manipulate variables just as in experimental designs but does not use random assignment

questionnaire   a form or instrument used in survey research that contains questions that participants are asked to answer

quota sampling   a type of nonprobability sampling in which participants are "chosen in approximate proportion to the population traits they are to represent" (McDermott & Sarvela, 1999, p. 271, Chapter 7)

random assignment   the assignment of the participants to groups such that each participant has an equal chance of being assigned to any of the groups (Neutens & Rubinson, 2010, Chapter 7)

random selection   when every member of the population has an equal chance to be selected as part of the sample

randomization   the process of randomly assigning research participants to group

rater reliability   also called observer reliability; associated with the consistent measurement (or rating) of an observed event by different individuals (or judges or raters) or by the same individual (McDermott & Sarvela, 1999, Chapter 8)

ratio measures/scales/data   put data into categories that are mutually exclusive and exhaustive, rank order the categories, and allow for equal intervals between the categories that can be measured; in addition, there is an absolute zero value

recommendations   a section found in a research article or in Chapter V of a thesis or dissertation where the writer offers suggestions to the reader concerning practical implications of the research, how the research could be improved, and ideas for future research

redundancy   also called **saturation**; seeing or hearing the same things over again while conducting a literature review

refereed journals   also called **peer-reviewed journals**; only publish articles that have been reviewed and accepted by an independent panel of reviewers or referees made up of individuals in the same or a closely related profession

reference list   an alphabetical listing by first author's last name of all sources cited in an article, thesis, or dissertation

reflexivity   understanding how the research conducted was or could have been affected by the researcher

reinforcing learning objectives   support or encourage new desirable behavior or remove support and encouragement from current undesirable behavior

reliable or reliability   the extent to which a measurement instrument will produce the same or nearly the same result (measure or score) each time it is used

research ethics   "comprises principles and standards that, along with underlying values, guide appropriate conduct relevant to research decisions" (Kimmel, 2007, p. 6, Chapter 6)

research participant   see **human subject**

research problem   question or issue that someone wants to investigate

research question   interrogative sentences that clearly and succinctly state the major question or questions to be answered in the study

return services   a postage-paid, self-addressed return envelope, included with a mailed questionnaire

rigor   employing a systematic approach to research design

rule of sufficiency   including adequate objectives and interventions for a successful program

running reference list   a list of citations placed alphabetically into the reference list while writing the document

sample   some of the potential participants

sampling   the process by which the sample is selected (Babbie, 1995, Chapter 7)

sampling bias   a sampling process that ends with a group that is biased

sampling error   the difference between the sampling estimate (the statistic) and the actual study population value (the parameter)

sampling frame   see **frame**

sampling unit   the element or set of elements considered for selection as part of a sample (Babbie, 1992, Chapter 7)

saturation   also called **redundancy** or sufficient redundancy; seeing or hearing the same things over again

scientific method   time-honored method of inquiry that involves the following steps: stating the problem; stating testable or measurable hypotheses; designing a study to test the hypotheses; conducting the study; analyzing the data using appropriate statistical tests; stating conclusions based on the findings; identifying new research questions (Berg & Latin, 2004, Chapter 1).

secondary source   one that reports on or summarizes a primary source or sources

selection bias   threat to validity that occurs when study participants are selected in a nonrandom manner

selection maturation effect   threat to validity that occurs when intact groups are used and the groups vary on their maturation level

selection treatment interaction   external threat to validity that concerns the ability of a researcher to generalize the results of a study beyond the groups involved in the study due to the way the study groups were selected

selective coding   use of initial codes that reappear frequently to sort large amounts of data

self-report   the person from whom data are being collected creates the answer

seminal works   the most important or critical works in a given subject area

sensitivity   "the ability of the test to identify correctly all screened individuals who actually have the disease" (Friis & Sellers, 2009, p. 422, Chapter 8)

simple random sample (SRS)   the most basic probability sampling process

snowball sampling   a type of nonprobability multistage sampling in which participants with certain characteristics are selected and then asked if they know others with the same characteristics that could be included in the sample

specificity   "the ability of the test to identify only nondiseased individuals who actually do not have the disease" (Friis & Sellers, 2009, p. 424, Chapter 8)

standardized effect size   small, medium, and large effect sizes expressed in standard deviation units

statistical inferences   estimating parameters from statistics

statistical regression   when participants are selected on the basis of their extremely high or low scores they will tend to regress toward the norm

statistical significance   indicates that noted differences are real differences and not the result of chance

strata   groups within the study population determined by specific variables

stratified random sample   a type of probability sampling in which several simple random samples are selected from strata

strict replication   duplicates in every way the methodology of an original research study to determine if the same results will occur

structured (or selected-response) items   instrument items in which the respondents are required to choose from the possible answers provided

study population   those in the population who are accessible to the researcher, who had the potential of being selected for the study, and to whom the results can be generalized

summative evaluation   assess the final effects or benefits of a program on its participants (Patten, 2009, Chapter 10)

survey research   involves using questionnaires or structured interviews for data collection, often with the intent of generalizing from a sample to a population related to their attitudes, opinions, beliefs, values, behaviors, or characteristics

systematic sampling   a type of probability sampling in which participants are selected from the frame at a constant interval determined by dividing the study population size *(N)* by the desired sample size *(n)* beginning with a randomly selected individual from the frame

telephone survey   a personal interview that takes place over the telephone

testing effect   learning that results from taking a pretest causes one to do better on a posttest

test-retest (or stability) reliability   "used to generate evidence of stability over a period" (Torabi, 1994, p. 57, Chapter 8) of time.

tests of significance   determine if observed differences are real differences or simply the result of chance

test-wise   learning techniques or strategies for taking a test that improve one's test scores

theories/models of change   "specify the relationships among causal processes operating both within and across levels of analysis" (McLeroy, Steckler, Goodman, & Burdine, 1992, p. 3, Chapter 4)

theory   "a set of interrelated concepts, definitions, and propositions that present a *systematic* view of events or situations by specifying relations among variables in order to *explain* and *predict* the events or situations" (Glanz, Rimer, & Viswanath, 2008b, p. 26, Chapter 4)

theory-based endeavors   processes (i.e., theory-based research and theory-based practice) in which theoretical constructs serve as the foundation or framework for the endeavor

theory-based research   see **theory-based endeavors**

threats to internal validity   any aspect of a study that causes one to question if the results are true and accurate

Title 45, Code of Federal Regulations, Part 46, Protection of Human Subjects (45 CFR Part 46) an HHS policy that reaffirmed that all research studies involving human subjects and receiving federal funds must be reviewed by an institutional review board (IRB) to ensure compliance with the requirements set forth in the policy

trend study   a type of longitudinal study that examines similar groups over time but not the same individuals, such as the senior class of 2000, 2001, and 2002

triangulation   in qualitative research, using multiple methods of data collection and analysis to identify consistencies among methods used

triangulation mixed method design   both quantitative and qualitative data are collected at the same time and the results are examined simultaneously to develop conclusions related to the initial research question

Tuskegee Syphilis Study   a study that began in 1932, sponsored by the U.S. Public Health Service, to investigate the long-term effects of untreated syphilis in poor, semiliterate African American men of Macon County, Alabama

type I error   the rejection of a null hypothesis when it is actually true

type II error   failure to reject a null hypothesis that is false

undue influence   excessive, unwarranted, inappropriate, or improper reward or other overture in order to get someone to participate

Universal Declaration of Human Rights   the world's first effort to create a collective view of the rights that go along with human existence

universe   all the participants with the given inclusion criteria that are unspecified by place or time

unobtrusive observation the person being studied is not aware that he or she is being measured, assessed, or tested

unstructured (or constructed-response) items instrument items where the respondent is required to generate or construct the answer

untreated control group a group that is not being exposed to an intervention

valid or validity concerned with whether the instrument "actually does measure the underlying attribute or not" (Bowling, 2005, p. 11, Chapter 8)

variable "a characteristic or attribute of an individual or an organization that can be measured or observed by the researcher and varies among individuals or organizations studied" (Creswell, 2005, p. 600, Chapter 5)

variables the empirical counterparts or operational (practical use) forms of constructs

voluntary participation "the participants' rights to freely choose to subject themselves to the scrutiny inherent in research" (Dane, 1990, p. 39, Chapter 6)

volunteer sampling a type of nonprobability sampling in which participants are motivated enough to self-select for the study

vulnerable groups may include the elderly, minors, pregnant women, the unborn, institutionalized persons, the emotionally or physically disabled, prisoners, the poor, the illiterate, or those with terminal diseases

INDEX

Boxes, figures, and tables are indicated with b, f, and t following the page number.